D1351601

IMAGES OF RULE

Painting possesses a truly divine power in that not only does it make the absent present (as they say of friendship), but it also represents the dead to the living many centuries later, so that they are recognized by spectators with pleasure and deep admiration for the artist. Plutarch tells us that Cassandrus, one of Alexander's commanders, trembled all over at the sight of a portrait of the deceased Alexander, in which he recognized the majesty of his king. He also tells us how Agesilaus the Lacedaemonian, realizing that he was very ugly, refused to allow his likeness to be known to posterity, and so would not be painted or modelled by anyone. Through painting, the faces of the dead go on living for a very long time. We should also consider it a very great gift to men that painting has represented the gods they worship, for painting has contributed considerably to the piety which binds us to the gods, and to filling our minds with sound religious beliefs. It is said that Phidias made a statue of Jove in Elis, whose beauty added not a little to the received religion.

Alberti *On Painting*, Book II. Trans. Cecil Grayson.
Introduction and Notes by Martin Kemp (Penguin 1991)

IMAGES OF RULE

Art and Politics in the English Renaissance, 1485–1649

David Howarth

Senior Lecturer in Fine Art,
University of Edinburgh

First published 1997 by
MACMILLAN PRESS LTD
Houndmills, Basingstoke, Hampshire RG21 6XS
and London
Companies and representatives
throughout the world

ISBN 0–333–51913–2 hardcover
ISBN 0–333–51914–0 paperback

A catalogue record for this book is available
from the British Library.

This book is printed on paper suitable for recycling and
made from fully managed and sustained forest sources.

10 9 8 7 6 5 4 3 2 1
06 05 04 03 02 01 00 99 98 97

Typeset by Footnote Graphics, Warminster, Wilts
Printed in Hong Kong

For my daughters
Jessica, Naomi and Alice

Contents

List of Plates

Foreword

Many people have given me help with the somewhat slow and painful progress of this book. First I would like to thank Vanessa Graham, formerly of Macmillan, who gave a contract to the idea and then proceeded to show exemplary patience as various deadlines glided past. Vanessa's successor, Simon Winder, took over when matters were getting into shape. Simon has combined acuity and alertness with optimism and reassurance in balanced, equal and most welcome measures. I thought naively that once the manuscript was submitted that was that. However the ensuing months devoted to obtaining photographs and related copyright from places as far afield as Edinburgh and Boston, were made bearable by the calm efficiency of Melanie Assinder-Smith, Editorial Services Controller at Macmillan.

Amongst academic colleagues I owe a great deal to Graham Parry and Jeremy Wood, both of whom read the manuscript and who alerted me not only to errors of fact but to some larger confusions. I am, too, especially grateful to Kevin Sharpe who lent me his own microfilms of the Strafford Papers at Wentworth Woodhouse with his characteristic and expansive generosity. These served to open the door to the world of Caroline Ireland. I have to thank Olive, Countess Fitzwilliam's Wentworth Settlement Trustees and the Director, Sheffield City Libraries for permission to quote from the documents cited as the Wentworth Woodhouse Muniments in Sheffield City Libraries. Bernard Nurse, Librarian and custodian of the prints and drawings of The Society of Antiquaries of London, is someone whose instinct is to say 'yes'. As indeed he did on all occasions when, as I fear was too often the case, I made inconvenient or awkward requests for help in tracking much of the illustrative material. Without Bernard's help, the painful business of gathering illustrative material would have been even more laborious. Colin Davis and Crystal Webster of the Edinburgh University Computing Services always seemed to have time for my alarms and excursions over missing files, blank screens, dropped footnotes or the index. Their kindness made the button pressing business much less stressful than would have been the case otherwise. Others have patiently answered queries to do with the text, agreed to the publication of their manuscripts, or obliged by generous loan of photographs: John Adamson, David Alexander, Toby Barnard, Christopher Brown, Michael Bury, the Dowager Countess of Denbigh, Geoffrey Fisher, Susan Foister, Alastair Fowler, Derek Johns, David Hemsoll, James Holloway, Alan Hood, Peter Humfrey, Hilton Kelliher, Susanna Kerr, John Leighton, Lowell Libson, Jules Lubbock, Andrew Malkiewicz, John Newman, Tom Nicholl, Stuart Piggott, Belinda Poli, Elizabeth Powis, Joe Rock, Michael Russell, Charles Saumarez-Smith, David Starkey, Anne Thackray, Simon Thurley, Jessica White, Joanna Woodall and Christopher Wright.

I would also like to express my gratitude to The Moray Fund of The University of Edinburgh, The Marc Fitch Trust and Alex Wengraf Ltd, all of whom have provided generous funding for the illustrations.

Finally my wife Alex has been endlessly patient and supportive. She has looked after our three small daughters. It has been an experience possibly not enhanced by the presence of a distracted academic at home.

Acknowledgements

The author and publisher wish to thank the following for permission to use copyright material.

Plates 1, 2, 10, 13, 14, 17, 67, 69, 84, By courtesy of The Conway Library, Courtauld Institute of Art; 3, 4, 11, 15, 18, 23, 36, 41, 51, 59–63, 65, 68, 70, Reproduced by permission of The Society of Antiquaries of London; 5, 6, RCHME © Crown Copyright; 7, 12, 39, 42, 66, 78–79, 94, Copyright British Museum; 8, 9, 22, 29, 38, 43, 64, 75, Joe Rock, Department of Fine Art, Edinburgh University; 13, 14, 67, By courtesy of The Conway Library, Courtauld Institute, and The Provost and Fellows of Worcester College, Oxford; 16, By courtesy of The Courtauld Institute Survey of Private Collections and Devonshire Collection, Chatsworth; 19, 31, 50, 85, The National Gallery, London; 20, 25, 26, 30, 34, 45, 52, 54, 86, 91, The Royal Collection © Her Majesty The Queen; 21, 33, 77, The Prado, Madrid; 24, 28, 58, 82, By courtesy of the National Portrait Gallery, London; 27, 47, 56, The University Library, Edinburgh; 32, 49, Réunion des Musées Nationaux, France; 35, Board of Trustees of The National Museums and Galleries on Merseyside (Walker Art Gallery, Liverpool); 37, By courtesy of The Marquess of Salisbury; 40, The Victoria and Albert Museum; 44, Thomas Photos Oxford; 46, Reproduced by permission of His Grace The Duke of Buccleuch; 48, The Metropolitan Museum of Art, Purchase, Joseph Pulitzer Bequest, 1944. (44.27); 53, Scuola Grande Arciconfraternita di S. Rocco, Venice; 55, Collection of The Earl of Rosebery – On loan to The Scottish National Portrait Gallery; 57, 1948 Fund and Otis Norcross Fund, Courtesy, Museum of Fine Arts, Boston; 71, John Crook; 72, 73, Reproduced by kind permission of The Warden and Fellows of All Souls College, Oxford; 74, Reproduced by permission of the Trustees of the Rt. Hon. Olive, Countess Fitzwilliam's Chattels Settlement, and Lady Juliet de Chair; 76, Devonshire Collection, Chatsworth, Reproduced by permission of the Chatsworth Settlement Trustees; 80, Private Collection, Courtesy of Harari and Johns, London; 81, National Galleries of Scotland;

83, The Metropolitan Museum of Art, The Jules S. Bache Collection, 1949. (49.7.26); 87, 88, The Uffizi, Florence; 89, 90, Reproduced by permission of His Grace The Duke of Norfolk; 92, The Ashmolean Museum, Oxford; 93, The Bodleian Library, Oxford (Poole Portrait, 151).

Introduction

The purpose of this book is to consider the relationship between political power and the visual arts in Renaissance Britain. It is a commonplace that the adoption of an Italianate Renaissance style came late to Britain; adopted tardily and only in part, by artists and craftsmen.

The orthodox view would have us believe that there were few great artists in Britain during the Renaissance period, and consequently a small number of works, if any, which can bear comparison with what was produced by contemporaries in Europe. This is a view which may, however, belittle the achievements of native-born artists and craftsmen. Inigo Jones was sufficiently highly regarded after student days in Italy to accompany the Earl of Rutland on an important embassy to Denmark, at that time arguably the most sophisticated of the northern courts.[1]

William Trumbull, English agent to the Archdukes at Brussels for twenty years at the beginning of the seventeenth century, was well placed to observe the autumn of the great Antwerp Mannerist school of painting. He came to know Rubens personally. The English miniaturist Nicholas Hilliard was not a Rubens but his work created a great deal of admiration amongst courtiers in Brussels as Trumbull reported to the Bishop of London in May 1613. It was a period when rumours of conspiracies and projected assassinations reached the ears of the credulous from various European capitals. In the process of clearing up just such an alarm, Trumbull suggests that the English miniature travelled well:

> Being informed by one Hickes an English domestic servant to these princes that . . . his mother-in-law brought over for her daughter, now his wife, a portrait of her husband by Hilliard the painter which, for the fame of the workman and curiosity of the science, was much admired by this people, things of that nature being here in great estimation, and by himself shewed to some of the archdukes' pages and others of his acquaintance.[2]

Nicholas Hilliard is the most English of English painters, and certainly the pre-eminent expositor of the miniature as an art form. But lesser practitioners, indeed artists who remain no more than a name to us, seem to have penetrated even to Florence. Five years before Trumbull had reported Hilliard's success in Brussels, Sir Henry Wotton had been busy arguing for the merits of native-born artists whilst acting as English ambassador in Venice. On 8 September 1607, Wotton had written to Ferdinand I, Grand Duke of Florence, to recommend a certain Mr Bilford, Wotton's secretary at the embassy in Venice. In that letter Wotton confidently claimed that Bilford was 'nella sua professione di ritrarre in miniatura forse non inferiore a nessun altro vivente'.[3] Ferdinand may or may not have been impressed – it is not known. What we can be certain of however is that Wotton continued to market this commodity. When Wotton was in England in 1611, between his posting in Venice and his subsequent appointment as ambassador at the Hague, he bet 'three of his choice pictures against three of the prince's [Henry's] horses, that he shall draw or portray the prince better than Isaac [Oliver] the French painter'.[4]

The issue of intrinsic quality is separate from the question of the skill and sophistication shown by patrons in manipulating art for persuasion or social status: something that Yorkist courtiers of the late fifteenth century were able to do at the same time as Leonardo da Vinci was completing *The Last Supper* in Milan. It is a point which has been made by Sir Roy Strong. He has claimed that the Burgundian tradition of chivalry was relocated in England where it was easily assimilated at court by virtue of Edward IV's exile in the Low Countries, a process of cultural fusion confirmed by the translations of Caxton which resulted in the two cultures coming to share a common civilisation.[5] One might not go this far, but Strong is saying something important which needs to be reiterated throughout the period we shall be examining. Historians of early modern English culture have tended to be distracted by the pursuit of originality. It has been thought that for the arts to be both affective and effective, they have always had to be 'original'. But originality is surely a post-Romantic distraction and even at the end of our period, and with Rubens, the greatest of the artists to figure prominently in this book, such a preoccupation would have seemed almost literally eccentric. For art to be at the centre of public affairs in Rubens' lifetime as indeed before then, it had to set up resonances, to pluck strings already strung.

A century after the reign of Edward IV England broke with Rome. Difficulties in presenting a full exegesis of monarchical authority without the support of a Catholic framework were, however, overcome. The English monarchy either adapted or simply continued to accommodate the evolving conventions of Continental state entries and triumphs. Strong summarises the skilful way in which the new Protestant, Elizabethan regime grafted a new growth onto an old tree when writing of how Elizabeth's state entry into London (1559):

> was a triumph for the Protestant Reformation and yet in style it was wholly a child of the preceding Gothic ages. Stripped of its Catholic trappings, the remnants of the archaic repertory were made use of: the legitimacy of descent appeared in the usual form of a tree, this time the family rose tree of the house of York and Lancaster culminating in the Tudors; the virtues of the *speculum princeps* tradition were re-worked to a protestant ethic, with a tableau of biblical beatitudes and a triumph of virtue over vice; the typological tradition was deployed to depict the young queen as Deborah, 'the judge and restorer of the house of Israel'. Catholic cosmological visions gave way to monarchy cast as Old Testament kingship revived.[6]

Thereafter Elizabeth promoted a range of public festivities not only for herself but for foreign suitors and ambassadors. These show perhaps more clearly than anything the extent to which England not only remained in touch with Europe during the years of religious isolation, but actively contributed to what united all rulers of whatever religious persuasion. Elizabeth I, that consummate Mistress of Ceremonies, knew as well as any Medici, Habsburg or Valois, the truth of Vitruvius' adage that festivities had to be cast in such a way as 'to please the eye of the people'. That meant a nice balance between the familiar, the novel and the sensational.

And so it went on. Whereas, early in the reign of Elizabeth, the Accession Day of the monarch was declared a holy day by a Protestant church in reassuring imitation of the old conventions of Catholic saints' days, gradually the emphasis shifted. As memories of the old dispensation faded with the death of the generation who had lived through the tumult of the Reformation, so the Accession/Holy Day gradually evolved into a chivalric celebration of the monarchy in the form of the tilt. In the Tilt Yard which ran down the centre of Whitehall, heroes of the Elizabethan age played out a charade of mock heroics. As jousting knights they created a neo-medieval world. Such a turning back may be seen as evidence of the insulated nature of the Elizabethan regime following the promulgation of the Papal Bull *Regnans in Excelsis* in 1570 which encouraged Elizabeth's subjects to depose her. It could be argued that the revival of aspects of medieval culture in England as the Baroque style in Italy was beginning to take hold, can be seen more usefully as a healthy capacity to adapt to the changed circumstances of the monarchy. If so then such a capacity to change is surely evidence of that kind of adaptability in the presentation of authority which finds a parallel in sixteenth-century Europe in the different but no less distinct changes whereby the crowned heads of the Continental regimes were presented to their peoples.

The tilt in turn passed with the passing of the Tudors, to be replaced by the masque. This new way of celebrating the virtues of a prince in England reached its most confident and sophisticated expression in 1634 in the great public celebration of the unity of the Kingdom, *The Triumph of*

Peace. This was the joint endeavour of Inigo Jones and James Shirley, and a great spectacle which anyone who saw it recognised as the finest of Inigo Jones' productions. It appears to have impressed the subjects of Charles I quite as much as Florentines had been moved by what became a legendary exposition of the splendour of the Medici court, the festivities in Florence in 1589 to celebrate the nuptials of Grand Duke Ferdinand of Tuscany and Christina of Lorraine. *The Triumph of Peace* represented the high point of the Stuart masque and it was staged just a year before Rubens' last contribution to the public life of the Spanish Netherlands. This was the *Pompa Introitus Ferdinandi* put on to greet the arrival of the new governor, the Cardinal Archduke Ferdinand. it was the last of the great Netherlandish state entries. In England Jones went on producing important masques for a further five years, but thereafter they stopped here also. Just as state entries ceased throughout Europe at much the same time, that is to say about the middle of the seventeenth century, so too they had begun more or less simultaneously in the gothic north as in the humanist south. The festivals for the coronation of Alfonso II of Naples in 1494 occurred a mere seven years before the joyous entry of Catherine of Aragon to London to celebrate her marriage to Prince Arthur. The point is made. England was little if at all different in the way in which it employed spectacle in a union of the arts to reinforce rulership.

What follows is a study of the *use* of art in Renaissance Britain. The reader will not find an account of the genesis of works of art; still less an analysis of artefacts in terms of quality. I shall argue that the emphasis art historians have tended to put upon the modest accomplishment of the visual arts of the Renaissance in Britain, has obscured a much more important achievement. Writers have yet to do justice to the way in which patrons in the highly competitive world of the court in London understood and exploited what artists could achieve. What is attempted here is to ask questions about the deployment of the visual arts in early modern Britain adopting a broader chronological time span than hitherto. To ask some of the questions which cultural historians writing about aspects of the visual arts in Europe have long been concerned with.

Jacob Burckhardt's *The Civilization of The Renaissance in Italy*, published in 1860, is perhaps the first and certainly the most celebrated attempt to understand the social and political use to which the visual arts were put by the princes and *condottieri* of Italy. Though very far from a critical success when it appeared, Burckhardt's book created a methodology and an approach which is emulated to this day; though not equalled if only because of Burckhardt's exceptional range of cultural reference.

Burckhardt was followed by Warburg and his disciple Gombrich both of whom shared or share his fascination with the Italian Renaissance. It was no coincidence that Johan Huizinga writing against the sombre background of the Nazi rape of Europe made his greatest impact as a cultural historian in his examination of the decline of Burgundian civilisation.

More recently Michael Baxandall has written illuminatingly about Italy and his *Painting and Experience in Fifteenth Century Italy* (Oxford, 1972) opens with the thought-provoking sentence 'A Fifteenth-Century painting is the deposit of a social relationship.' A century of scholarly writing on the social context of art already existed before Baxandall's book appeared; much of it to do with the same chronology and the same geography as interested Baxandall. However, many of the influential writers of Baxandall's generation who had thought of image-making as a form of social exchange had been in thrall to an ideology or a social theory such as Marxism or the *zeitgeist* – the most famous, Arnold Hauser, whose influential *The Social History of Art* was published in 1951. That book rapidly established itself as a canonical text at universities running courses on the 'great writers' of art history.

Other recent art historians have followed Baxandall in letting art speak for itself; in asking similar questions to those raised in Baxandall's justly celebrated book: David Freedberg ranged widely, quixotically even, to explore in diverse cultures what the title of his 1984 Slade Lectures at Oxford described as *The Power of Images* (Chicago and London, 1989). John Elliott and Jonathan Brown, sometimes in collaboration, sometimes separately, have scrutinised the patronage of the Spanish Habsburgs in a series of books of which *Philip IV and the Buen Retiro* (New Haven and London, 1980), a joint production, deals specifically with Philip IV's campaign of self-aggrandisement.

More recently French art has been approached in something of the same spirit: Peter Burke's *The Fabrication of Louis XIV* (New Haven and London, 1992), is a rich essay on the self-fashioning of the Sun-King; Thomas Crow in *Painters and Public Life in Eighteenth-Century Paris* (New Haven and London, 1985), and Albert Boime in *Art in an Age of Revolution* (Chicago and London, 1987); the latter significantly heralded as the first volume in A Social History of Modern Art – all have made distinguished contributions to a new appreciation of French Rococo and Neo-Classical art and how it was received by the French public. Svetlana Alpers and Simon Schama in turn have also opened, perhaps to some extent forced open, windows to give us an expansive if hazy view over the landscape of the culture of the Low Countries in the seventeenth century: Schama's *The Embarrassment of Riches* (London, 1987), and Alpers' *The Art of Describing* (Chicago, 1983), are characteristic of the separate but complementary approaches of two brilliantly imaginative writers.

Clearly there has developed something of an industry in studying the social impact of art in Europe in the early modern era. So much so indeed that the weather-vane may be turning. Theodore Rabb, Professor of History at Princeton, has published an essay in *The Times Literary Supplement* (November 10, 1995), entitled 'Play, not politics, Who really understood the symbolism of Renaissance Art?' That may be his title or the editor's. What is clear however is the scepticism with which Rabb treats assumptions made by many recent cultural historians. Rabb considers the processions, the portraits, the allegories – the stuff of which this book is made – as little more than 'shows of learning, homages to antiquity, or *jeux d'esprit*'. Rabb is not convinced that they meant very much at all to an audience beyond the initiates of a given court circle.

I disagree. If I didn't it would all be rather awkward. 'Play, not politics' is merely a fore-taste of a book yet to be published but it looks as if Rabb will bring his baton down sharply enough to call the orchestra to order, if not stop the music. Rabb's essay came to my notice when this book was in press, and evidently there is more to come. For these reasons it is not appropriate to take issue with what Rabb has to say about early modern Britain in what follows. It may be predicted however that those of us interested in this kind of history may have to sit up when the book appears.

Part of the intention of this book is to consider English Renaissance artefacts whatever they may be – buildings, tombs, portraits, subject pictures, masques or plays – as deposits of social relationships to paraphrase Baxandall's memorable apothegm; to look at what has survived, as the sediment of a rich social fabric.

In the last twenty years there has been much change in the writing of social history in early modern England: fruitful cross-fertilisation between disciplines which previously had been studies unto themselves. A wider appreciation of the importance of image-making has served to push back the moment when it is thought Englishmen understood the potential of visual culture. The recent biography of Lady Margaret Beaufort by Jones and Underwood, Gunn and Lindley, and Gwyn on Cardinal Wolsey, Thurley and Starkey writing separately about the court of Henry VIII, all serve to redress an important imbalance. In the early 1970s in a series of exhibitions devoted to the court of Charles I, it came to be understood that early Stuart England was an age without precedent in English cultural history as regards the visual arts. Twenty years later, it is now believed that there was perhaps more uniting the court of Henry VIII with that of Charles I than divided them; a unity of purpose symbolised by the employment of Holbein in the 1520s, and Van Dyck exactly one hundred years later. From the perspective of the 1990s, it now looks as if too much emphasis may have been placed upon the cultural achievements of the early Stuart period, not enough on that of the Tudors.

Despite the distinguished contribution of Strong to an understanding of the brittle aesthetic of the Elizabethan age, there still remains a consensus that the second half of the sixteenth century was a period of contraction. Elizabeth built very little: content to remain a cuckoo in the nest and dependent on the hospitality of others. She built no new royal residences; she conducted her progresses on the basis of eating her courtiers out of house and home; her painters owed rather more to the past than to their European contemporaries. The emphasis given by Strong on the medievalism beneath the surface of Elizabethan art, suggests that the culture of Elizabeth I cannot bear comparison with either the aggressive splendour of Henry VIII or the fastidious connoisseurship of Charles I.

Strong's interpretation of the Elizabethan court has yet to attract significant revisionists; unlike the earlier Tudor period or that which came after. As for tensions in early Stuart society, these can no longer be considered simply in the light of a dress rehearsal for the dramatic struggle over political rights, the curtain for which was raised with the outbreak of Civil War in 1642. Rule without parliament, the issue of ship money, religious controversy: all continue to be freshly analysed but there is a difference. A cadre within recent historiography vehemently rejects the 'inevitable' theory of the causes of the English Civil War: the view that the well-springs of the conflict reach far back to the revolution in government effected by Thomas Cromwell in the 1530s. The old argument that civil war was inevitable carried within it the implicit assumption that Charles I was the helpless victim of forces larger than himself: his actions made no essential difference since conflict between the Crown and Parliament was as certain as the sparks fly up. Such Hegelianism has had many distinguished advocates.[7] By contrast, revisionists of our generation, of which John Adamson, John Morrill, Conrad Russell and Kevin Sharpe are perhaps most prominent, have presented radical new appraisals. Studying the reign of Charles I with forensic intensity, they have argued that analysis of men and measures on a daily basis holds the key to an understanding of the causes of the Civil War. They argue that the Civil War was not inevitable. What caused it were the temperaments of the protagonists, misjudgements about short-term policies, and sheer misfortune. According to this perspective, the whole thing was more in the nature of a surprising tragedy, rather than something which had long been waiting to happen.

Reappraisal requires a new ordering of priorities and a new emphasis. It is indeed time that the visual arts of the Tudor period were looked at afresh as those of the Stuart era have been.

The contrast between old and new approaches to the Stuarts if not the Tudors can be vividly appreciated by a brief consideration of the Victorian high priest of early Stuart history, the magisterial Samuel Rawson Gardiner. In pandects which appeared between 1863 and 1882 in five series of two volumes each, under the title *History of England from the Accession of James I to the Outbreak of Civil War, 1603–1642*, Gardiner created the orthodoxy about the English Civil War for a generation of late Victorians. Gardiner wrote thousands of pages on high politics – the law, the church, the army, trade – but Van Dyck and Rubens do not appear in his index.

Historians now view the period very differently. Political history has become cultural history. One of the first and most accessible examples of this new approach is Graham Parry's *The Golden Age restor'd*: a synoptic account of the courts of James I and Charles I in which the author reaches up to many different shelves: politics, poetry, plays and masques, paintings, architecture, the theatre, sculpture, to explain what happened in the period 1603–42. A more recent example of a new emphasis on 'court' culture, is Kevin Sharpe's expansive, one-thousand-page study, *The Personal Rule of Charles I.*

In *The Personal Rule of Charles I* Sharpe examines every aspect of royal bureaucracy but there is, too, reference to the impact of the visual arts and literature in what represents the fullest reappraisal of the peacetime years of the reign of Charles I since Gardiner. Sharpe reveals himself as a master of archives which tell us of the Caroline Privy Council or the Justices of the Peace.

But it is symptomatic of the new priority given to cultural history that much of Sharpe's previous work has had to do with looking not at the returns of local tax officials, but at the texts of poets and masque writers for what a volume of poetry or a copy of a play may reveal of the wider social and political concerns at the court of Charles I.

An indication of this important shift in early Stuart historiography is that Sharpe's first book, *Sir Robert Cotton* (Oxford, 1979), was on Cotton (d. 1629), who had the broadest culture of any man in early Stuart England. It was the first study devoted to an English scholar who had enjoyed international fame in his lifetime since James Howell published his *Cottoni Posthuma: divers choice pieces of that renowned antiquary, Sir Robert Cotton* in 1651.

A contemporary of Cotton described his library as Helicon's fountain. Cotton's correspondent was referring to the Hippocrene fountain located on Mount Helicon, a spot sacred to the muses. The Cotton library was of inestimable value for politicians and lawyers who consulted its records to arm themselves with precedents in pursuit of favourite policies. However, it was no less valuable to Inigo Jones and Ben Jonson, who also consulted it for emblem books, architectural folios, and descriptions of state entries. These provided rich inspiration indeed for the creation of their own buildings, masques and plays, which they moulded to take the stamp of values and ambitions dear to the king's circle. Although Cotton's library was carefully organised and divided up under the headings of the Roman emperors – each section had the bust of a Roman emperor above it – there was no distinction in the mind of a Jacobean scholar-gentleman between the legal and political sources on the one hand, and what, at the risk of sounding anachronistic, might be described as cultural material on the other. So too it has been one of the distinctions of the present generation of early Stuart historians to have broken down the barriers between 'political', 'ecclesiastical', 'economic' and 'cultural' history. Anyone who now set about a study of Charles I in the 1630s who did not take cognisance of court interest in the arts would be writing at their peril.

For historians like Tawney, Hill, Hexter and Stone, the road to Civil War was full of Protestants, tradesmen and money lenders jostling and thrusting a powerless and decrepit aristocracy out of their path as they marched forward to claim the dominance which forces beyond their control ensured they were bound to grasp. Now, however, that orthodoxy has been shattered. John Adamson in close analyses of the English aristocracy has argued that the peers of the realm were neither powerless nor decrepit. Just as the arts in the broadest sense have belatedly received due, perhaps undue, attention among historians writing in the last twenty years, so too Adamson argues that far from being thrust into the bushes, the aristocracy played a central part in the struggles which led to war. Adamson's arguments, like those of Sharpe, are based on a close knowledge of archives but also on the perception that an important gauge of the relative vigour of the early Stuart aristocracy is an awareness of how much they built and how much they spent on luxuries, not only before but even during the Civil War. Adamson's study of the building ambitions if not the achievements of the Earl of Pembroke, erstwhile Lord Chamberlain to Charles I, in Civil War London, gives the lie to the view that the aristocracy in those times of trouble were merely reactive, never proactive.

The study of fashion, regarded until recently as the province of the amateur historian, has also come into its own. Janet Arnold, Malcolm Smuts, Diana Scarisbrick, Rosalind Marshall, all have contributed valuable studies on costume and jewellery, and the ways in which they were displayed. The researches of costume historians have checked others in their easy assumption that what matters to us, mattered in the Renaissance: that is to say because many of us see a Titian painting as a kind of substitute religion, so too did the court of Charles I. Titian was regarded by the early Stuart connoisseur with awe but, despite what Puritan critics of visual imagery claimed, Charles I and his courtiers could look to a hidden world of the spirit beyond a canvas. By contrast perhaps for us what we see on the surface of a Titian is indeed the confines of our spiritual world.

Malcolm Smuts especially, has set out to cut canvases down to size by arguing that because Charles and his courtiers spent a great deal more money on clothes than paintings, then we must re-order our understanding of cultural priorities (see Appendix I). Dress sent out far more important signals than a painted masterpiece. This is a valuable corrective. Smuts has served to temper the enthusiasm of those who have placed too much emphasis on the value the early Stuart court placed upon the high arts. However, Smuts's argument must be treated in its own turn with a certain degree of scepticism. A suit of clothes belonging to Buckingham was bound to be valued more highly in monetary terms than most if not all the paintings Buckingham himself displayed with such sumptuary splendour at his London residence York House. This was not because an English courtier in 1620 responded to trunk and hose more than to a Titian but simply because the hundreds of pearls and the gold and silver thread which made up a dazzling trousseau could be converted very easily into a sizeable pile of gold. But men then as now do not live by gold alone.

Psychology too has been used, sometimes intelligently, sometimes less so, in an analysis of motive and influence. Charles Carlton's analyses of the characters of Charles I and Laud are well known examples of the genre. Once again the contrast between methods of late twentieth-century historians compared with those of the late nineteenth, is startling. Psychoanalysis had not even been invented when Gardiner was writing.

What is attempted in this book is a survey of recent writing on visual culture of the early modern period in England. Its purpose is to assess how much weight we should give to visual artefacts in Renaissance Britain in understanding how people understood themselves and the times they lived in. What did a painting or a tomb mean to artificer, supplier and client?[8] It will be argued that the patron mattered rather more than the artist in the complicated process of making statements, claims, justifications or pretensions; that is to say, the various uses to which the rich and the great put art. This is not to discount the real growth in what art historians refer to as connoisseurship; the appreciation of a picture and its distinguishing characteristics for its own sake. As the work of Oliver Millar and a younger generation of scholars has made clear, the early seventeenth century was indeed an exceptional time for such pursuits. However, the issue is a complicated one since it is doubtful whether Charles I whose every action the people did 'gazingly behold', could be a connoisseur, appreciating art for its own virtue. The tastes of Charles, hardly less than his actions, had effects. Art collecting was a political activity when it was conducted at a court. This book is, then, about the politics of art.

Chapter One
The Royal Palace

Henry VIII was the most energetic of all English royal builders though from his accession in 1509 until the late 1520s he was rather more pre-occupied with violent competitive gymnastics than with palace building. To the late twentieth-century mind it seems curious that the joust and the tilt, wrestling and hunting were so important to the Renaissance monarchy; surprising that is until we read *The Courtier*, in which Castiglione devotes chapters to the pursuit of physical prowess as a defining and necessary characteristic of his model. These pursuits were a prelude to battle and in those early years of his reign, Henry was also keen to go to war with France. War itself was something Cardinal Wolsey was able to wean Henry from and this shift of priorities, combined with a serious accident in the jousting field, all helped to nurture an interest in patronising the arts; something which Machiavelli and Castiglione considered ruler and courtier alike should be well versed in. A great impetus to Henry VIII as a royal builder was the disgrace of Wolsey in 1529, which resulted in a number of splendid residences falling into the hands of the Crown.

Hampton Court today provides the touchstone not merely of the king himself but of the whole Tudor age. The size of a modern industrial site, its six acres are a miraculous survival from the English Renaissance. However, the significance which Hampton Court has for trying to understand the values of Tudor England owes much to the accident that this palace has survived in a more complete form than any of the other royal residences of the period. Hampton Court was just one of nearly sixty residences which Henry came to own by the time of his death in 1547.

At Hampton Court Henry was building on the work of others. The palace had been begun by Cardinal Wolsey in 1514 and what Henry added in the 1530s was development beyond the original nucleus of two main courtyards – the Base Court and the Inner Court – which had been left by Wolsey when he had been forced to hand it over to the Crown. But metaphorically speaking Henry VIII was building upon still earlier work;

upon foundations which went deeper than those left by Wolsey. Phenomenal in the context of Tudor and Stuart history as Henry's building programmes were, he was continuing a time-hallowed tradition; not following bookish precepts from a Renaissance manual urging the prince to display 'magnificence'.

Every English dynasty had built on a grand scale from the Conquest onwards. Henry VIII's father, Henry VII, had become increasingly interested in architecture but even he gave impetus to an existing momentum. In the secular field Henry VII's most interesting building was Richmond Palace, which grew out of the shell of the old royal palace of Sheen.[1] Here he was following the precepts of earlier kings who had built on this site. Henry VII's Richmond had interesting features, including what is thought to have been the location of an important library which in scope and ambition surpassed those at The Tower and Westminster.

The Tudor royal palace was a theatre of kingship, which had to employ new scenery, sometimes at short notice, when play, players or plot changed. Good architecture can be defined as building which meets the needs of the client efficiently or can be adapted to do so without undue delay or expense. That was certainly the case with the palaces of Henry VIII. In a volatile world like the English court in the 1530s, it was necessary to build in a material which could be produced cheaply; to use materials to be found or manufactured on or near the site. Brick was certainly a more versatile material than stone and at Hampton Court, where kilns were established, there were none of the logistical problems of quarrying, dressing and transporting stone which Inigo Jones would encounter when building the Banqueting House at Whitehall in 1620. The net effect of employing brick at Hampton Court in the 1530s for all but the occasional dressing of the corners or framing of the windows, was that new ranges, or the reshaping of existing lay-outs, could be accomplished comparatively easily when Henry created new protocols or discarded old wives. Stone palaces would have been relatively inflexible; whereas brick residences were like monstrous crustacea which shed outer shells to grow more fearsome claws, or put out longer antennae to catch the unwary. Tudor brick exactly suited the needs of its clients; no other material could have given expression to the rapid and powerful changes of the Henrician court.

Henry VIII got a building type and pattern of use which reflected the idiosyncrasies of his court. The needs of the English court were not the same as those of France and therefore we must resist the temptation to judge what was happening in the two countries in terms merely of narrow stylistic criteria. To the architectural historian, Fontainebleau is more 'progressive' than Hampton Court but, in terms of function, there was perhaps less to choose between them than has been thought.

In what ways can the political and social pressures which made Henry VIII tyrant but also slave at his own court be seen reflected in Hampton Court? That he was both is something to have emerged from Thurley's work in reconstructing the appearance and use of Hampton Court. The Henrician court was a lethal context for power politics. Someone whose position had seemed unassailable one day could be thrown down and executed at the king's whim the next week. However, throughout the early modern period in England the relationship between sovereign and subject was one of reciprocity. Henry was to some degree at the mercy of the pressure for access to his person demanded by an ever increasing circle of dependants and petitioners. Much time was spent both by Henry himself and by his builders in devising barriers which could be erected within the privy chambers to ensure an effective filtering system.

Ways in which these pressures can be seen reflected in what might be termed the archaeology of the Tudor palace are not easily traced and anyway, their interpretation is made more complicated because Henry VIII had been taught to build by the example of Wolsey.

Some of the features which Henry included in his building programmes at Hampton Court in the 1530s were aspects of the palace which had been conceived by the Cardinal. For example the State Staircase, which today is perceived as intrinsic to palatial architecture, was a feature Wolsey had first introduced at this site.[2]

Nevertheless there is a clear sense from the 6,000 pages of building accounts which cover Henry's alterations and expansion at Wolsey's Hampton Court, that the palace was an organic growth. Henry spent much time contriving architectural means to escape the publicity of court life, paradoxical though that may seem given the unforgettable images of dominance which Holbein created of him.[3] Amidst all the confusions, vacillations and impatience which the king showed during 1529–39 – that tremendous decade of building – one clear intention is discernible. This was to reinforce a trend first established by his father to create a clear demarcation between the privy chambers of the king, his family and the most important of the court officials, and the rest of the court.

Hampton Court was made to reflect the needs of a married king rather than a single prelate. This was expressed most obviously in the abandonment of the stacked lodgings created by Wolsey to receive the king and his consort.[4] Henry VIII abandoned the Queen's Lodgings which were above his own and built a new court on the same level and to the east of the King's Lodgings. The replacement of stacked lodgings by courtyards might appear to have reduced rather than increased privacy; one floor above another surely concentrates living quarters and therefore makes them easier to 'defend'. However, separate balanced and symmetrical courts thrown out laterally provided a more effective filtering system. It worked on the principle of the Swiss bank vault; many steel doors had to be opened before the diamonds could be seen.

There is a sense in which Henry's radical redisposition of the lay-out of Hampton Court rendered some of the most remarkable features of Wolsey's palace redundant; the State Staircase most notably. However, such a judgement may be false because it depends on how redundancy is defined. Certainly the State Staircase could no longer be justified in terms of the need to get from one set of royal apartments to another. And yet it continued to be an aspect of royal palace building under Henry VIII despite the fact that he thought about the disposition of households in quite different ways from Wolsey. The State Staircase was retained because Henry kept his eye on his rival Francis I, whose staircase in the Cour de l'Ovale at Fontainebleau of 1531 seems to have provided inspiration. The retention of the staircase is therefore a remarkable example of how elements in English royal palace building could be conditioned by show rather than function.

As Thurley has recently demonstrated, many of the most memorable features of Hampton Court today do not and indeed never did reflect life as it was lived by the Tudors. The celebrated terracotta heads of Roman emperors in their bay-leaved roundels were not mounted on the gates as they are now: the so-called 'Wolsey's Closet', which to us seems most richly evocative of Tudor interior decoration, is an historicist Victorian reconstruction; but more importantly, the chapel built by Henry, and decorated to be fit for a king, was used by the ecclesiastical household while Henry habitually worshipped in a closet above the nave; he was almost never seen in the chapel itself.

The Great Hall at Hampton Court must have been the most splendid part of the palace. But although Henry VIII built it he never used it; he dined elsewhere and it served as the most glorious of works canteens. Why then did Henry furnish a dining hall for others to a standard appropriate for the entertainment of a king rather than his groom?

A Great Hall had always had a central place in the mystique of kingship. The preservation of what had become a redundant aspect of princely living was something which stemmed from a growing perception of precedent and history. But it was more complicated than that. Though the incorporation of the Great Hall at Hampton Court may have been more medieval than Renaissance, the virtues which it embodied – hospitality, splendour and magnificence – were authentic aspects of a Renaissance prince; virtues which were being spelt out just at this very moment by Sir Thomas Elyot in his *The Boke named the Gouernour* of 1531 (Plate 91, page 266). What Elyot promoted, Ben Jonson celebrated a hundred years later when he lamented the dissolution of the old order of hospitality. In his poem *Penshurst* he praised the Sidneys:

. . . Whose liberal board doth flow:
With all, that hospitality doth know!
Where comes no guest, but is allowed to eat,
Without his fear, and of thy lord's own meat:
Where the same beer, and bread, and self-same wine,
That is his lordship's, shall be also mine.[5]

There is a crucial distinction here. Henry never dined in his Hall; Jonson's patron was being praised for being the centre of a community whose meetings in the Hall symbolised a well ordered world. Nevertheless, Henry VIII created his own magnificent dining chamber at Hampton Court to provide board and that was an important obligation. He embellished the Hall with one of the finest hammer-beam ceilings in England; spending generously to sustain princely 'liberalitie' as required by writers on manners like Elyot. Myth was as important as reality to images of rule.

The Great Hall at Hampton Court is a very splendid example of survivalism if not revivalism; an element of continuity during the English Renaissance. It may well be that the association of the present with the past was every bit as important to Henry at Hampton Court as the need to establish his credentials as a master of a new style.

Preference for the old is something which can often be detected during the English Renaissance. When, in the early seventeenth century, John Williams, Bishop of Lincoln, offered to build the new library at St John's College, Cambridge he rejected a classical scheme in favour of something with a distinctly gothic flavour. This was because he had been told by Bishop Cary of Exeter that 'the old fashion of church window' was 'most meet for such a building'; presumably, one assumes, because this academically-minded bishop associated learning with monks and monks with the gothic style.[6] At that time too, and also in Cambridge, Peterhouse built a chapel in a kind of bastard Gothic, the stylistic idiosyncrasies of which can perhaps be explained by suggesting that it was an attempt to express solidarity with an authentic and primitive Anglicanism; a national style for a national church; the origins of which, it was claimed, went back beyond the arrival of St Augustine and the Roman Liturgy in 597. A famous building to students of the 'Gothick' style, Peterhouse chapel is as rich in its historiography as it is in its form. Its builders saw that form both as fitting academic robes for seventeenth-century scholars, and as proclamation of a primitive, native and authentic religion called Anglicanism. Archbishop Laud, the moving spirit behind Caroline church building, saw Anglicanism and Catholicism as competing religions. To prove the superiority of the former, to prove how it was that Anglicanism represented the true church before it had become corrupted by the Papacy, it was necessary to build in Gothic; a style which most Englishmen associated with the early uncorrupted church.

By contrast, Augustus Welby Pugin, the great Victorian apologist for a 'christian style' in architecture, shared the assumption of the Cambridge Puritans about Peterhouse chapel; though he certainly did not share their religious viewpoint. To Pugin, as to Fenland church breakers of the Civil War, Peterhouse was a Catholic building with a capital 'C'. In his vastly influential *An Apology for the Revival of Christian Architecture in England* of 1843, Pugin turned his mind to what he described as the 'collegiate establishments' of Oxford and Cambridge; writing of how 'there cannot exist a

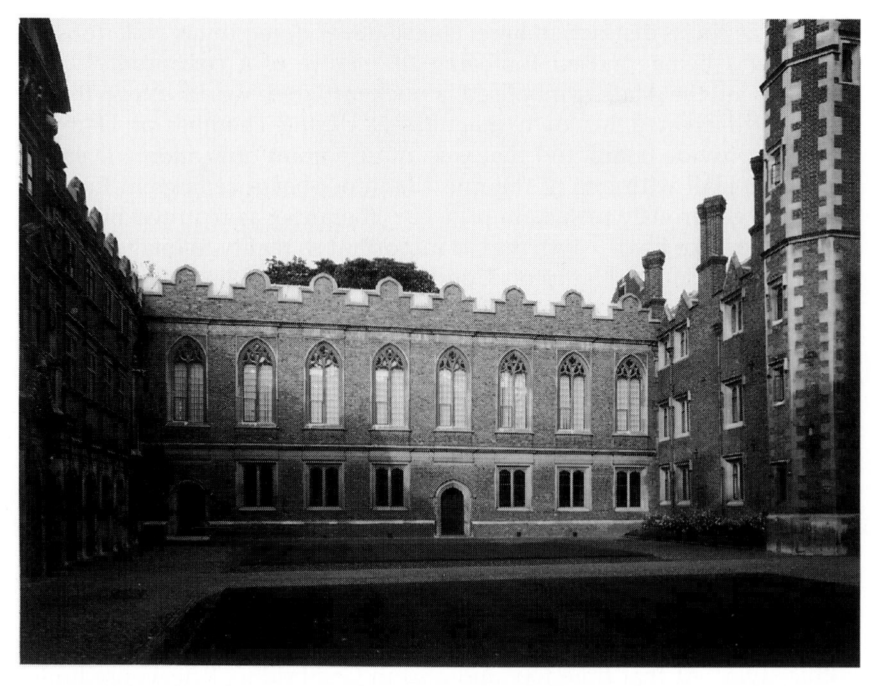

St John's College, Cambridge, The Library, 1623–5 (Courtauld Institute of Art)

doubt as to the propriety, if not the absolute duty', of erecting buildings 'in the same style and spirit' as the originals because 'Any departure from Catholic antiquity in a college is unpardonable.' Pugin then went on to single out Peterhouse chapel precisely because of what he claimed to see was the consistency of spirit between the seventeenth-century chapel, and the buildings of the original thirteenth-century foundation.[7] Herein lies an irony. Although the Laudians built in a style associated with Catholicism because they saw themselves as competing with the Vicar of Rome for exclusive claims to be the purest expression of Christ's church on earth, their very position in English society depended on recognition of the fact that they were not Catholics but High Church Anglicans.

A hundred years before St John's and Peterhouse got two of the most notable Renaissance buildings in Cambridge, Henry VIII was concerned to keep contact with the past whilst also trying to rival the patronage of Francis I and Charles V. These were distinct not to say mutually exclusive priorities which may go some way to explaining why Henrician architecture is such a hybrid growth.

Henry's most brazen attempt to compete with others is to be identified not with the various campaigns at Hampton Court, but rather with the building from new of Nonsuch Palace. Work began at this palace near Esher in 1538 and was only finished when Henry died in 1547. Although

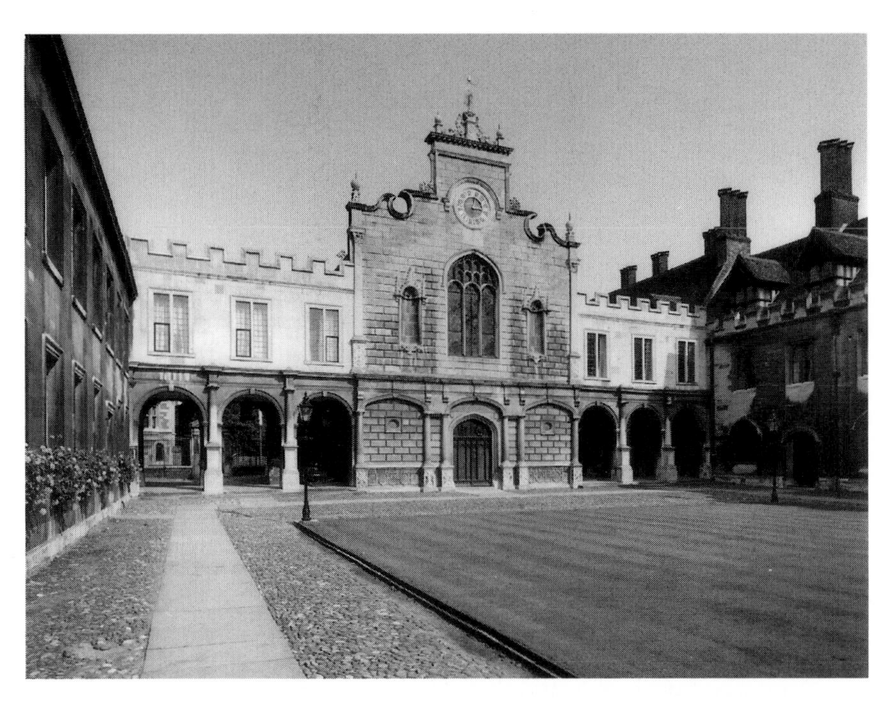

Peterhouse, Cambridge, The Chapel, 1628–32 (Courtauld Institute of Art)

the structure survived barely more than a century, it was much admired. John Evelyn's record of a visit early in 1666 offers a vivid sense of its bulk, so curiously appropriate for the sovereign for whom it was created. It had a surfeit of dense decoration which made it a coral reef of bewildering forms and materials:

> I supped in *None-such* house . . . at my good friends Mr. *Packer*: and tooke an exact view of the Plaster Statues and *Bass-relievos* inserted twixt the timbers and *poincons* of the outside walles of the Court, which must needes have ben the work of some excellent *Italian*: admire I did much how it had lasted so well and entire as since the time of *Hen*: 8, exposed, as they are to the aire, and pitty it is they are not taken out, and (preservd) in some dry place, a gallerie would become them: there are some *Mezzo relievi* as big as the life, and the storie is of the heathen Gods, Emblems, Compartiments, etc.
>
> The Palace concists of two Courts, of which the first is of stone Castle like, by the Lord *Lumlies* (of whom 'twas purchas'd) the other of Timber a Gotique fabric, but these walls incomparably beautified: I also observed that the appearing timber *punchions*, *entretices* etc were all so covered with Scales of Slate, that it seemed carved in the Wood, and painted, the Slat fastned on the timber in pretty figures, that has pre-

served it from rotting like a coate of armour. There stand in the Garden two handsome stone *Pyramids*, and the *avvenue* planted with rows of faire *Elmes*, but the rest of those goodly Trees both of this and of *Worcester*-Park adjoyning were fell'd by those destructive and avaritious Rebells in the late Warr, which defac'd one of the stateliest seates his Majestie had.[8]

Nonsuch stands apart from other palaces in terms of decoration as well as function. It was never intended to accommodate the entire court, which numbered some 1,500 people by the 1540s: it existed as a pleasurable retreat for Henry VIII, his Privy Councillors, and his favourites. Its connection with the king's intimates accounts for its peculiarly exuberant, extravagant decorations. In Joris Hoefnagel's 1568 view of the south front, the external walls look like stamped and embossed leather (engraving 1582). Everything was a writhing pattern of swirling arabesques with hardly a still interval the whole length of the façade. The inner court was hung with great carved slate tiles and the tower, under which Henry's bedroom was located, had a curious astronomical clock by Nicholas Kratzer. Kratzer, friend and sitter to Holbein, was something of a mechanical wizard; someone to whom Henry with his love of mechanics may have responded rather better than to Holbein himself. Nonsuch was the last of Henry VIII's architectural essays. It was the final, the most exuberant expression of a fantastic builder.

Predictably enough reaction followed. Edward VI was only nine when he became king; too young to embark on a building programme. Though it is doubtful whether he would ever have taken that step since he inherited too many houses. With Edward's accession in 1547 building became less the concern of the monarch than of the subject. Never again would the Crown dominate building practice to the extent that it had done under Henry VIII. Now it would be a case of the subject trying to impress the sovereign, not the other way round.

Edward Seymour, Earl of Hertford, Duke of Somerset, and as Lord Protector 1547–9, the dominant figure in the first two years of the new reign, is one of the most intriguing figures in the history of English architecture. He understood classicism in something of the same way that Inigo Jones was to do half a century later. Henry VIII and Wolsey, Burghley and Salisbury, all built more, but none had Somerset's grasp of what a classical building was all about.

What is known of Somerset's buildings suggests that he favoured understatement and reticence, simple proportions and a sense of the subordination of the parts to the whole. By contrast to such a coherent grasp of classical principles, Henry VIII's understanding of architectural design had been decidedly confused; except perhaps in the technical sphere of fortification in which he may have schooled himself by a serious study of Renaissance manuals.

For instance, Nonsuch had more in common with a Tudor warship than

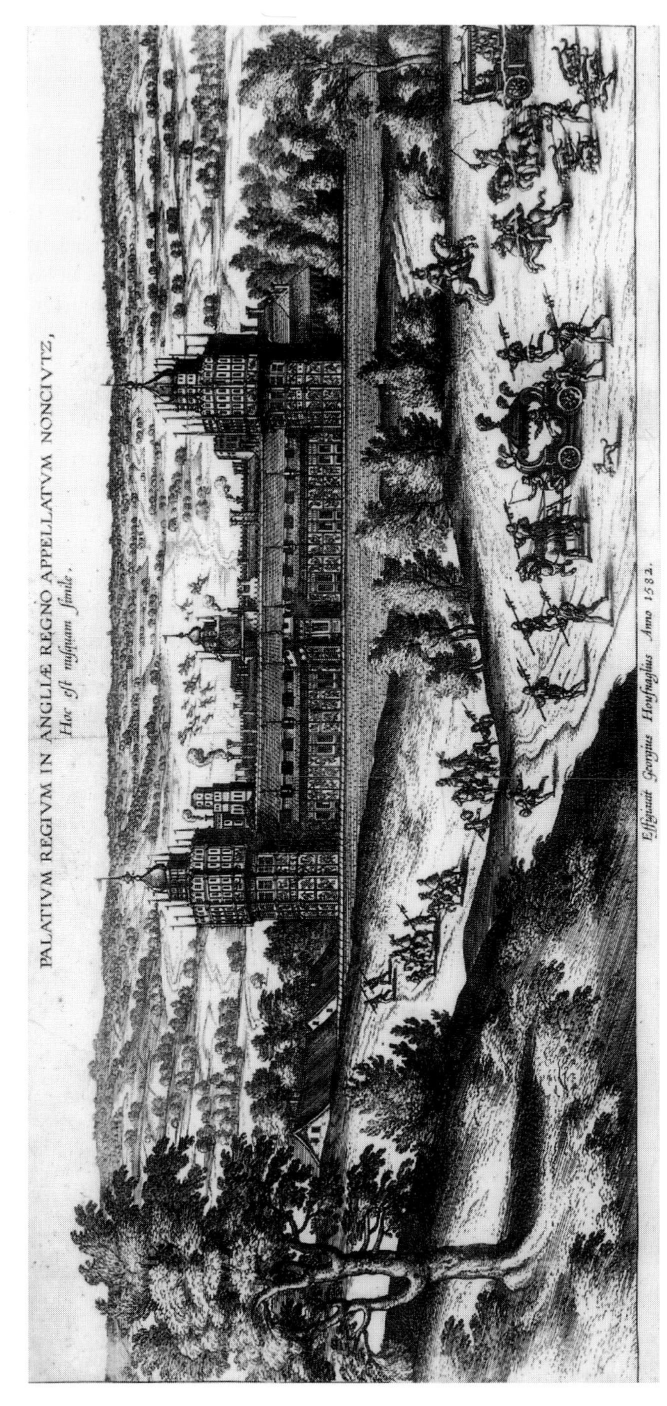

Joris Hoefnagel, *Nonsuch*, engraving, 1582 (Society of Antiquaries of London)

a Renaissance palace. Hoefnagel's view suggests the stern of the *Mary Rose* with those overhanging galleries comparable to stern cabins, whereas by contrast, views of Somerset House, put up in the Strand between 1547 and 1552, reveal a cool abstracted mastery of design which gave England its first classical building comparable in sophistication with what was being designed in Europe at the time. Somerset House had features not seen in England before. Of these the most conspicuous was the three-storied entrance gateway with its remarkable ground floor of a triumphal arch, complete with three-quarter columns on plinths and niches between.

Exciting though it is to compare the exuberant excess of Nonsuch with the assured understatement of well bred Somerset House, the one would not have been possible without the other. William Cure and Giles Gering, the Nonsuch 'molde-maker', moved on from one building to the other.

In the reign of Edward VI life was more uncertain than it had been under Henry VIII and yet Somerset House was informed with a functional logic and consistency of style not seen in English architecture since the completion of Henry VII's Chapel at Westminster *c.* 1512. The quality of this great London palace would suggest that crude connections between political power and how it is expressed in building are to be avoided. There could hardly have been more of a contrast between the serene conviction of the building and the hazardous life of the builder, who was to be demolished after only two years as Lord Protector; though his building would survive almost unaltered until *c.* 1777.

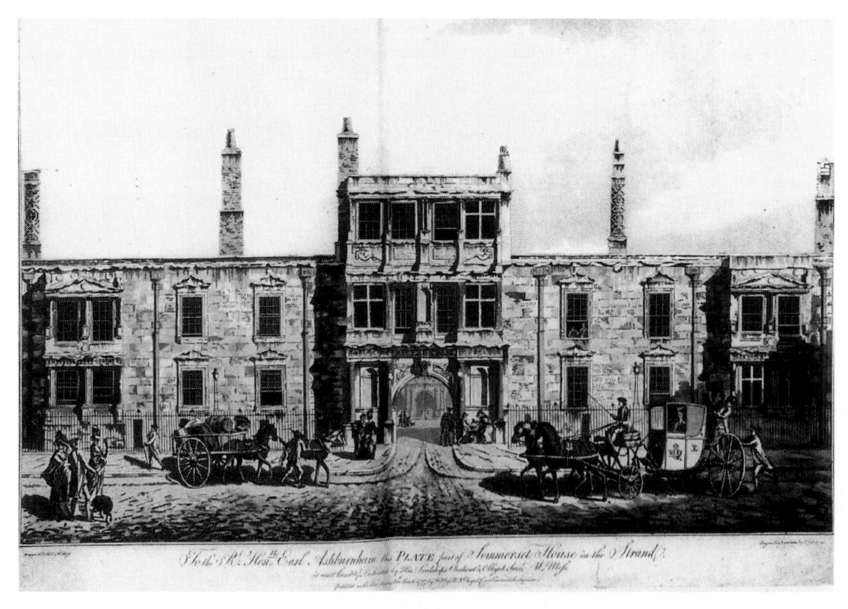

James Basire the Elder, *Somerset House*, 1547–52, pen and ink with wash (Society of Antiquaries of London)

But Somerset House was only the most ambitious of a number of Edwardian buildings with certain things in common. These were put up by a close-knit group of courtiers who owed good fortunes, metaphorically and literally, to Somerset himself. The group was sympathetic to Genevan Protestantism, which Henry VIII had set his face against, while their buildings were in the same advanced architectural vein as Somerset House itself.

Who were these men, and what was their relationship to the Protector? The most sharply focused is William Sharington; somewhat surprisingly since he was a relatively minor courtier though a major clipper of coinage and debaser of currency in his days as controller of the Bristol Mint. What Sharington built was rather less extensive than Longleat, put up by Sir John Thynne, steward to Protector Somerset. By contrast to Thynne, who had held the key post of steward to the Protector, Sharington ended his days in 1553 merely as Sheriff of Wiltshire. Nevertheless Sharington had been one of the many gainers from the Dissolution of the Monasteries when he had acquired Lacock Abbey in Wiltshire in 1540, which he would transform into what remains one of the most romantic houses in England.

Lacock is the creation of the final years of the reign of Henry VIII and the onset of the Edwardian Protestant regime. That is to say the transformation of the old monastery was begun in 1540 and essentially finished in 1549. John Chapman was the most prominent artisan to work on the conversion and his presence connects Lacock firmly with the Henrician

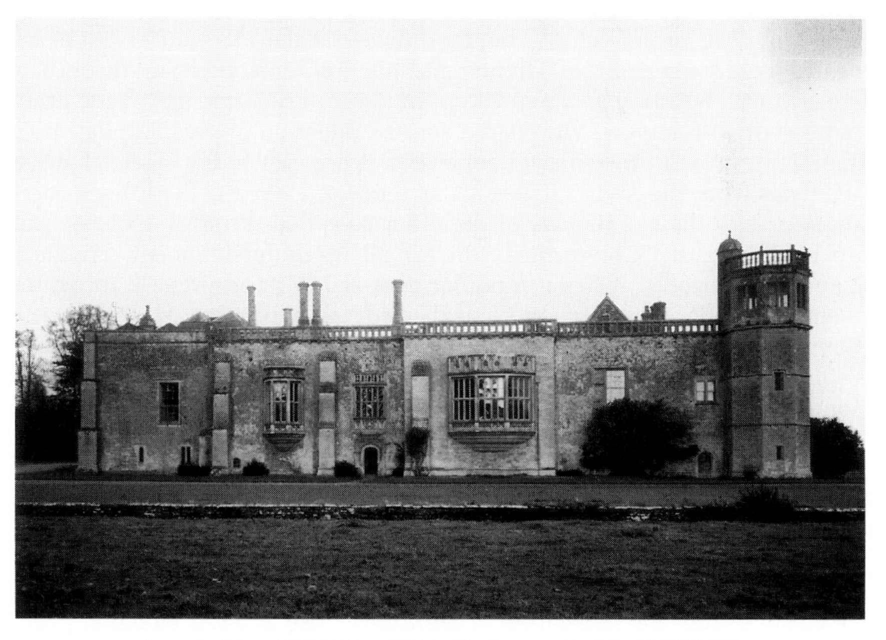

Lacock Abbey, Wiltshire, 1540–49, the south side (RCHME)

period since Chapman, like Cure and Gering, emerged from the Henrician Royal Works to create this mid-century classical interlude.

Lacock contains much very fine classical detailing seen through the prism of French taste. But it is not the Gallic qualities which make it one of the very best Tudor buildings; after all, Nonsuch was a confused response to French Renaissance architecture. What makes Lacock exceptional is its innate sense of 'fitness' or 'decorum'. Renaissance epithets, used to describe what should appear in good architecture, 'fitness' and 'decorum' also denoted the good carriage and manners of a well-bred courtier. This should not surprise us since Sir Thomas Hoby published his celebrated translation of Castiglione's *Il Cortegiano* in 1561; that is to say, between the completion of Lacock in 1549 and the appearance of the first English treatise on architecture: John Shute's *First and Chief Groundes of Architecture* (1563). There was much in Hoby about how and when to bend the ear of the prince. There was much too at Lacock which had to do with an instinct for discretion, of when and where to leave off, when to let ornamentation speak for itself; all skills, one might add, necessary for the courtier.

Sir John Thynne, Somerset's man, left London to retire to Wiltshire where he produced his own rural essay in the new classicism, the first Longleat House (1554–67); just a few miles from Lacock, and like it, built upon a monastic foundation. Unfortunately we know nothing of what the original Longleat looked like because it was destroyed by fire in 1567. Undeterred, Thynne then set about building again. The appearance of the new Longleat, probably only finally finished in the 1580s, after Thynne's death, would suggest that Thynne and his builder Robert Smythson had thought of a building as a whole and in the round; a rare gift at the time, but essential to anyone who had a serious intention of grasping the rudiments of classical proportion. Longleat as it appears today (and what we see dates from the 1570s) strikes us as reticent, even a trifle dull by comparison with the exuberance of the other so-called 'Prodigy Houses' put up by Elizabeth I's favourites. But for all its understatement, Longleat commands respect. It has a modular proportion informing all: measurements are rational, ornament controlled, detail subordinated. Indeed the house has more in common with the architecture of Jones than with say Wollaton, that ornament to the Tudor taste for the *grotesque* also designed somewhat surprisingly by Robert Smythson.

John Dudley, Duke of Northumberland replaced Somerset in 1549, after which he dominated the kingdom until his own fall with the accession of Mary Tudor in 1553. Although Northumberland built nothing comparable to the importance of Somerset House, like Somerset before him, he too combined Protestantism with what appears to have been a real interest at least in the mathematical and theoretical aspects of architecture. This can be gleaned from the dedication of Shute's treatise of 1563, which appears to have been composed in Northumberland's lifetime, though not actually

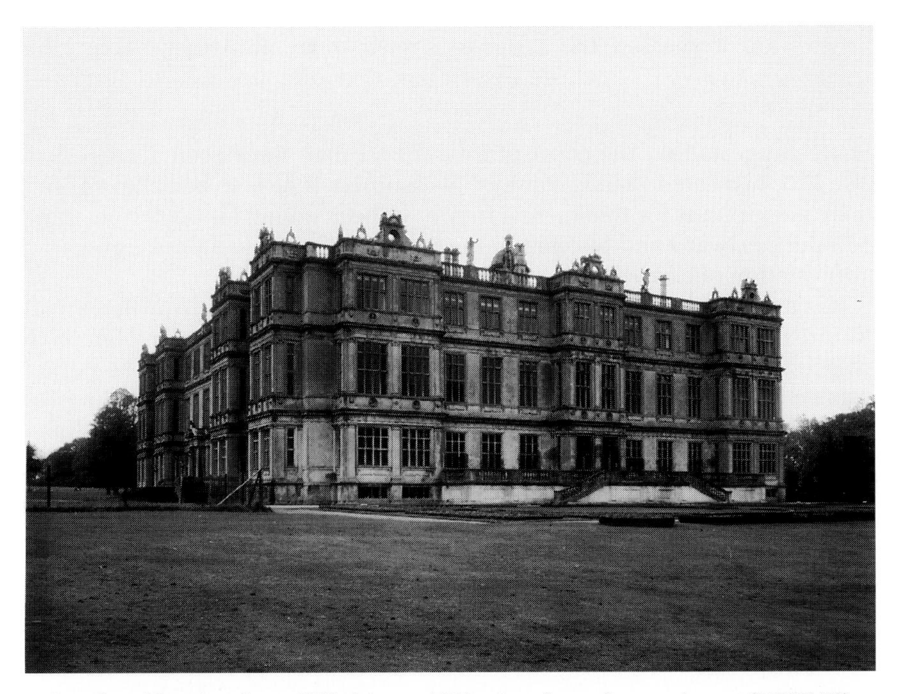

Longleat, Horningsham, Wiltshire, *c.* 1580, view from the south-east (RCHME)

published until 1563. Shute's book lifts the corner of the curtain on what is otherwise a dark area in the history of English architecture. Although we cannot help wishing that he had told us more about who built what, and where inspiration for these fine Edwardian classical buildings came from, he demonstrates how he has read and consulted widely, but more interestingly, he also reveals a critical mind. He relishes his independence from his sources; taking pride in stressing where he parts company from Vitruvius, Serlio and others. Where he does do so is over fundamentals: such as the best method to compute the proportions of the classical column. If a capacity to think for yourself represents intellectual maturity, then with Shute, English classicism might appear to have come of age at last, though his independence of thought did not of course result in the adoption of a sophisticated classical language of architecture. That was to take a great deal longer to achieve. Nevertheless Shute's book is so important that the passage in which he refers to Northumberland must be quoted:

> . . . being servant unto the Right honorable Duke of Northumberland. 1550. It pleased his grace for my forther knowledg to maintaine me in Italie ther to confer wt the doinges of ye skilful maisters in architecture, & also to view such auncient Monumentes hereof as are yet extant. wherupon at my retourne, presenting his grace with the fruites of my

> travailes, it pleased the same to shewe them unto that noble king Edward the VI . . . whose delectation and pleasure was to se it and suche like.[9]

Shute suggests that the court of Edward VI may have been a great deal more sophisticated than is commonly assumed. If he is to be believed, and there are grounds for thinking he may have been giving his book something of a puff, Edward and his chief ministers led the way to a thorough-going appreciation of classicism.

It is not possible to obtain a clearly focused picture of Edwardian architecture in the way that can be done with more success for Henrician palaces. Nevertheless, there is enough evidence to suggest that the period was an interlude of exceptional importance in the history of buildings of state. For example, we have a record from within the precincts of Whitehall Palace of the so-called 'Preaching Place'. This is in the form of a woodcut which if it is indeed an accurate record of what once existed in this important location, suggests that its architect really understood the principles of classical design; someone whose vision of building was not confined to lifting decorative motifs from printed pattern books.

The Preaching Place appears in a woodcut in Foxe's *Actes and Monu-*

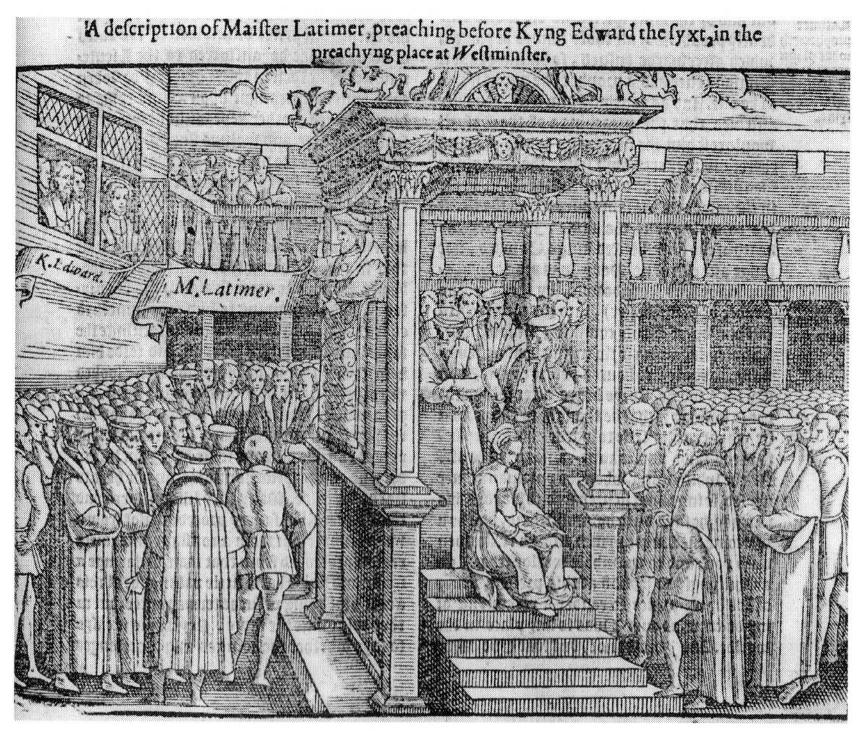

The Preaching Place, Whitehall, from Foxe's *Actes and Monumentes,* 1563 (British Museum)

mentes of 1563, commonly known as 'Foxe's Book of Martyrs', as a free-standing stone pulpit in the centre of a surrounding courtyard. Four Corinthian piers support a heavy entablature ornamented with a frieze of banded laurel or bay, suspended from masks. Above, a niche frames a classical bust, while four winged horses give emphasis to the corners. To the right and behind this courtyard pulpit, is a balcony with elegant balusters supported on plain well-proportioned piers. Beyond and above the temple-like building itself, we can see Bishop Latimer directing his invective at Edward and Northumberland.

It is surely going too far to suggest that Jones found inspiration here for his Banqueting House, but the architectural distinction of the 'Preaching Place' points to an interesting paradox.[10] The reign of Edward VI was one of great excitement and experimentation in architecture but it was also a period exceptional for the wholesale destruction of monuments.

Northumberland headed the junta which minded the sickly king and it would appear that he was absorbed by Italy and the classical tradition. Once again therefore we seem to have a repeat of the pattern established thirty years earlier when Cardinal Wolsey had combined the highest office with the largest ambitions as a patron of the arts. However, there is a fundamental difference between Wolsey, and Somerset and Northumberland: Wolsey was a cardinal whereas these Edwardian power brokers were fanatically anti-Catholic. What then can we make of this? What did this group of Edwardian classicists have in common? Is there a case for arguing that the new, cleaner, more sophisticated classicism, much admired by architectural historians, was an architecture for Protestantism? In other words was architecture politicised?

There is not a shred of evidence that the purity and simplicity of the particular type of classicism which these men favoured was chosen because it was felt to mirror a religion itself simpler and purified from the snares of Rome. We only have to think of the number of adherents to the new religion who did well out of converting monastic buildings to appreciate that architectural style was value-free in terms of religious or political allegiance. The only suggestion that can be put forward was that Edwardian classicism was promoted most vigorously by those who dominated the political scene. To that extent Somerset House and Longleat, and the lesser buildings discussed above, were indeed conscious images of rule.

The reign of Mary Tudor was so turbulent, short and unhappy that no coherent policy for promoting the image of the monarch emerged. In her turn, Mary's sister Elizabeth never did more than add embellishments to existing palaces like Windsor Castle. She was not concerned with building; she had no need to be, with so many of her father's palaces still in the possession of the Crown.

Elizabeth I had had one of the best schoolings in a great age of education. But whereas it was thought seemly for a woman to know Greek and Latin, or to play the virginals – all of which Elizabeth mastered – building was not part of the curriculum of the gentler sex. The first significant royal patroness of architecture in the Renaissance was Marie de' Medici, who would greatly extend the Louvre shortly after the assassination of her husband in 1610.

It is said that Elizabeth was a woman of the word not of the eye; she was a quite insignificant patroness of the visual arts. Ostensibly that is true. She built nothing noteworthy, whilst it is her courtiers like the Earl of Leicester, Lord Burghley and Sir Christopher Hatton who have been credited with promoting the careers of architects and painters. But the situation is perhaps rather more complicated than has been realised.

The truth has been obscured by a tacit assumption that great buildings must always be summoned up by direct intervention. But the so-called 'prodigy houses' of the Elizabethan period – Wollaton, Hardwick, Burghley, Holdenby – achieved their fantastic appearance as frames for Elizabeth's image; their owners were merely the glass through which she was to be viewed. Elizabeth was their creator in a sense which the Renaissance mind would have had no problem in grasping. On the numerous occasions when Elizabeth was greeted by an anxious, unctuous owner with the claim that all she saw was hers, this was in an important sense true. She reshaped accommodation and ordered the redecoration of a Long Gallery although she visited the site only when the job was done and always left without paying. Elizabeth knew how building could be manipulated just as well as her father but did so vicariously and a great deal more economically.

Henry VIII had shifted with bewildering speed from one palace to another. Elizabeth moved about too, though in quite different ways. Henry restlessly exchanged one hunting lodge for another in a desperate effort to preserve privacy and escape an overmighty court. His frequent removal from one residence to another was a chase, a charge, until, that was, ulcers and gout made him a prisoner of his own magnificence.

By contrast, Elizabeth headed a caravan which lumbered about the home counties in search of someone else's estate where tents could be pitched literally as well as metaphorically. The contrast between Henry and Elizabeth was one between the hare and the tortoise. Elizabeth saw the value of combining two important but distinct aspects of rule at the same time: exposition of herself to the people as a sacrament of sovereignty, and the obeisance of her most favoured courtiers. But Elizabeth was no Byzantine emperor who required her subjects to prostrate themselves on the ground before her. She was acutely aware of the need to flatter her subjects and paid far more attention to the business of making herself accessible to them than James I, who was positively frightened of contact with the baser sort. Elizabeth well understood what was described earlier as the reciprocity central to the patron–client relationship in the Renaissance. Nevertheless it was the Queen, not the Earl of Leicester or the mayor of Oxford, who held the aces.

Elizabeth's goal of reminding her favourites that their rivalry was because all rewards stemmed from her was achieved that much more effectively because rituals of deference were enacted within the context of a courtier's own demesne. Although the physical environment in which Elizabeth would be received at a great house was one of Renaissance fantasy and exuberance, the act of fealty was medieval. So too was the way in which she was seen by her loving subjects outside the pale of the courtier's deer park. Older men and women watching Elizabeth riding under the town hall or carried round the square in a litter must have been reminded of the Corpus Christi processions which they would have seen enacted under the old Catholic dispensation. As for Elizabeth herself, it was no accident that she played the card of the virgin princess for all it was worth. No one knew better how strong were the attachments to the old religion. Just as she manipulated and exploited what belonged to others by provoking a great spate of competitive building, so too she stole the imagery of the Virgin Mary while ignoring her subjects who plucked down crucifixes in their churches.

James I was not interested in architecture; so orthodoxy would have us believe. But the truth is that whereas Elizabeth may be said to have been manipulative in her willingness to get others to build for her, James built on his own account and, what is more, got maximum return on his investment. Like Henry VII, James decided what his priorities were to be and turned them to good effect. But whereas Henry spent the vast majority of his funds for building on pious enterprises, James had an aversion to church architecture and concentrated on promoting building projects which would either enhance the dynasty, or reinforce what he considered to be the key aspects of his kingship. James was concerned to ensure that government buildings were made eloquent. Although James's appearance and habits left a great deal to be desired, he was concerned that the instruments of government – the Courts, the Privy Council, the 'magnificent and metropolitan city of London' – should properly reflect the dignity of his kingship. He believed that it was from his own sacred person that they derived their authority.

At the very outset of James's reign, the splendour and wealth of London had been brought to his notice when he had processed through the streets as part of his reception of welcome. As the royal cavalcade advanced, it had been regaled by triumphal arches depicting the virtues of the City companies, and the merchant communities of foreigners. Such an entry was a cliché on a monumental, indeed a European scale; the arches which had both flattered and petitioned offered no surprises; nevertheless such an education in civic splendour may have had its effects on a man who had been tutored by the image-hating Calvinists of Edinburgh.

A constant feature of the reign was James's serious, sustained and partially successful attempt to raise the standards of hygiene and building in London through a series of Royal Proclamations; an impetus given an extra thrust with the creation of the Jacobean Commission for new Buildings in 1618, which soon established itself as an important instrument of social control under the effective dominance of Inigo Jones. Ninety per cent of Commission work was mundane: meetings were about drains not dentils. The Commission had come about through a long-term fear that unless the expansion of London was brought under control, disease and disorder would erupt more frequently than was already the case. Its business included such matters as: disputes with overseers of a market to regulate open-air stalls; inspection of the Fleet River to devise better methods of sewage disposal, or measuring out a land plot in Chancery Lane to check for abuse of a building licence.

Inigo Jones crouched in a drain is a vision far removed from the reception Sir Henry Lee provided for Elizabeth I at Woodstock in 1575 where she was conducted to a banqueting house in the woods, bedecked with ivy boughs and gold plates, and where the Fairy Queen made her first appearance in Elizabethan England. Yet in its mundane way, the work of the Jacobean Commission for New Buildings was as vital to the image of the monarchy as the most elaborate picnics laid on for a travelling queen. The Stuarts felt London was a direct reflection on their own magnificence. The palaces of Greenwich and Whitehall were central to image-making in a very obvious way: foreign ambassadors had to be impressed as they waited for an audience with the king. But hardly less important was somewhere like Cheapside in the City of London. Cheapside housed the jewellers and purveyors of luxury goods; important because it was a famous resort of tourists. For this reason alone the Jacobean Commission was given wide-ranging powers to interfere officiously with communities within the metropolis at large.

The very existence of the Commission, and tensions between the Crown and the City, suggest that the appearance, the function, and the good government of London mattered greatly to James I. London was the seat of government and the setting of kingship. It should be noted too that the life of the courtier and the life of the carter impinged upon one another in ways which now seem eccentric. A public thoroughfare leading west from the City of Westminster drove a path through the precincts of Whitehall Palace, and under the arch of the so-called Holbein Gate. At street level carriages and carts became locked together as they fought for rights of passage, while within earshot a stately royal train would be progressing from one part of the palace to another.

James I believed that London had to be clean, hygienic, fire-resistant, rich and splendid, as a whole series of his proclamations makes abundantly clear. But that was not the entire story. The Commission for New Buildings came into being when the best philosopher of the age and the most experienced diplomat of the Jacobean era respectively, both published on architecture.

Sir Francis Bacon, sometime Lord Chancellor, and advocate in print of the rational scientific method, wrote a series of famous essays which included one on architecture.[11] In his essay Bacon takes what may be termed a pragmatic, practical approach to the problem of how the great and good should set about building. The tone of his short essay is established with the opening sentence:

> Houses are built to Live in, and not to Looke on: Therefore let Use bee preferred before Uniformitie; Except where both may be had.

Thereafter the rest of the discourse is taken up with advice as to where each element required in a house should be placed according to the function it was intended to perform and its relationship with complementary rooms and spaces. Bacon's apothegms are, appropriately enough, short and pithy but their brevity should not belie the novelty of approaching the whole issue of building in terms of appropriateness or, as the Renaissance mind would have defined it, decorum. Bacon's essay was the fruit of much experience since he knew intimately many of the great houses of the period. His father Sir Nicholas, had built the important Elizabethan house Gorhambury, whilst Bacon himself had lived in York House whilst his father had been Lord Keeper. Furthermore there is evidence that Sir Francis had tried his hand at various architectural schemes; though these might be regarded as modest in scope, having more to do with the laying out of summer houses and walks than with houses *per se*.[12]

What Bacon had to offer was then followed by Sir Henry Wotton, whose two separate residencies in the embassy in Venice had given him unrivalled opportunities to acquaint himself with Renaissance architecture. Wotton's *The Elements of Architecture* came out in 1624 and with it, the most abiding definition of good architecture in the English language. Wotton believed that what was needed was 'Commoditie, Firmness and Delight'. These were criteria which were not lost on the members of the Commission. They recommended the replacement of wattle and plaster with new and commodious materials like brick and stone to prevent the spread of fire. But these new durable materials, to the extent that they were used in any quantity, were also much more 'commodious' and 'delightful' than jerry-built structures run up by a property developer interested only in squeezing people into his tenements. Thus the work of the Commission was not merely an aspect of the early Stuarts' preference for paternalistic intervention, but was informed too by a wish to promote good style.

This is a thesis which has been put forward in a stimulating book by Jules Lubbock on the politics of architecture and design in England from 1550 to 1960.[13] Lubbock sees a thread in English cultural history from the mid-sixteenth century until the advent of post-Modernism in our own day. Perhaps it might be better described not as a thread but a rope which bound architect and patron alike to a value system which meant as far as

James I and Inigo Jones were concerned, that 'The purpose of monumental or public architecture was to civilise a country . . . to assist the constitutional ambition of unifying the two different races of Magna Britannia.'[14] For Lubbock the existence of an 'agenda' in public building is something which can be traced throughout the centuries which he surveys. It is not our purpose to consider Lubbock's arguments beyond the time-span of our own study. But so far as this book is concerned, Lubbock is surely right to see James I and his surveyor as thinking of architecture not in terms of alternative styles but for how it could be made to improve society and express its most important priorities and values.

In considering the role of Inigo Jones in the promotion of a social and political programme of royal building, Lubbock rightly pauses to consider Jones' famous criticism of Mannerist architecture for what Jones considered its 'licentious' nature. By this Jones meant the way in which Michelangelo perverted the 'rules' of classicism to produce buildings of an unhelpful idiosyncrasy. In Jones's own words:

> And to saie trew all thes composed ornaments the wch Proceed out of ye aboundance of dessigners and wear brought in by Michill Angell and his followers in my oppignion do not well in sollid Architecture and ye fasciati of houses, but in gardens loggis stucco or ornaments of chimnies peeces or in the inner parts of houses thos compositiones are of necessety to be yoused. For as outwarly every wyse ma carrieth a graviti in Publicke Places, whear there is nothing els looked for, yet inwardly hath his immaginacy set on fire, and sumtimes licenciously flying out, as nature hir sealf doeth often tymes stravagantly, to dellight, amase us sumtimes moufe us to laughter, sumtimes to contemplation and horror, so in architecture ye outward ornaments oft [ought] to be sollid, proporsionable according to the rulles, masculine and unaffected.[16]

This is Jones's most important dictum on the affective nature of architecture. When Jones applied such values to the context of public building in London, it is hard to imagine a more paternalistic attitude. The whole passage is shot through with words to suggest a highly articulate moral code: solidity, gravity, wisdom, licentiousness, rules, masculinity, straightforwardness. All these were then moral attributes or temperamental weaknesses associated with the human condition and their crowding together makes it abundantly clear that for Jones style could not speak for itself. It had to be used to express moral and ethical qualities.

Lubbock responds to what Jones had to say for himself by writing:

> We can see that Jones perceived himself not as the man who merely restored to Britain a classical architecture, but as the man who restored it in its truest and purest Roman form, purged of all the licentious ornament of Michelangelo and his mannerist followers.[16]

Two things follow from this. The first is that a reading of Lubbock locates the key to opening up the meaning of the portrait of Jones which was executed while he was in Rome in 1614. The second is that Lubbock's discussion of Jones suggests why Jones seems to have turned his back on what might loosely be termed the 'Baroque' architecture of Continental Europe, although as we should expect, this was something he was interested in. Lady Arundel's Italian secretary, in a letter written in Antwerp to the Earl of Arundel, asked the Earl to tell Jones that Lady Arundel 'has seen the Church of the Jesuits and finds it marvellous'. This is a reference to S. Carlo Borromeo in Antwerp, for which Rubens had obtained a contract to paint thirty-nine ceiling paintings and two altarpieces just months before.[17]

And yet despite such vicarious evidence that Jones was alert and interested in what was being designed in the great cities of Europe, there is something of a paradox here. Although Jones was open to contemporary architecture, his own practice produced very little work which made concessions to the achievements of his European peers. In his catafalque design for the hearse of James I of 1625, it is true that he looked closely at the work of architects like Fontana who were practising in Rome, but beyond his 1634 proposal for the west front of Old St Paul's, there is surprisingly little in his oeuvre of the 1630s to show that he was aware of the young Bernini or the output of Pietro da Cortona who were then the principal exponents of Baroque architecture.

But to return to a closer focus, let us consider the image of Jones. Here we have an etching of Jones by the fashionable engraver Francesco Villamena, who had a modest but relatively successful practice as an illustrator in Rome in the early seventeenth century. Curiously enough justice has never been done to this portrait although it is of a famous architect and the only portrait of an Englishman which we can be certain was made in Rome prior to the arrival of Van Dyck in Italy in the 1620s.

A slightly rebarbative, aggressive looking man stares out of the image to fix the spectator with his gimlet eye. It is an altogether challenging image; challenging because it portrays future intentions as much as current looks. The most curious aspect to the whole thing is that Jones is framed by an architectural construction which is in fact an antique funerary monument. This can be understood in the context of the inscription chiselled onto the stone plinth beneath the head of Jones himself. It proclaims Jones 'Architector Magnae Britanniae' and it is laid out as if on stone, in a clear antique script. The confluence of these two details, the funerary monument and the antique inscription, suggests that Jones, so evidently alive, has rewakened the spirit of classical design which, through the allusion to death in the framing of his head, we are to take as having been dead in Great Britain until now. Until that was, Jones had come to Rome and mastered the art of building in the true style. Hereafter, it may be inferred, Jones is to return to Great Britain, to Magnae Britanniae, to promote an architectural style which will be classicism reborn.

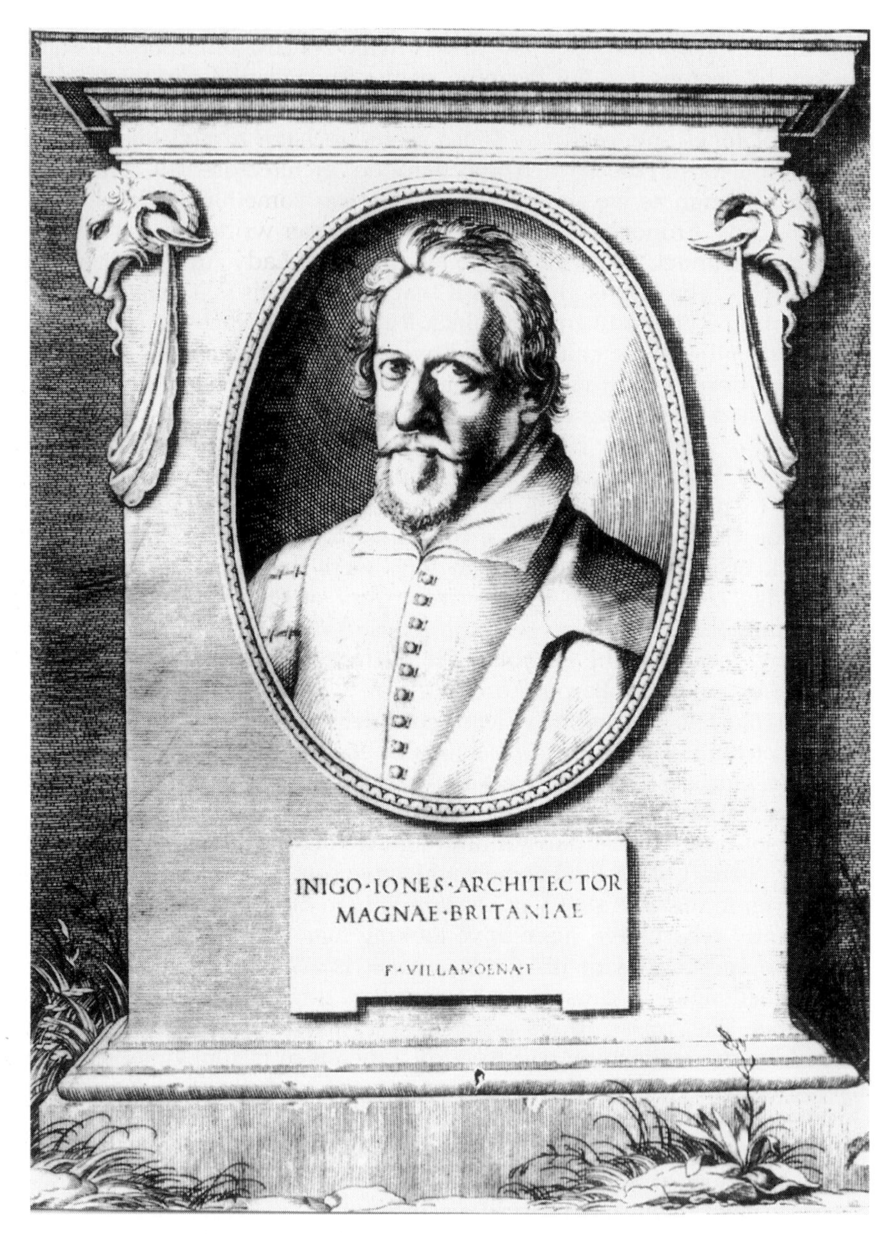

Francesco Villamena, *Inigo Jones*, 1614 (Joe Rock)

What we are presented with therefore is a prospectus of Jones' intentions. The challenging appearance of the architect is precisely because he is addressing a select band of friends back home or in other parts of Italy: men like Wotton, Bacon and Cotton, who were rare in England in understanding the principles of classical architecture but still looked for its rebirth following their own studies of Roman Britain.

Jones' reflections on what constituted good architecture explains too the paradox that he seems to have been deeply interested in new buildings in Europe though he consistently chose to build in an idiom which had been given its most perfect expression by Palladio fifty years before. The point is that Jones in his doctrinaire and inflexible way had decided early on that the Palladian style was the 'true' style and thus he consciously rejected alternatives. Given his extraordinary powers of design, and his deep absorption in the literature of architecture, it would be absurd to suggest that somehow he was incapable of change. Lubbock is surely right in suggesting that to understand Jones we have to see him at the beginning of a trend in architectural thinking in England which extends at least as far as the Victorian world of Ruskin and Pugin. Jones and Pugin had more in common than Jones and Palladio since both Englishmen were peculiarly susceptible to that very English concept of a 'right' style.[18]

Although James I became absorbed by subjects as varied as the American colonies and witches, architectural theory interested him not at all. The fact that in all his voluminous writings there is not a sentence to be found on architecture or painting accounts for why what was in reality his acute awareness of the propaganda value of things visual has been wholly ignored even in recent times when his reputation and the impact he made on English society has been the subject of much exciting new work. But is this even true? James certainly prided himself on what he took to be authoritative statements on a whole host of issues which were genuinely of concern to him if not, as he fondly deluded himself, to the Jacobean literati. But what James left to posterity was never intended to be wholly confined within the leather covers of the printed book. A whole series of proclamations on building show his close personal involvement both in the sentiments they express, the philosophy they declare and the ambitions they set out.

Furthermore James I was intensely proud of his achievement as a builder. His most wide-ranging proclamation about what was desirable in architecture was issued in July 1618 to coincide with the launch of the Jacobean Commission on New Buildings, of which Jones was to become the keystone. That proclamation drew a parallel between King James of Great Britain and the Emperor Augustus. With typical vanity James conceived of himself as a second Augustus, for just as Augustus had found Rome of brick but transformed it into marble, so James claimed that he had found London of sticks and was encouraging his subjects to build in brick.

Paper claims such as these may well have been given more permanent form thereafter. There is an inscription in Latin which proclaims James's distinction in commissioning the Banqueting House which replaced the first Jacobean banqueting house, destroyed by fire in 1619.

Although there is no evidence that the inscription was actually chiselled into marble on the walls of the building itself, there is no reason to suppose not. What is certain is that if such an inscription once adorned the building it has vanished. It probably wore away and was not replaced during the extensive and disastrous campaigns of restoration the building suffered at the hands of some of the most eminent Georgian architects.

The inscription, which has been tentatively dated 1621, once again takes up the Augustan parallel, echoing Suetonius' life of Augustus. A literal though certainly not poetical translation of the Latin might be rendered as follows:

> The genius of the place, to the observer-guest.
> This ⟨building⟩, which strikes the eye by its majesty and
> speaks most magnificently of the soul of its Lord,
> razed when scarcely previously made of brick, but now the
> equal of any marble buildings throughout Europe,
> JAMES, first monarch of Great Britain, built up from the
> ground; intended for festive occasions, for formal spectacles,
> and for the ceremonials
> of the British court; to the eternal glory of his/its name and
> of his/its most peaceful empire, he left it for posterity.
> In the year 1621.[19]

Self-advertisement enough surely to suggest that James I should not be thought to have been indifferent to the visual arts though we look in vain for evidence of direct interest. As will be proposed later, James was the willing subject of Rubens' celebration of his reign in the scheme for the painting of the Banqueting House ceiling. This and his constant and close interest in supporting the work of his Building Commission should be taken as a sign of his awareness of what marble and paint could do for the image of a monarch.

Building, painting, but also sculpture and tapestry, all were part of the repertoire of regal advertisement during the earliest years of the Stuart dynasty. James I often looked to France when he wanted to take social or economic initiatives, and to judge from a scheme to erect statues of himself and the Prince of Wales in London, it would seem that he had taken notice of the admiration the equestrian, life-size bronze statue of Henri IV of France provoked among tourists in Paris. That famous image had been cast by Pietro Tacca, and set up on the Pont Neuf in Paris, following the assassination of Henri in 1610.

James I seems to have encouraged the idea of having statues of himself and the Prince of Wales in London as a permanent and public advertisement of the greatness of the dynasty. This was not something the Crown initiated but the proposal once made seems to have met with approval. The idea came as a gesture of gratitude from the Houses of Parliament, who were delighted by James agreeing to act against monopolists in 1621.

The House of Lords took the lead and debated the feasibility of erecting a 'Statue of brasse . . . to the Kyng and prynce out of a general contribution by us [the House of Lords] . . . to be erected here in the parlement house . . .'. Apparently the figures were to be 'in roabes' and there was also to be '2 in the olde pallace on horseback at the costes of the Lords and lower house'. Arundel was then instructed to 'wryte beyonde seas for thess statua to be sett on worke'.[20] Nothing came of all this, but that the idea was taken seriously suggests that Jacobeans and their king were well attuned to the social impact of statuary in public places.

James was, then, well aware of the public utility of the visual arts, although they were not something which moved him like the religious controversies of the day, to which he made his own published contributions. Nevertheless, James took advantage of, though he made no attempt to master, the new and revolutionary grasp of classical principles which Inigo Jones revealed on his return from Italy in the winter of 1614–15. In his capacity as Surveyor of The Royal Works, Jones undertook a series of commissions to enhance the status of the royal prerogative.

The most significant project which reveals what might be thought of as a conscious programme to enhance the royal prerogative, was in fact the Banqueting House. This began as a replacement for an earlier building which dated from the beginning of the reign. The building history of the Banqueting House is complicated. It is clear that the interior as it is now, is a relatively faithful reflection of what it looked like when the Rubens ceiling was put in place in 1635. It does not however correspond to what the interior looked like when the building had been completed in 1622. Between then and 1635, Jones radically altered it and thereby changed its symbolism. Specifically it has been suggested that the wall behind the throne, as the visitor looks down the hall from the entrance, originally contained a smaller window above and a niche below.[21] The niche had been put there to locate the interior within what Renaissance theorists defined as the *basilica*. According to Palladio in his *I Quattro Libri* (1570), the most famous treatise on architecture of the Renaissance, in the ancient world the basilica had been the location of public administration.

It was appropriate that James I should have been triple framed as he sat in the Banqueting House performing the sacred rites of a priest king. He was framed by his throne, and by the canopy of state vaulting over his head, and behind that, by the niche or exedra in the masonry of the wall behind. Those who progressed up the central gang-way of the basilical hall, must have been conscious of how the ensemble itself would have been focused by the deep shadow of the niche excavated out of the wall

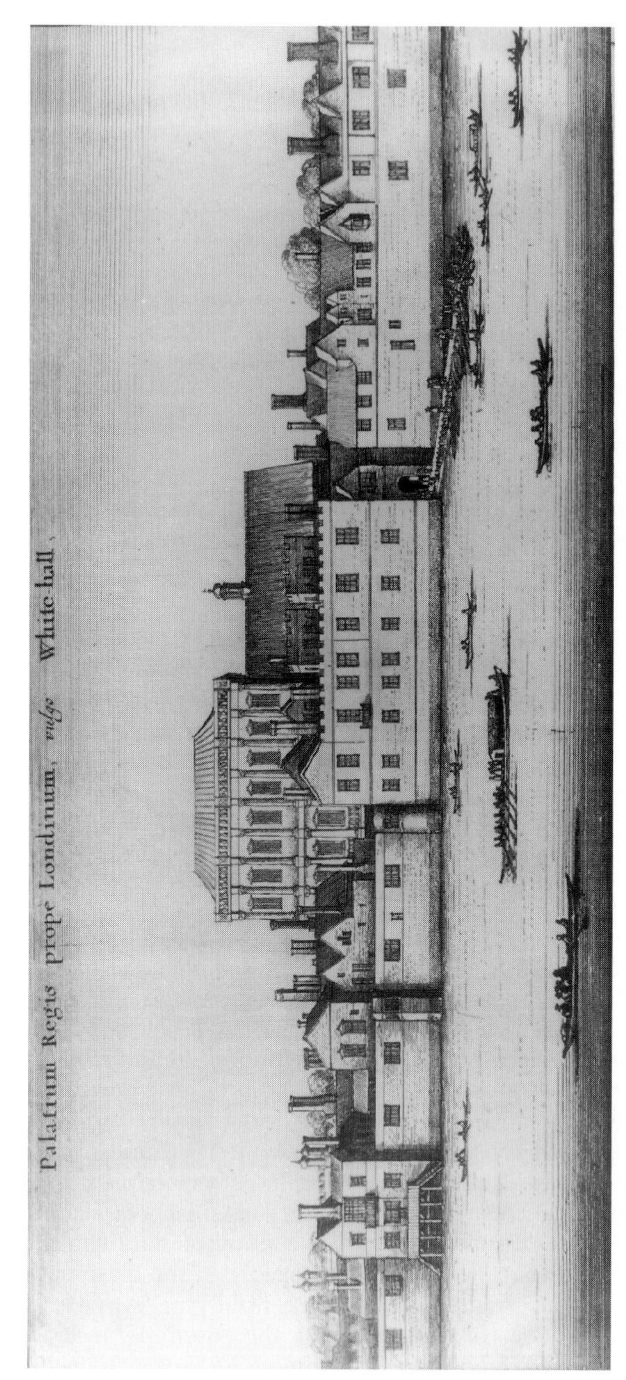

Wenceslaus Hollar, Elevation of *The Banqueting House*, designed and built 1619–22 (Joe Rock)

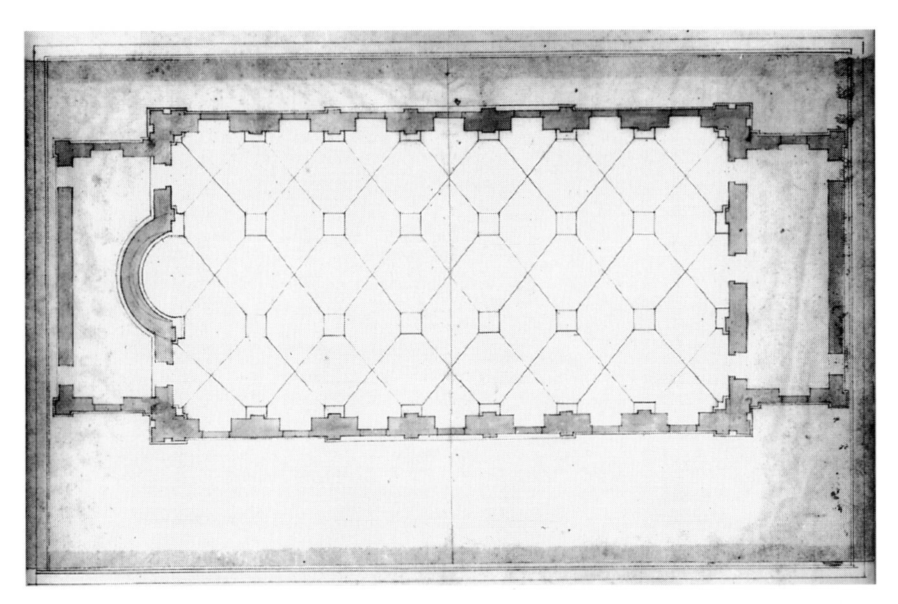

Plan of mainfloor and basement of Banqueting House (Courtauld Institute of Art)

behind. James loved to compare himself with those heroes of The Book of Judges from the Old Testament; priest kings who had been famed for their wisdom and good judgement and who had sat in the Temple at Jerusalem. To the humanist mind of the English Renaissance, the niche denoted the basilica, and customarily the basilica had been the location for the promulgation and application of law in the ancient world.

It has been suggested that the niche which acted as a backdrop to the king was removed by Jones within a few years of the completion of the building because more space was needed behind the scenes for a processional way. But a reminiscence if not an echo of that niche remains to this day in Rubens' canvas of *The Benefits of the Reign of James I*. Here James divides the good from the bad in anticipation of the Day of Judgement; pivoting athletically within a great niche supported by bold rusticated Salomonic columns. The canvas was arranged in such a way as to be 'readable' by the King seated under the canopy of state. That is to say with the feet of the king nearest the throne and thus the niche illusionistically framing him, as if hoisted aloft from the wall of the building below. The great central oval of *The Apotheosis* was again arranged so that James himself appeared to be borne aloft, with foreshortened body and head facing towards the seated sovereign waiting for a supplicant below making his measured approach to the throne along the middle of the hall from the entrance. From this it then followed that the *Union of the Two Crowns* was aligned in the *opposite* direction to the *Benefits* in order for it to be 'readable' by those waiting to approach the throne ahead of them. To

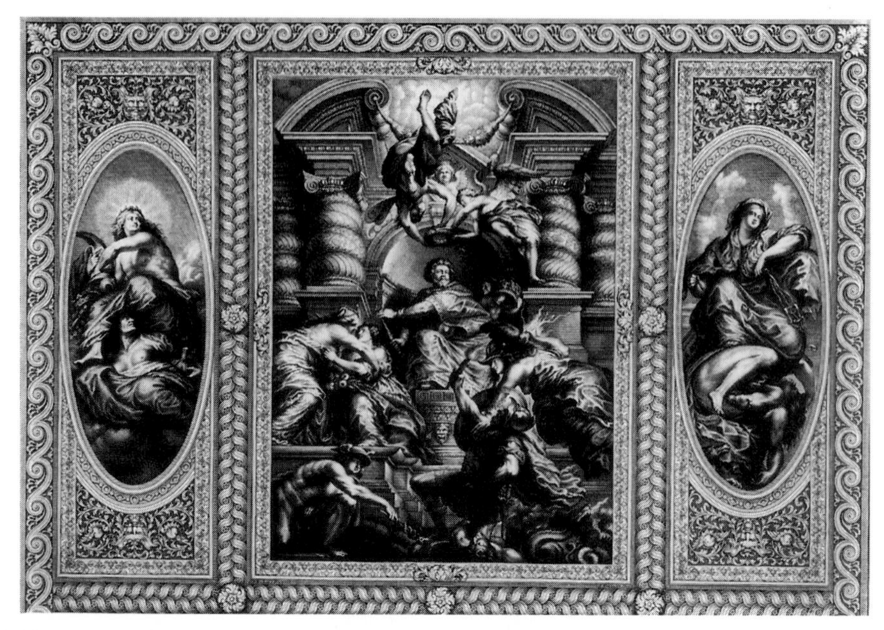

Simon Gribelin, 1720 engraving after Rubens, *The Benefits of the Reign of James I* (Society of Antiquaries of London)

illustrate these points the Gribelin engraving has been re-arranged in a montage to demonstrate how the ensemble would have appeared to a monarch seated under the canopy of state opposite the main entrance to the Banqueting Hall.[22]

James I justified the exercise of the royal prerogative and the divine right of kings both in *Basilikon Doron* and in speeches to Parliament. To apologists of the theory of kingship, and of these Inigo Jones was one, it was fitness itself that authority and justice were to be located in the Banqueting House, that theatre of early Stuart ceremonial.

Solomon was the favourite paradigm for James I. Always susceptible to flattery, nothing pleased him more than when one of his divines preached before him comparing his virtues with those of the patriarchal king of the Jews. Solomon was favoured above all for wisdom exemplified through the exercise of good judgement. But James was not content simply to listen to the honeyed words of preachers because, probably in the summer of 1617, he had ordered that rex as lex be given permanent expression in stone. While plans were formulated for the setting up of the Commission for New Buildings, Jones began to design a new building to house the Court of Star Chamber; thus named because the committee which formed the 'court' habitually met in a room decorated with a roof with a gilded star in its centre.

The Star Chamber consisted of a committee of the Privy Council which

The Ambassadors' Entrance
[Coat of Arms and Inscription
as seen on Gribelin Engraving]

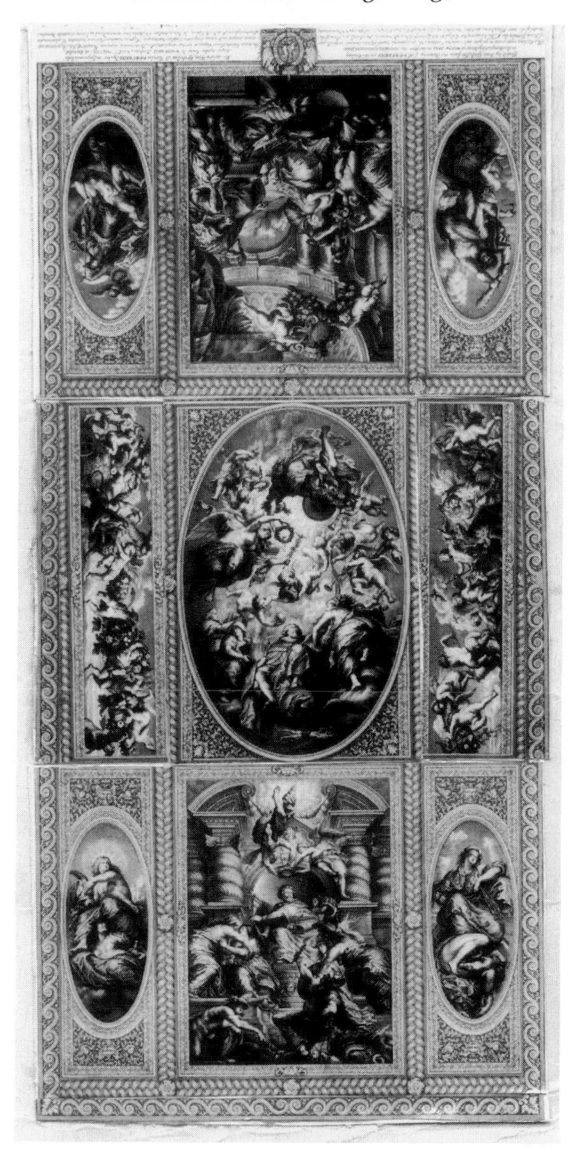

The Throne and
Canopy of State

Reconstruction of Rubens' Banqueting House ceiling as originally hung; after Julius Held (British Museum)

met to try cases which most frequently involved breaches of the peace. Though notorious in the Whig view of history, revisionists have come to a rather more positive view of its activities. But whatever the achievements and effects of the Star Chamber, its powers had been enhanced with the accession of James I in 1602.[23]

The Court of Star Chamber had been an important organ of government during the Tudor period. This is clear from the frequency with which the chamber had been refurbished: 1500–2, 1517, 1535, 1565–70, 1579–80, and lastly 1588–9, when it had received a new roof with 'a verie large starre'. Nevertheless all previous campaigns had been undertaken within the original chamber, whereas what James I envisaged in 1617 was an entirely new building which was to have had a giant order of Corinthian columns rising nearly fifty feet.

There is a ground plan of a new Star Chamber together with 'edited' elevations worked up later by Jones's disciple and amanuensis John Webb; enough to make it clear that if the new Jacobean Star Chamber had been realised, something yet more splendid than the Banqueting House might have thrust itself through the gables and crockets of a medieval

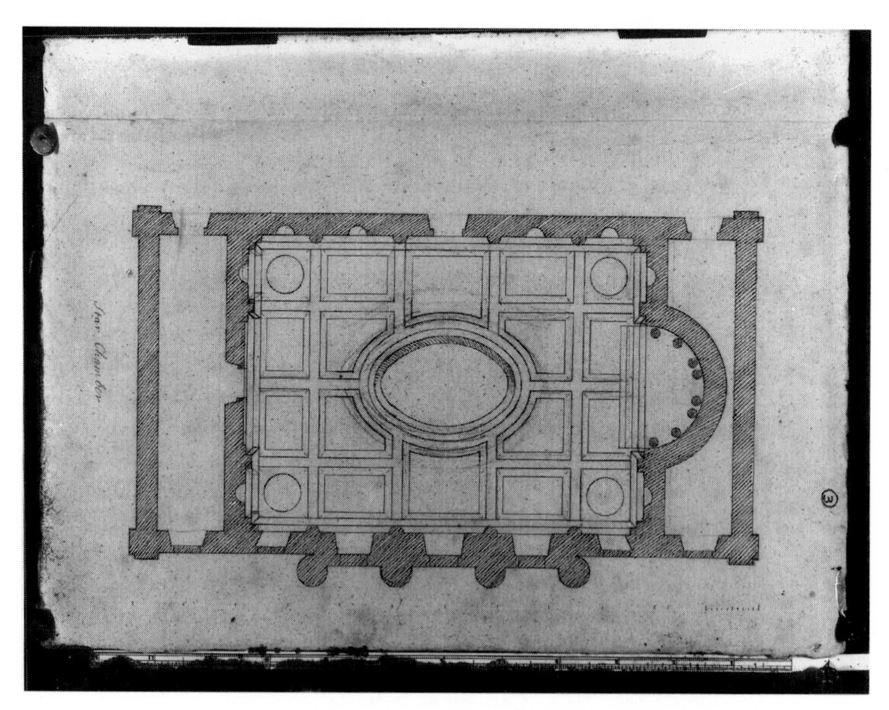

John Webb (after Inigo Jones), Groundplan of *The Star Chamber*, designed 1617 (Courtauld Institute of Art/The Provost and Fellows of Worcester College, Oxford)

London sky-line. Jones's ground plan was cut in half at some point, but when the two pieces are carefully aligned, the genesis of the Banqueting House lies revealed. However, there are different emphases. The earliest Star Chamber design has a basilical niche articulated at regular intervals with columns carrying a circular entablature and, behind these, square and round niches alternating on the concave space behind.[24] It is much more polyphonic than the design for the niche which was to stand for a few years behind the throne in the Banqueting House. These are differences in design which reflect differences in function; examples of design as both an expression of function and, as such, the hallmark of someone who really understood classicism; a subordination of parts which had never been grasped by the pattern book purveyors of Elizabethan classicism.

The contrast with what had been achieved in the previous generation was fundamental. With rare exceptions, Elizabethan architects, if architects they can be called for they were mostly master masons, had little or no capacity to see that certain elements which made up the classical language of architecture were more important than others. It was most unusual to find an Elizabethan builder who understood that the column had to be used like scanning in Latin verse: to break up the line and to give emphasis where required. Instead they piled obelisk on column and scroll upon pier in a wildly picturesque but essentially confusing medley. The Elizabethans could produce artefacts of great romance, but the deeper and more abstract qualities of classicism which have to do with proportional balance and a totality of design were beyond their grasp.

The Court of Star Chamber not only administered the common law, but passed judgement in certain types of legal dispute; the king enthroned in the Banqueting House merely reminded the subject that it was from him that judicial authority stemmed. Perhaps for us it is the difference between a judgement and the wig, robes and buckles of the judge. One was and still is a matter of a man's livelihood and reputation, the other, that is to say, the ceremonial dress, certainly meant much in the seventeenth century but to most observers now seems merely anachronistic. Justice was embodied when the king was enthroned in the Banqueting House but the Banqueting House was never a court. It was used for a host of court ceremonials: the masque, court feasts connected with the great holidays of what had once been the Catholic liturgical year, touching for the King's Evil, the reception of foreign ambassadors, as a gallery to view spectacles in the Tilt Yard outside, and the weddings of court favourites.

If Webb's street façade of the Court of Star Chamber can be trusted as an accurate record of what Jones had intended, it suggests that Jones was wanting to give fixed expression to his view as to what architecture was really about. It will be recalled that when Jones had been in Rome he had anticipated Bacon and Wotton, whose considered views on architecture were not to be given to the world until the mid-1620s, in seeing an

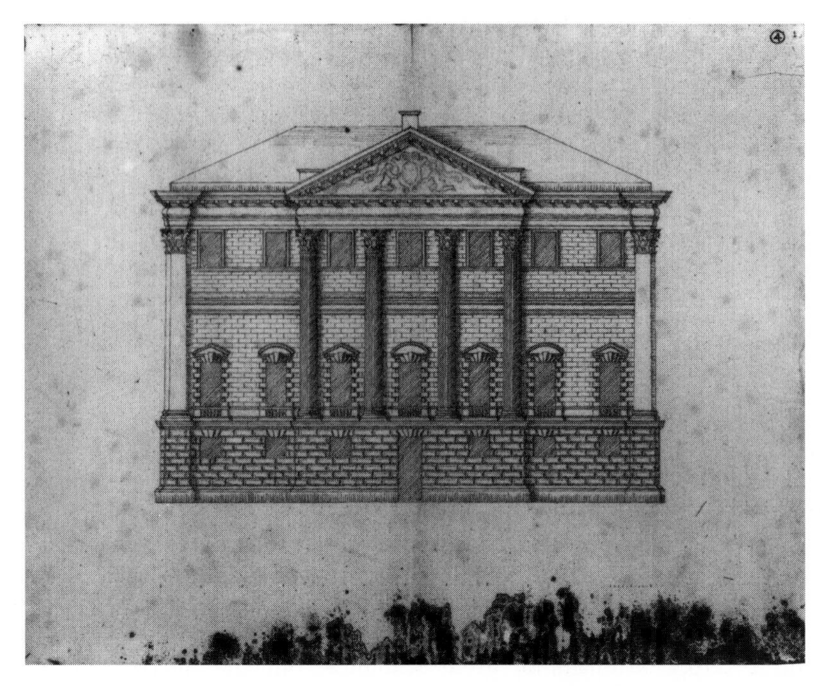

John Webb (after Inigo Jones), Elevation of *The Star Chamber* (Courtauld Institute of Art/The Provost and Fellows of Worcester College, Oxford)

analogue between human deportment and architectural decorum. To repeat what Jones had written, he had then considered that:

> in architecture ye outward ornaments oft [ought] to be sollid, proporsionable according to the rulles, masculine and unaffected.

That is precisely what the Court of Star Chamber would have been. The language would have expressed the values which Jones saw the Star Chamber as embodying. The elevation was to have combined a forthright aspect in the rough basement and heavily channelled stonework of the piano nobile, with a grandeur and joyous triumphalism in the deployment of a giant order of four attached Corinthian columns supporting a central pediment. Here Jones would have shown himself an impresario of rare accomplishment; an architect capable of uniting opposite qualities in a building which surely would have been replete with richly anthropomorphic suggestiveness. The stern incorruptible face of law as the basis of all systems of natural justice was to have been expressed through a rusticated base to the building; here the unhewn face of the stone providing an analogue to the origins of law as stemming from nature. But above, those who came to the building seeking or indeed receiving justice would have beheld the weight, the significance and the reassurance of a law properly ennacted and a law properly applied. The façade would have been the most splendid in London because it was to have been articulated with a huge Corinthian order; an order traditionally reserved for the most important buildings associated with rule. But it was also an order associated with the Roman triumphs in which the victorious Emperor received accolade and reaffirmation at the hands of the people.

Although James I was aware of how to use architecture to give visual expression to imperium, he was little if at all concerned with the palace life of the sovereign. The contrast between himself and Henry VIII could hardly have been more marked. Whereas the aggressive, tyrannical Henry kept on building because he kept on trying to devise methods of controlling his volatile court, James did not seem to mind how much exposure he was subjected to. By contrast to Henry VIII, who had half a dozen building projects on the go at once, James confined his interest to single public buildings where he got Jones to express a view which was much more articulate than that of the early Tudors. The projected Star Chamber or the completed Banqueting House had a learnedly classical, consistent and all-embracing allusion which came to provide a rather different form of persuasion than the badges and beasts, the bosses and beams of a Tudor Great Hall. Symbolism in the architecture of the early Stuart court was of a quite distinct order from that employed in Tudor royal architecture; though both epochs depended upon evoking lost worlds. The stained glass windows and the heraldic beasts of Hampton Court should really be seen as a natural outgrowth of *opus anglicanum*, understood in its widest sense; that is to say, the marvellously wrought skills of the English medieval craftsmen whose artefacts were regarded so highly that they found a place even in the Vatican Treasury.[25]

By contrast to the after-life of medieval art, Jacobean architecture was the product of a world of antiquity; monuments to a learned and well informed class of patrons and architects who had been busy collecting architectural folios, latterly even visiting Italy at first hand, since John Shute had published his treatise half a century before. English royal architecture bore quite a different meaning in 1520 from what it was to express in 1620. But that is not to say that the one was more effective than the other. Henry VIII depended upon tradition, sumptuousness, repetition and assertiveness; James I, on an educated elite who could appreciate the eloquence of proportion, clarity, decorum and a well judged display of awesome splendour.

The reputation of James I has soared in recent years.[26] Now historians discount the more lurid aspects of a weak character and such of his policies as flopped conspicuously. Today there is an acknowledgement that he handled theological disputes adroitly, while his determination to play the peace-broker in Europe appeals to our age of the international peace-keeping force. Such a significant rethink about the nature and achievements of his kingship invites a fresh look too at his role as a patron of the arts. Almost all the public work undertaken by Inigo Jones for the Crown was actually conceived or begun in the reign of James I; a point that needs emphasis when the exposure of The Royal Collection through a series of splendid exhibitions and television series has created the fixed impression that Charles I created a golden age of the arts. It has always been assumed, wrongly as I believe, that James did not care for a picture. Indeed on one occasion he actively set about diminishing the royal stock. It happened when the king was showing the Spanish ambassador round Whitehall in the winter of 1620. The party stopped in front of a 'history piece' which showed the defeat of the Spanish at Kinsale twenty years before. The ambassador was offended and so James 'caused several pieces to be cut out of the pictures in the gallery, which reflected on the Spaniards'.[27] Coarse but hardly uncaring might be how James's attitude to painting could be described. Arguably James cared sufficiently for pictures to see that what he did not like, he had destroyed. It would be quite wrong to think that a man who had seen bonfires of pictures when a boy in Scotland was unaware of just how persuasive a visual image could be. This is suggested in a creative if derivative way by a document cited by Chamberlain, whose two-volume biography of Holbein, though eighty years old, remains the definitive study of the painter. Chamberlain noted that on 13 January 1618, James wrote from Newmarket to the Company of Barber-Surgeons asking that Holbein's mural of Henry VIII granting a charter to the company should be lent to him, as he was anxious to have a copy made of it:

> We are informed there is a table of Painting in your Hall whereon is the Picture of our Predecessor of famous memorie K. Henry the 8th., together wth diverse of y^r^ Companie, wch being both like him and well done Wee are desirous to have copyd.[28]

Whatever view we take of James's attitude to painting, there is no doubt about architecture: the variety and ambition of projects initiated if never realised by Jones under the patronage of James suggests that James certainly saw buildings as eloquent images of rule.

Priorities were reversed with James's son Charles I. He was not as fond of building as he was of pictures. Why was this so? The answer may lie in part at least in differences of character. Disputatious, garrulous, articulate, promiscuously fond of robust company though personally timorous, James was a marked contrast to his fastidious, shy and sensitive son; a figure who felt most at ease in the intimate surroundings of a cabinet room inspecting medals to the sound of the lute. By contrast, James I loved to be the riotous centaur, to 'wallow in beastly delights' as he did so famously at Theobalds in 1606 when entertaining his brother-in-law,

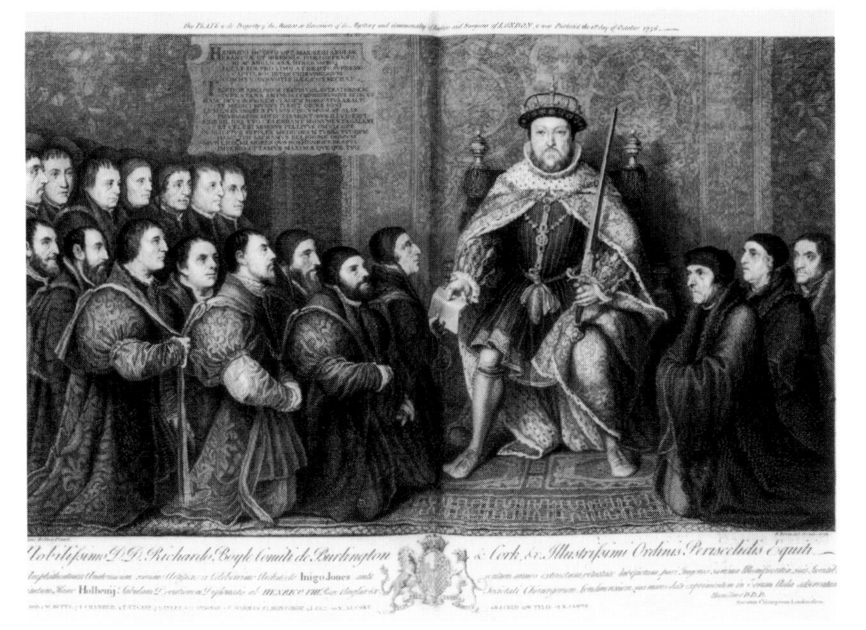

Bernard Baron, 1736 engraving after Hans Holbein, *Henry VIII and the Barber Surgeons*, 1541 (Society of Antiquaries of London)

Christian IV of Denmark.[29] Loss of control pleased James, where it made his son shudder. Such differences have a bearing on why James built and Charles did not. Charles was not a man for the expansive gesture; there was no progress through London to greet the onset of his reign as there had been when his father entered into his new kingdom. Charles I lacked confidence and to have built on a princely scale demanded it. James I was a coward physically but essentially a confident man. His son was the reverse.

So too with the court masque, now valued, overvalued perhaps, as an expression of the Stuart mind. The masque is intimately associated with the early Stuarts. It developed into an ambitious and sophisticated expression of regal values within a few years of the accession of James I, but then there was a hiatus following the accession of Charles I in March 1625. Although the occasional pastoral was enacted by Charles I's wife Henrietta Maria, the full splendour of the Jacobean masque was only to be equalled again with the performance of *Love's Triumph Through Callipolis* in 1631.

Inigo Jones built more for James I than for Charles I. Momentum slowed down with the accession of the new king in the early spring of 1625. Of course the Crown still remained an important source of work for the building trades in the 1620s; there was a never-ending round of repairs and decoration to be done. However, in so far as there was challenging work from the Crown, it tended to come from Henrietta Maria not Charles. Henrietta Maria summoned Jones frequently for much of the early thirties when work began again on the Queen's House; there was, too, Somerset House chapel to design, and by 1638–9, that fascinating rural retreat which needed major refurbishment, Wimbledon House – originally a Cecil property and one about which we know tantalisingly little.

Charles I liked privacy and intimacy and it may be that he found Jones's peremptory judgements on royal pictures more interesting than his views on architecture.[30] Jones had begun life as a painter and by the 1630s his reputation as a connoisseur was formidable. Indeed it may have been his skills as a judge of painting as much as his contribution to royal building which led to the offer of a knighthood; an honour he turned down in April 1633. He probably refused it because of the expense entailed for those who put their foot on this first rung of the ladder to social elevation.[31] Jones refused at the time when he was described as a 'Puritanissimo fiero' by Monsignor Gregorio Panzani, a Vatican official who obviously disliked him. It is a famous epithet which historians have found understandably difficult to reconcile with the persistent myth that Jones was a Roman Catholic.

What Panzani was really referring to surely had nothing to do with the supposed religious affiliations of this high priest of taste; Jones was no Puritan hiding under a Roman Catholic cloak; that would have been a strange disguise indeed. Rather, Panzani simply meant that Jones was dogmatic like most connoisseurs then as indeed today. Jones was a Precisian not a Puritan; according to the *Oxford English Dictionary*, a definition current in the late sixteenth century meant that a Puritan was perceived as a man 'given to excessive (or affected) strictness or preciseness like that of the Puritans'. Affected preciseness, or a dogmatic certainty, perfectly summarises what poor Panzani felt and what Jones embodied. Thus the reference to Jones as a Puritan had everything to do with temperament; nothing with men in black hats.

Henrietta Maria was an enthusiast for architecture: in the thirties she restarted building at The Queen's House, which had been abandoned with the death of Anne of Denmark back in 1618. That was a perfectly turned essay in the Italian villa style to the east of the metropolis. As if in deliberate contrast, Henrietta Maria then created a French-style villa at Wimbledon to the west of London; modifying a pre-existing structure which had been acquired from the Cecils. When Jones came to be assessed by Parliament for fines connected with his support for the Crown during the Civil War, he had to make a declaration of his estate; including money he was owed. Some of these lists survive and show Henrietta Maria owed him significant amounts.[32]

There is however one respect in which Charles can be compared with Henry VIII, the greatest royal builder, and this has to do with the use, not construction of buildings. Henry had changed the protocol of Tudor court life with the enactment of the Eltham Ordinances of 1526. Although this initiative really came from Wolsey, it certainly had the enthusiastic support of the Crown. The Eltham Ordinances were elaborate instructions aimed at making the life of the court more ordered, regular and decorous. A century later Charles I again concerned himself with how people conducted themselves within the precincts of the royal palaces.[33] Just as the Eltham Ordinances can be seen as evidence of a king now restive at being dominated by his chief minister, so Charles may well have felt the need to stamp his own personality on a court he found antipathetic.

However, there appears to be a major difficulty in assuming that Charles was a king for pictures not palaces. This is found in a corpus of some seventy drawings by Jones' assistant John Webb. These are now taken to represent two separate schemes from the 1630s for a palace which was to have been located either in St James's Park or along the Thames.[34] But impressive though these schemes may be on paper, they were nothing more than a *jeu d'esprit*. Some believe that the drawings allow us to conclude that James and Charles intended the Banqueting House to be part of a classical enfilade of buildings; a flagship waiting for its squadron of classically dressed buildings floating along the river.

Castles in the air or palaces on the river if you will, these were things of almost obsessive interest to Baroque princes. The quest for a great new

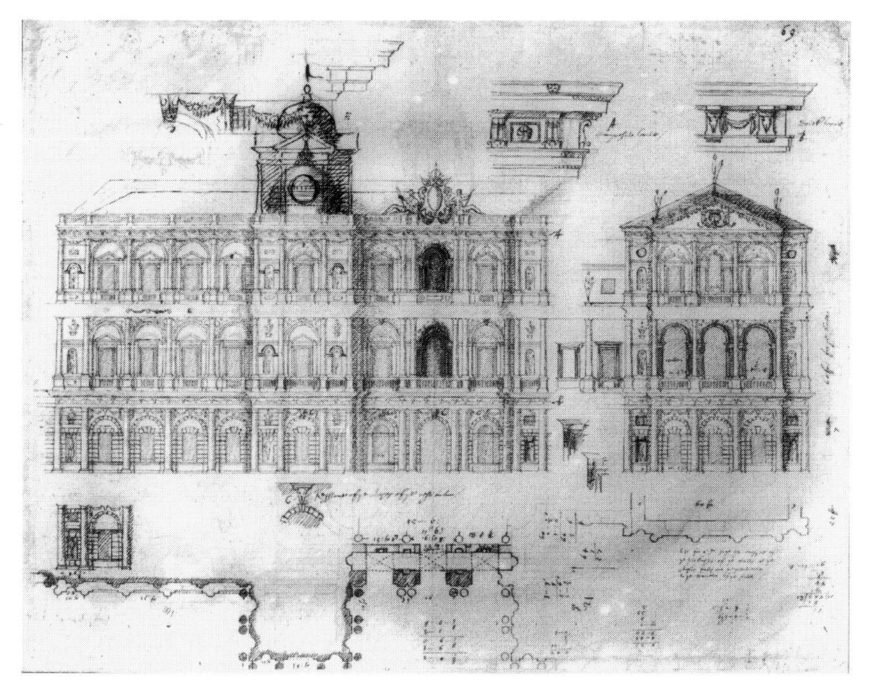

John Webb, *Whitehall Palace*, sketch plans and elevation, late 1630s onwards (Courtauld Institute of Art)

palace was an opiate paralleled in its fascination at that time only by the interest 'chymists' took in discovering the philosopher's stone. The palace compulsion stemmed from the extraordinary pull exercised by the plans for the Escorial, which had been published by the architect Juan de Herrera, in 1589, and entitled *Las Estampas de la Fábrica de San Lorenzo el Real de El Escorial*; a publicity exercise in part bound up with the work of two Jesuits, Jerónimo Pardo and Juan Bautista Villalpando. In 1580 the two priests had set themselves the task of reconstructing the ancient temple in Jerusalem. This bizarre exercise in 'archaeological' reconstruction eventually bore fruit over the next twenty-five years when their ruminations appeared in various learned and illustrated volumes.[35] But how many megalomaniac schemes influenced by the Escorial and the Temple in Jerusalem, which absorbed so much of the creative imagination of princes, ever led to one stone being placed upon another, let alone to the point of completion? Surely Charles I liked to discuss such plans as a pleasing diversion from the hard, conscientious and relentless attention to detail he gave to government without Parliament. He encouraged these schemes because they flattered him; like the children's fairy tale in which the mirror obligingly tells the wicked princess that she is the fairest of them all. It was the same illusion which allowed the king to be duped by the rhetoric of his own masques.

There is not a shred of evidence of Charles annotating these plans, which there would have been had he been serious about having them used in a masons' yard. He usually added marginalia when engaged in a serious practical way with business, but he is nowhere to be seen in these late essays by Jones and Webb. This is in stark contrast to his scrutiny of accounts for works of art. Francis Cleyn, who produced coloured designs for the Mortlake tapestries, Hubert Le Sueur, the most productive of the sculptors working for Charles – or 'Praxiteles' Le Sueur as he liked to call himself, an inflation of status to match what have been described aptly as his Michelin men – even the great Sir Anthony Van Dyck when presenting his account for *Charles I à la chasse*, one and all, had their bills cut down to size by the stroke of the regal pen. It was not however quite as humiliating as it seems. It has been suggested that artists deliberately inflated their accounts knowing full well that they were never going to get what they asked for.[36] Since Charles I found time to scrutinise the paper work sent up by his artists, because visual propaganda in whatever guise it came was a priority for him, we should expect marginalia on these Jonesian drawings for megalithic palaces if what was drawn was to have been for real. But these we do not have.

Oliver Cromwell made Charles I walk to his death against the tragic backdrop of a stone curtain in a symbolic gesture of humiliation. The doomed king emerged onto the scaffold of his execution from a window of the Banqueting House, the scene of so many ceremonies to elevate the Stuart monarchy to a heavenly sphere. Cromwell, too, chose to steal majesty from within that paradigmatic building. He favoured it for his own elaborate court rituals, which differed in many respects so little from those of the Stuarts. In so doing, the republican regime of seventeenth-century England was distinct from the *sans-culottes* of the French Revolution. In France a mass programme of the destruction of royal buildings was thought to be a more effective means of extinguishing the old regime. But whether state buildings were claimed by an alien regime or destroyed by the rabble, each response demonstrates the potency of buildings as images of rule.

Chapter Two
The God that Rules

The Church was the First Estate of the Realm, churches the most controversial buildings in early modern Britain. John Morrill has argued that men cared more about their religion than anything else by the 1630s.[1] This has been proposed on the grounds that most pamphlets produced in the war of words which preceded Civil War were about religion and freedom of worship. To those who find it hard to believe that men could care more for what is unseen than seen, an examination of the issues raised about church architecture certainly seems to support this argument. It is then the purpose of this chapter to consider in what ways the appearance and furnishing of churches really mattered to people, and how disagreements on these issues reveal values of the period.

An ecclesiastical building was much more than a church in early modern England. Today most churches are locked, and many out of business. In 1600 it was very different. The parish church acted as school, library, public noticeboard, MP's surgery, village hall, and mortuary. All, from earl to village idiot, were expected to congregate.

The break with Rome made the church in England a state church and so began a fatal partnership between state and church which saw the survival of the former but very nearly the extinction of the latter. The rejection of Catholicism which began with Henry VIII divorcing Catherine of Aragon was one of the most audacious robberies in the history of England. It succeeded against all the odds. At a stroke people were deprived of a thousand years of tradition; the lion and the unicorn chased Christ away as the royal arms came to replace the rood screen and its carvings of the Passion. The Anglican Settlement, fully established on paper only with the statutory sanction of the Thirty-Nine Articles by Convocation in 1571, but actually never properly settled, was one of the most unlikely revolutions in the cultural history of Europe. It just succeeded, but only because it claimed to be a restoration. There was constant pressure on its apologists to justify what had been done by an appeal to the past. The ways in which ecclesiastical building in the first century of Anglicanism expressed the intimate relationship between church and state is a major theme of this chapter.

Elizabeth I made it certain that the monarchy and the Church would stand or fall together when she commanded that the royal arms should substitute for the rood screen. Thereafter however, she proceeded with caution. Although she had her own strong views about church furnishing, she was careful not to get embroiled in such heated debates as where altars should be placed in churches.

She built little for herself in the secular sphere and nothing at all in the ecclesiastical. No royal chapels were built in the reign and only nineteen churches in all England in a forty-five-year reign. On the face of it this seems surprising since a new religion which recognised only the two sacraments of Baptism and the Eucharist, and which put far greater emphasis on the word in the form of the sermon, might be supposed to have been ill-served by buildings originally designed to articulate a richer and more complicated system of belief. However, the church authorities felt that pre-existing structures could be adapted to meet new requirements. But this is by no means a complete explanation.

At first the challenge which the Anglican Settlement had to meet had come from Catholics; though, with the passage of time, the Establishment came to be threatened rather more by Presbyterians. Presbyterians held the view that a separate and specially dedicated building in which to worship was not only unnecessary but positively wrong. This led to great tension and hostility with the official church. It also promoted the view within the Church establishment that the building of 'Anglican' churches would serve only to exacerbate an already tense situation. Caught as the Anglican Church was between the quagmire of Catholics and the briars of Calvinism, the best thing was to do nothing, or so the authorities inclined to believe. The Anglican Church was not a city upon a hill as its optimists believed, but a city besieged on every side. Somehow it survived.

It was a successful policy of inactivity and as such, something of a contrast to what had happened in the educational sphere. Because the educational resources of early Tudor England had been so closely identified with the church, changes in worship had had very significant effects. The old chantry schools had been swept away by the Edwardian Chantries Act which resulted in the Edwardian Grammar Schools; although in many cases the actual structures in which a Catholic education had been provided survived.

With the church itself, Anglican ministers adapted old buildings as the laity did also. For example Sir Richard Rich turned part of St Bartholomew's Priory, Smithfield, into tenements, or Sharington moved into the abbey at Lacock.[2] A strong incentive whether in the sphere of the houses of the nobility or the ordinary parish church had been the money saved in adaptation. Nevertheless the paucity of church building in the later sixteenth century was because the authorities were afraid of stirring up controversy. There could hardly be a more marked contrast between how Elizabethans responded and what the Victorians were to do when they came to be confronted by threats to the state church. Following the repeal of the Test and Corporation Acts in 1828 and the Roman Catholic Emancipation Act of 1829, a significant campaign of church building was undertaken to try to sustain the continued dominance of Anglicanism.

In the reign of Elizabeth, the best energies of Matthew Parker, the Archbishop of Canterbury who presided over the Anglican Settlement, and of Whitgift who later policed it, were directed towards damping down controversy and rooting out schismatics. The life of the Elizabethan church was directed rather more from the pulpit than from the altar, as was to become the case under the Stuarts. The crisis period for Anglicanism was the 1550s until the mid-1580s. The threat was from Cambridge Presbyterians. These were the years when Cartwright and Travers, erstwhile Cambridge academics deprived of their fellowships for their unsound views, attacked Anglicanism through the eloquence of their preaching; helped so to do by Leicester and Burghley who protected them. Through Burghley's means, Travers was appointed afternoon lecturer at the Temple Church. It was a key preferment since the Temple served the Inns of Court, the greatest concentration of intelligence in the realm. Travers' opponent there was Richard Hooker, whose great work of *the Laws of Ecclesiastical Polity*, published from 1594 onwards, was the purest distillation of Anglican apologetics. Towards the end of the reign however, furious pulpit controversy died away for several reasons: Hooker's compendious and comprehensive defence of Anglicanism won many converts through its learning and mild reasonableness; Travers died, and Cartwright lost his fire; while a wave of Catholic missionaries began once more to threaten the integrity of the state Church.

The pulpit was where theological controversy was to be located; though it was to move to the altar under Elizabeth's successors. James did much to make men think with acerbity about religion again; it pleased his vanity and his Scottish taste for disputatious theology to weigh in on his own account. His first initiative was the Hampton Court Conference of 1604, the purpose of which was to reconcile the differences between Anglicans and Puritans. Having treated the 'painful men' of the Low Church with marked rudeness, he followed this excursion into one thicket with a long trek in search of an accommodation with a more flexible Papacy. James proposed mutual respect through mutual recognition of separate but equal jurisdiction. This however was too much for Paul V, and James's principal adversary, Cardinal Robert Bellarmine.

Earlier James I had declared when irritated by Dr John Rainolds, a Puritan and the Professor of Divinity at Oxford, in a famously exasperated moment during the course of the Hampton Court Conference of

1604, how, were the bishops to be ousted by the Puritans, 'I know what would become of my supremacy. No bishop, no King. When I mean to live under a presbytery I will go into Scotland again.'[3] It is therefore to the ecclesiastical bench we turn for a clear example of how the church, its fabric and its glorious furnishings, became identified with an authority felt by many as increasingly alien.

Lancelot Andrewes was a curious mixture of the worldly and the saintly. Although James felt that Andrewes' High churchmanship would probably have been divisive in a nation which was floating on a current if not a tide of Calvinism, he might still have become Archbishop of Canterbury had he not refused two bishoprics in the reign of Elizabeth on the grounds that they could not be properly ordered while the Queen herself had alienated their revenues. This may have been a case of admirable integrity in the face of cynical exploitation of what properly belonged to the ecclesiastical estate, and certainly such gestures also show the degree to which Andrewes felt the necessity of upholding the full dignity and authority of the Church as by law established.

Despite his high-minded stance over ecclesiastical promotion, Andrewes did eventually become Bishop of Winchester. That office made him chaplain to the Order of the Garter, the principal order of chivalry in England; the dignity of which Charles I was greatly to enhance. Certainly devout, and even by the pre-eminent standards of Tudor and Stuart divines, a great preacher, Andrewes was no ascetic. He loved ceremony and he loved a High Church.

Andrewes stands as the first prominent churchman to be described as an Arminian by enemies of Anglicanism. Nobody quite knew then, any more than they seem to do now, what exactly was meant by an English Arminian; though the only safe assumption which can be made is that they turned their faces against the Calvinist doctrine of Predestination, against the idea that a man was saved or not, according to the arbitrary and inscrutable nature of an unpredictable Deity. Arminians tended toward a liking for ceremonial and what tended rulers toward a liking for them was Arminius' own inclination to stress the absolute authority of the state.

Andrewes certainly decorated churches and chapels with provocative richness. He felt this correct because God's holy house was the most important building on earth. This being so, the church should be distinguished by the finest works of art, by way paradoxically, of revealing man's humility and reverence in the face of the Creator, the Universal Architect of nature.

But another motive for sumptuous splendour has an important bearing on ways in which ecclesiastical architecture became an image of rule. Church and state were branches of a stem which had been planted by Henry VIII. Henry had ended the judicial links between England and Rome in 1533 by declaring 'Where by divers sundry old authentic histories and chronicles it is manifestly declared and expressed that this realm of England is an Empire'.[4] Such a resounding opening to the Act of Appeals, a drum roll for an emergent nation state, proclaimed the dignity of the state and the splendour of the prince. But it also knocked away the buttresses of a church which had been national but crucially too, supra-national.

When Thomas à Becket had quarrelled with Henry II after his appointment to the see of Canterbury in 1162, the Church in England had called up the support of the Papacy. A year or two after Becket was chased out of England he had appealed to Alexander III who was then at Sens. The intervention of the Papacy meant that Henry had to give ground over the issue of how far ecclesiastical authority ran. Although Henry eventually provoked the most famous assassination in English history at Christmas 1170 and so removed what he had perceived to be a great impediment to his rulership, the Papacy acted immediately and decisively in defence of its church in England. Within three years of Becket's assassination, Alexander III had had Becket canonised and the very next year Henry himself did public penance at the site of the murder in Canterbury Cathedral. Henry prostrated himself at what had already become one of the great shrines of Christendom; an act which signalled that for the church, triumph had issued out of disaster. Within thirty years Innocent III was to be elected to the Holy See, a man who saw his office as semi-divine and himself as one 'set in the midst between God and man, below God but above man'.

The murder of Becket was the most famous quarrel between church and state in pre-Reformation England but there were other less lurid and well publicised occasions when the most powerful weapons in the armoury of the Roman Curia were brought up to lay siege to the monarchy in England. Once Henry broke with Rome, however, there was no longer the prospect of sending for powerful reinforcements. Although Henry proceeded cautiously in dismantling the Roman Church in England, it had in effect become an isolated target.

Following the Act of Appeals of 1533 in England, there began a gradual but decisive inflation in the presentation of the ceremony and context of worship. This would have much to do with the dignity though little with the sanctity of what had become a state religion. The very phrase 'state church' reveals a contradiction between the demands of this world and the next which by the mid-seventeenth century could not be resolved. Therefore such insuperable difficulties led to the temporary destruction of a system which had been so painstakingly nurtured by Elizabeth and her first primate Matthew Parker.

The application of silk and marble to interiors, a willingness to dramatise ceremonial so as to make theatre out of worship, which Elizabeth avoided but an influential early Stuart divine like Lancelot Andrewes emphasised, could be justified certainly, but it was a perilous undertaking. It made High churchmen vulnerable to accusations of covert sympathy towards Roman Catholicism.

The drama of High church Jacobean worship, the sight of an Arminian bishop prostrating himself before the doors of a church, is encapsulated in a celebrated phrase 'The beauty of holiness'. It referred to a powerful body of clerics who became dominant within Anglicanism by the time of the death of James, and who felt that the Church was best served by the deployment of the most eloquent and affecting arts. They wished to impress upon all the ineffable beauty of the sacred mysteries. But what it is vital to appreciate is that the conviction which this phrase seeks to describe was not and should not be equated with 'the holiness of beauty'. The phrase was not a prescription for beautifying English churches for it was holiness not beauty which mattered to the likes of Andrewes, a man of great personal piety. Beauty was not an end in itself, but rather a means to an end which was infinitely more important than the silver candlesticks to be found in Bishop Andrewes' private chapel at Winchester. Unhappily for those who saw beauty as a powerful instrument of persuasion, Puritans either could not, or more probably would not, see a Thomist distinction between 'essentials' and 'inessentials'.

The central figure in the early Stuart Church was not however Andrewes but William Laud, who became Bishop of London in 1628, and Archbishop of Canterbury in 1633. During the twenty-five years when Laud was either a persuasive or dominant figure in Anglicanism, from his appointment to the Deanery of Gloucester in 1616 until his removal to the Tower in 1641, material changes occurred in churches which transformed many into jewelled caskets. Stained glass windows were inserted into college chapels, marble pavements and turned walnut rails put up before the altars of City of London churches. Where plain and moveable 'tables' had satisfied the Elizabethan gentleman, communicants came to be pressured into taking the eucharist on their knees, upon plum velvet cushions and at a decorous interval from the sanctuary.

Curiously enough although richly visual embellishments and theatrical ceremonies were encouraged by Laud, personally he had little relish for the visual arts. We know a great deal about what Laud thought because his papers were minutely searched for evidence to be used against him by William Prynne, the fanatic lawyer who had been persecuted by Laud for intemperate attacks on the Anglican Church. Much of this material Prynne then proceeded to publish in a highly selective way.

One of the most revealing of these documents was Laud's private diary.[5] At no point does it suggest that he was moved by the visual arts for their own sake. Abrasive and impatient, though not without humour and flexibility, he had little time to discuss irresolvable questions of taste. Temperamentally inclined to feel satisfied when things were done rather than discussed, changed and discussed again, he might well have found the editorial line of *The Ecclesiologist* sympathetic. In 1854 the editor of what was then an influential journal wrote: 'Church architecture . . . is admitted to be the subject not so much of taste as of facts.'[6] Whereas for the Victorians there was a 'right' style for ecclesiastical architecture and decoration which had all to do with 'rightness' and little to do with style, for Laud and his fellow bishops, what mattered more than a particular style was that churches should exist where they were wanting and, where they did exist, should be decent and comely.

Laud encouraged splendour in the Anglican Church believing that it provided an elevated frame for the enactment of the liturgy. However, for Laud, art remained first and last, a frame for something much more important; for the commemoration of Christ's death through the word made flesh in the case of the Eucharist celebrated at a marble altar, or for new birth symbolised in the sacrament of Baptism conducted under a canopy as high as a market cross. There is an irony about the predicament the Laudian church was to find itself in. It was because Laud personally was largely indifferent to material objects that he was prepared to have them erected or not, provided that was, the building offered an efficient context for the enactment of divine service. Difficulties arose however because whereas most of his enemies shared his indifference to works of art in a secular setting, they differed from him in believing that the erection of a picture over an altar broke the Commandment that 'Thou shalt not take to thyself any graven image'. To do so was idolatrous because it induced men to worship the object and not what the object symbolised.

The tragedy of Archbishop Laud stemmed from his lack of imagination. He thought it no scandal to have an image of God the Father as an old man, making the world with a pair of compasses, as a stained glass window in the parish church of St Edmund, Salisbury. For him that window would have been merely an aid to worship; as schoolboys might use an abacus. Unfortunately not everyone agreed and especially not Henry Sherfield, the Recorder of Salisbury. Sherfield was scandalised by the window, and unable to bear the imagery any longer, knocked it out, and himself also in the perilous business of hanging off a ladder, hammer in hand. When he had recovered, his vandalism landed him in the Court of Star Chamber in February 1633, where predictably enough, Laud flew about him like an angry wasp; demanding a fine of £1,000 and public acknowledgement by Sherfield of his offence.

What made Laud implacable was not the destruction of an old window, but rather the assault on the dignity of the church. Laud was not interested in taking a stand on the great issue of the legitimacy of sacred imagery since the window was replaced with plain glass. Sherfield had committed a more serious crime than the destruction of imagery by daring to question the authority of the established Church. Interestingly enough, Laud was supported by Sherfield's bishop, John Davenant, who was much more disposed to be sympathetic to Puritanism. Privately, Davenant was himself doubtful as to the legitimacy and efficacy of sacred imagery, but he too felt that the real issue was the authority of the state Church. In his capacity as Bishop of Salisbury, Davenant felt bound to support Laud.[7]

In general Laud shared much the same view as Elizabeth I, who had defended the Anglican Settlement so Francis Bacon had said, by not opening windows into mens' souls. But although Laud too was prepared to leave the individual conscience alone, provided men conformed to outward and public acts of worship, there the comparison ended. Laud simply did not possess Elizabeth's capacity to compromise and retreat. The Sherfield case reveals the fatal extent to which he perceived Anglicanism as a buttress of order.

Laud's emphasis on ceremony encouraged the literal elevation of the host and the metaphorical elevation of the priesthood. Laudians urged communicants to kneel because they believed such a physical gesture induced a proper awe for the central mystery of the Christian faith, while for his part, the Laudian minister inhabited a sanctified area within the chancel. Laudians tended to follow a recommendation made by High Church bishops on their Visitations, which was to rail off the area immediately around the altar. The net result was to enhance the superiority of the priest over the laity.

Laudians made the service a work of art and not merely its physical setting. The conduct and deportment of Laudian priests was a daily, peripatetic image of order defined by the presence of a caste, deriving its authority from the Imperial monarch of Great Britain. It was a caste and indeed a cast for the theatrical enactment of ritual splendour; words apt for describing the elaborate protocol of court life in Renaissance England.

The impact Laud made is clear from descriptions of what had happened in January 1631 when he had consecrated St Katherine Cree in his capacity as Bishop of London. St Katherine's was one of the few new churches to be built in the City since the Reformation. Here we encounter what those of Puritan sympathies found profoundly distasteful; a ceremony which they saw as Catholic, and Catholic in the most elaborate and theatrical vein; if, that is, Prynne's account can be regarded as trustworthy. It occurs in *Canterburies Doom* – a publication which passes as a book though it partakes more of a pamphlet. Like a dishevelled crow crowing upon a dunghill, Prynne exults over his enemy whose blood had hardly dried on the axe when his book came out. He writes a lively not to say hilarious account of the bowings and scrapings which went on. Such is the vividness of the passage in which he describes the consecration that it is tempting to believe he would have been better served had he written comedies rather than denounced them:

> [Laud] came in the morning about nine of the clock in a pompous manner to *Creed-church*, accompanied with Sir *Henry Martin*, Dr *Rive*, Dr *Duck*, and many other *High-commissioners* and *Civillians*, there being a very great concourse of people to behold this novelty: the Church doores were garded with many Halbeders; at the Bishops approaching near the West door of the Church, the hangbies of the Bishop cryed out

> with a loud voyce, *Open, open, ye everlasting doores, that the King of glory may enter in*; and presently (as by miracle) the doores flew open, and the Bishop with three or four great Doctors and many other principall men entred in; and as soon as they were in the Church, the Bishop fell down upon his knees with his eyes lifted up, and his hands and armes spread abroad, uttering many words, and saying, *This place is holy, and this ground is holy: In the name of the Father, the Sonne, and the Holy Ghost I pronounce it holy*; and then he took up some of the earth or dust and threw it up into the aire (as the frantick persecuting Jewes did, when they were raging mad against *Paul*). . . . After all this, the Bishop betook himselfe, to sit under a cloath of State in an Isle of the chancell neare the Communion Table, and taking a written book in his hand . . . *He pronounced many curses upon all those which should hereafter any way prophane that holy and sacred place*. . . . When the *Curses* were ended, he then pronounced the like number of *Blessings* to all *those that had any hand in the culture, framing and building of that holy*, sacred and *beautifull Church and pronounced Blessings to all those that had given any Challices, Plate, Ornaments, or Vtensills*. . . . Then he came to one of the corners of the Table, and there bowed himselfe three times; . . . but, when he came to the side of the Table where the bread and wine was, he bowed himselfe seven times, and then, after the reading of many praiers by himselfe and his fat chaplins . . . he himself came neare the Bread . . . and then he gently lifted up one of the corners of the said napkin, and peeped into it till hee saw the bread (like a boy that peeped after a bird-nest in a bush) and presently clapped it down againe, and flew backe a step or two . . . then hee came neere againe, and lifting up the cover of the Cupp peeped into it, and seeing the wine, he let fall the cover on it againe, and flew nimbly backe and bowed as before: After these and many other Apish Anticke Gesturs he himselfe received, and then gave the Sacrament to some principall men onely they devoutly kneeling neere the Table, after which more praiers being said, this Sceane and Enterlude ended.[8]

Prynne concludes his description of proceedings that Sunday morning in 1631, with the words 'Sceane' and 'Enterlude'. It is the language of the theatre; the language Jones was to use just weeks later in his stage directions for *Chloridia*; along with *Love's Triumph through Callipolis* its accompaniment for the 1630/1 season, the first great masque of the reign, and the last collaborative offering of Jones and Jonson. It is impossible to know which Prynne found more offensive – the consecration of St Katherine's or bare-breasted Chloris capering about the Banqueting House – but for him they were the same thing: theatrical conspiracies to support a tyranny and scandalise the godly.

The most provocative statement of the Laudian manipulation of art came however with the renewing of Old St Paul's and not with the consecration of parish churches; actually a ceremony Laud performed rarely. The whole St Paul's project, and as always with anything Laud touched, the unfortunate manner in which it was prosecuted, played a far more fundamental part in the alienation of the City of London than his occasional appearances in the City in full episcopal regalia.

There are parallels between how the Crown looked on Old St Paul's and how it was then trying to control building in London. Just as Elizabeth had made a series of ineffectual attempts to supervise London building, so too desultory efforts had been made to repair the disgraceful condition of the metropolitan church. In 1561 the spire had collapsed after a thunder storm and although the wooden roof was replaced by 1566, thereafter little had been done. For nearly seventy years its appearance had manifestly failed to support its historic importance. Indeed, by the time Laud succeeded to the bishopric in 1628, it had become a temple for money lenders. Business was done there and it was there too that people met to exchange City and court gossip.

Laud was scandalised. Reasonably enough. Sweeping away the affairs of men from the Temple of Jerusalem was something that could be done relatively easily. The re-edification of the fabric was however altogether more challenging. But it was something which appealed to Laud enormously because it revived an early crusade which had been frustrated. As Dean of Gloucester he had preached before James I in June 1621 when he had resorted to a cliché of Jacobean court flattery by comparing this new British Solomon to the Solomon of the Old Testament. Laud's purpose had been to get something done about the physical state of Old St Paul's. The analogy between the two Solomons was apposite because the Old Testament king had built the Temple in Jerusalem; in the same way, or so Laud had wanted his audience to believe, it was the intention of James I, this latter-day Solomon, to build a new Temple in London. Nothing expressed so eloquently the indivisibility of church and state in the mind of Laud than that sermon. During the course of his address Laud had reminded his listeners of the fact that God's House and the King's House were both comprised under the one designation; that was to say, the new Jerusalem: 'And it is fit, very fit it should be so; the Court, and the Great Temple of Gods service together; that God and the King may be neighbours: That as God is always neere to preserve the King, so the King might be neere to serve God.'[9]

A few years later John Williams, Bishop of Lincoln, was called upon to deliver a funeral oration for James. On this occasion too, ways in which the act of building could induce a proper regard for the actual building of a church did not go unnoticed. In his sermon Williams looked back on the achievements of James I; reminding his audience of the late King's constant wish to provide a proper, dignified setting for the acts of state and worship. Consequently Williams made much of the close relationship in Latin between *edificare* and *aedificare*: the one meaning to edify, the other to build. For Williams they were etymologically related because they were manifestations of the same quest for order and decency.

The road to Old St Paul's was paved with good intentions but it was only when the obsessive, tireless energy of Laud combined with the elevated vision of Charles I that the great restoration actually began. The renovation preoccupied Inigo Jones more than any other building project of his entire career. One of his earliest architectural drawings, of *c.* 1608, shows his first encounter with the old building; an inept design for the rebuilding of the spire of the church, which had been left in an unsatisfactory state since the fire of 1561.[10] But his drawing which comes nearest of all to an accommodation with the Baroque, is a solution to the west front which he evolved in 1634 and which provided the basis for the great building campaign that was to be pressed on right up until the Civil War. The drawing represents something of a new flotation for a company since the king was offering to pay for the refurbishment of the west front by way of giving a new impetus to the campaign for restoration of the building as a whole, which had begun in 1631 but which had started to flag by the spring of 1634 when Charles I had informed Laud that the Exchequer would foot the bill for a new giant portico. Such an expansive gesture was

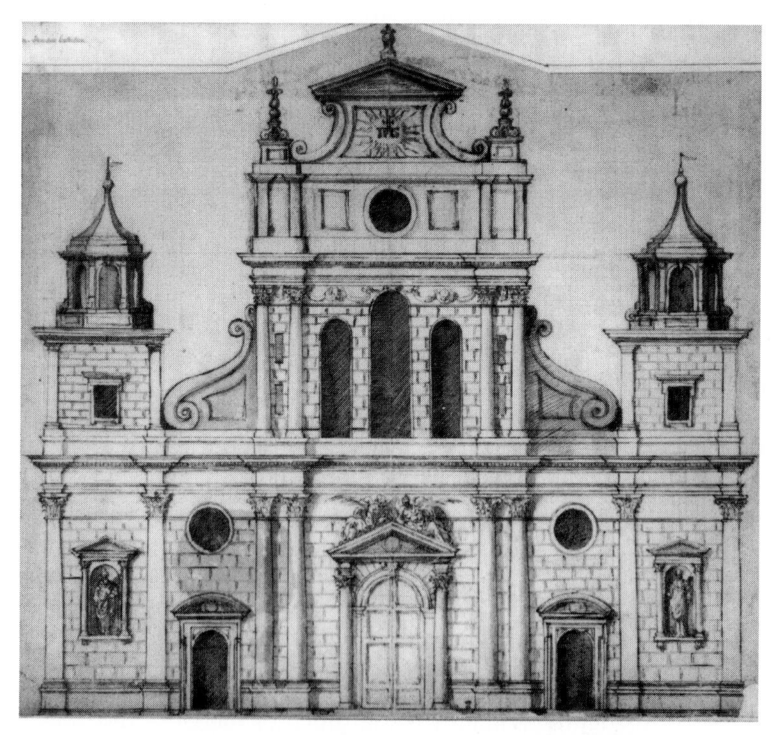

Inigo Jones, Elevation of *Old St Paul's*, 1634 (Courtauld Institute of Art)

then combined over the next few years with various methods of taxation and coercion throughout the kingdom aimed at inducing rich and poor alike to disgorge.

Although people did not respond with the generosity which Charles and Laud had hoped for, the Cathedral emerged transformed. The medieval nave was encased with round arched windows to create an air of reticent classicism, while the front was screened by a classical façade with a giant order of Corinthian columns, creating the most imposing front north of Rome. But despite the size of Jones's giant portico, and as Summerson pointed out, not even the portico of the British Museum comes near to what was realised by Jones,[11] it never bore symbolically the full weight of what apologists claimed was the centuries-old authenticity of Anglicanism.

A problem for Anglicans had been how to establish that the break with Rome was legitimate. They had set about doing this partly by an elaborate claim that the Established Church was a return to the pure church as it had existed before St Augustine arrived at Canterbury and began to corrupt the purity of the well with his poisonous, heretical Romanism. Augustinian Catholicism, so the line went, was in fact a corruption of the original church and it was the Anglicans who were the true heirs of the evangelical church. By these curious thought processes therefore, it was claimed that the Church of England was not heretical at all, but rather the true, undefiled, Apostolic church. It was also argued that the church in England received authentic apostolic authority by virtue of having been established by Joseph of Arimathaea who had arrived centuries before St Augustine, and at Glastonbury not Canterbury. Incredible though this farrago of myth may seem to us now, it was widely believed at the time. In order to persuade enemies that Papists and not Anglicans were in error, it became necessary to mount a defence of the role of the monarchy as Supreme Governor of this state religion. Jones therefore may have intended that the attic of his portico should be surmounted by ten statues of the kings of Great Britain to emphasise the extent to which the English monarchy had been identified with the church since earliest times;[12] though in the event only statues of James I and Charles I were actually put up.

The idea of a splendid new frontispiece for St Paul's was something Jones had been considering since shortly after the accession of James I, but nothing had got beyond the sketch stage until Charles offered to pay for a new front in the spring of 1634. Although Jones' sole surviving 1634 autograph drawing of the west front does not include statues on a balustrade such as we see in William Kent's 1727 presentation of Jones's thoughts in his *The Designs of Inigo Jones*, that 1634 drawing by Jones is just one of what must have been many if not scores. Supposing therefore the Kent design does indeed represent a now lost alternative scheme, as must surely be the case, then Jones' inspiration for having statues to greet those who processed to the building was close at hand. In the reign of Charles I, the west front of Westminster Abbey had its own statues of kings. It would have seemed entirely appropriate therefore that the other great London church should be adorned likewise. The distinguished eighteenth-century historian of the printing press in England, James Bagford, noted in one of his common place books:

> On ye outside of ye Abby have been ye figures of several of our Kinges, Bishops and Abbots and some remain to this day; as y[t] of K: James ye 1st set up at his first coming into England.[13]

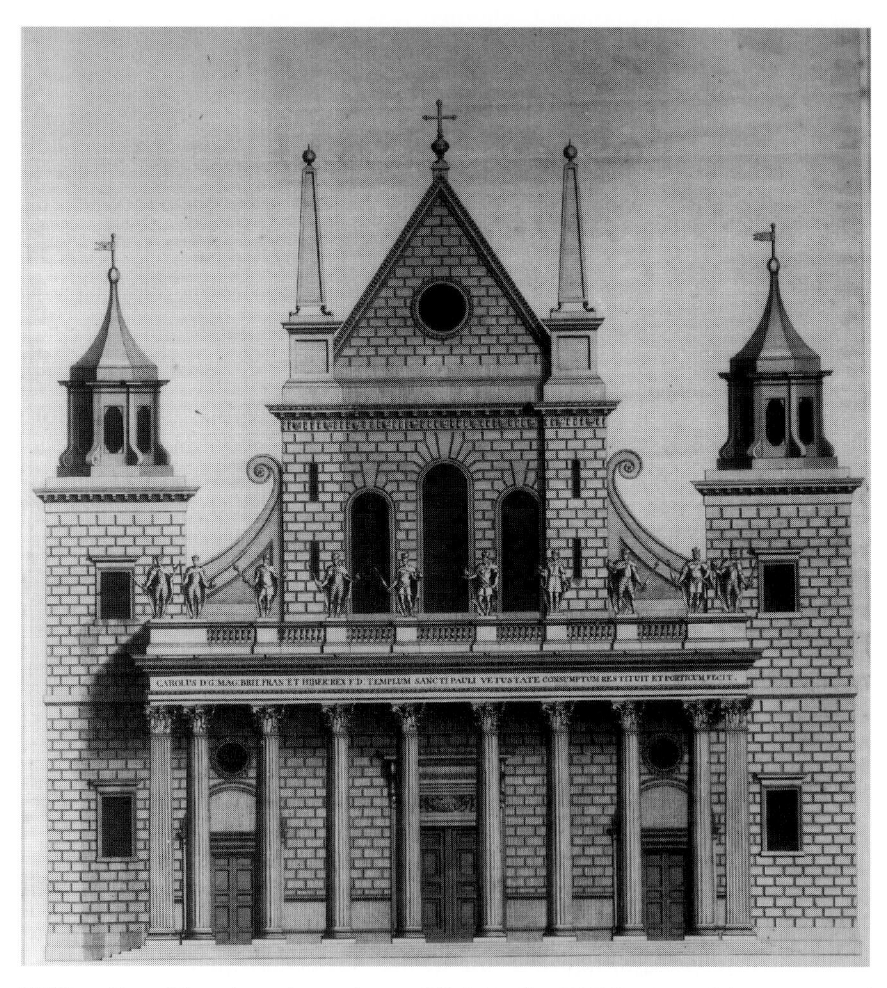

William Kent, Elevation of west front, *Old St Paul's*, 1727 (Society of Antiquaries of London)

The renovation of Old St Paul's was held by its promoters to be a triumph for the Anglican Church and though there were many who refused to subscribe, much money was raised; a powerful testimony to the capacity of ministers of the Crown to get things done during the years of Personal Rule. But it was a victory achieved at a high cost. The expense was not just a question of money required to see the renovation through, but more ominously perhaps, there was a heavy price paid in respect for the Established Church at large. What had been intended to set the metropolitan church on a secure foundation of respect and outward decency, actually served to turn men away from Anglicanism. This was partly because of the pressure exerted by the Crown to raise money through means of questionable legality, once it had become clear that free gifts were not forthcoming in sufficient quantity. But just as important was the effect the campaign had within the bishopric of London in encouraging London parishes to defy the authority of the hierarchy. The case of St Gregory the Great was just one instance of how things could go badly wrong.

St Gregory's was a modest parish church within the shadow of the west end of the Cathedral. There was pressure from above for Jones to recommend that it be removed once work began on the Cathedral. When the arguments proceeded upwards and into the Court of Arches, Charles, for his part, began to play a central part in the vexed question as to what to do with it.

The high-handed way in which the Crown attempted to expunge St Gregory's was a famous and well-aired case of central government threats to parish life. It was an important incident in growing tensions between the Crown and the City. What happened was this. On 5 January 1631 the decision to renovate St Paul's had been taken. On 31 May of that year, Inigo Jones was directed by the Commissioners for Pious Uses to report on whether the fabric of St Gregory's was likely to constitute a threat to the renovation programme. The Commissioners wished to know whether St Gregory's should be removed. Jones visited the site and wrote:

> As for the neerness of the Situac̄on Joyning to the walls of St Paules: I conceave it no way hurtfull to the foundac̄on, or walls of the said church. . . .
>
> Touching the taking away the beauty of thaspect of St Paules, when it shalbe repaired and the howses demolished; it butteth on an auntient Tower, called the Lollards Tower, the wch is answered on the other side wth an other Tower, unto wch my lo: Bishopps hall doth adioyne: And I doe conceave, that neither of them are any hinderance to the beauty of thaspect of the said Church;.[14]

So the matter would have ended but for a recommendation which Jones appended to his report which he thought the parishioners had agreed to, but which he subsequently discovered they had conveniently forgotten.

He had recommended that whereas the parishioners could keep their church, they were to stop excavating a burial vault which they had already begun and which Jones, not unreasonably, believed threatened the foundations of the Cathedral. In February 1632 Jones reported his discovery that the parishioners had ignored his order and gone on digging. In what seems a fair-minded response Jones wrote:

> although I cannot say there is any presente danger to ye church or tower by digginge the sayd vaulte, yet in my opinion I hold it not fitte that the foundac̄on of soe great and noble a worke should be underwroughte upon any occasion whatsoeer, seeinge the parishioners might have digged their vaulte towards their churchyard, . . .[15]

Still they would not stop and Jones became vindictive. He proceeded to recommend the removal of the whole building. The matter did not end there however because although St Gregory's duly disappeared, the issue returned to haunt Jones when government broke down and civil war threatened. In December 1641 he was ordered to appear before the House of Lords to hear a petition against him sent up from the Commons. The parishioners of St Gregory's had complained:

> The said Inigo Jones, being Surveyor of His Majestie's Works, and particularly those to be designed for the re-edifying of the said Church of St Paul's, would not undertake the work, unless he might be, as he termed it, the Sole Monarch, or might have the Principality thereof, conceiving that the work would not be well done, without pulling down the said Church of St Gregorie's, presented a Plott to his Majesty accordingly.[16]

Apparently the king had been persuaded that the church had to be rooted out and so probably in March 1639, Jones

> did pull down and caused to be pulled down part of the Church, and threatened that if the parishioners would not take down the rest of it, then the Galleries should be sawed down, and with skrews the materials of the said Church should be thrown down into the street . . . that if they did not take down the said Church they should be laid by the heels.[17]

Here we have a resonance of the issues connected with St Edmund's Salisbury. In Salisbury as in London, what mattered was authority not aesthetics. Strangely Jones seems to have been prepared to allow St Gregory's to threaten the symmetry of his splendid classical portico, but he could not tolerate the questioning of authority.

The quarrel fits a pattern of disputes between the Crown and other

London parishes. The sources of friction differed but matters tended to boil down to who had authority within the parish; the parish itself, or the Bishop of London from whom the minister derived his licence.

Continuities of conflict can be illustrated by the row with the much richer parish of St Michael le Querne or, as it later came to be known, St Michael's Cornhill. By the mid-1630s the parishioners wished to enlarge their church; a measure which was approved by Jones sitting with two other members of the Building Commission. However, beyond agreeing in principle the two sides could not go: the parish promoting the designs of their favoured architect, Jones proposing his own. The Commissioners, reflecting the wishes of the king, thought this an excellent opportunity to remove a number of unsightly structures which impeded the view of Cheapside where St Michael's was located and which was one of the tourist attractions of London as the location of goldsmiths and jewellers' shops. The parish however did not wish to contribute to civic amenities. They merely wanted to make their own church better fitted to new demands placed upon it by an increase in the size of the parish. In the end Jones, with the full support of the Privy Council, forced his own designs on the parish; having rejected the rather more modest proposals submitted by a certain Mr Binion who led the campaign from within the parish itself. The net result was that the parishioners were forced to pay £3,000 more for the remodelling of their church.[18]

The Anglican Church as mediated by Whitehall and Lambeth Palace, came to be seen by many as oppressive, remote and proudly scornful of local sensitivities. Laud and Juxon, the reigning Bishop of London during the years of Personal Rule, tried to make the daughters conform to their mother's will; the City parishes should follow the lead of the great metropolitan church of St Paul's.[19] Both Laud and Juxon were important Privy Councillors, indeed, Juxon held one of the great offices of state as Lord Treasurer. Both were inextricably bound up with the main thrust of governmental policy in the years of Personal Rule with the result that initiatives taken in the ecclesiastical sphere came to be seen as an aspect of that quest for regularity and efficiency which Charles needed to impose if he was to sustain life without Parliament.

Controversies which arose from the renovation of St Paul's had the net effect of politicising the Church. It became identified with a regime which we now know was a lot more effective and acceptable than was once believed, but which became dangerously isolated and increasingly ineffective from the autumn of 1637 onwards. The importance of Old St Paul's, by appointment, symbolic purveyor of good rule and conformity to the Crown, is attested by Peter Heylyn, who has the last word. Heylyn was chaplain and secretary to Laud, and therefore inclined to interpret the actions of his master in the most positive light. And yet Heylyn had no illusions about the widespread damage done to the image of the Supreme Governor of the Church of England. Looking back on the events of the

1630s from the other side of the Civil War, Heylyn was in no doubt that the campaign to raise money for the renovation of Old St Paul's had been disastrous. It contributed significantly to strained relations between the court and the City. Writing of the repairs to the Cathedral, Heylyn concluded 'yet it cannot be denied, but that it met with many rubs, and mighty enemies'.[20]

John Milton was one of those who felt that rub, and his attacks on the ecclesiastical policies of Charles I were the more biting for being staked out on ground favoured by those faithful apologists of the sovereign, the King's chaplains. It will be recalled that court divines had been much taken with the parallel between the early Stuarts and Solomon. Milton surveying the scene from beyond the Civil War, was to make the same comparison in his *Pro Populo Anglicano Defensio* (1651); though with him it was an opportunity to criticise Solomon and condemn Charles:

> Still, if you take such pleasure in Parallels, let us compare King Charles and King Solomon. . . . Solomon 'oppressed the people with heavy taxes,' but he spent that money upon the temple of God and other public buildings; King Charles spent his in extravagances.

Ten years before Milton was to publish his *Defence of the People of England* he had attacked directly the system of episcopacy in his *Of Reformation Touching Church-Discipline in England* (1641). Waxing to his theme he had denounced the material splendour and visual extravagance of William Laud's church:

> Now I appeale to all wise men what an excessive wast of Treasury hath beene within these few yeares in this Land nott in the expedient, but in the Idolatrous erection of Temples beautified exquisitely to out-vie the Papists, the costly and deare-bought Scandals, and snares of Images, Pictures, rich Coaps, gorgeous Altar-clothes. . . . If the splendor of *Gold* and *Silver* begin to Lorde it once againe in the Church of *England*, wee shall see *Antichrist* shortly wallow heere, though his cheife Kennell be at *Rome*. If they had one thought upon *Gods glory* and the advancement of Christian Faith, they would be a meanes that with these expences thus profusely throwne away in trash, rather *Churches* and *Schools* might be built, where they cry out for want, and more added where too few are; a moderate maintenance distributed to every painfull Minister, that now scarse sustaines his Family with Bread, while the *Prelats* revell like *Belshazzar* with their full carouses in *Goblets*, and *vessels* of *gold* snatcht from *Gods Temple*.[21]

Milton's views are important for revealing the extent to which the 'beauty of holiness' led Puritans into believing a Laudian Eucharist was a monstrous Belshazzar's Feast. These passages are valuable too because they make us realise that something very important to a proper understanding of the outrage a Laudian church could provoke has been lost forever.

It was the candlesticks, hassocks, pyxes, crosses, copes, monstrances and such like gew-gaws, tossed on a thousand bonfires of iconoclasm after Charles I left London in 1642, which caused the real offence. Costly furnishings scandalised those with Puritan sympathies. Laudians were not architects, they were superb interior decorators with an eye for what would appeal to the emotional and the theatrical. The Laudian era was the greatest age for church furnishing in the history of Anglicanism until the Camden Society and the manic Pugin set to work in Victorian England. Caroline bishops were smothered by their own hassocks not stoned by rocks from new-built churches.

Charles I and Laud were Anglicans. That is what they were and they had never contemplated apostasy. Charles had sent Henrietta Maria's entourage of friars packing and Laud was profoundly shocked when it was claimed at his trial that he had wanted to manoeuvre the king into the arms of Rome. He responded to this outrage by reminding his accusers that a decisive event in his preferment had been a summons in 1622 to save the Duke of Buckingham's mother from conversion, by refuting Father John Fisher, a subtle Jesuit casuist.

Laud defended the credentials of the Anglican creed with genuine conviction and painful conscientiousness, but as can be inferred from Milton, the appearance of a Laudian church made it an easy thing for its enemies to claim that the king and his archbishop were crypto-Catholics. In this respect, it was unfortunate for the reputation of the king that many of the art connoisseurs whose company he found particularly congenial were indeed Catholics. The connection is understandable to us, but it was panic-making to seventeenth-century Puritans. The king loved pictures and those best qualified to talk authoritatively on them were men who felt at ease travelling at will in Europe. Now although Rome in 1630 was an altogether more accessible place than it had been in 1580, it was still a great deal easier to see the private collections of the Papal Curia if a traveller was a Catholic. Predictably therefore Charles spent more time closeted with Catholics than was good for his image. A case in point was his intimacy with Father George Gage, who caused the darkest suspicions in the hearts of stouter Protestants at home.

George Gage came from an ancient Catholic Sussex family.[22] Gage had been in Rome with the Earl of Arundel and Inigo Jones, when he had been ordained a Jesuit in 1614 by none other than James I's old theological adversary, Cardinal Robert Bellarmine. Thereafter he spent years gliding from one European capital to another, picking up an impressive mastery of European languages, and an unrivalled eye for a picture. Such was his feel for painting indeed, that he appears to have been the only Englishman whose views on his own art Rubens really respected.[23]

When Gage eventually resurfaced in London, he was just the type to

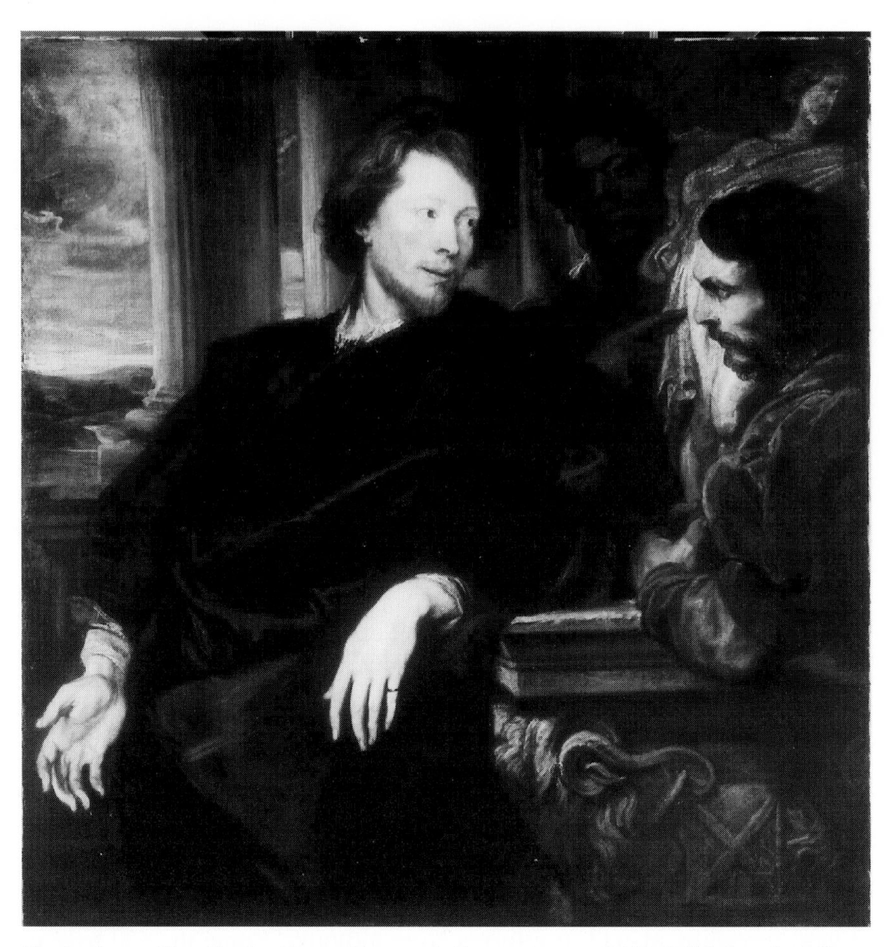

Sir Anthony Van Dyck, *George Gage and Companions*, *c.* 1620–3 (National Gallery, London)

appeal to Charles I. That was when Charles' interest in art really began to blossom: Van Dyck, the 'famous allievo' of Rubens, had arrived in London in October 1620 and Charles was keen to have examples of Rubens' work, about which Gage could talk in thrilling and vivid detail. It was one thing for the Prince of Wales to make George Gage a confidant, but it was quite another for Gage to be entrusted by the Crown with the weightiest concerns of international politics. That though was exactly what happened. Gage was appointed chief go-between in the negotiations for a marriage between Charles and the Infanta of Spain. This was typical of the way in which the early Stuarts could put first things last and last things first; appointing someone to a position of great influence on the doubtful qualifications of either good looks, charm or sympathetic conversation.

No sooner had Gage ingratiated his way into royal favour than he was entrusted with the most delicate aspects of the marriage negotiations. He began a strenuous period of shuttle diplomacy in May 1621: travelling between London, Madrid and Rome carrying secret missives – though Gage's game was quickly understood by the ambassadors who found him habitually irritating. Sir Isaac Wake at the court of Savoy in Turin took a certain wry pleasure in the discomfiture of a man he seems to have disliked. He wrote from Turin in June 1623:

> Upon Satirday last the 3 of this month Mr George Gage arrived at Turin, having finished (as he doth say) the great negotiation at Rome, and complyed with ye Dukes of Florence and Parma in ye name of his M^{atie}. It should seeme that he hath receaved good presents, for he doth glorifye himselfe much in speaking of them, but yet here they would not let him passe as a publique Minister, nor free his stuff from paying of dacio untill he procured a Fede from mee; wch accident did a little mortifye him, as being unwilling to owe unto a third person the justification of his quality which he did presume to have been of such eminencye that he might better have given than taken certificats.[24]

The presents for which Gage was forced to pay in Turin were doubtless splendid. Great hopes were invested in them. For the Papacy at least the summer of 1622 was the high point in negotiations which would later collapse: a moment when Gregory XV saw a possibility of the reconversion of England. We do not know what Gage presented to Charles but it might have been like the imagery which would be intercepted by the Parliamentary Colonel Morley, 'hard by Arundel Castle', during the Civil War, and which it had been intended was to have been spirited away to Spain. What Morley was to discover gets the flavour of the Counter-Reformation art which must have appeared in London in significant quantities in the reign of Charles I. It was imagery which fatally compromised Charles's presentation of Anglicanism as something distinct from, and uncorrupted by Rome. Morley addressed his letter to William Lenthall, Speaker of the House of Commons:

> Amongst the goods taken from the Dunkirk ships we have found certain pictures which contain most gross idolatory; upon one the Trinity pictured in monstrous shapes like giants; upon another is painted the Virgin Mary as sitting in heaven with her babe in her arms, underneath is the Pope on whose left stands our king perfectly limned [painted] and completely armed, with his cavaliers attending him; on the Pope's right hand stands the Queen accompanied with her ladies, the King tenders his sceptre to the Queen, she accepts it not, but directs it to be delivered to the Pope. This picture was to be set up in the chief church in Seville in Spain as appears by the direction on the outside of the box,

> in which it is inclosed. I look upon this picture as an hieroglyphic of the causes and intents of our present troubles and the opinion of the neighbouring nations concerning them and if the House please to command the picture to London and there permit it to the public view, I conceive 'twould very much convince the Malignants and open the eyes of all that are not wilfully blind.[25]

'An hieroglyphic of the causes and intents of our present troubles'. Evidently nothing was clearer in Morley's mind. For him, and as he supposed, for the godly zealots in Parliament, religious imagery played a vital part in tearing the Commonwealth apart.

Whether it was God falling out of a window in Salisbury, the destruction of an ancient parish church in the City of London, or the sight of the King of England rubbing shoulders with the Pope, people reacted with horror. The painting which so offended Morley had been hung in a Catholic household, and it was Catholic centres of worship which attracted the most scandal. The overt public observation of Catholic rites in the chapels associated with Henrietta Maria was sufficient proof for those who wished to see the court as a seed-bed for conversions.

There were three places of worship provided for the Queen: the new chapel at Somerset House, designed by Jones 1632–36, the most important; also by Jones the chapel at St James's, originally designed for the Infanta of Spain in 1623 when the Spanish Match looked likely, and finished in 1625; and finally an oratory at Whitehall. These three venues were popular not only with Catholics but with High Anglicans too. Unwisely Charles was seen in them too and that can have done his reputation little good. Just how splendid their interiors must have been can be sensed from a description of the appearance of the east end of Somerset House chapel, based upon an account by Père Cyprian Gamache, a Capuchin attached to the household of Henrietta Maria. There the worshipper was confronted with:

> 'a paradise of glory, about 40 feet in height.' There was a great arch, supported by two pillars, about 5½ feet from the two side walls of the chapel. The spaces between the pillars and the wall served for passages between the sacristy and the altar, and the choir, with the organ and other instruments, was on either side over these vacant places. The altar stood outside the arch, and there were six steps leading up to it. Behind the altar was a dove holding the Blessed Sacrament, and forming the centre of a series of separate oval frames painted with angels seated on clouds, most ingeniously contrived, with the aid of perspective and hidden lights, so to deceive the eye and to produce the illusion of a considerable space occupied by a great number of figures. There were seven of these ovals – the outer and larger ones consisting of angels playing on musical instruments, the central ones of angels vested as deacons, and

> carrying censors, and the inner ones with child angels in various attitudes of devotion. Immediately round the dove were cherubim and seraphim in glory, surrounded by rays of light.[26]

It has been suggested by Erica Veevers in a remarkable study of the role of Henrietta Maria at the peacetime court of Charles I that this ensemble represented the most fully developed expression of a Roman Baroque tableau to be seen in London prior to the Civil War.[27] Veevers points to the parallel between what could be seen at Somerset House chapel and the great *quarantore* temporary altarpiece which had been erected by Pietro da Cortona in the church of S. Lorenzo in Damaso in Rome at the prompting of Cardinal Barberini. As Veevers notes, Barberini was also Protector of the English Nation, that is to say, the cardinal entrusted with nurturing the interests of English Catholics at the Vatican. As for the *quarantore* itself, this was an aid to the faithful, who were encouraged to meditate upon the forty hours which Catholics believed had elapsed between the Death and Resurrection of Christ.

Cortona's temporary structure was erected in 1633, three years before the unveiling of the permanent high altar in Somerset House chapel. Veevers also points out that Monsignor George Conn, who arrived in London in July 1636, a few months before the unveiling of the Somerset House altar, was a canon of S. Lorenzo and must therefore have known of Cortona's work. His appearance in London at just the moment when serious thought was being given to the embellishment of Henrietta Maria's chapel suggests that the Roman canon may well have been called upon for advice by Jones, the chapel architect, and François Dieussart, the sculptor who created the altarpiece, and who had himself been called from Rome by Arundel in 1635.

The Dieussart high altar created a sensation when it was unveiled. On the third night after it had been revealed, the king himself came to view it. It was reported that having gazed at it for a long time the king 'said aloud, that he had never seen anything more beautiful or more ingeniously designed'.[28] Even when allowance has been made for the hyperbole of Catholic reporters enthusiastic to please their masters in the Vatican, the high altar of the Queen's Chapel in Somerset House stands as symbol of the role Henrietta Maria performed jointly with her husband in promoting the arts at court. The Mantuan sale, and the quality of Renaissance masters thus acquired, means that a conscious effort has to be made to realise that both the king and his consort were as keen on Reni as Raphael, indeed just as capable of appreciating what was being created in Baroque Rome as what had been hallowed by tradition. Haskell has pointed out that one of the very first acts Charles initiated when he came to the throne in 1625 had been to try to persuade Guercino to come to London.[29] That had not happened but Charles soon came to own works by Rembrandt and later by Bernini, whilst Henrietta Maria was to have her house at Greenwich decorated by Orazio Gentileschi with an ambitious allegory in the form of a ceiling painting depicting *Peace and Arts under the English Crown*.

Although many of the pictures presented by Cardinal Barberini ostensibly to the Catholic Henrietta Maria were in fact expected to be handed on to the king, there can be no doubt of her own real enthusiasm for contemporary art. Giovanni Baglione is now more famous as a commentator on the artistic scene in Rome during the seventeenth century than as a painter, but in his own lifetime he enjoyed a real following as an artist in the merciless world of the Roman artistic scene. Baglione's *Virgin and Child* was evidently much admired by Henrietta Maria since it is recorded as hanging in her bedroom at Denmark House at the time of her death.[30]

The active, confident role Henrietta Maria played in promoting the arts during the years of Personal Rule was, I believe, given most poetical expression in the famous painting by Rubens, *Landscape with St George and the Dragon*. Veevers considers this at some length and offers a fresh interpretation of its meaning. She argues that it expresses Rubens' view after ten hectic years of diplomacy that the way out of the impasse of pan-European religious conflict was for a compromise between Catholicism and Protestantism, a compromise which Veevers sees Rubens celebrating in the chivalrous encounter between Charles I, a Protestant king, and Henrietta Maria, his Catholic consort. In the painting Charles is St George and Henrietta Maria the maiden whom St George has rescued from the dragon which lies slain in the forefront of the painting. For Veevers the dragon is a symbol of the devil, not as it had been in the past, as heresy for Catholics, and the anti-Christ for Protestants.

This is an interesting view but there may be still more to extract from the painting if we pause to consider the pose of Henrietta Maria in relation to an earlier version of the theme by Rubens. This was created perhaps in Genoa *c.* 1606 and though the picture is splendidly florid, it fails as a narrative since the eye is very largely absorbed by St George, who takes up the front of the canvas as he appears to leap out at the spectator in the act of slaying the dragon. Rubens was evidently so pleased with the athleticism of his mounted warrior that he repeated the pose in the greatest of his hunting pieces, the Munich *Lion Hunt* painted for the Scottish aristocrat the Marquess of Hamilton, in *c.* 1621–22, whilst understandably forgetting the figure of the maiden. In the original version of the subject, the lady for whom this feat or arms was undertaken appears as a redundant, etiolated figure whose presence right at the back of the picture combines a precious gesture of mild surprise at all the commotion going on around her, with what St George might have considered, reasonably enough, a lamentable failure to express gratitude for her deliverance.

Rubens may well have regarded the 1606 essay as what in another context and in relation to another picture he had once excused as a 'work

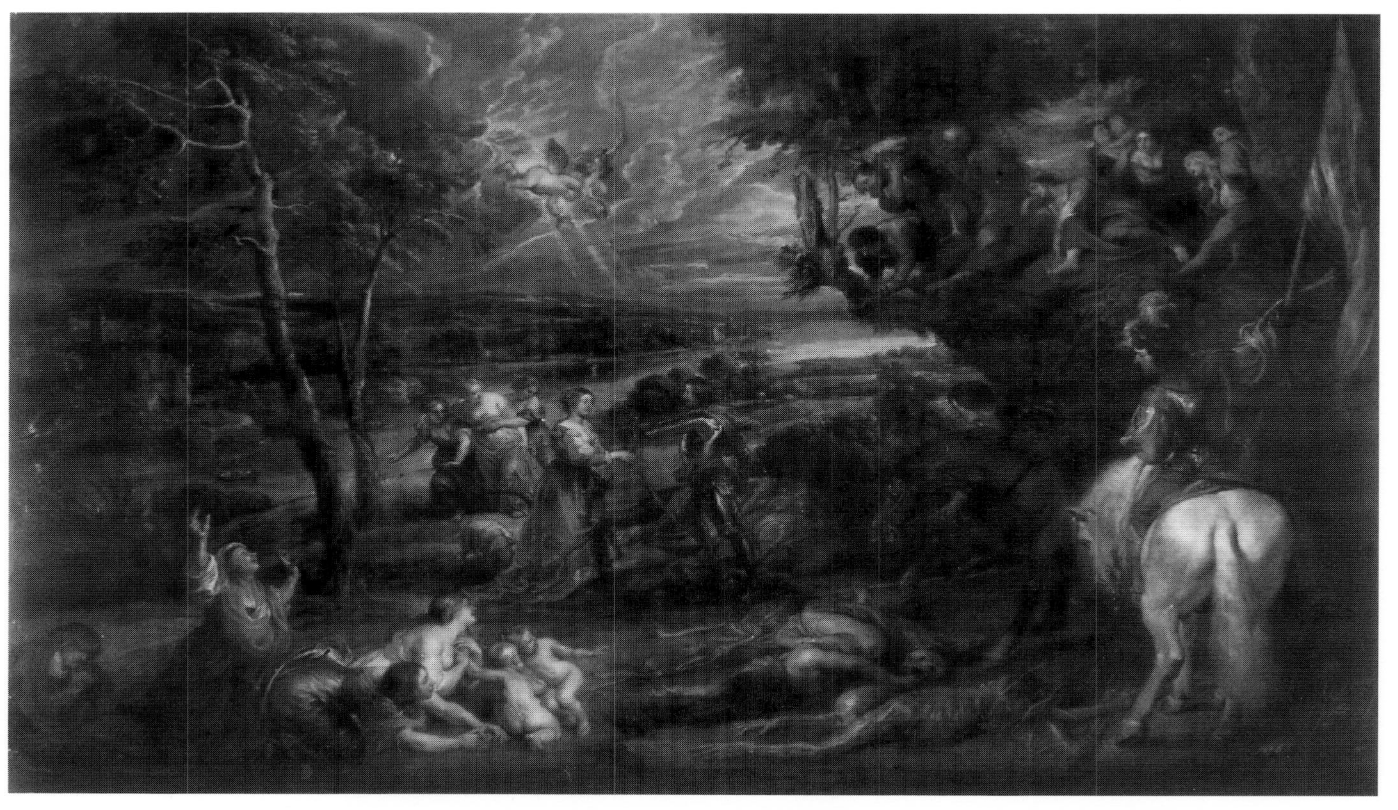

Sir Peter Paul Rubens, *Landscape with St George and the Dragon*, *c.* 1630 (The Royal Collection)

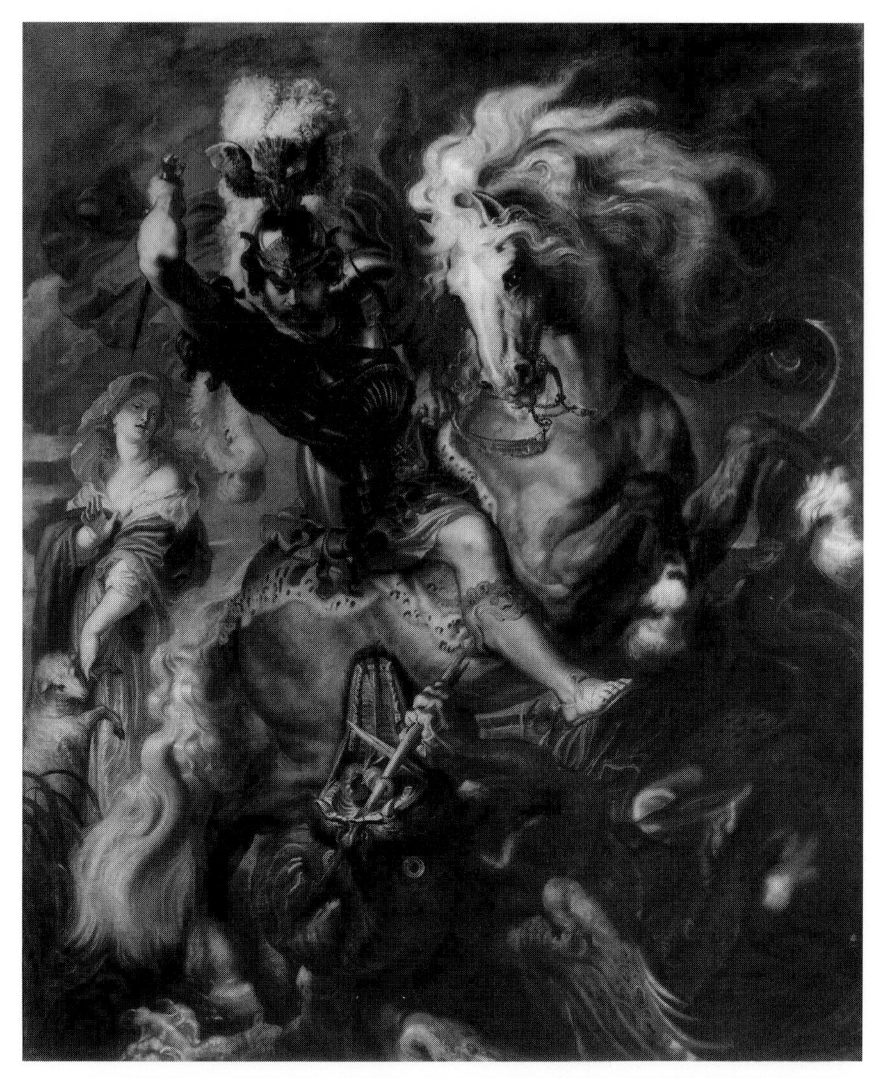

Sir Peter Paul Rubens, *St George and the Dragon*, *c.* 1606 (The Prado, Madrid)

of my youth', whereas the picture painted for the English royal couple represented a master at the height of his powers. In the later version Henrietta Maria is a heroine whilst Charles is more supplicant than hero. What is so startling is that Henrietta Maria dominates the painting psychologically. Indeed in some sense the way in which she appears wholly unaffected by the heat and dust of battle just stilled, is every bit as odd in terms of a convincing narrative as the lack of response on the part of the maiden in the earlier version. However, the difference is that after

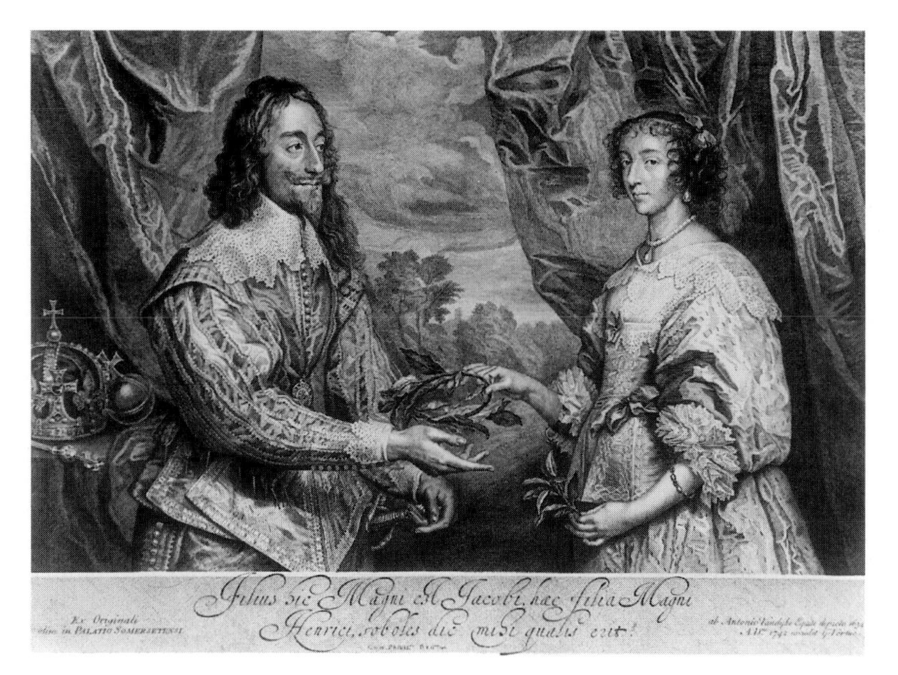

George Vertue engraving (1742) after Van Dyck, *Charles I and Henrietta Maria*, 1632 (Joe Rock)

the passage of a quarter of a century the painter had learned to mask narrative inconsistency.

Surely the message Rubens wishes to convey in his second version has less to do with a putative way through the maze of religious controversy than with a celebration of the joint endeavours and joint achievement of Charles I and Henrietta Maria in promoting peace and consequently the arts. For Rubens, the envious observer of a nation at peace, what symbolised the concord established by the royal pair, for whom the artist seems to have had real admiration, was the English countryside.

At first it may seem odd that the promotion of civilisation in the *Landscape with St George* should have been located in a world given over to nature rather than the arts. Yet many descriptions of the rapine of the Thirty Years War, as of the titanic struggle between the Spanish Netherlands and the United Provinces before that, centred upon the destruction of agriculture and the frighting of Ceres. Thus the dominance of the countryside in this picture should be seen not as a distraction but rather as a felicitous and singularly poetic reinforcement of the central message, which is the union of the happy pair and its fecund consequences.

A marriage of true minds described by Rubens topographically, Van Dyck expressed more intimately and more reciprocally. Whereas in the Rubens, Charles hands Henrietta Maria the trophy of his victory in the form of a symbolic bridle to control the passions, in Van Dyck's portrait of the royal couple, Charles has just handed Henrietta Maria an olive sprig, she is about to hand him a laurel wreath (Kromeriz). The meaning is clear. The fruits of victory and peace are a *joint* achievement and together they nurture those qualities which made of Great Britain 'a people rich and happy in the lap of peace' as Rubens put it.

So much then for the role of Henrietta Maria as a patroness of the arts and a promoter of her religion. As with Laud's theatrical performance in consecrating St Katherine's, there seems a compelling parallel in what was erected in the Queen's chapels by way of an aid to worship and belief, and the techniques of 'light and motion' Jones was manipulating in his masques to make his audience believe in the semi-divine status of the king and his consort.

This chapter has been devoted to the impact of Laud's policies on Anglicanism, and the effect which imagery had on the outward observance of religion, and religious conflict, in the reign of Charles I. We have come full circle. We began by remarking that differences in religion are now regarded by some as the most important explanation for the conflict, and we end by finding heart-felt endorsement for that view from those who saw these images of religion as provocative. We switch now to portraiture and specifically to portraits of the monarchy. Because such things were almost all securely located in the secular sphere they were never as provocative as church imagery. Nevertheless portraits speak eloquently of a sovereign's natural instinct for dignity and majesty; qualities which Elizabeth and her Archbishop Whitgift, and Charles and his favourite prelate Laud, united in wishing to see in the state church.

Chapter Three
The Royal Portrait: The Tudors

In this chapter we shall be examining the portrayal of the monarchy. Holbein and Van Dyck dominate the history of royal portraiture in the English Renaissance as artists of international stature; the only ones who have ever been persuaded to settle in England. The visions of Holbein and Van Dyck have created imagery of two kings surpassing that of any other English sovereign. Queen Victoria was on the throne for significantly longer than the reigns of Henry VIII and Charles I combined, but it is to the old copper penny and not to a lush Winterhalter portrait we turn to recall the image of a Queen who ruled a land-mass greater than the Roman Empire. Neither Gainsborough nor Reynolds, both of whom owed so much to the inspiration of Van Dyck, could give George III immortality, and even Elizabeth I, popularly regarded as the most successful of our sovereigns, lacks a magic talisman such as we have in Henry VIII with legs like a sawing horse, or Charles I as finely bred as the Arabs upon which he sat.

The parallel between Holbein and Van Dyck is illuminating. Both were northerners and both had two distinct periods in London; separated with much the same interval between visits. Although each seems to have had a successful career in England, here both compromised their artistic integrity and ambitions. Holbein was certainly employed on extensive, intellectually challenging work for the Crown: preparing theatres of splendour for the reception of ambassadors or marriage festivities for Anne Boleyn, but as was to be the case with Van Dyck, most of his royal work consisted of portraiture.

It is probable that both artists produced more religious imagery than records reveal: with Holbein, murals and relatively small easel paintings like *Christ in the Garden*, still in The Royal Collection; in Van Dyck's case, altarpieces for the chapels of Henrietta Maria, destroyed or taken abroad during the disruption which followed the death of the artist in 1641. But even when allowance has been made for an unknown corpus of lost works, both artists reduced their ambitions when they settled in England in 1532 and 1632 respectively.

Just before Van Dyck first visited England in 1620, he had been principal assistant to Rubens, who had been commissioned to decorate S. Carlo Borromeo in Antwerp; the most important Jesuit church of northern Europe. With Van Dyck at hand, Rubens executed thirty-nine ceiling paintings and two large altarpieces for the Jesuits. This was one of the most ambitious undertakings of Rubens' entire career, and one with which Van Dyck was involved in the complicated process of transforming sketches no bigger than an exercise book into canvases several feet in diameter.

Both Van Dyck and Holbein had produced work of extraordinary range before either was to set foot in England. Holbein had painted altarpieces of great pathos before he was first received in England by Sir Thomas More into his community of souls at Chelsea. Holbein had also frescoed house fronts in Basle comparable in splendour to the painted palaces of Giorgione and Titian on the Grand Canal in Venice.

Van Dyck was at his most inventive during the four years spent in Antwerp after his return from Italy in 1627 and before he settled finally in London. Where are the pictures from his London period to equal the *Rinaldo and Armida*, painted in Antwerp in 1629? That was created for Charles I himself, but it was created where Van Dyck could find the intellectual nourishment to envisage one of the greatest of all works of romance. Van Dyck would never be able to repeat such a tour de force in England. The setting was not right, the insistent demand of Englishmen for their portraits too overpowering. The artist capitulated. He never produced a painting comparable in ripeness and burnished sensuality to the great *Rinaldo and Armida* of his last Antwerp days.

But although London was to confine Van Dyck as it had diminished Holbein, their English portraits are certainly amongst the greatest produced in all Europe; masterpieces which served their owners supremely well. They are powerful images of rule and they can be compared effectively.

The most famous image of kingship by Holbein, the so-called 'Great Picture', was once a fresco, perhaps located in the Privy Chamber in Whitehall. It was the most ambitious image of Henry VIII of which record survives; something which 'Holbein's biographer van Mander said would "abash and annihilate" those who looked at it'.[1]

To understand both the expectations of what it was hoped Holbein would produce, and the nature of his achievement here, we turn to Richmond Palace, and to an important image of kingship which once dominated the decoration of the Great Hall in that lost building. Richmond was admired: especially a fresco which had been painted on the orders of Henry VIII. The fresco looked back to what the medieval kings had done in the Palace of Westminster, and forward to Henry VIII in the Privy Chamber at Whitehall.

At Richmond, Henry VII had a whole series of the kings of England

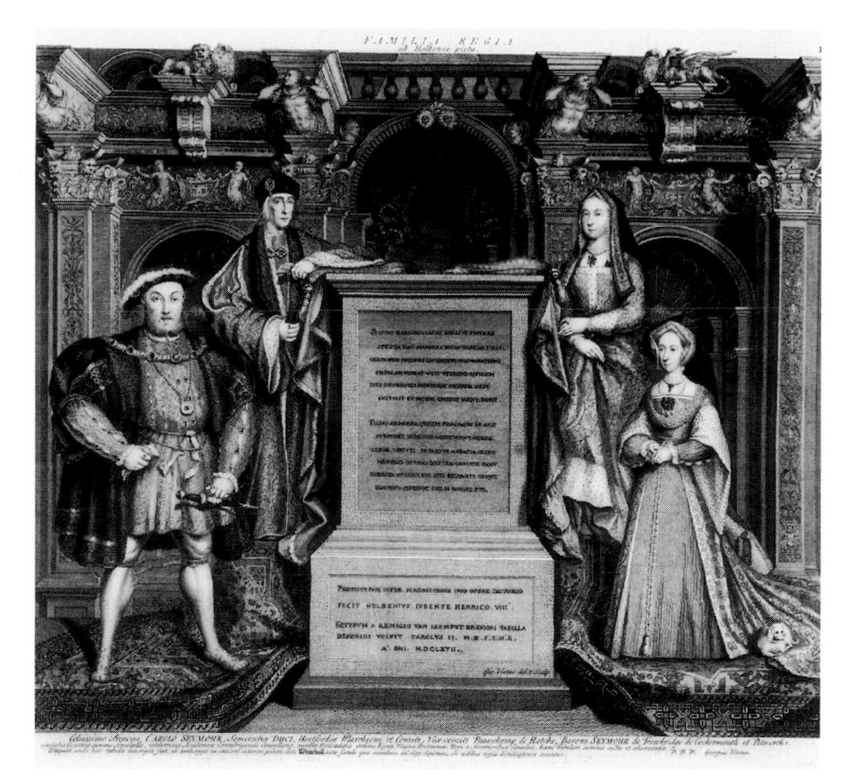

'The Great Picture', George Vertue *c.* 1737, engraving after Remigius van Leemput's copy of Holbein's *Henry VIII and Family* (Society of Antiquaries of London)

painted between the windows in imitation of similar ensembles which the Angevin and Plantagenet kings had provided for the Palace of Westminster. Henry's Richmond imagery culminated in the 'seemly picture and personage of our moost excellent and heyghe Suffrayn . . . King Henry the VIIth'.[2] If this had survived we would have a far more certain impression of painting in England between the Eton College frescoes of *c.* 1479 and Holbein's own work, but even so, bald archival description of what existed at Richmond is of the greatest importance. It allows us to see Holbein's achievement in the Privy Chamber at Whitehall as part of an historical continuum rather than the ambitious expression of a Renaissance prince set upon creating a 'new' style.

We do not know the date of the Richmond frescoes nor for that matter who painted them. But in the case of the Whitehall fresco by Holbein, the relationship between patron and painter becomes much clearer. Two couples flank an altar in the middle ground, whilst behind is an indeterminate loggia-like structure embellished with classical detail reminiscent of the Italy of Mantegna and Bramante.

The couple in the background of Holbein's fresco consist of Henry VII to the left, and flanking the altar on the other side, his wife, Elizabeth of York. On a step below, at elbow height, Henry VIII stands beneath his father, and below Elizabeth on the other side, Jane Seymour, who may have been carrying the hope of the dynasty, the unborn male heir, the future Edward VI.

At first glance it seems that the principal concern of Henry VIII was to stress the fecund nature of the Tudor dynasty. Holbein's preliminary thoughts about how to group his quartet, suggest that he had intended to give the consorts equal prominence. It was to have been a painting about dynasty, expressed through the realisation and the potential of fruitful union. Here it must be recalled that Henry VII had bound the wounds of England after the Wars of the Roses by marrying a tribal enemy. Henry, of the Lancastrian camp, had killed the Yorkist King Richard III at Bosworth, but had rapidly made a *politique* alliance by marrying Elizabeth from the Yorkist faction. The marriage proved an early and a decisive success.

Henry VIII too had had much to be grateful for in his marriage to Jane Seymour, whose death as a result of giving birth to a longed for male heir is, most believe, the reason for the commission to Holbein. By 1537, the date of the picture, Henry had already discarded two wives and there would be no less than three more after Jane Seymour herself. But what had made Jane special at this juncture was that she, unlike the two previous consorts of the king, had actually produced a male child. For Henry there was hope.

We only know what the picture looked like because it was copied in the seventeenth century by the obscure Remigius van Leemput, before the original disappeared in the disastrous Whitehall fire of 1698. There is too a precious fragment of Holbein's original preparatory drawing in the National Portrait Gallery in London. That happens to cover the most important area of the painting: the likenesses of Henry VII and Henry VIII. This cartoon, that is to say a carefully worked drawing corresponding to the size of the intended painting so that it could be used to trace outlines onto panel, provides precious insight into the evolution of royal propaganda. In the dress rehearsal, as this cartoon fragment might be termed, Henry VII leans elegantly against a classical plinth, staring nonchalantly out of the picture as generations of landed gentlemen would do later in the portraits of Van Dyck and Gainsborough. It is possible to imagine Henry VII like his dreamy, ineffective but saintly forebear Henry VI whom he revered, and tried repeatedly to get sanctified. But as Henry VII came on stage for the performance, he changed character; Leemput records a rather different persona: quizzical, knowing, very much the politician who keeps his counsel according to the precepts of Machiavelli. The change in Henry VIII was still more decisive. In the cartoon he looks at us out of the corner of his small eyes; almost slyly we might be tempted to think. He is the range finder. In the fresco he becomes the marksman looking straight down the barrels.

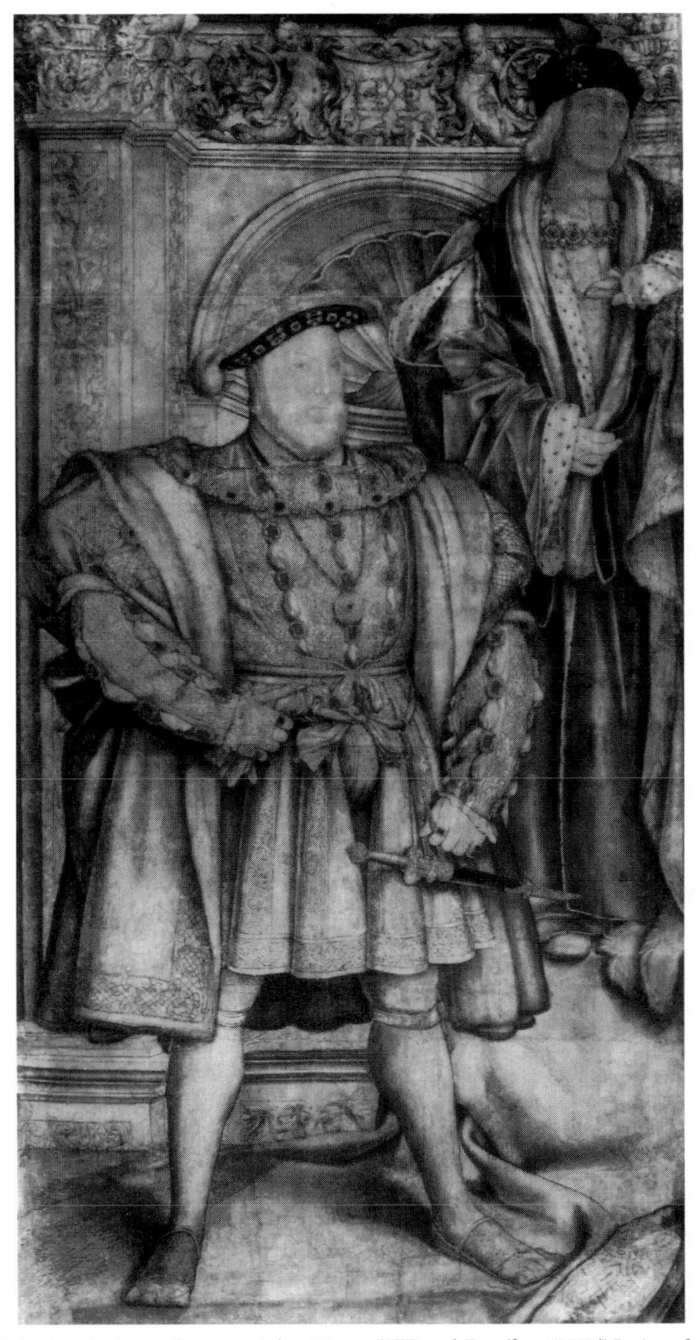

Hans Holbein, Cartoon fragment for *Henry VIII and Family*, 1537 (National Portrait Gallery, London)

We have no documents for 'the Great Picture' but it may be that the decisive changes between cartoon and fresco were the result of Holbein showing his cartoon to Henry VIII. There is some support for this view because the head of Henry VIII in the cartoon has been pasted on so that we are looking at a Renaissance collage. This may be the result of Henry suggesting to Holbein that he wanted a more direct confrontation with the spectator than in the cartoon. So the artist came to substitute a new head for the original. Such intervention would have been entirely in keeping with how Henry VIII dealt with his artists. Henry certainly took a close, not to say maddening interest in the progress of his buildings; he drew up some 'platts' or plans of coastal defences even if he did not involve himself in the Thames-side palaces.[3] Surely then, he would have been deeply interested in this dynastic banner floating above one of his thrones.

What of Elizabeth of York and Jane Seymour? Holbein has orchestrated them with subtlety. They are given a degree of presence as befitted those who bore offspring which gave legitimacy and permanence to the dynasty. Yet they are subservient to their husbands. Their perceptible inferiority is emphasised because they do not engage the eye of the spectator but look out of the picture. As if to underscore their recessive function, their hands are self-enclosing, neither eloquent nor aggressive as in the case of the two kings.

The architectural backdrop to the mural has caused considerable interest: the composite pilasters, shell-niches, mermen, and canonically proportioned classical altar, have been taken as evidence of the new aesthetic which Henry VIII did so much to promote with his building campaigns of the 1530s.

'The Great Picture' was probably the most powerful image of rule Holbein painted for Henry VIII, but it was certainly not the first. Of his works which have survived, *Solomon and the Queen of Sheba* takes chronological precedence. We now know this only as a miniature the size of a photograph frame. It combines portraiture, allegory and sacred art; all fused together in the service of propaganda dedicated to the defence of a state religion which according to its defenders had just cast off a thousand years of servitude. It is tempting to take up the suggestion first made by K. T. Parker exactly fifty years ago, in his catalogue of Holbein drawings in The Royal Collection, when he made the tentative proposal that *Solomon and the Queen of Sheba* records a lost wall painting;[4] though to others, the exquisite finish of the miniature militates against it being regarded as a design for a fresco. Whatever the purpose to which the miniature was put, most scholars are agreed that the image which has come down to us reflects Henry's position as Supreme Head of a church purged of the corruption of Rome.[5]

The miniature of *Solomon and the Queen of Sheba* is important because it contains the first surviving painted record of the entry of Solomon into the repertoire of Henrician propaganda; though Henry VIII had featured

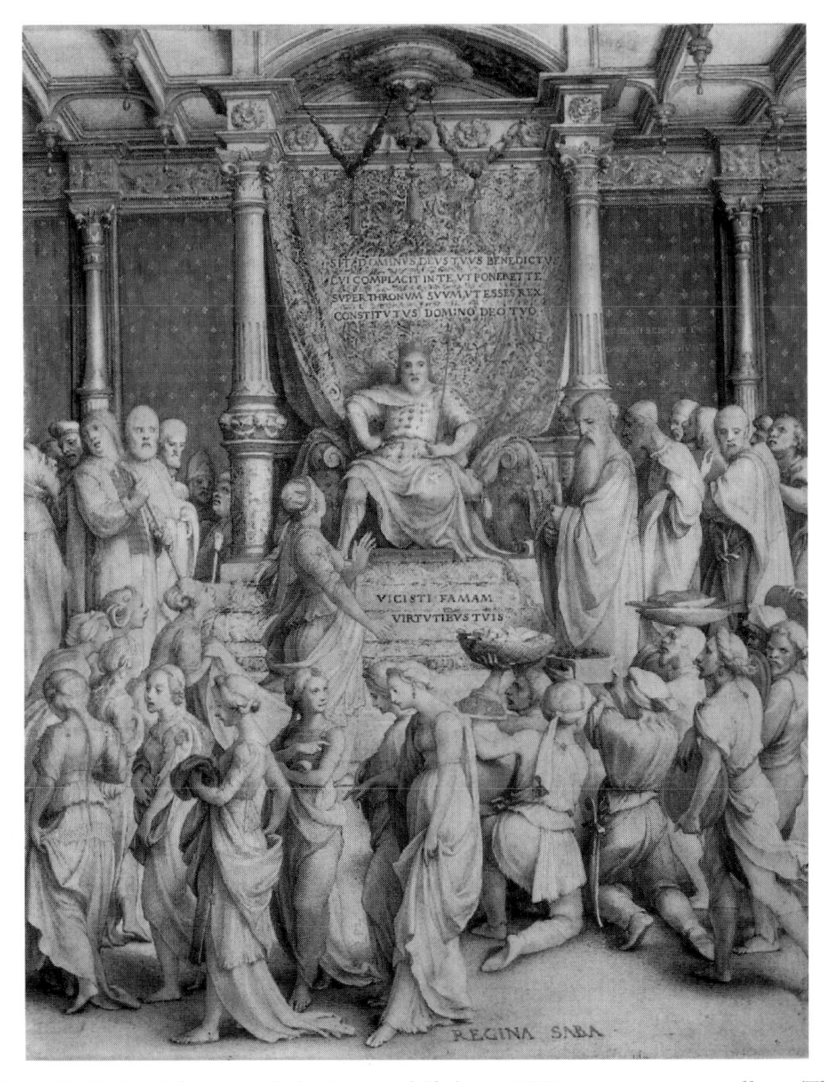

Hans Holbein, *Solomon and the Queen of Sheba*, *c.* 1535, miniature on vellum (The Royal Collection)

in this role in one of the stained glass windows of King's College Cambridge chapel, made some ten years earlier.

The parallel between Solomon and the British monarchy was one which would become a cliché with James I and one we have already encountered; James likened himself to Solomon as he set out to resolve some of the religious disputes which Henry VIII, the first English Solomon, had done so much to inflame.

Holbein's image of *Solomon and the Queen of Sheba* is not entirely successful because the painter was overfilling his picture. In order to make the portrait of Henry himself stand out in what is a many-figured narrative, Holbein has him writhing like some miniature body-builder, with the consequence that the bearded, diminutive figure appears trivialised beneath an all too splendid canopy. Henry is surrounded by a Latin inscription, based upon the Old Testament Book of Chronicles, justifying the break with Rome. In translation it reads:

> Blessed be the Lord thy God, who delighted in thee, to set thee upon his throne, to be king (elected) by the Lord thy God.[6]

Beneath Henry, a flight of steps leads to his throne where the Queen of Sheba, arrested in motion, is caught in awesome contemplation of this priest king. The Queen suggests admiration and homage with her left hand, while with the other, she gestures downwards and towards the tributes she has brought to the famous encounter.

It is an image of the greatest richness and one in which Holbein draws upon his previous experience of palace decoration in Basle, as well as his acquaintance with the frescoes of Raphael and the prints of Dürer. *Solomon and the Queen of Sheba* is Janus-like: looking back to High Renaissance narrative painting, but forwards also to the artist's frontispiece to *Coverdale's Bible* of 1535.

The influence of *Solomon and the Queen of Sheba* may have been felt beyond the parameters of Holbein's own professional life. It seems to have fascinated Rubens when he was in London for ten months from May 1629 to March 1630; where he could have seen it at Arundel House, his spiritual home when in London. Rubens then began at last to think seriously about the Banqueting House which he had been commissioned to paint eight years earlier. Holbein's image of Henry as Solomon was surely a component in Rubens' *The Benefits of the Reign of James I*, one of the three great central canvases of the ceiling (Plate 11, page 38).

The matrix in both is the same. A central, powerfully athletic figure provides the hub of a wheel, which moves clockwise. At the same place in relation to the single dominant figures, vectors of energetic forms thrust themselves towards the respective kings, while on the other side in both, figural groups are discharged before gathering to return to centre stage. Similarities between the two cannot I think be explained by dependence on a common source. Although it is clear that Rubens was recalling *The Last Judgement* by Michelangelo when designing his canvas, something he had studied when in Rome some twenty years earlier, Holbein painted his miniature ten years before the Michelangelo was unveiled.

If the miniature is a record of a lost wall-painting, where was it?[7] The central theme of a righteous king placed over the church by God, might suggest the Convocation House. That had been the physical headquarters of the ecclesiastical establishment; a bastion which had abjectly surrendered when Henry VIII had laid siege to it. Although the ecclesiastical revolution had been forged in Parliament not Convocation, the forum of Convocation remained the most prominent physical symbol of church government even after the break with Rome. Perhaps, then, if the miniature does indeed represent the record of a lost fresco we should think of its setting as some building associated with the proceedings of Convocation. Such an environment would have been an appropriate setting for a painted affirmation of Henry's claim to be the Supreme Head of the Church of England.

But although Convocation remains a possible venue for a putative lost fresco of *Solomon and the Queen of Sheba*, there is another site which must also be considered. The presence of gilded stars on the cerulean blue hangings behind Henry, may suggest the Tudor Court of Star Chamber. Traditionally the miniature is dated 1535; interestingly enough this was when the Chamber underwent one of its many refurbishments.

Holbein's Privy Chamber fresco makes an interesting comparison with *Charles I with Henrietta Maria, Prince Charles and Princess Mary* by Van Dyck. The titles by which the two paintings have been known, the Holbein since the mid-eighteenth century and the Van Dyck since its inception, encourage us to see them together. The Holbein was referred to as 'the Great Picture', the Van Dyck as 'The Great Peice'. Both were located in Whitehall Palace: the Holbein possibly in what had been the Privy Chamber of Henry VIII, the Van Dyck in the Long Gallery of Charles I. But connections between them extend beyond nomenclature and physical proximity, to a real possibility that one was inspired by the other.

'The Great Peice' of 1632 is the first in the monumental series of Van Dyck portraits of the Stuarts which the artist was to undertake over the next eight years. Surely he would have been anxious to establish his reputation by showing that he could match the achievements of the last great court artist to immortalise the English monarchy.

Van Dyck has Charles seated towards the left of the centre line, wearing the ribbon and the star of the Garter; confidently scrutinising the spectator, while one arm rests on the table as the other encloses the small figure of Prince Charles. To the right, Henrietta Maria looks intently at her husband while her baby daughter, Princess Mary, stares out of the painting at us.

The background consists of a splendid theatrical curtain wound up against cold immovable marble; its lustrous sheen providing a foil to the solemnities of good order evoked by the drums of a giant column. Just behind the figure of the king, a table covered with rich cloth displays the sceptre and orb, symbols of the legitimacy of Charles I himself. Behind this, in the far distance, the outline of the Parliament House can be made out in indistinct but certain silhouette. The visual continuity between the sceptre and the orb, and the legislative centre of the kingdom, is surely no

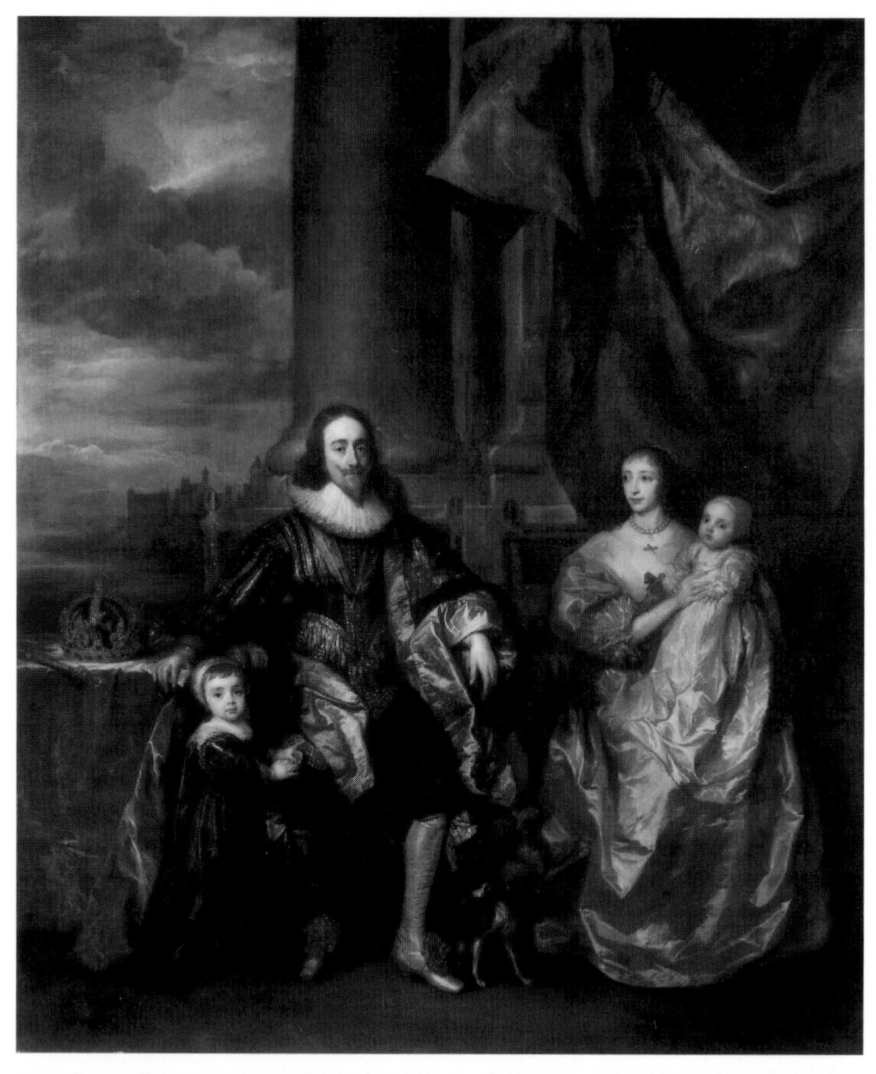

'The Greate Peice', Sir Anthony Van Dyck, *Charles I with Henrietta Maria, Prince Charles and Princess Mary*, 1632 (The Royal Collection)

accident. Nor for that matter is the weather. The Parliament House is at the centre of an aureole of light surrounded by dark banks of rain clouds. Beautiful in itself, this passage of landscape has too a symbolic meaning. The weather had often been used to underscore meaning in a picture and it continued to be so in the High Baroque period. We only have to think of the *Rainbow Portrait* of Elizabeth I to remind ourselves of this. This famous image, still at Hatfield, the house for which it was created, has been

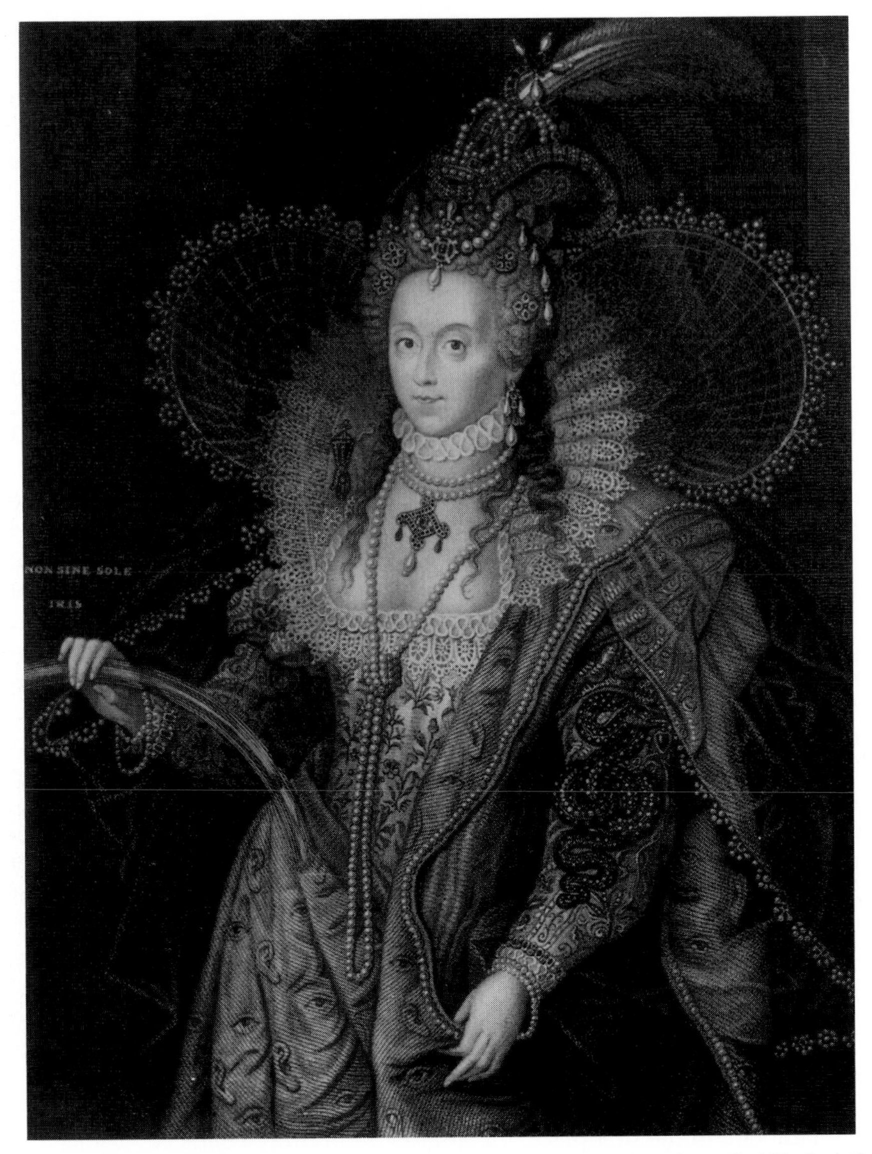

'The Rainbow Portrait', engraving after Marcus Gheeraerts (attributed), *Elizabeth I*, *c.* 1602 (Edinburgh University Library)

described by Strong as 'the most amazing of all these final visions of Elizabeth as "Queen of Love and beauty"'.[8] Serpents, carbuncles, gilly-flowers, disembodied eyes and ears, are all thrown into a witches' cauldron of symbolism.

Yet the most emphatic emblem within that picture is the rainbow which the Queen holds as if it were the neck of a viol. Reinforcement of the motif is provided by the Latin motto *Non Sine Sole Iris*, which translated means 'No rainbow without the sun'. That tag carries the implication that the sun comes after storms – for the rainbow requires the sun to irradiate the passing storm clouds. So too in Van Dyck's 'Great Peice', it is perhaps possible that the artist intended us to infer that illumination, brightness and calm, will break through those other storm clouds which had engulfed and obscured the proceedings of Parliament during the stormy sessions which had characterised its conduct during the unhappy period of The Petition of Right and the impeachment of the royal favourite Buckingham.

The painting is the first grand essay in self-justification, if not self-delusion, ordered by Charles since his acrimonious break with Parliament in 1629. It must have been Charles himself who contrived this alignment. Van Dyck was certainly in no position to understand what was required by a sympathetic but as yet unfamiliar new master. Moving from meteorology to metallurgy, Charles is making the point that it was through the powers vested in him as sovereign – proof of which lies at hand in the sceptre and orb lying upon the table – that he has allocated a subordinate role to Parliament; subordinate rather than non-existent that is, since the visual relationship accurately mirrored his own thinking. Charles had protested that he did not intend to dispense with this partner in government. He had told Parliament, as indeed he had told those who were more hostile to the institution than he was, that when Parliament came to its senses, then and only then, would there be a place for it in what would have become a properly ordered Commonwealth.[9] For this reason the Parliament building appears in an indistinct shadowy form in the background, which precisely measured its place in the kingdom when this painting was created in 1632. 'The Great Peice' is therefore a prospectus for the future as much as it is a celebration of the fecundity and felicity of the Stuart line. Van Dyck, acting as visual secretary to the King, is taking down dictation; emphasising the two things which mattered most to his new-found patron: his sovereignty and his family.

This Van Dyck painting, and the Holbein fresco we have already analysed, are not obviously related. Nevertheless, there are final adjustments, nudges such as a photographer makes in setting up a family photograph, which suggest how interested Van Dyck may have been in the Holbein. In the first place, the quartet is carefully balanced, just as it is in the Holbein. In the Van Dyck there is a deeply shadowed recess in the columnar architecture which creates a caesura: it has the same effect as the altar around which Henry VIII and his family are gathered. The figures in both, create a solid pyramid with an upward angle to the placing of the heads of about 45°. Van Dyck chose to set off his figures in their silks and gold braid by the generous sweep of a great brocaded curtain. Holbein too wanted to suggest wealth and splendour but instead of hanging tapestry from a ceiling, the equivalent to the Italian silk in the Van Dyck, he placed his sitters on an immense Turkey rug. Turkey carpets were distinct luxuries in the 1530s; one this size, of almost legendary status. Van Dyck, the son of an Antwerp silk merchant, knew the value of 'stuffs' and so, for his part, includes yards of extremely expensive silk hangings to suggest exceptional material splendour.

The architectural setting of the two pictures creates different moods. Holbein's sitters stand in a claustrophobic world which is paradoxically empty despite the presence of four full-length figures. Although Holbein does not appear to have been painting a portrait of an actual loggia or room, he meant the onlooker to be impressed by the wealth of detail to provide a digest of the architectural form Henry was then incorporating into the alterations he was making to Hampton Court and other residences. Van Dyck places his group in an airy loggia, the scale of which suggests that this too is setting a tone rather than portraying a real palace.

Van Dyck and Holbein adjust relationships between their figures with considerable sensitivity and here too there are close similarities. In her glance Elizabeth of York anticipates Henrietta Maria. The two male figures at left in the Holbein are a foretaste of how Van Dyck would cast the males in his group portrait. These are all modulations which suggest that Van Dyck studied the Holbein before embarking on his own picture. If so that is understandable. When Van Dyck began 'the Great Peice', he was almost literally finding his way; dependent for advice about England and English mores, upon cosmopolitan connoisseurs like George Gage and the royal organ-builder Edward Norgate, the precocious connoisseur of Flemish landscape drawings with whom Van Dyck lodged when he first came to England. Van Dyck, newly arrived in England when he set about 'the Great Peice', was surely in need of guidance by a patron with firm views. For although Van Dyck may have already proved himself master of the group portrait to the satisfaction of clients as far apart as the Hague and Palermo, it may be suspected that Charles I led him towards the Holbein mural as the desired point of departure.

Designs by Inigo Jones for the King's masques suggest that Tudor portraits were much admired in the Stuart era. Arundel, to whom Jones was closer than any of the other great English aristocrats, had a room with over fifty Holbeins; in addition to owning the incomparable album of Holbein portrait drawings now in The Royal Library at Windsor. Reminiscences of Tudor fashions in some of Jones' costume designs suggest that like many artists, he found the Arundel Holbeins a real inspiration.

Interest in the Tudors taken by Rubens, Van Dyck and Inigo Jones, may seem surprising. But then we should recall that Henry VIII had declared himself Emperor, and Charles I followed suit. Charles was the beneficiary of Henry's palaces, the result of the greatest building programme in the history of the English monarchy and the most vivid and permanent memorial to the achievements of the Tudors. Charles I, part Danish, part

Scottish, but only remotely English, modelled himself on the first English prince to live on a European scale of splendour.

At the end of his life, Holbein painted *Henry VIII and the Barber Surgeons;* never a wholly successful picture even when allowance has been made for the later, awkward insertion of figures, and smoke damage during the Fire of London in 1666 (Plate 15, page 45). But although Holbein's painting must always have ranked as one of his least successful English works, it is interesting because it is an early example of how the Tudors rifled sacred imagery for their own propaganda.

The stuffed, rigid appearance of Henry VIII is derived from the iconography of the Epiphany paintings, when the Magi journey to adore the Christ Child held in the arms of the Virgin. The Virgin with her maternal appeal had always been the most accessible figure to the layman, but towards the end of the reign of Henry VIII she proved to have great potential to the new secularised monarchy. When the crown passed to Elizabeth, not only a woman but a virgin, the attraction of the Virgin Mary to those whose job it was to suggest the presentation of her image, became irresistible. Before then, in Holbein's Barber Surgeons Company picture, there is a certain irony that the artist should have pilfered the iconography of the Virgin to depict one who was doing all he could to destroy her cult.

Images of the Virgin Mary were the single most influential source for Tudor propaganda and it is to her transition from this life to the next that we turn to examine the earthbound, threatening transition from the world of Henry VIII to that of Edward VI. We move from the twilight of late Henrician Catholicism in which men found it difficult to locate themselves, to a harsh dawn when everything was picked out in extremes. The most famous image of that transition is the painting known as *Edward VI and the Pope.*

The painting is anonymous; a visual equivalent to the Tudor royal proclamation. Although it is competently executed, the artist whoever he was, is more concerned with legibility than with sophisticated illusionism. To the left, Henry lies on his deathbed, pointing to his son who sits on an elaborately carved throne staring resolutely out at the spectator; intent upon facing down any possible doubts as to the legitimacy of his succession. Beneath lies the Pope, crumbled like a rag doll with 'All Fleshe is Grasse' inscribed across his chest. The Pope points helplessly to a monk and a friar who exit rapidly and fearfully.

Thanks to a brilliant analysis by Margaret Aston, this celebrated image has now to be seen in a very different way from how it has been understood hitherto.[10] The right hand is taken up with portraits of some of the most dominant figures in that turbulent period. But whereas it has always been assumed that these represent the Politburo of Edwardian England, the poker-faced men responsible for flushing out Catholicism, Aston has argued wholly convincingly that those with their backs to the viewer are adherents of the Old Faith, while the rest are indeed supporters

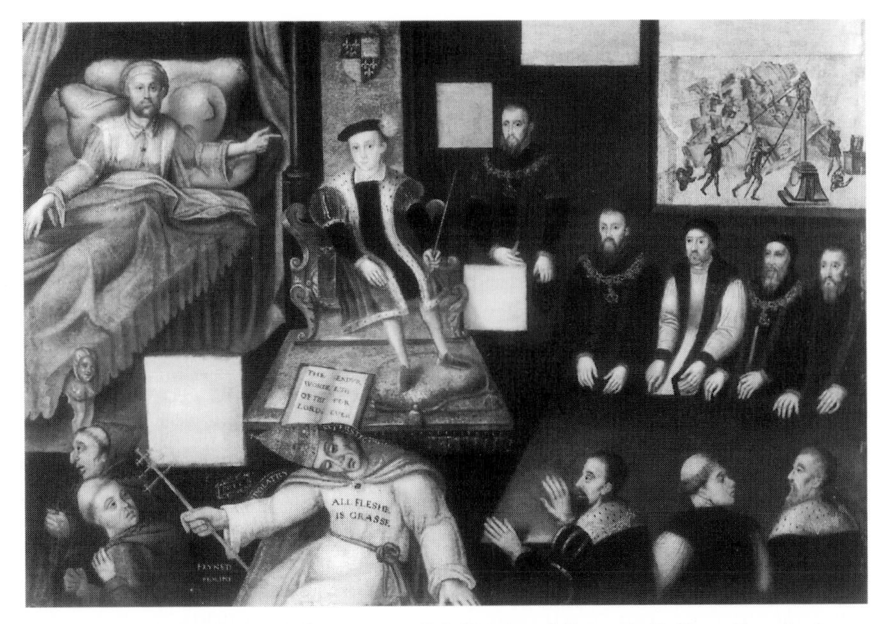

Anon., *Edward VI and the Pope*, c. 1570 (National Portrait Gallery, London)

of Protestantism. Aston is encouraged to see conflicting religious loyalties because the bottom left-hand figure seems to gesture with alarm and sympathy towards the Pope and his subordinates.

Aston demonstrates that the picture is Elizabethan not Henrician or Edwardian as previously assumed. She shows that it contains motifs from Dutch prints which only began to circulate in the mid-1560s. She then goes on to suggest a date of *c.* 1570 and argues that the painting was created as a petition to Elizabeth I. Such a proposed new dating, combined with the inset at the top right-hand corner, are central to a proper understanding of what is going on in this most famous image of English iconoclasm. The inset at the top right is a painting within a painting; not a window onto the outside world as has always been thought. It contains a scene of men toppling a statue while a building behind shivers into a thousand fragments like an exploding shell. This is not an accurate topographical vignette of one of the medieval crosses which had actually been destroyed in the reign of Edward VI, but a symbol to associate Elizabeth with a specific biblical figure. Energetic destruction of monuments is carried on with great gusto because whoever was responsible for putting this surreal collage together, wanted to remind Elizabeth that she was a second Hezekiah.

Hezekiah was a hero to Calvinists: a King of Judah who features prominently in The Second Book of Kings, and whose most successful role was as destroyer of the brazen serpents. Elizabeth is being urged to defend the purity of English Protestantism by becoming a latter-day Hezekiah; an epithet it is inferred she would earn by ensuring that the Papacy and all its works are cast away; as indeed happens so dramatically in what is in effect a strip-cartoon devoted to the violent excitements of iconoclasm.

Aston proves that *Edward VI and the Pope* was painted in the reign of Elizabeth; she then goes on to suggest that its purpose cannot have been to reinforce the succession of Edward VI, but to make Elizabeth hold fast to a revolution accomplished but perceived to be threatened. Where however her argument becomes doubtful is when she suggests that it was actually painted as a visual sermon for direct presentation to Elizabeth herself. Elizabeth liked neither painting nor iconoclasm and surely if anyone had had the temerity to present it, she would have had no compunction in having the thing destroyed.

It is tempting to think that the image was something of a triumph, not merely an admonition as Aston argues. Could it be that the painting was made to commemorate the granting of royal authority to the Thirty-Nine Articles in 1571; a date which falls within the period when Aston says it was executed?

Something else too should be added to Aston's brilliant analysis, which has transformed our understanding of a justly famous picture. The painting is both naive and sophisticated – it looks crude. And yet to dismiss it is to underestimate how skilfully the painter may have manipulated the preconceptions of those at whom it was aimed. The visual language of the Elizabethan had been built upon Catholic visual imagery and accordingly, consciously or unconsciously, the artist combines certain sacred archetypes.

The title of Aston's study, *The King's Bedpost*, derives from her discovery that the image of Henry is plagiarised from a Heemskerck print of *The Chronicles being read to King Ahasuerus*. But it is not the whole story. The very title of the painting should remind us there is another bed and another person to be accounted for besides an Old Testament king. Henry's predicament, and his relationship to others in the picture, derives from the iconography of the Death of the Virgin; a popular Northern subject at the time. Sixty years earlier, Dürer had etched his *Death of the Virgin*. In this the dying Virgin is seen propped up on pillows surrounded by a nimbus of light; not so near her end however that she cannot read the Bible open at the foot of the bed, while with demurely folded hands she awaits her end with didactic serenity.

The right-hand side of *Edward VI and the Pope* borrows a formula used in that most popular of all religious subjects, *The Last Supper*. Edward VI's posture derives from Christ's moment of revelation, while the gesture of the member of the Council of Regency nearest the spectator, confirms this. He raises his hands in surprised concern for the fate of the monk and friar, just as the Apostles traditionally respond with vehemence to what Christ has just told them of his coming betrayal. As for the monk and friar who

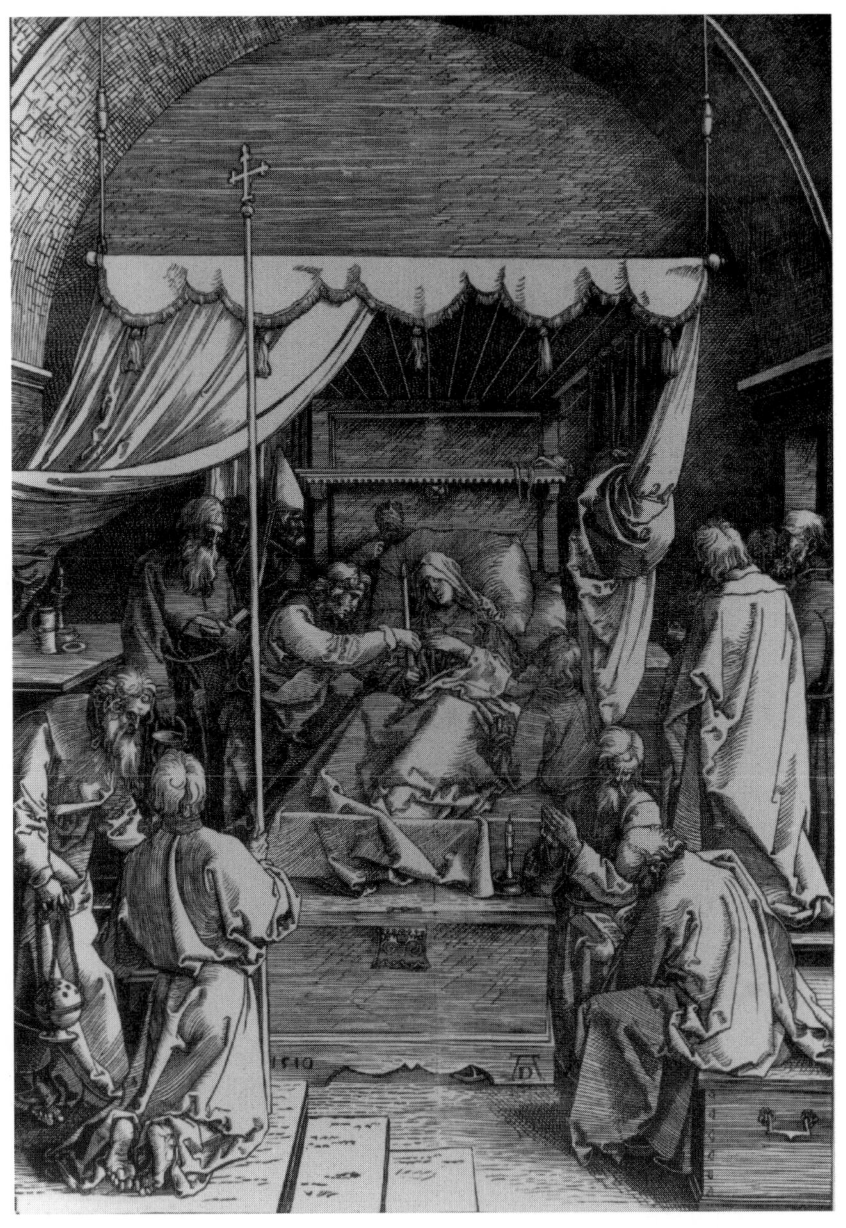

Albrecht Dürer, *Death of the Virgin* (engraving), 1510 (Joe Rock)

exit left, they surely suggest a composite Judas slipping from the Upper Room.

Edward VI and the Pope marks a new departure in narrative ambition. Holbein had struck a balance between the demands of art and those of propaganda; perhaps because the artist came to have equal mastery over both. Here however everything militates against the mesmeric effect of illusionism. In this type of picture (and dozens like it may have vanished), clarity and legibility become a great deal more important than illusionism or aesthetic effects. We can see where the solder is applied but a powerful current flows through the mechanism nonetheless.

How then do we account for the fact that imagery of the second half of the sixteenth century addressed the mind rather than the eye? In effect publicly accessible works of art became a visual counterpart to the Royal Proclamation. This may have been because the Bible, by then in English, had found its way into people's homes and with it, that great educational visual aid, the illustrated book. Although it has just been suggested that a medley of Biblical archetypes went to make up *Edward VI and the Pope*, the painting is essentially a book illustration writ, or rather painted, large.

Edward VI and the Pope is vastly more successful for the information it carries than for its aesthetic qualities; it must have looked like a school noticeboard because it once contained a cluster of inscriptions now erased. The clamorous nature of the painting means that it surely hung where its message could have been widely read. Although Aston's analysis makes it abundantly clear that it is taken up with the great affairs of church and state which were the concern of an elite, some of the methods employed to get over the various messages it sets out to broadcast had come into being in response to a perennial need to justify the Reformation to those beyond the court, the Universities and the legal Inns.

Whilst it can now be accepted that *Edward VI and the Pope* is an Elizabethan picture, there are a number of distinguished images of Edward himself and it is to these we now turn. Edward VI by William Scrots is one. This might well have become a standard image had the king lived long enough. It is the finest Mannerist portrait produced in England during the Renaissance and it demonstrates that those with stern Protestant sympathies were by no means hostile to the visual arts.

The portrait was probably painted in 1550. There is a payment of March 1552 to the artist for 'three great tables' or portraits, two of which were of Edward VI: perhaps sent abroad to Sir John Mason and Sir Thomas Hoby, diplomats in France, for presentation to the Valois court.[11] Mason was ambassador to France in 1550 and mention is made of a portrait of Edward VI sent to him in October that year. Early in 1551 it was reported that the Council was dispatching to France 'a certain painting, a portrait of the King of England, which the Vidame requested to be allowed to present to the King'. This was probably in connection with a proposed marriage between Edward and Henri II's eldest daughter. The other Scrots

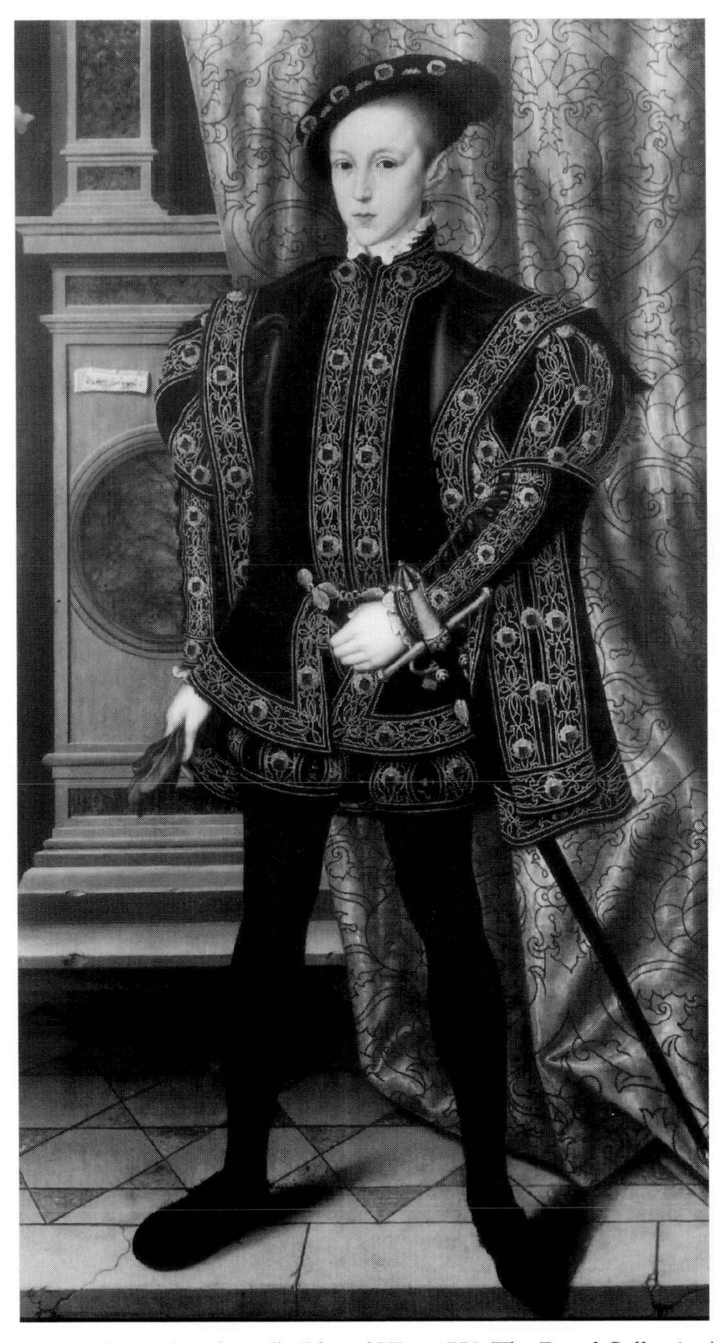

William Scrots (attributed), *Edward VI, c.* 1550 (The Royal Collection)

may well have been given to the Mareschal St André, who had visited London in July 1551, with the Order of St Michael for the English King.

The presentation of paintings as commodities in high-level diplomatic exchanges happened frequently and we have firm documentary evidence of such activity between the courts of England and France in the middle of the sixteenth century. However, myth can often tell us as much as facts about how people have thought those of an earlier generation perceived famous images. Thus it was that the legend grew up about a supposed famous exchange which, until recently, it was claimed took place between Henry VII and the Duke of Urbino in 1506. Henry, so tradition had it, had given the Garter to Guidobaldo of Urbino, who had responded by sending Baldassare Castiglione to England, with Raphael's painting of *St George and the Dragon*; chosen to flatter the English, who made a cult of St George as the patron saint of their most prestigious order, the Order of the Garter.[12]

In the next generation Holbein was called upon twice to play the role of marriage broker. First he was sent to Brussels to paint *Christina of Denmark* so that Henry VIII could decide whether her physique was likely to make her a good breeder. Holbein created one of the most winning female portraits of the Renaissance; fortunately for Christina, nothing came of the projected marriage.

Shortly afterwards Holbein was asked to do the same thing again and on this occasion was sent to paint Anne of Cleves. The enterprise was however disastrous for everyone concerned. Holbein produced a draft portrait, which was later worked up into a three-quarter length and a miniature. However, they seem to have been illusionistic in more senses than one because the king proceeded with the marriage on the basis of what Holbein offered up. When he met his future bride at Gravesend however, he was aghast; horrified by what he rudely described as this 'Flanders mare'.[13] It seemed by then too late to get out of the marriage but Henry simply could not face poor Anne and consequently underwent close questioning by the celebrated Dr Butts as to what had or had not happened in bed; an embarrassment he was willing to endure if it would provide a means of annulling the marriage on the basis of non-consummation. It would be of the greatest interest in understanding the role of Holbein as court artist to know what Henry said to him after this debacle and how Holbein defended himself.

Holbein's misfortunes demonstrate how artists were intimately involved with politics. It was a role best symbolised by Rubens. In *The Presentation of the Portrait*, one of twenty-four paintings from the Marie de' Medici cycle executed by Rubens for the Palais de Luxembourg in 1622–5, the artist paid tribute to the nuptials of Henri IV of France and Marie de' Medici but also, incidentally, to the role of himself as artist in international diplomacy.

No less than four of the Marie de' Medici cycle are concerned with the union of the two houses of the Valois and Medici: betrothal, legitimacy,

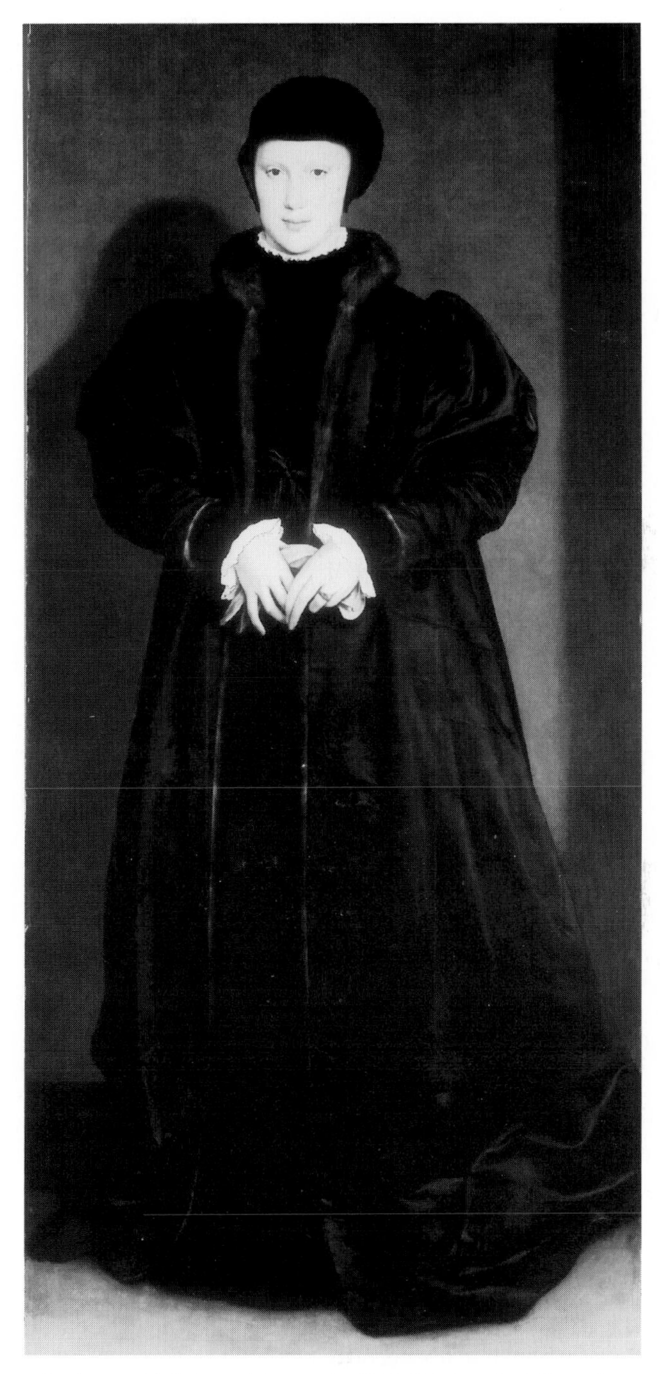

Hans Holbein, *Christina of Denmark*, 1538 (National Gallery, London)

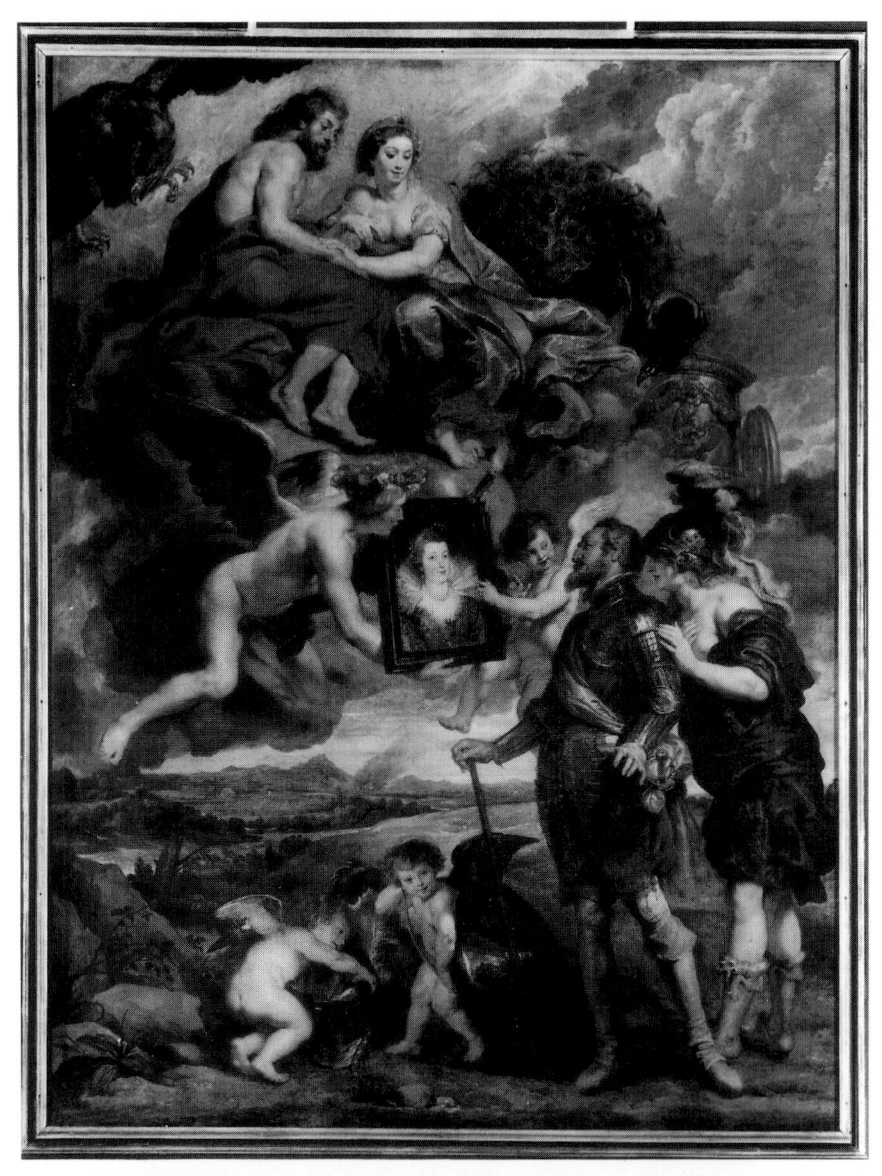

Sir Peter Paul Rubens, *The Presentation of the Portrait*, c. 1623 (The Louvre)

intentions and consequences: *The Presentation of the Portrait*, *The Marriage by Proxy*, *The Consummation*, and the felicitous end result, *The Birth of the Dauphin*. Marriage receives more emphasis in the Rubens cycle than treaties and triumphs of arms because everything was underpinned by its achievements and its consequences. Central to recording those priorities in early modern Europe was the artist, whose role could be almost as significant as those whose task was to negotiate the dowry; in the case of Marie, of such prodigality that the union had become of compelling attraction to a bankrupt French monarchy.

In the Medici cycle, Rubens says as much about the role of the artist as he does about the patrons whose merits he was commissioned to celebrate. In the very centre of *The Presentation of the Portrait*, Hymen, the God of Marriage, and a skittish Cupid, hold up a bust-length framed portrait of Marie. This is presented for the delectation of Henri who, like a rich connoisseur, considers the purchase of a great but expensive masterpiece. Cupid eloquently persuades Henri of the charms of his bride by pointing with his left hand at the face, while looking inquisitively but encouragingly at Henri. Henri appears captivated; his left hand suggesting surprise, delight and excitement. He is encouraged not only by Cupid, but by a décolletée female who hovers closely behind. She is France. With one hand, she lightly touches his shoulder to encourage; with the other she declares that she too is moved for she touches her breast. Although she is certainly France, she has another persona; she is strongly reminiscent of Minerva, the goddess of wisdom. This is a telling allusion since what Rubens is suggesting is that art can teach princes wisdom; a point reinforced not only by the look of wonderment on the face of Henri himself, but through France–Minerva's absorbed expression as she stares at the picture with the same rapt attention as her protégé Henri. As befitted the Master of Tact, Rubens flatters the parties to the negotiations by showing Jupiter and Juno in the clouds above, awaiting Henri's decision with deferential attention and in a rare interlude of marital harmony.

Rubens has given Juno her peacock and it has been suggested that he probably consulted Pierre Dinet's book of emblems, published in Paris in 1614.[14] Rubens was the most learned painter in the world and he was the last person who needed to look up the symbols of the gods. However, Dinet gave his peacock a meaning which was particularly apposite in the context of *The Presentation of the Portrait*; the thousand eyes of the tail represented 'the caution and vigilance required in any affair of consequence'. Caution and vigilance are qualities Rubens means the onlooker to see in Henri, but they are also qualities which the painter helps Henri to exercise when weighing up the merits of his future bride. To those who could afford a Rubens, and they tended to be the crowned heads of Europe, the artist was probably as significant in the role of diplomat as he was as a painter. Philip IV of Spain was affronted when informed by the Archduchess Isabella that she had chosen Rubens to represent her at the Spanish court in 1628, and could only be mollified when it was pointed out just how much experience Rubens had had.[15] Rubens was unique in the variety of his talents no less than in the demands made upon them, but Titian, Holbein, Scrots, Van Dyck and Velazquez, none were confined to their studios; all lived a public life.

Just how important a Holbein or a Rubens could be if they had the necessary gifts to sustain a dual life as painter and diplomat, is suggested by the career of Hans von Aachen, court painter to the Emperor Rudolf II. In 1603 he was sent into Italy by Rudolf, and the ambassador of the Estes tried to persuade his master to treat him nobly 'for he is one of the emperor's greatest favourites and most influential servants; with a fine portrait he would be able to win back your territory for you'.[16]

Baccio Giovannini, the Florentine resident in Paris, reported that Henri IV had finally met Marie at Lyons where numerous portraits were exchanged; though Henri found that his bride 'surpassed in beauty all the portraits that had been sent to him'.[17] Poor Holbein! If only that had been the case in England some eighty years before. *The Presentation of the Portrait* was not of course among the images referred to by Giovannini; Rubens' offering was not a marriage portrait like Holbein's *Anne of Cleves*, but rather, a flattering allegory to recall courtesies which had been exchanged twenty years before *The Presentation* was painted. Nevertheless Rubens had to cope with his most difficult client in Marie de' Medici; a woman whose unerring capacity for misjudgement meant that neither her career nor her character merited commemoration. The pressures on Rubens were different from those Holbein had had to face, but the offerings of both demonstrate clearly enough how much hung upon these ambassadorial 'dispatches'.

Mary Tudor, who succeeded her brother Edward VI in 1553, was married to Philip II, principal patron of Titian, the greatest living artist of that time. Although much might have come of this contact, nothing did because the marriage was barren in every sense. Mary cared passionately about religion not art. She sublimated her own consciousness beneath an obsessive devotion to Catholicism, to the extent indeed that it is doubtful whether she would ever have seen the potential for image-making had she lived longer. She benefited briefly and vicariously from her husband's ambitions though, because he sent the great Low Countries portraitist Antonis Mor to England in 1554 to paint her portrait as a prelude to their wedding.

The Mor portrait is an image of immense power.[18] It tells us at once that here is a daughter of Henry VIII. Mary sits at three-quarter length at an angle to the spectator, looking out to our left. The rudiments of the painting owe much to Titian's posthumous portrait of *Isabella of Portugal*, the wife of Charles V. Despite Mor's debt however, the Titian is much more abstracted; understandably given that it was done without the sitter. But even so, the gaze of Mary and the lighting make it a much more assertive image. Mary looks furiously at us; surrounded by intense diamond light which heightens an alarming physical presence and provides a fitting analogue to the intensity of her personality. The light is entirely different from the caressing, distinguished and reassuring illumination of a typical Titian portrait. It is tempting to think that Mor made play of this

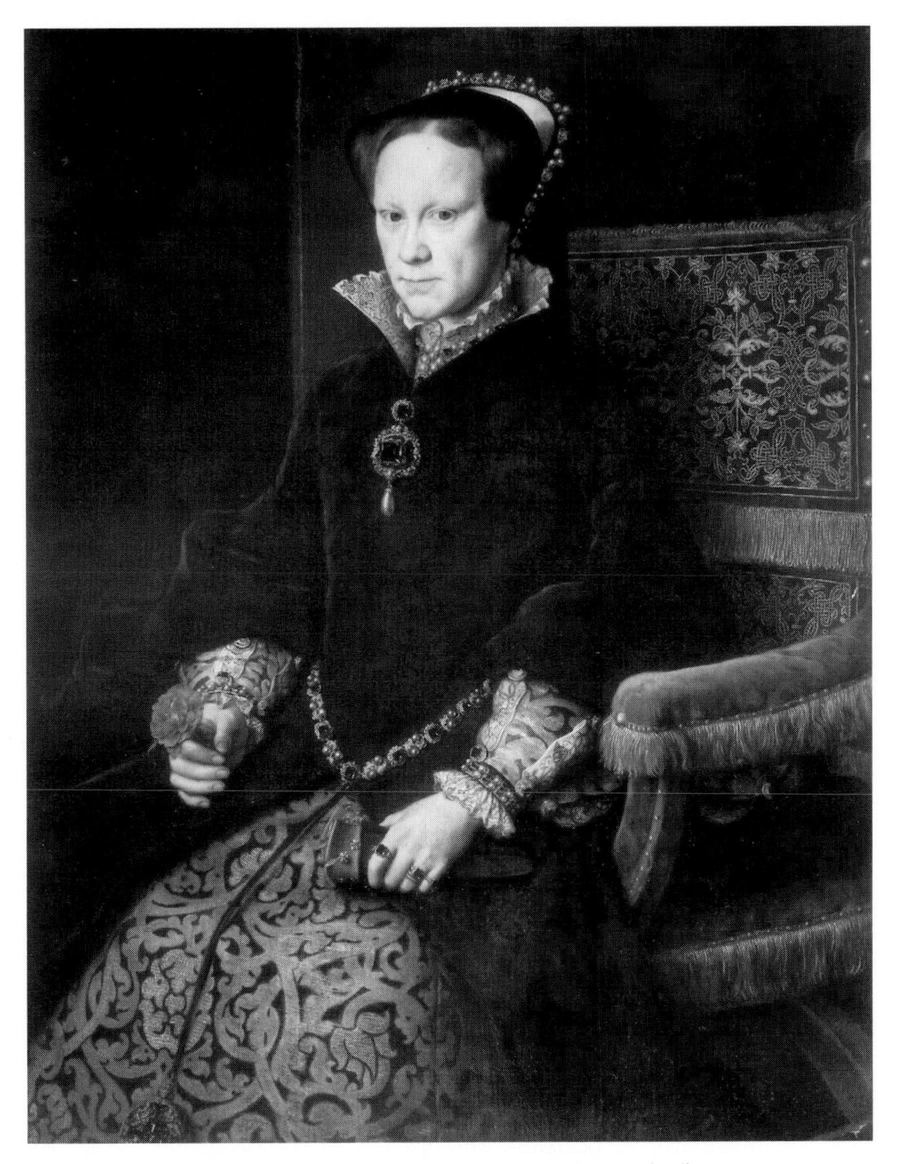

Antonis Mor, *Mary I*, 1554 (The Prado, Madrid)

to get over a powerful impression of fanaticism hinted at in other ways: the rod-like backbone, the pursed lips, the chisel-like chin, the meaty facial muscles, a stare more reminiscent of a gargoyle than of a woman of thirty-seven. The picture is positively frightening because it is a likeness without mercy. It has a menace only surpassed in English portraiture by Holbein's understanding of the character of her father; though a certain poignancy too, as revealing a character which made the woman 'The leading victim of her own persecution'.[19]

It is, too, a painting of great significance in the larger story of royal portraiture in England. It represents the last of its type for the Tudors. Mary's sister Elizabeth would set her face against this sort of image; with its combination of a sense of design derived from Titian and a northern intensity of finish. With portraits of Elizabeth we are presented with something new and something unexpected.

The earliest portrait of Elizabeth shows her as a princess not a queen. It is conventional enough. Painted when Elizabeth's future looked frighteningly uncertain, it shows her at the time when she was the vulnerable target of bishop Bonner, who consistently made her life a misery. Elizabeth stands three-quarter length; a thirteen-year-old with elegant, nubile figure clothed in warm pink. It is the only image which shows her with breasts and as an attractive adolescent on the verge of her sexual potential. Once however this princess became a queen, images of flesh and blood were not to be seen again.

The key to understanding the attitude of Elizabeth to her own image is to appreciate that she wanted to control it. In 1563 a draft Proclamation promoted an 'approved' portrait to which all were to subscribe. It acknowledged that 'all sorts of people both noble and mean' wanted a portrait of the new Queen, but then set about trying to check that gratifying enthusiasm by directing that nothing should be done until 'some special person, that shall be by her allowed, shall have first finished a portraiture thereof, after which finished, her Majesty will be content that all other painters, or gravers . . . shall and may at their pleasure follow the said pattern or first portraiture'.[20]

Such thinking was not so very different from the control which monarchs issued over the minting of money. It was not necessarily a sinister move. Indeed one of the tasks Velazquez was to perform regularly for Philip IV nearly a century later, was to scrutinize royal portraits which were not produced under his knowing eye at court to ensure that they were 'in keeping with the propriety and dignity of royal persons'.[21] It is therefore wholly inappropriate to conclude from a document which was not in fact issued that Elizabeth was antithetical to portraiture. Indeed it could be argued that Elizabeth's instinct for censorship is evidence of her awareness of the potency of portraits, though not of course of her liking for them. This was surely so since she made a second attempt to license her image in the last years of her reign when a portraitist could all too easily have revealed the truth. In July 1596 the Privy Council ordered that assistance should be given to the Sergeant Painter that all offensive images were to be destroyed.

What then came to replace a quest for the life-like such as we have described in the most sympathetic portrait of her, where she appears as a real princess? Portraits of Elizabeth I differ as they were bound to do over

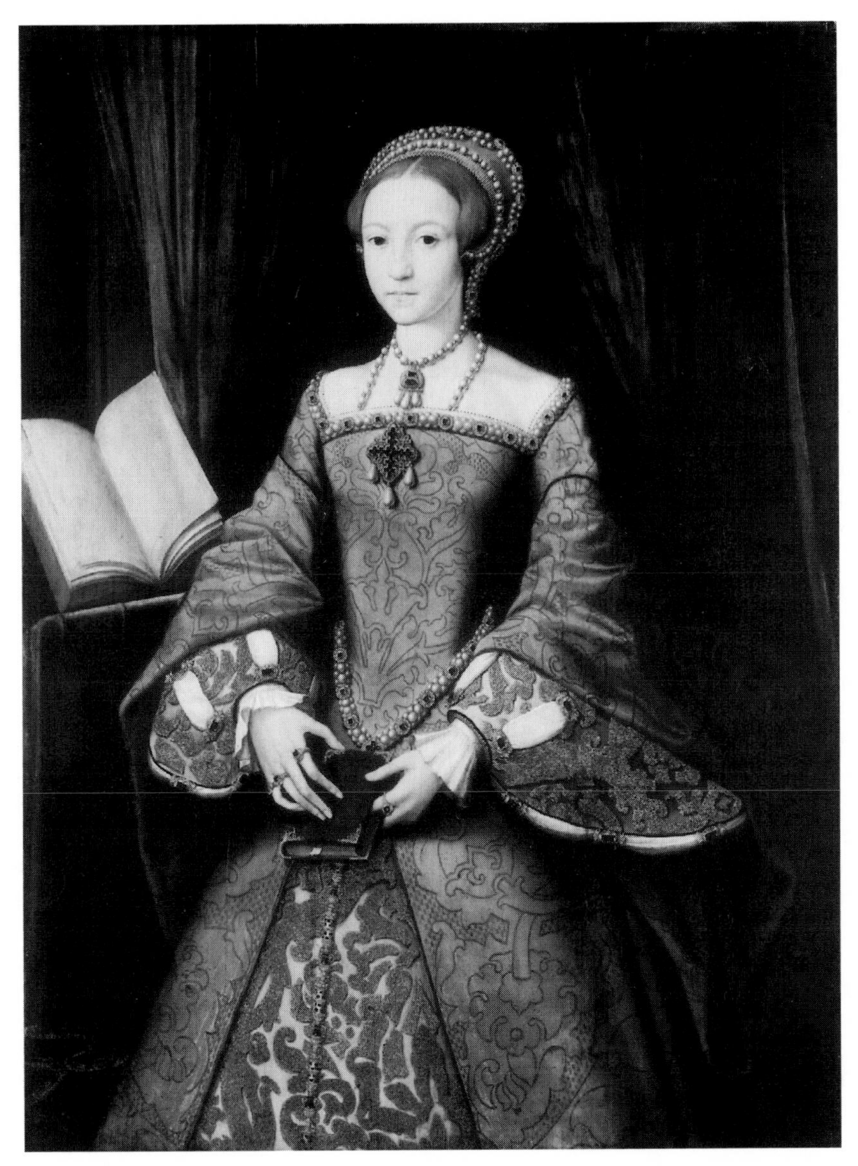

William Scrots (attributed), *Princess Elizabeth*, *c.* 1546 (The Royal Collection)

a reign which lasted forty-five years, but all tend to underplay any sense of her physical presence and the ravages of time. This may have had something to do with Elizabeth's wish to stress constancy and continuity; something she did by adopting the motto *Semper Eadem*, which translates as 'Always the same'. The Tudors had all lived dangerously and Elizabeth was no exception. Such was the skill of the dynasty in manipulating its image however, that it comes as a real surprise to discover, in an historical atlas of Tudor England, little hatchings of rebellion from Cornwall to Northumberland like some television weathermap. Tudor sovereigns inherited a country rife with potential chaos, or they invited turbulence by challenging the status quo. Elizabeth through her portraits tried to invent the myth that hers was an unchanging regime; just as her father may have favoured an aggressively forthright pose to suggest the firm anchorage of the kingdom amidst the pitch and toss of revolution.

With Elizabeth, the high-risk strategy of remaining a virgin and thereby placing the lid on the Tudor sarcophagus, is central to her imagery. At first it was important to stress that she remained a fecund virgin to sustain the possibility of marriage; hence the image of *Princess Elizabeth*. But in time art had to be recruited to conceal nature; to sustain the myth of fecundity in defiance of the laws of nature. When at last continuance of this fiction became positively damaging, it was time to make strength out of weakness; a virtue out of her failure to take a husband and settle the succession. This was when the old myths had to be painted out. What had once been a cosmetic image of a physical being came to be replaced by a face looking as indestructible as marble.

The failure of Elizabeth to marry was nothing less than a long-sighted and selfless devotion to her people; or so her propagandists proclaimed. Elizabeth co-operated in all this as we can see by turning to one of Hilliard's most effective life-size images, his so-called *Pelican Portrait*. Hilliard's portrait gets its name from the prominence with which he shows 'The Pelican Jewel', a favourite from the Royal Jewel house. The sculpted pendant shows the pelican plucking its breast to feed its fledglings with its own blood. The pelican symbolised the body of Christ who was sacrificed to offer spiritual nourishment, just as Elizabeth, the governor of God's true church on earth, sacrificed herself for the good of her subjects.

The face is a 'powdered Pharaoh', as Horace Walpole categorised the genus of the queen's portraits. Hilliard is concerned to emphasise the sacrificial and selfless nature of his subject. There is therefore a dependence of the secular on the sacred such as we have encountered already in other contexts and in other media. Elizabeth wears the badge of the pelican just as in a painting of pilgrims journeying to St James of Compostela, the identity of the figures can be established from the shell of St James worn on their breasts. But there is a fundamental difference. Whereas the presence of that symbol in pilgrimage iconography denotes the cult of that saint, Elizabeth has arrogated to herself a symbol which under the old religious order had been reserved for God himself. It was an audacious theft and an audacious, ironical blasphemy in the face of a sustained campaign mounted by Elizabeth and her house to expunge idolatry.

Giorgio Vasari published his definitive edition of *The Lives of the Artists* in 1568, just when the industry of Elizabethan propaganda was really

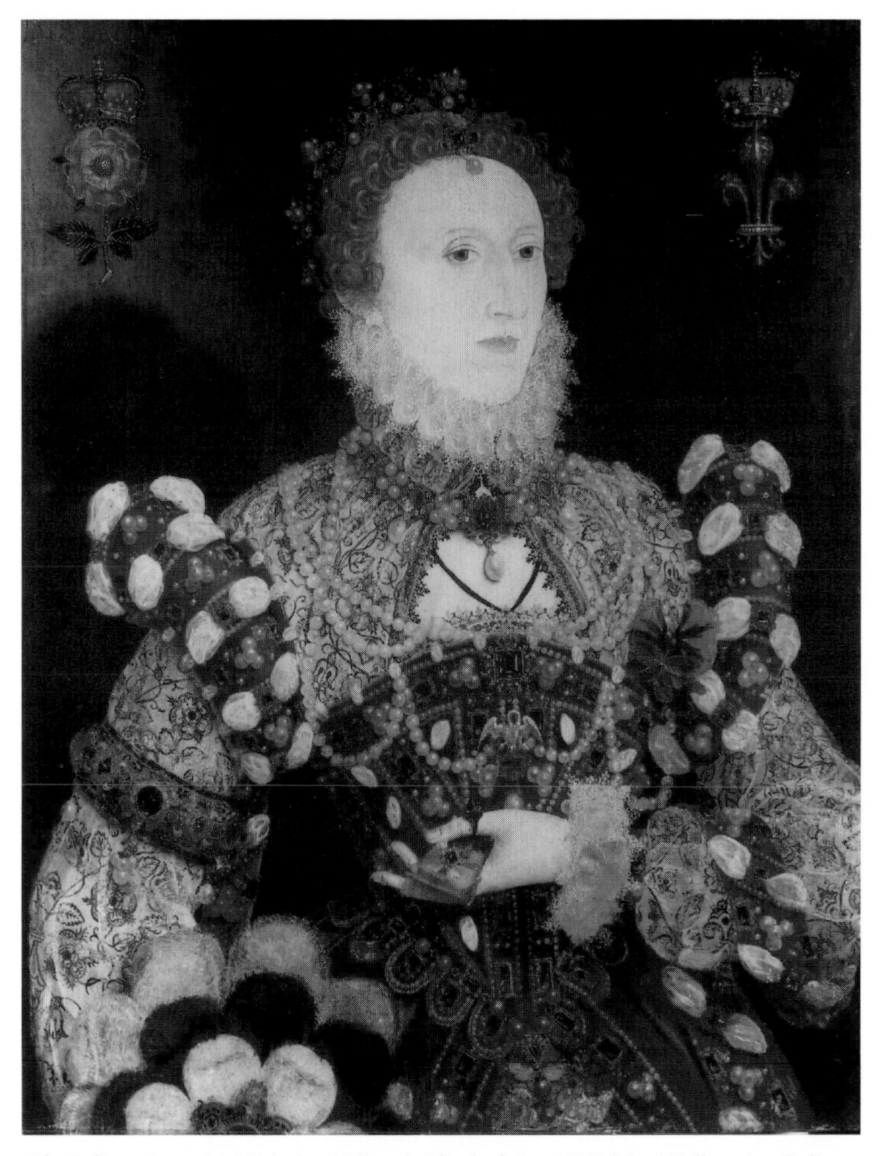

'The Pelican Portrait', Nicholas Hilliard, *Elizabeth I, c.* 1575 (The Walker Art Gallery, Liverpool)

getting into gear. By Vasarian standards, and they remain the dominant methodology in art history today, the portraiture of Elizabeth is inept, timid and confined. That has to be conceded if we wish to look at pictures narrowly; that is to say, to judge the effectiveness of imagery by the standard of illusionism. But surely there was something immensely daring in the way in which the armoury of sacred imagery was rifled to defend the new order of things. Seen in this light, the portraits by Hilliard and other approved masters are much more ambitious than the great illusionistic images of Titian or Holbein. Neither Charles V nor Francis I had dared to do what Elizabeth did by way of breaking into the sanctuary of sacred art. This may have much to do with the fact that they were Catholics and she a Protestant, inclined more to the old ways than the road to Geneva certainly, but precisely because she was free of the old shackles, she was the more able to pervert its propaganda to other uses.

Elizabethan portraiture has tended to be approached on the assumption that this was the best that could be done in England at the time. We are told that the isolation of the Elizabethan regime meant that great foreign portraitists could not be recruited. This is a myth. It is a myth based on the assumption that artists in Europe were Catholic and could not settle in a Protestant country.

In the first place the Catholic Church and Catholic patrons did not have a monopoly on image-making; the Low Countries had many distinguished artists who were Protestant. Secondly, artists did not divide along sectarian lines. The celebrated Italian Federigo Zuccaro entered the service of that great champion of Protestantism and favourite of Elizabeth, the Earl of Leicester. This may appear mildly surprising since Zuccaro had been working in Counter-Reformation Rome, and Leicester was the protector of some of the most rabidly Calvinist divines in all England. But still more surprising is to learn that Zuccaro owed his introduction to Leicester to the Marchese di Cortona, a general serving under the Duke of Alva who hanged Protestants in the Spanish Netherlands as women put out their washing to dry.[22] Furthermore, fifty years later Rubens would be quite prepared to produce propaganda for the Protestant Charles I. Thus, far from being cut off, England was positively attractive to cultural refugees who saw a society where profound religious differences did exist certainly, but where it was apparent that although the state executed people for their religious beliefs, and it should be remembered Elizabeth permitted the execution of a significant number of Catholic missionaries, the crucial difference was that men did not go into the streets to kill each other in the name of Christianity. Consequently painters did settle in England. Nevertheless it is true that no one of pre-eminent talent as an illusionist stayed. But this was because illusionism was not wanted.

This is clear from what happened to Zuccaro. Leicester recruited him in 1575 as one of the most successful European portraitists of his day. But he stayed for only three months and panel paintings of the Queen herself, and of Leicester, probably make up the sum total of what survives of his visit. Not a great deal it may be thought and certainly not very exciting. Zuccaro soon packed up his brushes and went home. His failure to establish a thriving practice was because he offered an art of illusion when what was required was an art of emblem.

The emblem book had had an extraordinary vogue throughout Europe since it had first appeared in the 1530s. Emblems aimed to fix in the mind's eye the nature of virtues, through the combination of a brief verbal definition which in time tended to be supported by a visual symbol: for instance, the virtue of indomitable strength and constancy, to be found in marriage portraiture, was symbolised by a bay tree which though struck by lightning remained unconsumed. That was how it was used by Elizabeth I for the obverse of a medal which would have been distributed amongst the less privileged of her supporters (see Plate 41, page 117); that is to say those who were not in line to receive a miniature splendidly mounted by Hilliard in a jewelled case; or a cameo portrait in sardonyx which, it was believed in the eighteenth century, Elizabeth had presented to her favourite Essex who had worn it in his cap.

Elizabethan portraiture was emblematic first and foremost. Patrons put a higher priority on the inner self than on outward appearance. Vasari was not a writer who evoked much interest; a Vatican official complained as late as the 1630s, that golden period in the history of collecting in England, of how he was having great difficulty locating a copy of *The Lives* in London.[23] By contrast however, people did read the much duller and more theoretical writings of Lomazzo. Lomazzo's treatise *Trattato dell'Arte de la Pittura* (Milan, 1584) was translated during the reign of Elizabeth, by the Oxford don Richard Haydocke. It appeared in 1598 under the title *A tracte containing the artes of curious painting . . .*

In his tedious but very influential book, Lomazzo was at pains to stress that it is the *idea* incorporated into a painting which is more important than any outward appearance. It was a theory much more in accord with the Elizabethan aesthetic than Vasari. Elizabethan patrons drew attention away from a face to an eloquent, complex symbolism expressed through jewel and dress. What they sought were 'interior' portraits. They shrank from the merely corporeal. It is therefore no surprise that Elizabethans responded to Lomazzo but ignored Vasari.

An Elizabethan portrait depends for its effect on 'reading' the emblems in jewels, clothes, animals, furniture, or objects held in the hand. It is a biography not merely a likeness. This can be seen in the *Ermine Portrait* of Elizabeth I. There is more information about this image than about many other portraits of Elizabeth I. The picture was painted by the herald and artist Sir William Segar in 1585 for that most faithful and astute of all the political advisers to the Queen, William Cecil, Lord Burghley. Its name, *The Ermine Portrait*, comes from the conspicuous presence of an ermine in the bottom right-hand corner, gazing adoringly into the face of Elizabeth like some diminutive lap dog. Now Elizabethans did not keep ermines as pets and so the animal has a symbolic meaning. Emblem writers told of how the ermine would rather shed its own blood than be sullied by uncleanness. Again we have a reference to the virtue of the Queen; to her purity of motive and action. When the painting was made,

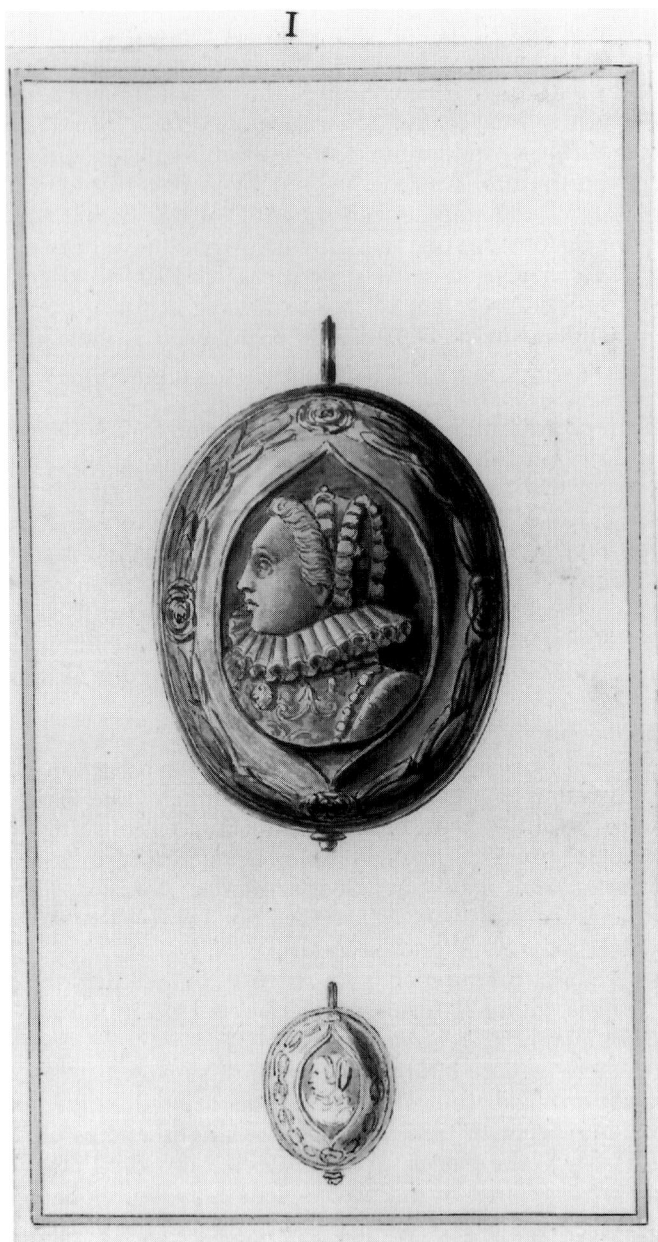

Elizabeth I, Water colour of a sardonyx cameo, Anon., 18th century (Society of Antiquaries of London)

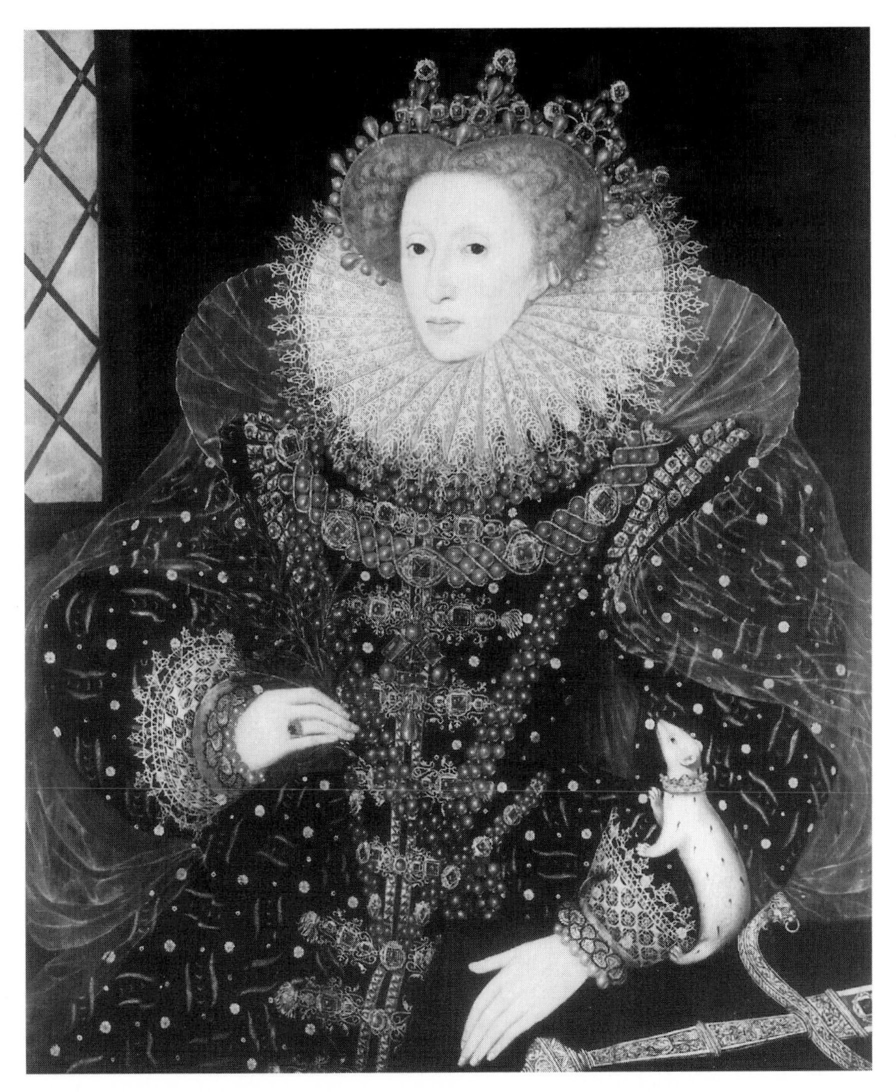

'The Emine Portrait', William Segar (attributed), *Elizabeth I*, 1585 (The Marquess of Salisbury)

Elizabeth's subjects were being asked to see her marital status as a positive virtue. The image is one plain on a many-faceted ball of allusive propaganda; a ball on which each face was angled slightly differently but together they made a weighty construction of sophisticated apologetics.

It was characteristic of those who painted Elizabeth that they did other things: Segar was a herald and illuminator; Hilliard a miniaturist, medallist, and jeweller. Heraldry was a form of social engineering in late Tudor England. It was the job of heralds to ensure that those who displayed arms were entitled to do so. Painting and heraldry were frequently intermingled in the portraits of the period; as, for example, in Hilliard's *Pelican Portrait*, which includes heraldic badges: the rose of England and the fleur de lys of France float disembodied to sustain the claims of Elizabeth to be Queen of both kingdoms.

Anti-naturalism was a powerful element in Elizabethan portraiture. But what these images lose in illusion, they gain in allusion. The *Ermine Portrait* is instantly recognisable as an image of Elizabeth. And yet this is not the woman as she really must have appeared in 1585 when the picture was painted. She looks in her thirties though she was over fifty.

So much for the mask of youth demanded by Elizabeth. Something else characteristic of so many of her portraits, and something noticeable in this one too, is the emphasis given to dress. Elizabeth took extraordinary care about what she wore and when.[24] The most famous expression of the importance of dress for Elizabeth concerned her persona as a desirable bride. In 1582 Elizabeth herself was still going through the charade of pretending to be interested in marrying her 'frog', as she called the hideous and pox-marked Duke of Alençon (later Anjou). Accordingly a full-length portrait of Elizabeth was shown at the Valois court when the size of the pearls was much admired: and it was noted that 'The great princesses did note and weare very muche satisfied to see her Majestie appear attired all over alla francoyse'.[25] Elizabeth would sometimes wear colours which would reflect the heraldry of whichever Continental house she favoured. This was meant to indicate which suitor was likely to win her hand.

The catalogue of portraits of Elizabeth consists of names culled not from the subject herself but from her accessories; inanimate objects of a symbolic nature. By contrast, the portraits of Charles I are identified by the liveliness and action of his figure: *Charles I in Three Positions*, *Charles I à la chasse*, or the *Charles I on Horseback with M. de St Antoine* – they are all action paintings, in which subsidiary figures are included as foils. Elizabeth is always alone. There are no double portraits and this cannot simply be accounted for because she was unmarried. Even in those paintings where she is accompanied by a retinue, such as the *Blackfriars Portrait*, she is conspicuously and hieratically elevated above strife and hurry. In the *Armada Portrait*, intended to celebrate a great national victory, she sits alone in an airless world; a world which anticipates empty shadowed squares in some Italian Futurist painting. The preternatural stillness of the *Armada Portrait* is because her portraits are archetypes. Attributes are suspended from her frame as the symbolic shields of her jousting courtiers were hung within the palace of Whitehall. Just as those presentation shields were not actually used in the running of the horses, so the illusion of Elizabeth's physical presence was not necessary for an effective expression of her self.

Prints of Elizabeth are bewildering in the variety of sources upon which they draw. Although they often appear crude, the same kind of adjustment is needed as for the heiratic, stiff and anti-illusionistic *Ermine Portrait*. Evidently many prints were aimed at an educated market, because they contain elaborate inscriptions in Latin. Although the level of literacy appears to have been high in England compared with Continental standards, few Elizabethans could read Latin.

One of the most famous prints of Elizabeth is by Crispin van de Passe Senior. The Queen stands between two pillars with sceptre in her right hand and orb in her left. One pillar is surmounted with the Pelican pecking its breast to feed its young, the other with the Phoenix arising from the flames. Escutcheons hang from each: on the left the Tudor royal arms, the portcullis on the right. Behind Elizabeth there is a world of seas and sailing boats, towns and turrets. Each element was familiar enough to the subjects of the Queen, but all the more effective for that.

In the de Passe print the two pillars stand for the pillars of Hercules, which were supposed to have marked the fullest extent of the ancient world. Although the appearance of the Pillars of Hercules was not all that common in the iconography of Elizabeth herself, it had been one of the favourite devices of the Emperor Charles V; seen on a thousand buildings and countless Imperial seals. The Pillars, taken in combination with the great panoramic world view, suggest that Elizabeth saw herself as an Imperial figure as her father had done before.

The symbolism of the pelican we have touched on. The phoenix, the mythical bird which was reputed to rise from the flames unscathed, was not only the subject of another famous pendant jewel, but the title, too, of a further celebrated panel painting of Elizabeth by Hilliard.

Periodically Elizabeth was the recipient of propaganda, to some of which she had a decidedly equivocal attitude. This applied especially to what was offered by the United Provinces; the seven northern provinces of the Low Countries who were trying to break free from Habsburg control with her help. As a politician she approved of those who fought for independence from Spanish rule, but as a sovereign she thoroughly disapproved of the principle of overthrowing ordained power. Thus she provided help by encouraging her subjects to fight in the Low Countries, while she kept the levelling Dutch well away from herself.

Never can she have been made angrier by visual imagery than when she discovered herself starring in the title role in a horror version of the story of Diana and Calisto. The intention of the Dutch rebels in casting her as Diana in a print issued in Holland with an accompanying text in Dutch was to establish Elizabeth as the champion of their cause. Its effect was to make her yet more doubtful of a strained alliance. Rarely can there have been such a mismatch between an image and its source.

The story of Calisto as told by Ovid, was a favourite of Renaissance

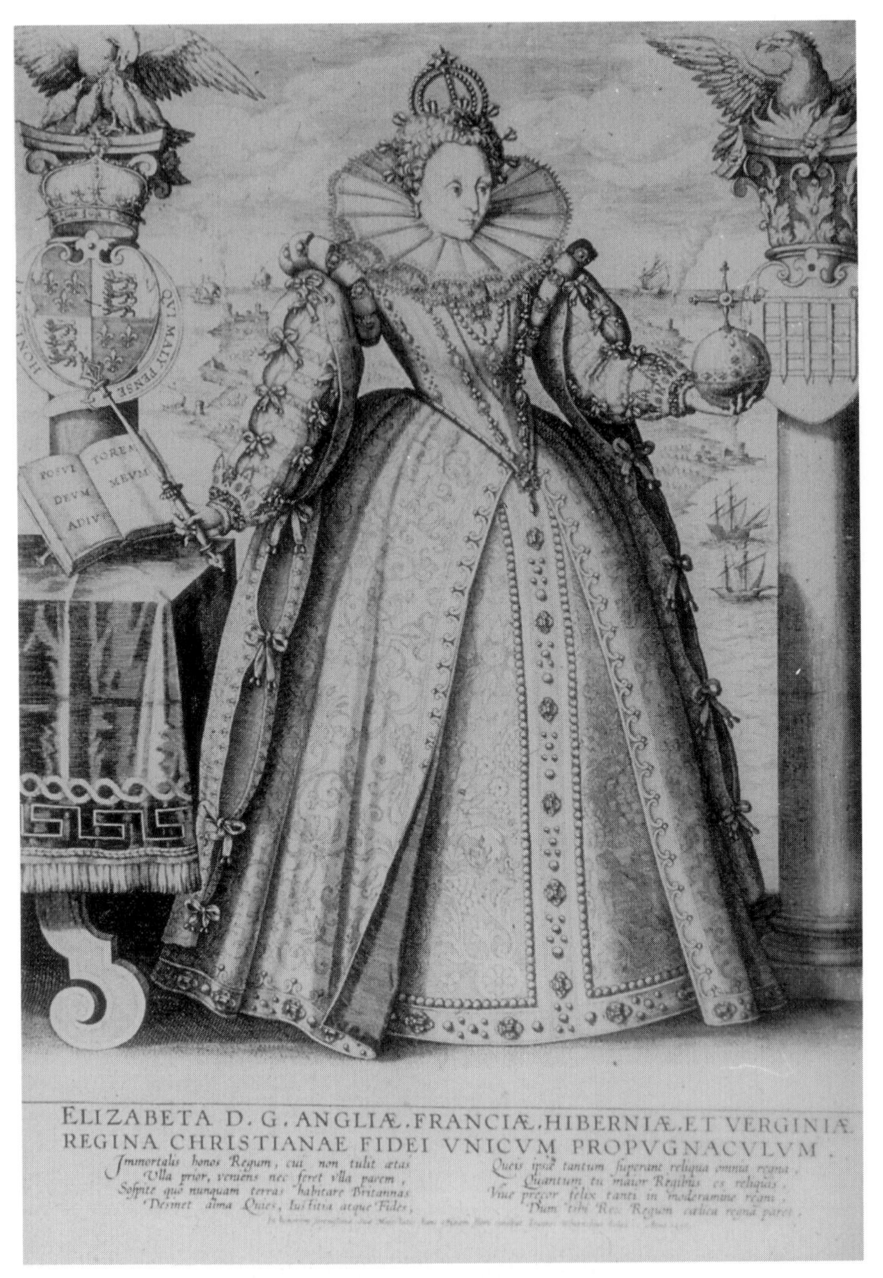

Crispin van de Passe, *Elizabeth I* (engraving), late 16th century (Joe Rock)

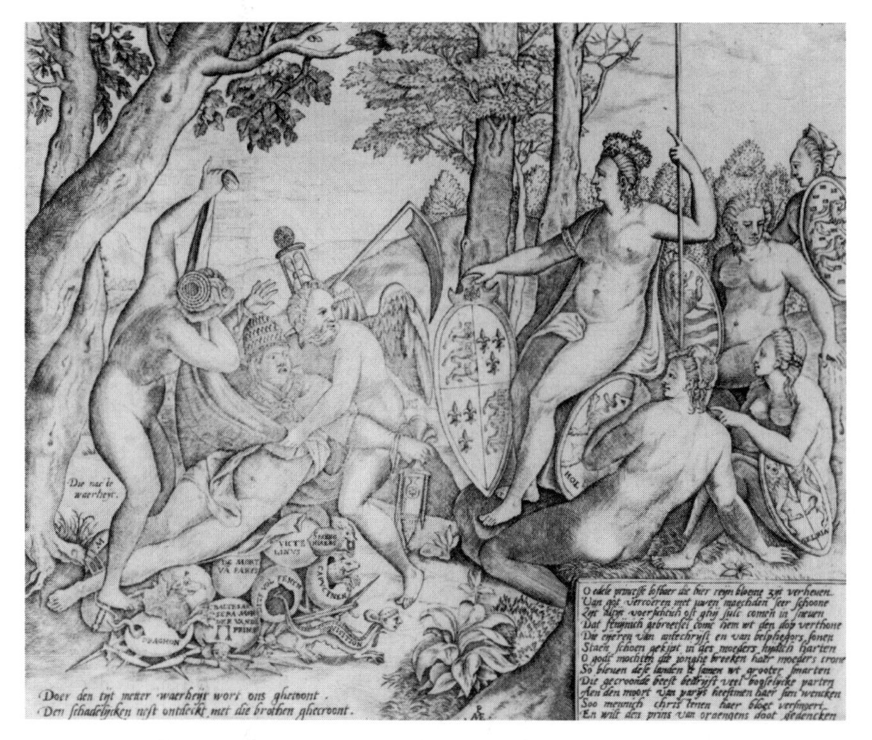

Pieter van der Heyden, *Diana and Calisto*, late 16th century (British Museum)

painters. Calisto, one of Diana's train, found herself alone, and, ravished by Jupiter, gave birth to Arcas. Titian had immortalised the scene as one of the *poesie* painted for Elizabeth's erstwhile brother-in-law Philip II. This design is the image the print-maker vulgarised for the crudest possible anti-Papal propaganda.

In the print an imperious and nude Diana sits enthroned; her true identity as Elizabeth confirmed by the extended right hand which grasps a shield bearing the Tudor arms. Elizabeth's finger points to the sprawling figure of the Pope who looks fearfully towards her. Father Time, substituted for one of the nymphs in the Titian original, has pulled back the cope which the Calisto–Pope wears. Humiliation is compounded because the physical posture of the Pope is decidedly undignified and made still more so when we notice that he still wears the Papal tiara. Father Time, vigorously assisted by a nymph, is undertaking a gynaecological inspection to reveal loss of virginity. But while this happens, the laws of nature are abandoned as a multiple birth takes place. Monstrous eggs of heresy lie in profusion as if issuing from some womb-like hell imagined by Hieronymus Bosch.

However misguidedly, the print-maker attempted to flatter Elizabeth. Surrounded by nymphs displaying the arms of the United Provinces,

Elizabeth is equated with Diana. There was nothing offensive about that: Elizabeth frequently identified herself with the Virgin Goddess. But there was a world of difference between emphasising virginity and proving it. Time conventionally revealed Truth; as anyone knew who was at all conversant with allegory in the Renaissance. Here however matters are inverted. Far from revealing Truth, Time reveals falsehood; the false religion of Rome. On this occasion and most unusually, Time is baffled and has to look towards Elizabeth for an interpretation of what he has uncovered; he does not know what he has found, but she does because she, being immortal and not subject to Time, is in fact the greater judge. It is the judgemental gesture of Diana–Elizabeth which condemns what Time has discovered but cannot interpret, just as she herself is revealed as the fount of Wisdom; not Time as convention had always had it. Elizabeth–Diana has a capacity for right judgement which goes beyond the mythical powers even of Father Time. The mental purity which allowed Elizabeth I to judge rightly, is the natural corollary of her own unviolated and unviolable physical being.

The *Diana and Calisto* print retains its capacity to shock when the issues it played upon are past history. How much more powerful must have been its impact at the time. Elizabeth cannot have relished this encouragement to her subjects to dwell upon her gross, corporeal nature. As a woman who had been forced to perform the difficult contortion of turning her status as a Virgin Queen into a positive source of strength, she must have found the crude and explicit reference to the fate of Calisto powerfully repugnant. Embarrassment was caused to the recipient, injury done to the painter, and insult heaped upon the patron for whom the original had been created. Whatever doubts Elizabeth herself might have felt about productions such as these, struck and sold in enormous quantities as part of the armoury of her defence, they certainly seem to have made an important contribution to political consciousness.

The *Diana and Calisto* print should however be related to another wholly different image of her, and one which is not only richly suggestive of her virtues and capacities, but in contrast to this print, entirely in keeping with propaganda of which she would have approved. It is the *Rainbow Portrait* to which reference was made earlier (see pages 86–8). It was painted probably by Marcus Gheeraerts, for Robert Cecil, 1st Earl of Salisbury, who succeeded his father Lord Burghley as chief minister. Strong dates it to a visit Elizabeth made to Salisbury at Cecil House in the Strand in December 1602, months before she died.[26]

Here she is seen wearing perhaps the most exotic creation of all from what was always her legendary wardrobe. Of the many symbols seen in this portrait, it is the embroidered eyes which are of especial interest. These Strong relates to *Hymns to Astraea*; a series of acrostics contrived by the lawyer–poet Sir John Davies, at the command of Salisbury for his reception of the aged Queen. The significance of the open eyes on Elizabeth's dress is spelt out by Davies in a key to understanding Gheeraerts' painted riddle:

> E ye of that mind most quick and clear,
> L ike Heaven's eye, which from his sphere
> I nto all things prieth;
> S ees through all things everywhere,
> A nd all their natures trieth.

The *Rainbow Portrait* and the *Diana and Calisto*, one a rarefied esoteric work of art, the other little more than a scatological cartoon, should however be seen together since both suggest Elizabeth's unique gifts of insight and perception. There is, then, common ground between an authorised image created for the Elizabethan Establishment at its most elevated, and this other quite different vision, concocted by a rabble with whom Elizabeth was forced to come to terms in the interests of *realpolitik*. Beyond that the connection ceases.

We turn briefly to miniatures; favourite flowers in the *hortus conclusus* of Elizabethan culture. Much has been written about the art of the miniature; the cultural setting brilliantly evoked by the work of Strong. Nevertheless the importance of the miniature may have been exaggerated. The miniature was an intimate, private expression of loyalty; one which was hidden inside a jewelled case or a turned box; something kept in every way close to the heart.

Occasionally we do have evidence that these acorns grew into oaks; when, for example, a miniature was presented to a specially favoured courtier in a public ceremony intended to impress the court at large. The celebrated *Armada Jewel* is a case in point. It was painted by Hilliard and mounted within a case of enamelled gold set with diamonds and rubies; the inside of the hinged lid decorated with the red Tudor rose. Tradition has always had it – and it is only tradition – that it was presented to Sir Thomas Heneage on the defeat of the Spanish Armada.[27] If that was really the case, we can envisage an Elizabethan equivalent to Queen Victoria pinning a Victoria Cross onto the swelling breast of some Mutiny hero.

Miniatures were not, however, medals, and medals had far more impact in the public sphere than those delicate paper-thin disks painted with squirrel hair. Miniatures belonged to that peculiarly late English Renaissance world of escapism and exclusivity, not to the requirement for a prince to show himself. Certainly the miniature helped to spin out the fine web of flattery; they sustained the charade of Elizabeth I as medieval princess whose hand was contended for by her brave knights long after she had become toothless and shrivelled. They can therefore be said to have been a device in the arsenal of weapons drawn out to sustain the identity of the sovereign at court. But the robust medal was much more significant as a propaganda device. They were made in metals of varying

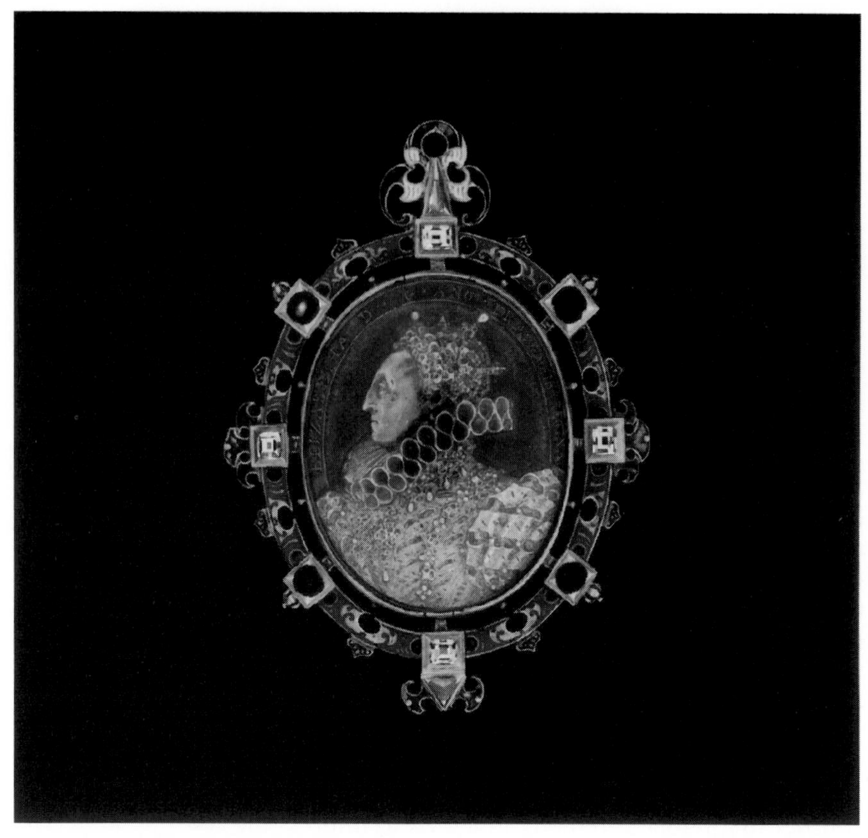

Nicholas Hilliard, *The Armada Jewel*, *c.* 1588 (Victoria and Albert Museum)

costs – suggesting a market aimed at different pockets – and they offered an iconography just as rich and varied as the exquisite and exclusive creations of Hilliard or Oliver. Medals offered interpretations not always found in other art forms and they were produced in infinitely greater quantities. It is impossible to know how many miniatures Hilliard produced in a given year, but in theory at least, the medal could have found its way into every Elizabethan doublet just like the coin of the realm. In considering the medal and the miniature as effective propaganda, we must think about the means of production and distribution. Propaganda depends as much on its capacity to penetrate a market as it does on any message it might carry. The Elizabethan miniature has captivated us by its beauty and we have come to value it still more because it is a miracle that something so exquisite, something so captivating, has survived this long; like finding birds' eggs in a long abandoned nest. Those sentiments have however served to inflate the importance of the miniature. It was the

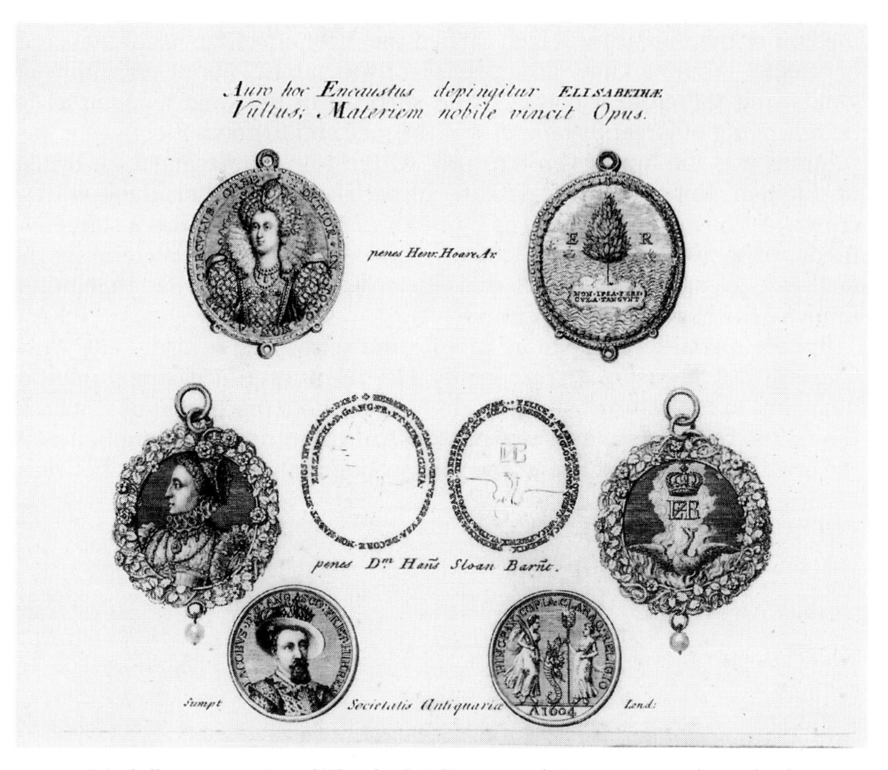

Medallion portraits of Elizabeth I (Society of Antiquaries of London)

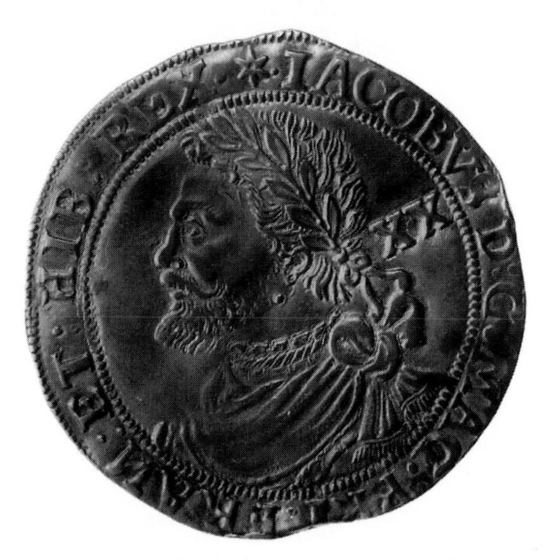

Gold laurel coin (obverse), *Head of James I*, 1619–20 (British Museum)

medal not the miniature which carried the most effective visual messages of a reign. We now know how percipient was James I about visual propaganda and therefore it comes as no surprise to find that as soon as he became King of Great Britain, he put the medium to good effect.

James was the first sovereign since Alfred to be represented on British or English coins 'with a wreath, imperial style, rather than with a crown'.[28] The medal of James as Emperor of Great Britain was a statement made for general not simply courtly consumption; both proclaiming the fact of a great new imperial dynasty and suggesting what that might imply at the head of a new century.

But the medal could be more private and retrospective also. Lady Anne Clifford was the last of a great family. Her relentless, unceasing pursuit of her claim to the Clifford lands might have found a place in *Bleak House*. In the 1640s, I would suggest when Lady Anne had finally triumphed over the law to win back what she had always doggedly insisted was her right

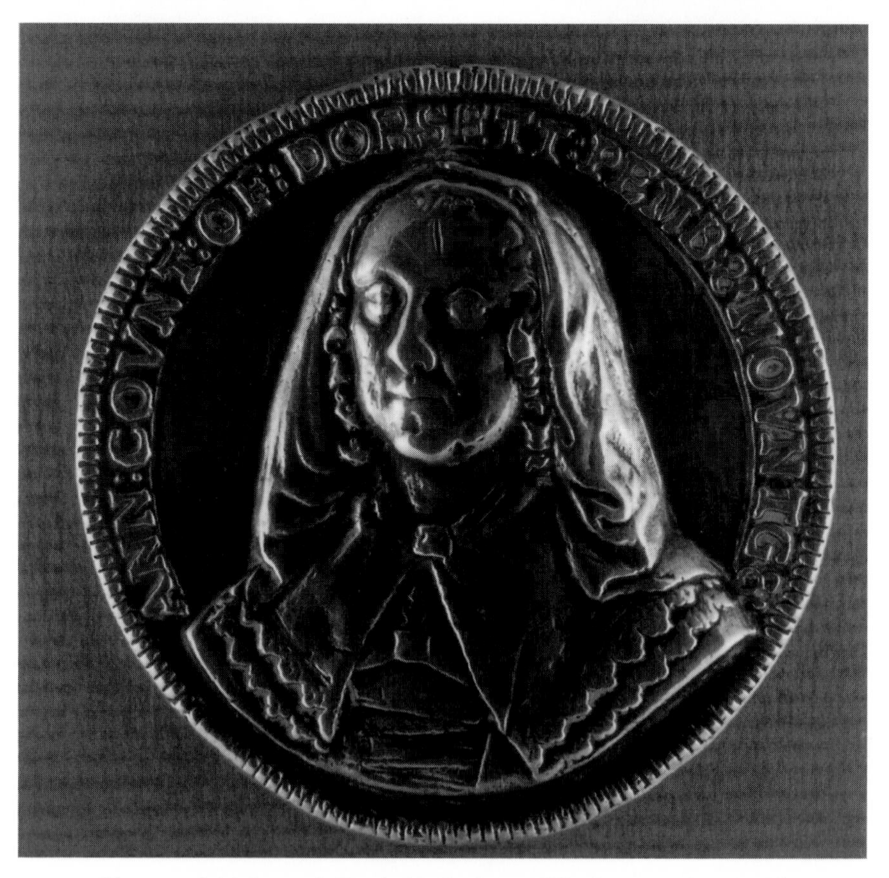

Silver medal (obverse), *Head of Lady Anne Clifford*, c. 1643 (Joe Rock)

to the Clifford estates in the north of England, this party to one of the great land law cases of the seventeenth century chose the medal to commemorate her triumph. By the time Lady Anne cast herself in silver, the miniature was rarely if ever biographical as it had been in the richly allusive days of Hilliard. By the 1640s it had been reduced to the simplicity of a portrait *tout court*. By contrast, the medal proved to be a much more widely exchangeable commodity. By the mid-nineteenth century, in Britain medals were struck for the jejune as well as the sublime since subjects included: the death of Nelson; the birth of a railway; the destruction of a famous building; a Swedish opera singer; and the arrival of a Chinese junk.

The cult of the miniature which has accompanied the retrieval of much of the magic of Elizabethan culture over the last thirty years has been a case of romance running away with reality. The miniature was and must remain an important part of that process of rediscovery, but there is a sense in which these exquisite objects have been made to bear more weight than their delicacy can sustain.

Chapter Four
The Royal Portrait: The Stuarts

This chapter begins with a sculptural group, not an easel painting. It is the effigy of James I which faces the main entrance of the Bodleian Library, on the inside of the Tower of the Five Orders described by Pevsner as 'a frontispiece prouder than any in England'. The sculpture was erected to commemorate the foundation of the library by Sir Thomas Bodley in the early years of the seventeenth century. It is a concentrated and richly allusive image of a king who responded to the book more than to visual imagery but who nevertheless well understood the power of art.

The anonymous sculptor has placed the king under a canopy to suggest a frontispiece; appropriately enough since the foundation over which James presides was dedicated to the book. James is seated in full regalia with a volume in each hand, which he presents to Fame blowing her trumpet on the left, while Oxford University kneels at the right. The attendants are lifted straight from an Annunciation of the Virgin. The results are distinctly comical. Fame, so suddenly transformed but so transparently the annunciate angel, looks upwards as she calls Heaven to witness the beneficence of a learned British king who has deigned to encourage this enterprise of learning. For the British Solomon, Fame solicits blessings but she appears to be distracted by someone at an upper window: the sculptor has been too incompetent or too lazy to modify the poses following his removal of the dove of the Holy Spirit.

James sits within a deep niche, or exedra. Its presence in this provincial sculptural context may recall the world of metropolitan architecture and specifically, the Banqueting House at Whitehall. It was suggested earlier that the presence of the exedra in that building alluded to the ancient basilica; the traditional seat of justice in antiquity. At the Bodleian and above the figure of James, this same allusion has been underscored by an actual personification of Justice standing upon a plinth holding a pair of scales. Between James and Justice is a massy, rounded canopy, like some high-precision drill head, but to the Jacobean undergraduate, a resonance

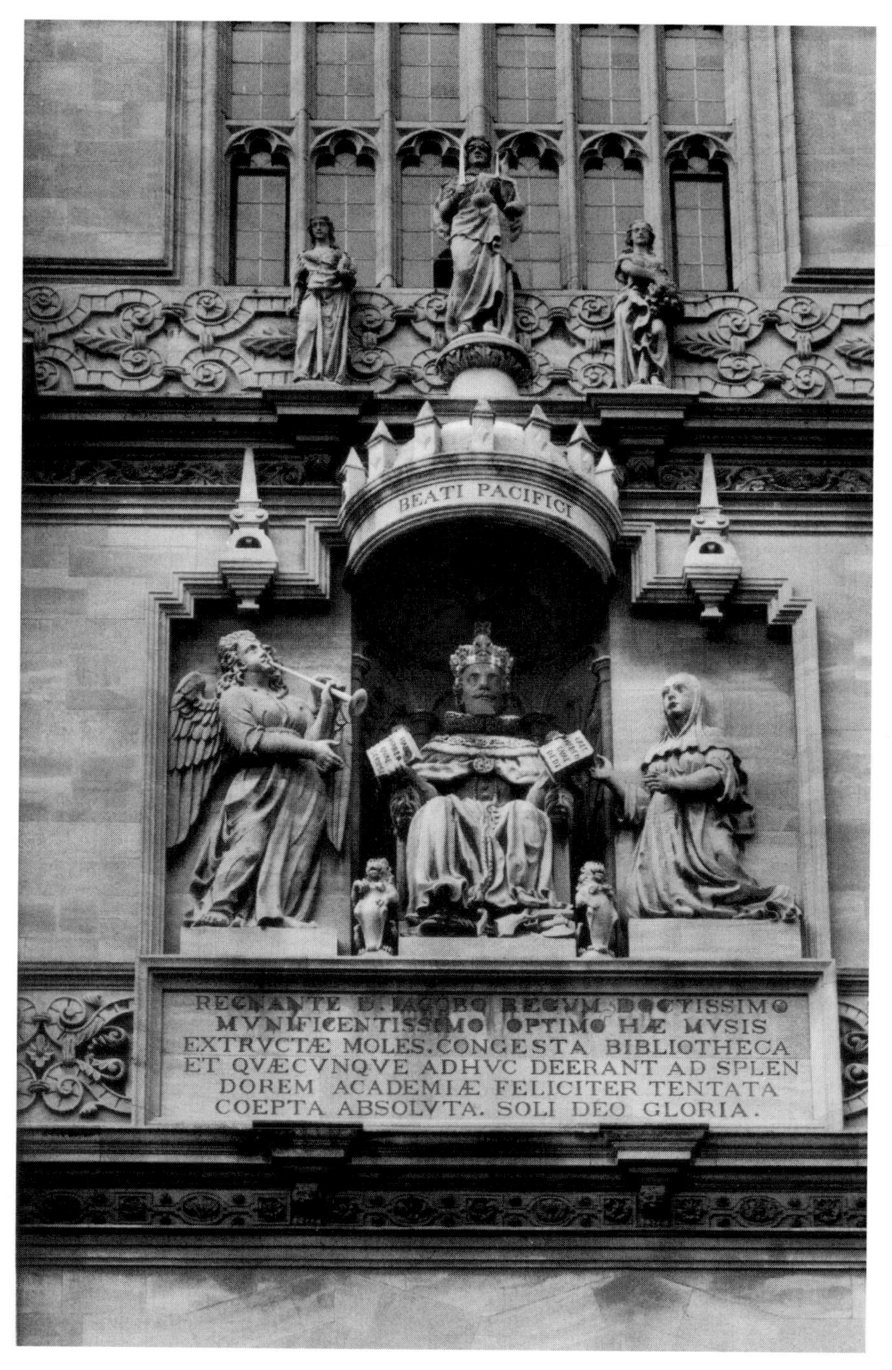

James I, Bodleian Library, Oxford, *c*. 1620 (Thomas Photos)

of the sounding board of a college pulpit. Just as the altar format of the whole ensemble was appropriate to a priest-king, so a reference to the 'word' was telling for those for whom the monument was intended. James I valued the word greatly: especially when spoken out of his own mouth, but also by those passing under Bodley's tower – Oxford divines like William Laud, the future Archbishop of Canterbury, but at the time of the inception of the Bodleian, President of St John's College, Oxford. Laud was a man whose preferment would be attributable to his industry and to his eloquence. The ensemble which presides over the Bodleian was addressed to Laud and his generation; men who would have to face the challenge of defending the Protestant Settlement, armed with books licensed by Oxford University.

Two words are deeply carved on the architrave of the sounding board above James: 'Beati Pacifici', 'Blessed are the Peacemakers'. It was a tag as familiar to Jacobeans as 'Peace in our Time' to inter-war Britons; proud claims which could not be sustained in either age and attracted derision in the face of the Thirty Years War and the Fall of France respectively. Although reality made a mockery of fond hopes, the pursuit of peace was James I's most consistent policy as it was his most serious endeavour. It failed but it brought considerable benefits to the Union of England and Scotland. James' identification with the peacemakers reveals a complex man whose character was at one and the same time shrewd and naive. There was never much hope of the European powers agreeing to peace, but James perceived the benefits which would accrue to his own kingdoms in keeping them out of wars; benefits which are alluded to in the Bodleian sculpture, an appropriate frontispiece to the reign.

Justice, presiding at the highest level of the monument, is accompanied by two figures half her size; suggesting that their significance is less than hers: Minerva with her owl nestling in the palm of the hand represents wisdom, and wisdom brings peace, while Plenty holds a cornucopia and plenty is the blessed consequence of peace. Reading the symbolism of the monument, Oxonians were taught that learning flourishes when promoted by a wise king. The main priority of a Solomon must be to promote the blessings of peace, of which the most abundant fruit is plenitude.

In this secular temple of learning, the fondness of the king for things of the mind is symbolised by the book. Peace, Wisdom, Plenty and the power of the printed word all feature because all were given positive expression in the real world of Jacobean politics. James was a controversialist with a European reputation for his own learning; he was drawn to paper wars rather than the exercise of arms; though he did try to end the banditry of the Scottish Borders while promoting religious toleration beyond the confines of his kingdoms. These were laudable aims and ones which his son set about immortalising in May 1625 when he revived an approach originally made to Rubens in 1621 for the Banqueting House scheme.

In 1621, Rubens had responded to a request from the English court asking him to create a decorative scheme for the ceiling of the new Banqueting House to replace the first Jacobean building, destroyed by fire in 1619. Rubens responded in a characteristically confident vein in a letter addressed to William Trumbull, English Agent to the court of the Archdukes in Brussels, a government official whom we shall encounter in a later chapter as an important go-between for English collectors buying the paintings of Rubens in significant quantities. Rubens accepted the commission in principle:

> As to His Majesty and H.R.H. The Prince of Wales, I shall always be pleased to receive the honour of their commands, and with respect to the Hall in the New Palace, I confess myself to be, by a natural instinct, better fitted to works of the largest size than little curiosities. Every one according to his gifts. My endowments are of such a nature that I have never wanted courage to undertake any design however vast in size or diversified in subject.[1]

Somewhat inappropriately given the tenor of the letter, Rubens then signed himself with a flourish 'Your very humble servant, Peter Paul Rubens'.

The problems of the Marie de' Medici cycle, Rubens' most challenging and difficult exercise in state propaganda, seem to have almost overmastered even the artist's seemingly limitless resources, and the English commission stalled. Two alternative programmes for the Banqueting House ceiling, the authorship of which is unknown, one contrived when James was still alive, the other after his death, were lodged with Sir John Coke, one of the two Secretaries of State. Although these alternative projects were abandoned, and probably only revived again when Rubens visited London in 1629, the rudiments of what would stand as the painted glory of the British Crown were established with these two separate but closely linked programmes, one of which certainly dates from before the death of James since he is referred to in the Latin in the present tense.

The programmes seem to have been drawn up between the time of Rubens' letter to Trumbull of 13 September 1621, quoted above, and a letter of Lord Danvers, also to Trumbull, dated 19 May 1625, in which Danvers reveals to Trumbull: 'His Majesty is now upon a design of building at Whitehall'; Danvers adding that once the design is settled 'this will give me the measure for Rubens' picture'. This is surely a reference to the fact that Jones was probably making those alterations to the throne room end of the chamber to which we referred in an earlier chapter, and thus, incidentally, a probable moment when the second projected programme for a painted ceiling might have been called for; the more so, given that the second proposal refers to James in the past tense.

In the central oval James is seen 'tending towards Eternity', as his appearance in this picture was described in the 1639 catalogue of The

Royal Collection. The very title of the centrepiece, *The Apotheosis of James I*, denotes a triumph – those who had been James's earth-bound subjects, invited to witness James's joining the Gods in their immortal sphere, which he does with something of the same wonderment which had possessed the Apostles as they stood on the Mount of Olives to witness the Ascension of Christ.

But is this all? Rubens gave the allegory an extra dimension which only his unique combination of skills as painter and diplomat could have accomplished. He portrays James well, but he portrays James' conception of kingship better. James had frequently defended the philosophy of 'divine right', the claim that a monarch was only answerable to the Almighty, by declaring that he was to be judged by his maker not by his subjects. Rubens underscores this by suggesting that now, at the hour of his death, James is indeed called to account. To emphasise the point, James appears much as Rubens would have imagined him to have been when ill and old. Here is a fearful, tousled, grey-haired old man; quite distinct from his appearance in the adjacent canvases, in which he appears altogether more robust.[2]

The outcome of judgement about to be enacted is not in question; nevertheless the complexity with which the painter has responded to his instructions shows his pre-eminent genius. The extra dimension of fear and doubt with which Rubens has invested his image of James I makes this indeed an allegory of the first Stuart kingship and not merely a portrait of the king.

Adjacent to the main field, two smaller square canvases expound on the themes of the Union of the Crowns of Scotland, and the Benefits of the Reign of James I. Long thin borders frame the main field; festive, exuberant and triumphant, with processions of putti and animals cavorting among swags of grapes and corn. Such themes were surely appropriate for the reception of the first Stuart king into Elysium.

The discovery of what for simplicity's sake might be termed programmes A and B, programmes to which reference was made earlier, reveals that these subsidiary fields are not merely decorative, as has always been assumed.[3] They have a serious didactic purpose stemming from Isaiah Chapter 11, verses 6–9. These new documents, outlining schemes for the programme, are based upon the passage from Isaiah:

> The wolfe also shall dwell wth the Lambe, and the Leopard shall lye downe wth the *Kidde*; and the Calfe and the yong Lyon, and the fatling together, and a little chyld shall leade them.
>
> And the Cowe and the Beare shall feed, theyr yong ones shall lye downe together, and the Lyon shall eate strawe like the oxe.
>
> And the sucking chylde shall play on the hole of the Aspe, and the weaned chylde shall putt his hand on the Cockatrice den.

They shall not hurt nor destroy in all my holy mountayne; for the earth shalbe full of the knowledge of the Lord, as the waters cover the sea.

In the foure small Ovalls.

The fower Evangelists.

These were noble sentiments, entirely in accord with the dearest hopes of a pacific king. They should not be dismissed lightly. James succeeded in keeping Britain out of war in Europe; ineffective though he was in persuading other nations to stop fighting. The success of this, his main policy, can be gauged by what happened after these programmes for the ceiling evolved. Charles I rapidly became embroiled in disastrous wars with both France and Spain which were to have the most profound consequences for his kingship.

Charles I made his father the subject of the greatest cycle of pictures ever to commemorate the British monarchy; providing him at the same time with a magnificent funerary monument although one which broke with convention in being of canvas not touchstone and metal. It was unconventional too in being a cenotaph rather than a tomb. Nevertheless James I would have found his vanity well served by such a gesture since it was he, not his son, who started the process of making the Banqueting House a chamber of memory for his own renown when he probably approved that eulogy of himself based upon Suetonius' life of Augustus.

It was said by a contemporary that James 'could never be brought to sit for the taking' of his picture, and certainly he never seems to have bought a single interesting picture. Judged by the criterion of acquisition therefore, the contrast between James I and Charles I could hardly have been greater. However, this is a somewhat narrow way of defining an interest in visual imagery since a number of highly competent portraitists created a repertoire of Jacobean regal imagery. Thus the claim that James was entirely unco-operative over the tedious business of sitting may be an exaggeration. One of the most interesting portraits of him, of *c*. 1620, is by the Dutchman Paul Van Somer. It is quaint and yet curiously impressive. James shows off his robes like a model on a cat walk, while the regalia is displayed in front of the new Banqueting House. The artist has recorded the mortice joints on the stonework with as much care as he has noticed the line of the sitter's mouth. The building has a more insistent presence than the Parliament House in the background of Van Dyck's 'Great Peice'. This is because sitter and his building are both portraits. In fact the actual appearance of the building would seem to have been different and this discrepancy may be accounted for by the suggestion that the Van Somer was painted in 1619 to commemorate the inception of the Banqueting House; before, that is to say, Jones' drawings were predictably modified by the masons on the scaffold. Van Somer himself died in the winter of 1621 and thus the detail remained unchanged and inaccurate.

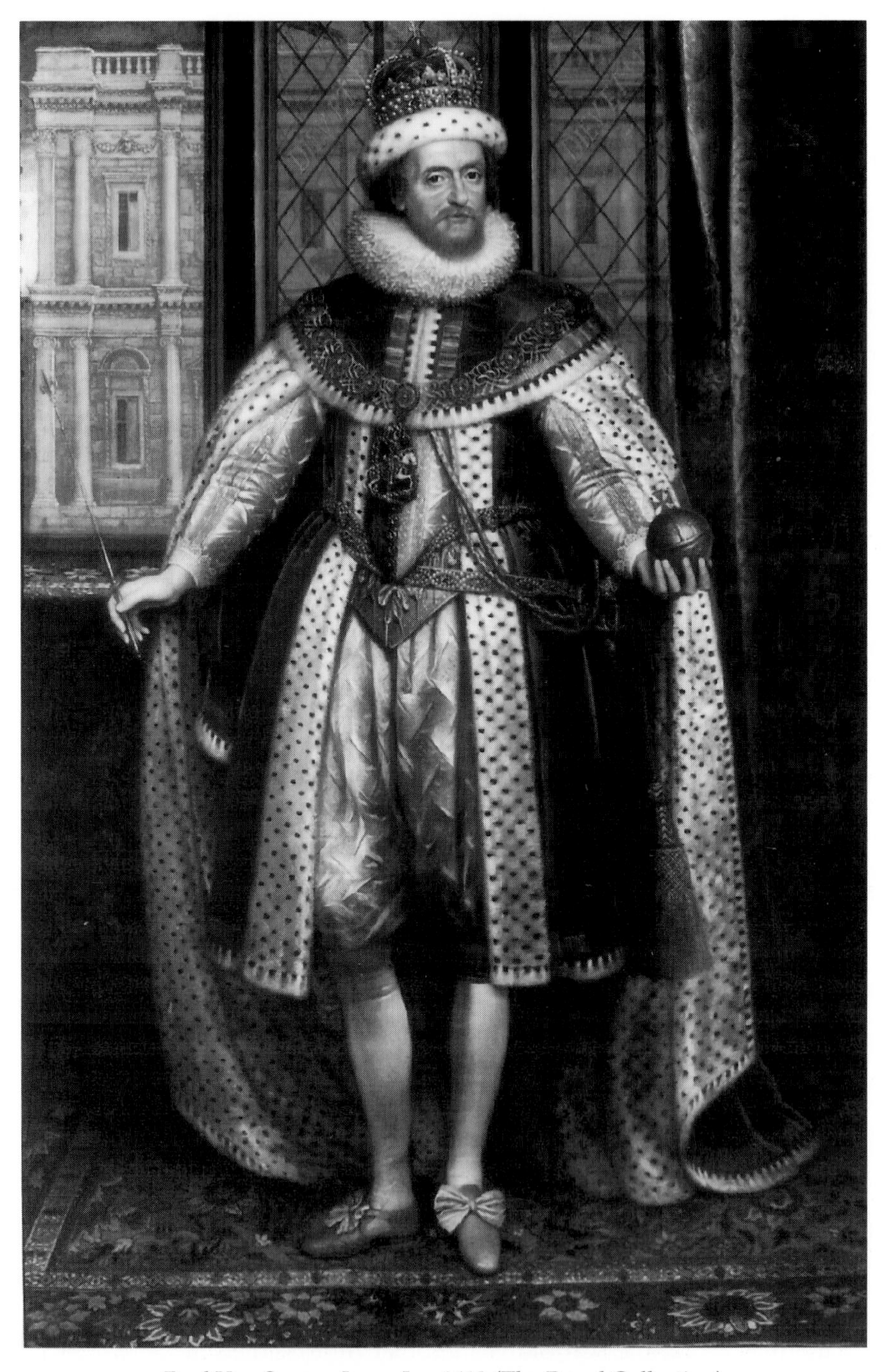

Paul Van Somer, *James I*, *c.* 1619 (The Royal Collection)

Van Somer's likeness of James is an important image for understanding how art was used as propaganda. It confirms what we know from the court masques; certain buildings were thought of as theatres of state. The Banqueting House is drawn to our attention because when James was in that building he performed the parts of majesty just as, at Epiphany, his subjects would dance in celebration of his beneficent rule in an allegory designed by Inigo Jones and Ben Jonson.

Modest though the Van Somer may seem as a work of art, its importance for James was that he took it to be a portrait of a king and his kingship. Portraitists in the Jacobean age were expected to be more than face painters for they had real status. They were required to visualise policy by expressing: summation, consummation, celebration and preparation. They were regarded in something of the same light as Jacobean antiquaries who began to act as apologists for the regime as portraitists became part of the propaganda machine. Here Van Somer celebrates King James as Sir Robert Cotton, described by a contemporary admirer as a 'magazine of history', justifying royal policies on the grounds of precedent, the evidence for which was to be found in Cotton's legendary manuscript library.

James I manipulated art, his wife Anne of Denmark worshipped it. Anne had a real passion for painting. When she died in 1619 she owed Van Somer £170, while the artist himself walked in her funeral procession as her 'picture maker' along with other 'Tradesmen and Artificers'; a mark of favour which is further evidence of the rise in the status of artists which took place in England at about this moment. Van Somer along with the court painters Marcus Gheeraerts and Peter Oliver were in attendance at her obsequies because picture makers had become necessary to the greatness of a sovereign or a consort. As courtiers who contributed to the status of royalty, they had a place in the most formal and solemn occasions of state.

Anne induced a competitive atmosphere as courtiers vied with each other to present her with a choice painting. Unlike her daughter-in-law Henrietta Maria who was to exercise significant backstairs influence in the next reign, Anne's role seems to have been minimal. Nevertheless she was a most important stimulus to that fashion for collecting which was to become such a marked feature of early Stuart life and which would play its part in alienating certain influential groups from the court.

What did Anne look for in her portraits? The answer is suggested in her own portrait by Van Somer, which exists in several versions. There are intriguing similarities between this image and the Van Somer of *James I*. Both have prominent buildings as background; though in the case of the portrait of Anne of Denmark, it is thought that the artist has included an architectural fantasy.

The Queen takes up three-quarters of the image. Her dominance is reinforced by her stance right at the front. A red curtain cuts off the top

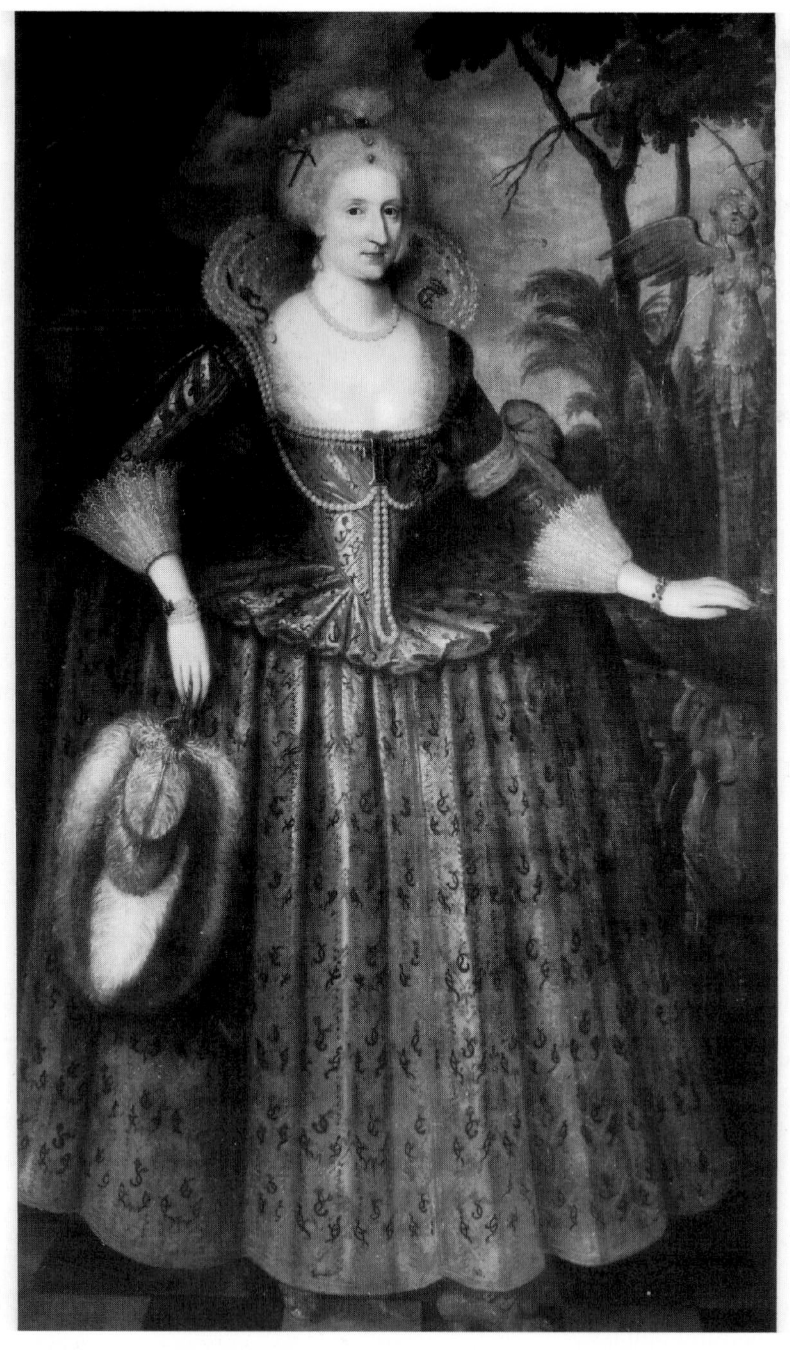

Paul Van Somer, *Anne of Denmark*, 1617–18 (His Grace The Duke of Buccleuch, Drumlanrig Castle, Dumfriesshire)

left-hand corner, while to the right are exotic trees clustering around a fountain of a winged herm-harpy, milk from whose melon-like breasts generously fill a shallow basin beneath. Intriguing as these details are, they do not hold the balance of the picture like the Banqueting House in the Van Somer of James I. The main concern for the artist is to show the clothing and especially the jewels. The elaboration and beauty of the dress which Queen Anne wears is certainly the most striking aspect of this painting, but as the eye takes it in, the jewels become noticeable. It is a world of emblems in sardonyx and emerald.

The sitter has the profile of some late gothic cathedral: nave consists of torso, aisles of hooped dress, arms act as buttresses. The pear-shaped pearls in the hair have the filigree delicacy of gothic tracery as they climb towards the central crocket of an aigrette pinned with a great table diamond. This may well represent the Mirror of France, which would become a favourite jewel of Henrietta Maria; appropriately enough, it might be thought, since Henrietta Maria was herself a daughter of France. Prominent in Anne's coiffure is a diamond crossbow. Anne had inherited just such an item from Elizabeth, but it is unlikely that this is it since Anne's is wholly of diamond, whereas Elizabeth's included 'a harte enamelled red at the string'. One of the few things Anne shared with her husband was a love of hunting and so this crossbow would have been appropriate. However, there may also have been a more emblematic explanation for its appearance in the painting. Whitney refers to the crossbow in his *A Choice of Emblemes*; an immensely popular book which had first been published at Leyden in 1586. Whitney writes:

Ingenium Superat Vires

Mans wisedome great, doth farre surpasse his strengthe,
For proofe, behoulde, no man could bende the bowe:
But yet, his witte deuised at the lengthe,
To winde the stringe so farre as it shoulde goe:
Then wisedome chiefe, and strengthe, must come behinde,
But bothe be good, and giftes from God assignde.[4]

We are map-reading with English Renaissance portraiture and we often have to do so in a mist if not a fog. The jewels here are the 'features of interest' on the ordnance survey map. Only by climbing and descending the contours of the dress, and stopping to view specific features, can we get an impression of the terrain. Let us look then at the other features of this landscape of diamond and taffeta.

The Queen has a collar of 'IHS' crowned, to remind those who were in any doubt that she was a woman of piety. It is a forthright statement of religious loyalty, although certainly not exclusively a badge to denote an affiliation with Rome since it appears in an aureole of glory in Jones' 1634

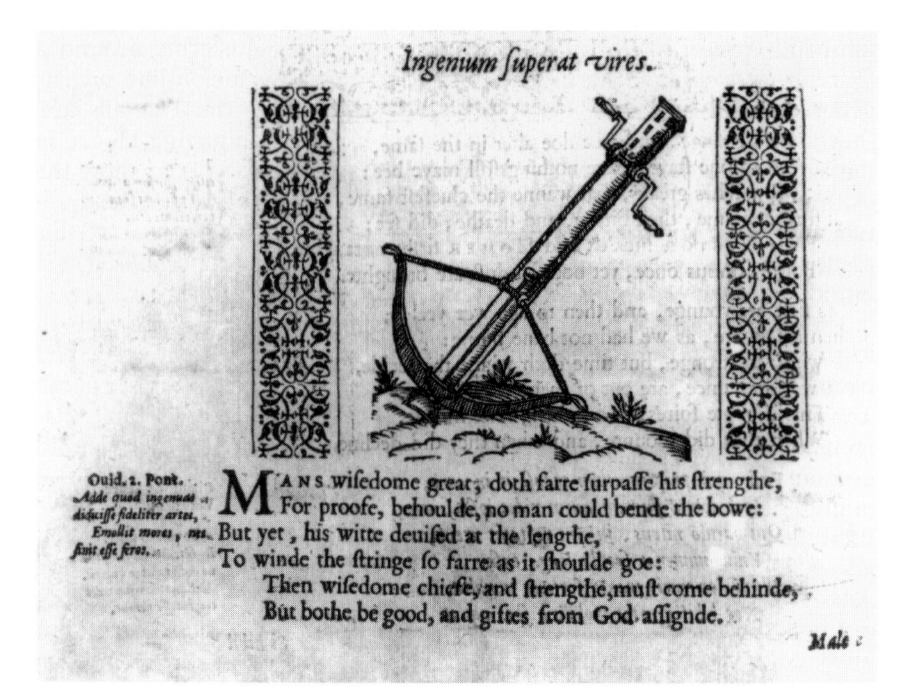
Ingenium ſuperat vires.

Ouid. 2. Pont.
Adde quod ingenuas didiciſſe fideliter artes,
Emollit mores, nec ſinit eſſe feros.

MANS wiſedome great, doth farre ſurpaſſe his ſtrengthe,
For proofe, behoulde, no man could bende the bowe:
But yet, his witte deuiſed at the lengthe,
To winde the ſtringe ſo farre as it ſhoulde goe:
Then wiſedome chiefe, and ſtrengthe, muſt come behinde,
But bothe be good, and giftes from God aſſignde.

Male

Crossbow, from Geoffrey Whitney's, *A Choice of Emblemes* 1586 (Edinburgh University Library)

design for the façade of Old St Paul's. Nevertheless in the case of its appearance in the portrait of Anne of Denmark it is sufficiently prominent to suggest she may have resented her husband's combative rebuttal of the truths of the old religion. It has been suggested too that it may be identifiable with a jewel sent out to Charles when he went to Madrid to woo the Spanish Infanta. If that was indeed so, it was doubtless selected to persuade that doleful lady she had nothing to fear from the old enemy.

Anne also has a great lace collar which rises like the earflaps of a monstrous lizard. To the left is pinned a crowned 'S'; reference perhaps to Anne's mother Sophie of Mecklenburg, or more simply, to her status as Sovereign. Finally there is the 'C4' on the other lobe of her collar. This jewel belonged to her brother Christian IV of Denmark who entrusted her with its safe-keeping when he went campaigning against Sweden; the Venetian ambassador reporting in 1611 how Anne 'wished him all success declaring that she desired nothing more than the increase of his glory and his state for between them is such perfect love and so sincere a correspondence that its like has never been seen'.[5]

Analysis of the Van Somer of Anne, with its symbolic small-scale detail, suggests that paintings of this nature were more ambitious than their immediate appearance suggests. Anne may have wished her brother increase of 'his glory and his state' but this image was her way of seeking the same for herself.

The more we delve into portraiture nurtured by emblem rather than illusion, the more it seems that Van Dyck would offer something wholly different. However, it is easy to exaggerate the novelty of expression which Van Dyck brought to the English court when he came to settle permanently in 1632. It should be appreciated that the 'action' picture was a mode of representation which had become firmly established in British portraiture before. The so-called *Blackfriars Portrait* of Elizabeth, where we see her borne aloft in a litter as she processes with a retinue of courtiers, is very much the exception in her iconography; normally she is as static as a chloroformed butterfly. By contrast the Jacobean sitter lives and moves and has a being. The formula of the warrior prince or the prince *à la chasse* had entered the repertoire of English portraiture years before Van Dyck gave it immortal expression in his famous image of Charles I (see Plate 49, page 134). Recently it has been argued with some force that this famous image is a visual poem in praise of the king as the presiding genius of what Rubens described in a letter from England as a country in which the 'people [are] rich and happy in the lap of peace' and not an 'action' picture of the king in the hunting field.[6] However, the earliest surviving inventories describe the painting in terms of the chase and furthermore there was a convention within the parameters of English royal portraiture, of the prince in the hunting field. Therefore there seems no compulsion to abandon the traditional interpretation of what appears to be going on in the portrait.[7]

Modern scholarship on Van Dyck suggests his portraiture is richer in hidden meaning than was once thought. Until now Van Dyck has not been appreciated for his capacity to fuse the emblematic with an astounding realism; as he surely did in fact. Of course it is surely true that Jacobean portraiture is a brittle, dry, bookish type of painting by comparison. Yet whilst the Jacobean precursors of Van Dyck were manifestly unable to touch his astounding naturalism, the best of them were surely his equals in putting over a richly allusive web of meaning.

Henry, Prince of Wales, the eldest surviving son of James I, was a considerable patron of the arts; though because of his early death, what he did or promised to do was exaggerated by his contemporaries as it continues to be by historians today.[8] Nevertheless there is certainly evidence to suggest that Henry did indeed see patronage of the arts as a pursuit worthy of a prince alongside the exercise of the martial arts, the maintenance of a good library, and the exploration of the military sciences.

One of the most interesting artists Prince Henry employed was the dilettante Robert Peake. Peake was involved with the production of a translation of Sebastiano Serlio's treatise on architecture (1611); the most popular and accessible book on the subject in English until Colen Campbell's *Vitruvius Britannicus* began to appear from 1715 onwards.

Although Serlio's work had entered the mainstream of English architectural practice long before it was translated, the value of this first English edition lay in its treatment of geometry and its application to building practice; hitherto, applied geometry had not been easy for builders to master who did not read foreign languages.

Peake also turned his hand to painting and to one ambitious portrait of the Prince in particular: *Henry, Prince of Wales and John, 2nd Lord Harington of Exton*. Despite the unconvincing appearance of the figures, it represents an important breakthrough in English portraiture. It is an 'action' painting; something which had been comparatively rare in the Tudor period. There are early anonymous campaigning pictures clearly shaped by the conventions of tapestry hangings: the important pair in The Royal Collection of *The Embarkation of Henry VIII,* and *The Field of the Cloth of Gold,* perhaps the most famous. Holbein had painted *The Battle of Thérouanne,* the celebration of an English victory over the French, which eccentrically, regaled the French ambassadors when they were received by Henry VIII in temporary banqueting houses at Greenwich in 1527. More battle pieces and sovereigns in procession may have been painted which have simply been lost, but for the whole reign of Elizabeth I, there may always have been very little. There is *Edward VI and the Pope,* now known to be an Elizabethan picture, but as for Elizabeth herself, so nimble in government, she never moves. The so-called *Blackfriars Portrait* shows her carried in a litter surrounded by court favourites. All around is bustle and procession, but she sits rigid and unmoving like a graven idol.

In his portrait of Prince Henry and John, Lord Harington, Peake created something of a fresh ambition in English royal portraiture. Peake shows Prince Henry aggressively triumphant in that most regal pursuit, the hunting of the stag. The picture is all about a masculine and martial world. Here the Prince is the apprentice making do with the vernal heroics of the chase; though from what we know of his intense admiration for his forebear Henry V, and the Gallic Hercules Henri IV, the Prince hoped in time to be seen astride the walls of Harfleur as a new Prince Hal.

The Peake portrait must have stood out from the dull ranks of Scandinavians on the walls of Whitehall. The challenge which it represented would be taken up by Van Dyck in his own portrait of Henry's younger brother, *Charles I à la chasse* of 1635. This Van Dyck has some claim to be the most finely tuned of all the portraits of Charles I. The artist shows preeminent skill in the subtlety with which he adjusts the body to create the desired tone. The eye-level is very low as the spectator has to ascend the high ground from which the King looks down with perfect composure. Van Dyck has brilliantly transposed a flight of steps, as it were from Whitehall Palace, into a natural contour to create a claim for innate greatness in his sitter; the superiority of Charles over his subjects is as God-given as the laws of nature which ordained the folding ground and surrounding trees crowding into a canopy of state above the blessed head

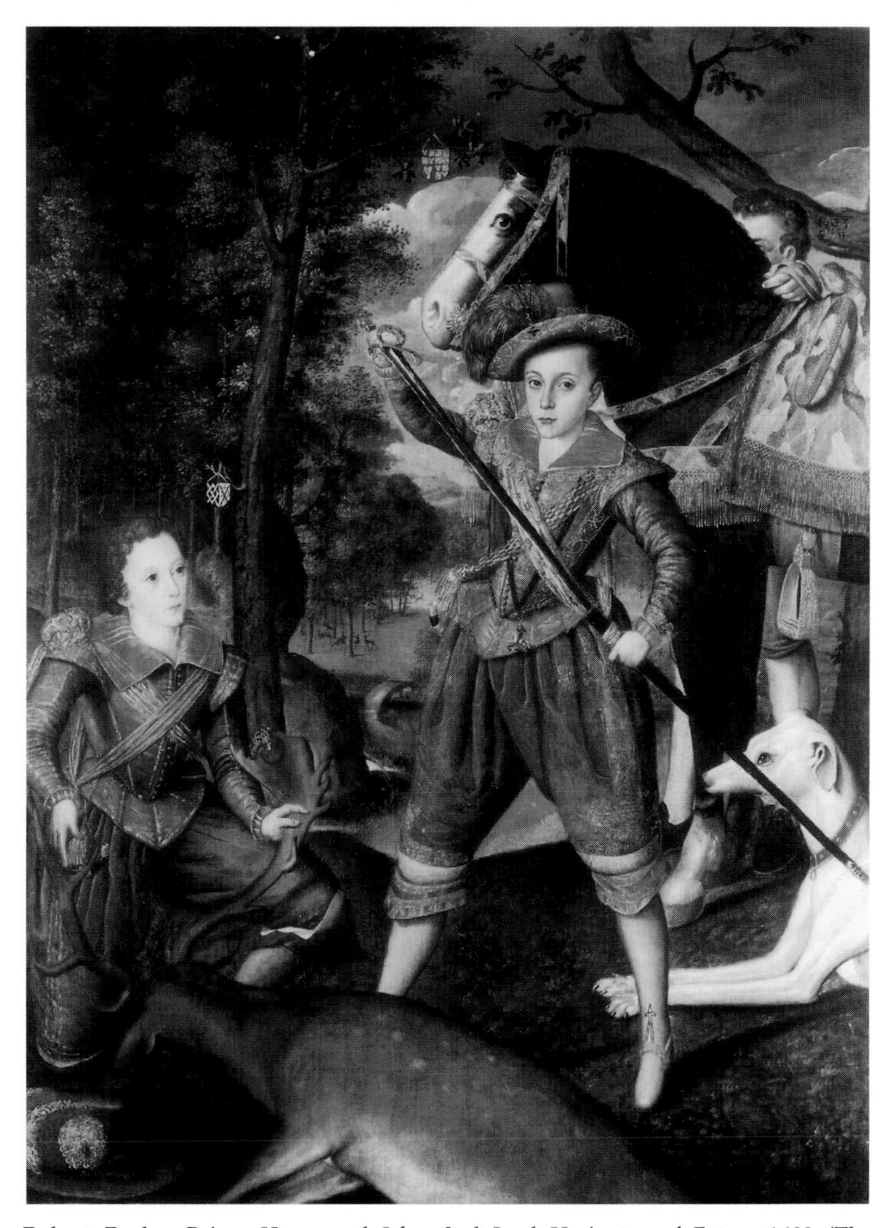

Robert Peake, *Prince Henry and John, 2nd Lord Harington of Exton*, 1603 (The Metropolitan Museum of Art, New York)

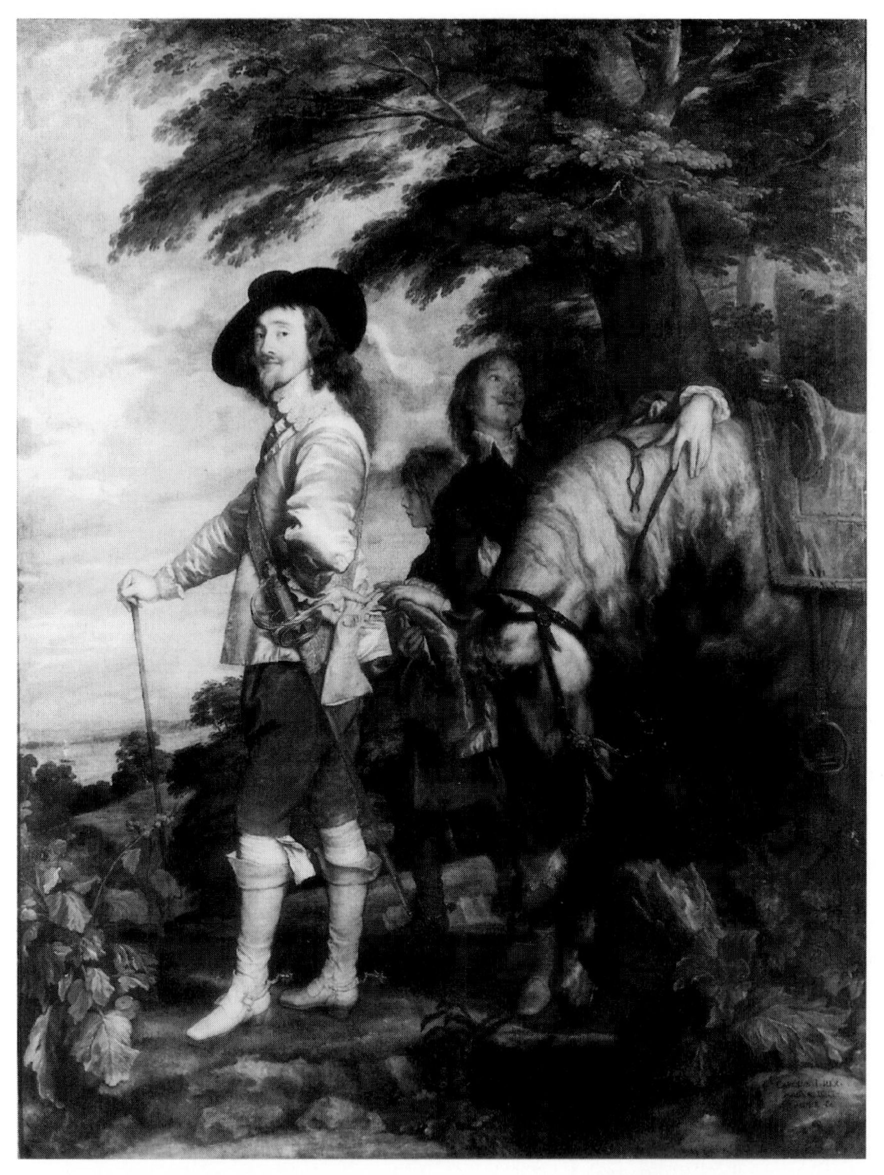

Sir Anthony Van Dyck, *Charles I à la chasse*, 1635 (The Louvre)

of the King. Charles exerts total command as his attention is momentarily caught by our interruption of a private, leisured world. His face miraculously combines encouragement and distance, condescension and command. The King waits upon our petition as one who listens to his subjects while commanding rapid action and timely departure. What the face suggests, the arm asserts. The left elbow is thrust out to give the measure of the King's distance from the frontal plane, but also to reinforce the message that petitioners should not approach too close. The King has divested himself of the trappings of outward regality but he can never divest himself of inherent majesty. What is an expression of natural law must be acknowledged by the laws of men.

So much for the person of the King himself, but what has the rest of the picture to tell us? The dappled grey horse is the most notable subsidiary element. It serves to explain the action of the painting as an interval in a hunting expedition, but it carries more upon its back. It is something of a nursery horse; though correctly proportioned in itself, its size in relation to other elements in the picture is not right. It is too small but it is necessarily so. If Van Dyck had painted it accurately, it would have dominated the person of the King. It paws the ground in tribute to its master as Van Dyck plays a variation upon a theme first composed by Titian as portraitist to the Habsburgs. Titian was fond of including great hunting dogs in submissive obedience to a master. Such stage-props suggested the social superiority of the sitter because hunting was the preserve of the great, but also because an animal subdued was testament to how the sitter subdued not only his own passions, but a world over which he had been given command.

The equestrian portrait was the oldest favourite in royal propaganda. Nothing in seventeenth-century England more powerfully signified superiority than horsemanship; as Nicholas Morgan suggested in *The Perfection of Horsemanship* (1609), in which he posed the rhetorical question 'Doth any earthly thing breed more wonder?'

The brilliance of *Charles I à la chasse* is partly to be accounted for by the way in which Van Dyck paints his rider dismounted without however surrendering the elan which we still associate with horsemanship. The horse could not have been depicted gazing adoringly into the face of Charles I because that would have resulted in a marked note of bathos. Nevertheless Van Dyck chose a hardly less perilous course by making his animal adopt the social mores of the court; inspired so to do by his admiration for Titian's *Adoration of the Magi*, one version of which the artist had sketched in Milan, the other Charles I himself had almost certainly seen in the Escorial. The horse bows deferentially to its master. It was a risky strategy but one which comes off. Van Dyck has succeeded in making his own contribution to the iconography of the equestrian portrait; just as Rubens had done thirty years earlier when, for the first time, in his portrait of *The Duke of Lerma* (1603), he had the simple but brilliant idea of making the animal face the spectator rather than perambulate in remote elegance across the picture.

In *Charles I à la chasse* the King is accompanied by two servants who do not look at him. The equerry looks back into the trees, not at the King; as if to suggest the imminent appearance of a cavalcade from out of the wood from which the King himself has just stepped like an actor coming on stage. A much younger page is behind. In strict profile, he stares intently out over the landscape; seemingly oblivious to the presence of the King. Neither attendant engages the principal figure. This is important to the mood. By avoiding an encounter, and yet by showing Charles I accompanied in a fertile but otherwise empty kingdom, the artist achieves a sense of the King's uniqueness without making him appear vulnerable because alone. It is a consummate example of how well Van Dyck understood a sitter who was personally reserved, but devoted on an abstracted level to the Commonwealth; a land and a landscape in which both he and his erstwhile master Rubens found true inspiration. It is, too, something which Van Dyck may have learned from looking at Caravaggio. In *The Conversion of Saul* Caravaggio had painted Saul accompanied by a groom who is also wholly absorbed in his own world; though he too, like the attendants in the Van Dyck, is in the same physical ambience. It suggests a barrier between Saul, an exceptional human being, and ordinary mortals. It may have inspired Van Dyck.

Charles I à la chasse was probably always in France; perhaps dispatched by Charles I himself as a gift for the French Crown. The most powerful testament to its impact is that it provided the starting point for Hyacinthe Rigaud's full-length portrait of Louis XIV (1701); the favourite portrait of a man who exploited image-makers with an obsessiveness anticipating the totalitarian rulers of the twentieth century.

Van Dyck's *Charles I on Horseback* is more firmly bedded within an iconographical tradition than *Charles I à la chasse.* It is based on the earliest example of a mounted ruler; the fourth-century AD equestrian bronze of Marcus Aurelius. In 1538 Michelangelo had moved it from outside the Lateran Palace to the centre of Roman civic pride, the Capitoline Hill. In 1536 the Emperor Charles V had visited Rome as an act of reconciliation following the sack of the city in 1527 by Imperial troops. The Papacy had felt embarrassed that the Capitoline Hill was not sufficiently splendid for a reception of symbolic import. Consequently Michelangelo had been commissioned to recast the civic centre by making the statue the nodal point of a Mannerist piazza; a plan which he had conceived by the winter of 1537.

Thereafter Marcus Aurelius became a symbol of secular authority; a model for all subsequent equestrian monuments. There was, however, a certain irony about this since the Marcus Aurelius had always been misidentified. The bronze had only escaped being melted down by iconoclasts because it had been thought wrongly to be a statue of Constantine, the first Christian Emperor. It was, however, a misconception under which Charles I and Van Dyck continued to labour since the true identity of the monument was only established long after they had died.

The bronze equestrian statue of Marcus Aurelius became the most influential source for state propaganda until the tank replaced the horse. The monument served Titian, Rubens, Van Dyck and Velazquez in paint;

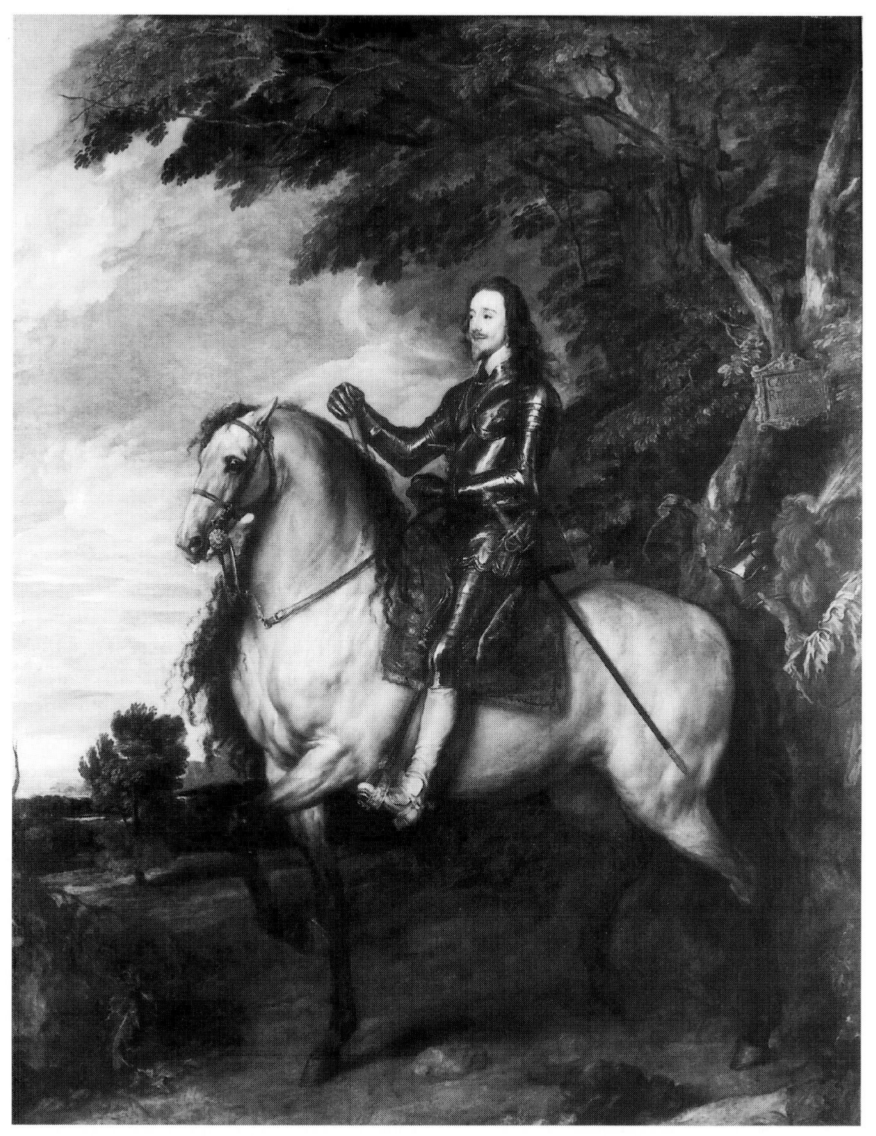

Sir Anthony Van Dyck, *Charles I on Horseback*, *c.* 1637 (National Gallery, London)

Giambologna, Tacca, Le Sueur and Girardon in bronze. It was a template from St Petersburg to Messina. And it was because it had been used to celebrate so many famous men, that Van Dyck was required to address the theme. Charles I wanted his image to rival if not surpass the overwhelmingly impressive *Charles V at the Battle of Muhlberg*, Titian's own homage to the prototype, which Charles had seen but Van Dyck not.

A consideration of the after-life of the Marcus Aurelius serves to emphasise an important point about the use of images in early modern Europe. The images which interest us have been described as clichés. But such a value judgement is unhistorical. Much of the effectiveness of an image depended on its capacity to emulate a prototype; to strike a resonant chord in the beholder. The art historian with racks of slides and boxes of photographs has been well-armed to track the influence of one artist on another, but because of so many images ready to hand, perhaps reluctant to reconstruct the impact an image had on those at whom it was aimed before those writers like Baxandall and others to whom reference was made in the introduction.

England was badly in need of its equestrian tributes to the Stuarts, as James I had realised well before artists arrived skilled enough to provide them. James kept a careful eye on what Henri IV had done to promote the arts, and when he established the Mortlake Tapestry Works in 1619, he specifically acknowledged the inspiration of the late French king in setting up a tapestry works in Paris in 1597.

The idea which came from the House of Lords that public statues of James I and the Prince of Wales should be erected in London, to which reference has already been made, may have had something to do with the fact that Henri had a splendid equestrian bronze of himself by Tacca on the Pont Neuf, to which it became customary for Parisians to doff their hats as they passed; a gesture which intrigued English visitors but which meant something serious to Parisians. Even before absolutism became the state religion of France under Louis XIV, such a gesture meant that where the King was in effigy, there too he was in spirit; that was certainly why courtiers never turned their backs on the Rigaud portrait of Louis XIV. When Louis XIV was absent from Versailles, Rigaud's picture stood in as substitute in the Throne Room.[9] The court was required to acknowledge the King's presence, as Catholics genuflect at the cross.

In obtaining the services of Tacca, Henri IV had emulated Cosimo I of Tuscany who had commissioned an equestrian portrait by Giambologna; a work which had always been much admired by the traveller to Tuscany. Not to be outdone, James I, or perhaps his son, had wanted to get on terms with Henri IV by summoning Tacca to London but he failed; a failure which must have been the more galling when Tacca went to Madrid instead and erected an equestrian monument of Philip III in the Plaza Mayor.[10]

Although Van Dyck's design for *Charles I on Horseback* depends upon the famed antique, however familiar the play, the performance is astoundingly brilliant. Van Dyck's rendering of a latter-day emperor is meltingly sensuous. Perhaps Van Dyck saw the commission as a *paragone*; a competition between painting and sculpture. Van Dyck may have been trying to suggest the miraculous powers of painting to summon up illusionism and in the process created one of his greatest works.

The *paragone* may have been more than merely theoretical. Charles was the first English monarch to collect sculpture and the passion grew. He possessed hundreds of busts and scores of statues, though almost all were late Hellenistic or Roman copies of works optimistically attributed to Phidias and Praxiteles. Besides the collection of works by dead hands, Charles also sustained a circle of sculptors. Of these the most productive and the most pretentious was Hubert Le Sueur, a Frenchman who had been brought over from Paris, probably by Buckingham after the proxy wedding of Charles I and Henrietta Maria in 1625. Le Sueur liked to sign documents 'Praxiteles le Sueur' because he saw himself as the reincarnation of that most famous of the antique masters; a grotesque comparison which served merely to irritate his employer, who harboured few illusions; at least in his realm of connoisseurship.

Le Sueur's pretensions to immortality must have been hard to bear. Nevertheless within the context of a court which had known almost no public sculpture, his productions and those of the much more gifted Italian sculptor Francesco Fanelli may have caused Van Dyck's competitive hackles to rise. By the time Van Dyck painted *Charles I on Horseback*, Le Sueur had cast his own variation on the theme of the celebrated Marcus Aurelius. This was not in Whitehall as it is now, but at Roehampton, in the garden of Charles I's Lord Treasurer, Richard Weston, Earl of Portland. Roehampton was close to Hampton Court, and Portland was close to the king. There can be no doubt therefore that the bronze was well known within court circles. That may have been sufficient to goad Van Dyck into a particularly scintillating performance.

In the painting, Charles emerges from right to left out of a darkened wood, as he does in *Charles I à la chasse*. There the similarity ends. Here he is a quite different person. He is elevated in every possible sense of the word; most obviously, he sits on top of his horse, but his own elevation of mood is hardly less striking. This is the portrait of a person who commands, but also of one who communes. Given the mood of confidence and optimism which Charles's expression seems to suggest, it may well be that the mounted sovereign in this context is a metaphor for the ruler in charge of his subjects since there was a long tradition in the Renaissance that the horse was an emblem for 'the people'.[11]

In the painting there is the tentative presence of a page nervously proffering a plumed helmet, but he is essentially redundant. His discreet presence does not vitiate the impact because the King is alone in spirit. That is important. The King is communing not with his subjects, but with his maker. Although there is not a single sacred reference, this is sacred as well as imperial art. This is The Lord's Anointed whose authority derives from God and whose servant he is; the *miles christianus* marching resolutely out of darkness into light as the length of his reign grows. There is movement, but we are spell-bound. Crucial to the mood of sublime and private communion is that the King notices no one. Although he advances resolutely he is abstracted. It is a vision which brings to mind one of the

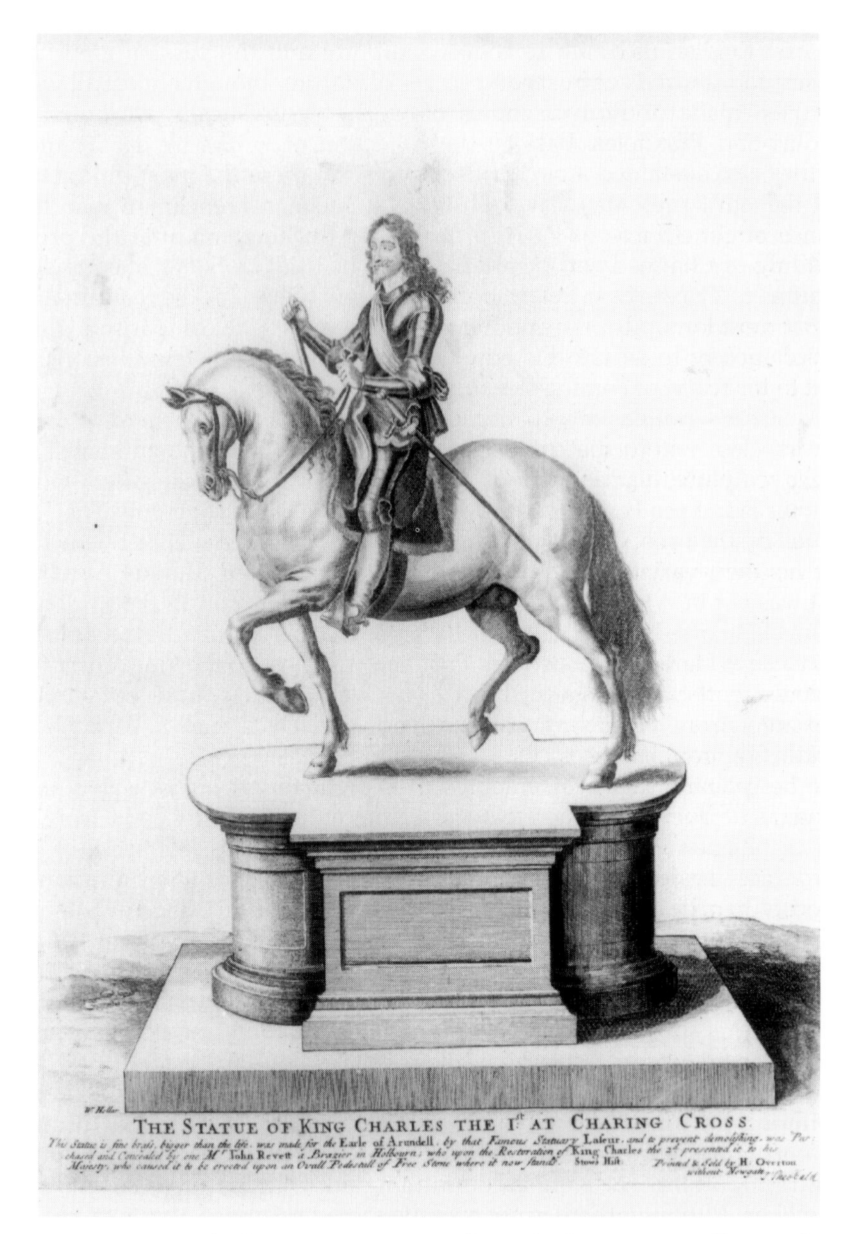

Hubert Le Sueur, *Charles I*, 1629–33; originally at Roehampton; at Charing Cross since 1674 (Society of Antiquaries of London)

most famous prints of the Renaissance: Dürer's *Knight, Death and the Devil.* In that too we are confronted with the Christian knight who moves forward in spite of the daemons which jostle and pluck him; an affirmation of Christian fortitude which anticipates the heroism of Bunyan's Pilgrim. As for the horse, this is not the pawing charger seen in *Charles I à la chasse*, but something as artificial and exquisite as the table bronzes which Francesco Fanelli was then casting for the King's closets.

We do not know how it was intended to display *Charles I on Horseback.* Abraham Van Der Doort, Keeper of Charles I's pictures, describes it in his 1639 inventory of The Royal Collection as being 'at present' in the Prince's Gallery at Hampton Court.[12] It would be fascinating to know what hung next to it and how it was framed.

We are on surer ground, however, with a third portrait by Van Dyck: *Charles I on Horseback with M. de St Antoine.* This appears to have been displayed with a masterly attention to the best possible theatrical effect. It was placed at the end of the Gallery at St James's. Unusually, we have a contemporary description of how it affected the court, since a member of the suite of Marie de' Medici who lodged at the palace in 1638 referred to it:

> At one of the ends of this Gallery . . . there is a portrait of the king . . . armed and on horseback, by the Chevalier Van Dyck. And, without exaggeration, in preserving the state of this great monarch, he has so skilfully brought him to life with his brush, that if our eyes alone were to be believed they would boldly assert that the king was alive in this portrait, so vivid is its appearance.[13]

It was the climax to an enfilade of 'portraits' of the Roman Emperors; a famous series of eleven paintings by Titian (with the twelfth by Bernardino Campi), acquired by Charles I when he had bought the collections of the Dukes of Mantua in 1628. The inspired idea of making seven of the Titians a guard of honour along with seven Giulio Romano equestrian 'portraits' of Roman emperors, demonstrates how collecting was an arsenal for regal propaganda. It is often stated that Charles I regarded his collections as a diversion, even a fatal diversion, from the more serious affair of ruling his kingdom. Certainly there were occasions when important business was delayed while Charles was closeted with Inigo Jones discussing the merits of the latest consignment of pictures from Italy, but it would be wrong to conclude that this was merely a distraction from affairs of state. Charles I saw his passion for art not as a distraction, but as a complement to politics. *Charles I on Horseback*, certainly the most triumphant expression of Charles's vision of his kingly status, was created as fitting climax to Titian's expression of imperialism. We may see Charles the art collector wishing to escape the burdens of rule, but he may have seen himself as fusing art and state-craft. The Gallery in St James's where

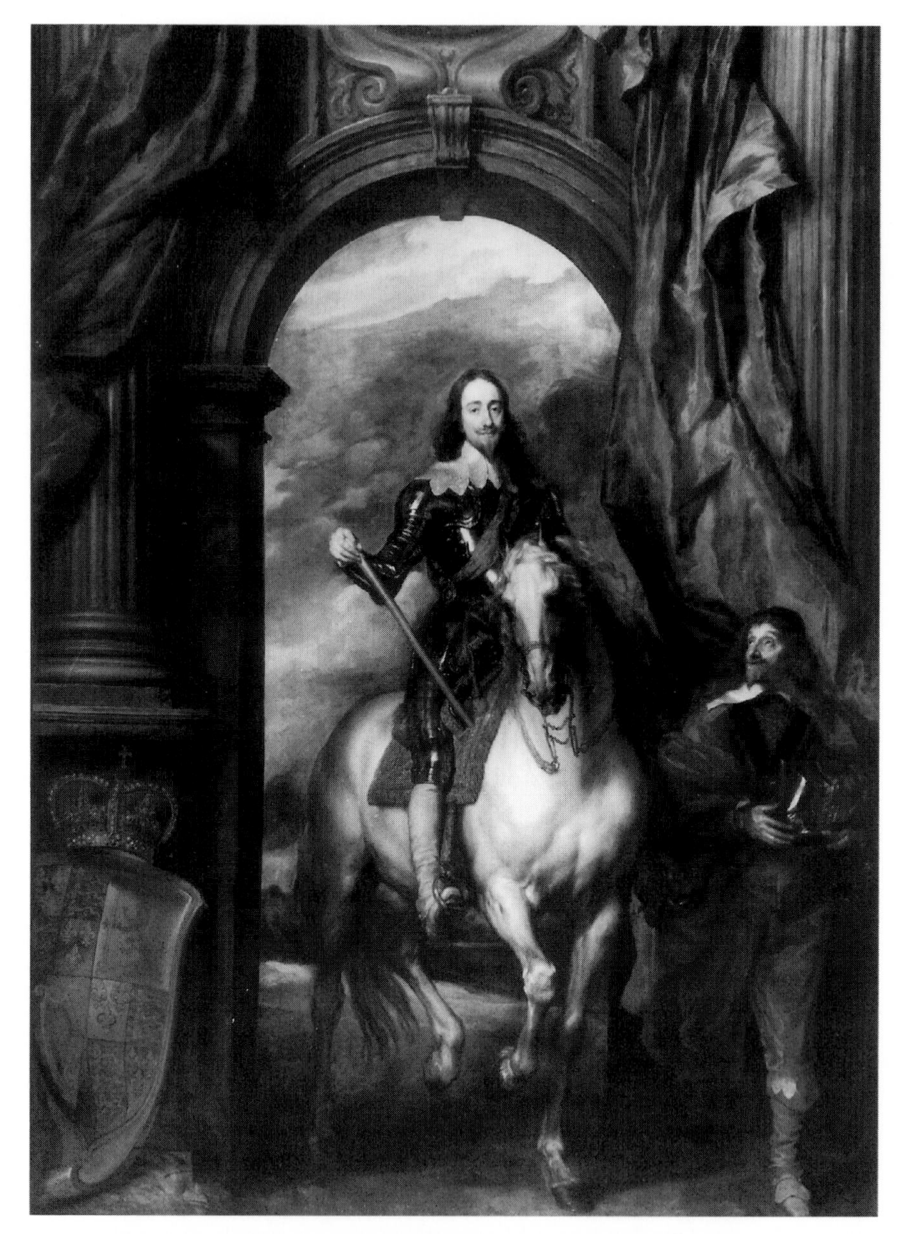

Sir Anthony Van Dyck, *Charles I on Horseback with M. de St Antoine*, 1633 (The Royal Collection)

this painting hung was strategically important to the ritual of kingship; it was a location for foreign dignitaries to assemble before being received in audience. Thus foreign ambassadors were left in no doubt as to the Imperial grandeur of the monarch at whose court they represented their own country.

The painting affirms a paradox offered to the consideration of his students by Sir Joshua Reynolds when speaking to them in his capacity as President of The Royal Academy. Reynolds believed, and Van Dyck had demonstrated, that the apprentice artist must be always copying the original.

The tremendous impact of *Charles I on Horseback* was partly to be accounted for by the fact that it was a distillation of works by Rubens and a further more fully worked development of previous essays by Van Dyck himself in the genre of equestrian imagery. Horsemanship is central to many Van Dycks of Charles I. Contemporaries rated horsemanship and hunting amongst the most important of all attributes of the noble life; priorities which account for why Rubens' great hunting scenes of the period 1615–1625 were so popular amongst English courtly collectors.

These Van Dycks share other important points of comparison. In all three, Van Dyck has taken religious iconography as his starting point; though the dependence is fainter in some cases than in others. In *Charles I à la chasse* Van Dyck has adapted the theme of the Adoration of the Magi out of his *Italian Sketchbook*, in which he had recorded impressions of Titian when travelling in Italy ten years earlier. The way in which the group moves from right to left, and the rapt attention of the page seen in profile, recalls the coming of the Wise Men. This is reinforced by the presence of the horse, reminiscent, albeit in reduction, of the entourage of animals which was part of its iconography. Mention has already been made of the dependence of the *Charles I on Horseback* upon Dürer's engraving of *Knight, Death and the Devil*, which though of course not a biblical theme, is nevertheless the most famous image of the fortitude of the Christian warrior.

In *Charles I on Horseback*, Van Dyck seems only to be drawing upon past achievements in the secular sphere. However, besides looking to his own repertoire and that of Rubens, the picture owes something perhaps to his celebrated early work of about 1620, the *St Martin and the Beggar*. The design also involved a return to the Bible and, specifically, to the theme of the Flight into Egypt. Tintoretto's moving interpretation of the story in the Scuola di St. Rocco suggests this. Tintoretto chose to have the Virgin being led straight out of the picture, as if into the path of the spectator, in much the same way as Charles emerges from under the arch. The energy and expression of awe-struck and devoted solicitation with which Joseph struggles in the Tintoretto is transposed by Van Dyck into the figure of Seigneur de St Antoine, whose balletic and energetic movement might be thought of as a reinterpretation of Tintoretto's Joseph. One of the most moving elements of the Tintoretto is the darkling trees which stress the toils and dangers of that flight from death; alleviated and

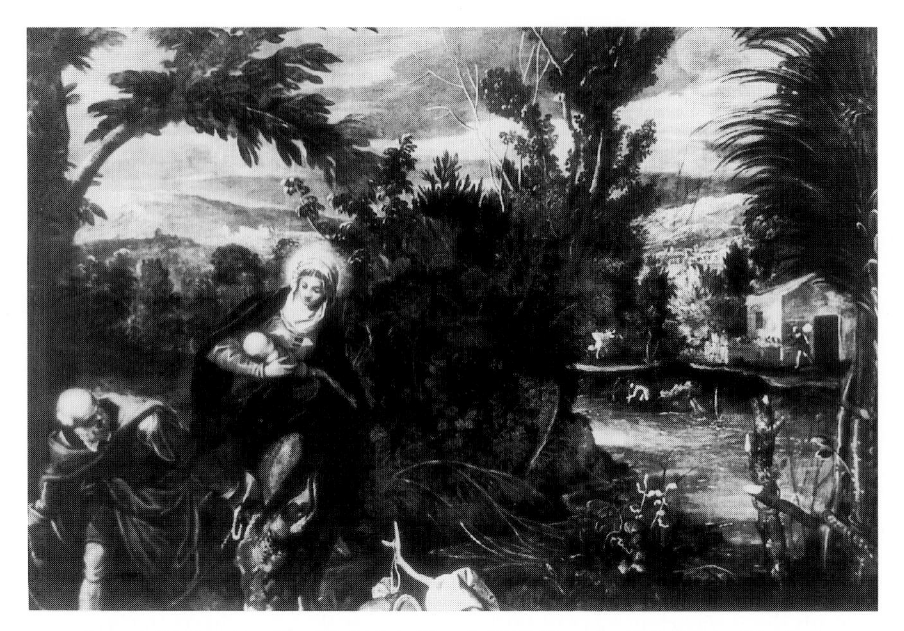

Jacopo Tintoretto, *The Flight into Egypt*, 1575 (Scuola di S. Rocco, Venice)

illuminated however by the nimbus of light in which the Holy group are enveloped. That central ellipse of light within vernal gloom, framed by a bending frond which seems to anticipate Poussin as an expression of sentiment, becomes the light in the aperture of the triumphal arch behind horse and rider in the Van Dyck.

What then are we to make of how Van Dyck has taken sacred art as his starting point? Perhaps he was encouraged because of the way in which the early Stuarts identified themselves with the divine. Time and again, from the *Basilikon Doron* to the *Eikon Basilike*, that is to say from the exposition to the expiation of Stuart kingship, the reader is regaled by the analogy between God and his lieutenant. Van Dyck, naturally sympathetic to a monarchical system of government, would have found his values reinforced when he arrived in London early in 1632. His landlord Edward Norgate, stepson of Nicholas Felton, a notably royalist Bishop of Ely, earned his living restoring, tuning and painting organs in royal chapels which gave the setting to anthems devoted to the theistic nature of the English Crown. Inigo Jones, with whom Van Dyck would have had frequent contact, was more concerned with the order implicit in good government than with the Orders of Vitruvius and he taught Van Dyck much about the social values of the court. Then there was the mildly disreputable Sir Balthazar Gerbier, English ambassador to the court of the Archduchess Isabella at Brussels. He had been responsible for pressurising the reluctant painter to come to London back in 1632. As a former major-domo at York House, Gerbier too would have impressed Van Dyck with the sanctity of English kingship. As Van Dyck switched from working for the canons of Antwerp to canonising a British sovereign, it was easy to transpose the Three Kings into one.

So much then for the English tutelage of the painter, but what about the sitter? What can we know, if anything, of Charles's thoughts of these portraits? On one level it is clear enough. He knighted Van Dyck on approval: that is to say, before Van Dyck had produced anything at court, he was given an honour which the more gifted Rubens had had to earn laboriously. How is this to be explained since Rubens was recognised as the greater painter? Van Dyck had of course agreed to come and work for the English court whereas Rubens, like Titian before him, always kept courts at arm's length. But perhaps too it had to do with the temperament of Charles I. Rubens was too robust for the fastidious English King for whom appearance meant more than substance. By contrast, there was no one to whom appearances mattered more than to Van Dyck.

We tend to think of Van Dyck as overwhelmingly a portraitist; as the founder of the British school of portrait painting. But in the Spanish Netherlands he had been perceived as a great master of the Counter-Reformation altarpiece. Exactly what his relationship in his early years with Rubens had been, seems to be impossible to unravel; though since he played a central part in Rubens' commission for the Jesuit Church, sacred art was certainly a language he had mastered by the time he was twenty. It would have been natural therefore for him to look to that genre as a means to give sanctity to secular majesty.

But what did Charles think of these expensive masterpieces? We do not know. But there is a hint. On 19 August 1647, a week before Charles took up residence at Hampton Court, an order for payment was made to 'Mr Remigius van Leumput for ye coppie of ye Great Peice at Whitehall'.[14] The request had originated with Charles I's turncoat Lord Chamberlain, Philip, 4th Earl of Pembroke, who had ordered it on behalf of the king in September 1643. It is tempting to believe that payment was authorised in August 1647, because the copy was then delivered to Hampton Court where the king had just become a close prisoner of Parliament. He wished to be consoled by a painted recollection of a shattered world. The marriage of Charles I and Henrietta Maria was an exception to the rule of marital discord which historically has tended to beset the English monarchy. It was because family life meant so much to this outwardly cold and aloof man that he may have had this image, the warmest of those created by Van Dyck, by way of consolation.

So we come to the closest scrutiny of Charles I by Van Dyck: his *Charles I in Three Positions*. Here Charles, taken at head-and-shoulders length, is painted three times in one canvas. The unusual format was because it was made for dispatch to Rome where it was to be used to make a bust of the king by Bernini, the leading sculptor in Italy.

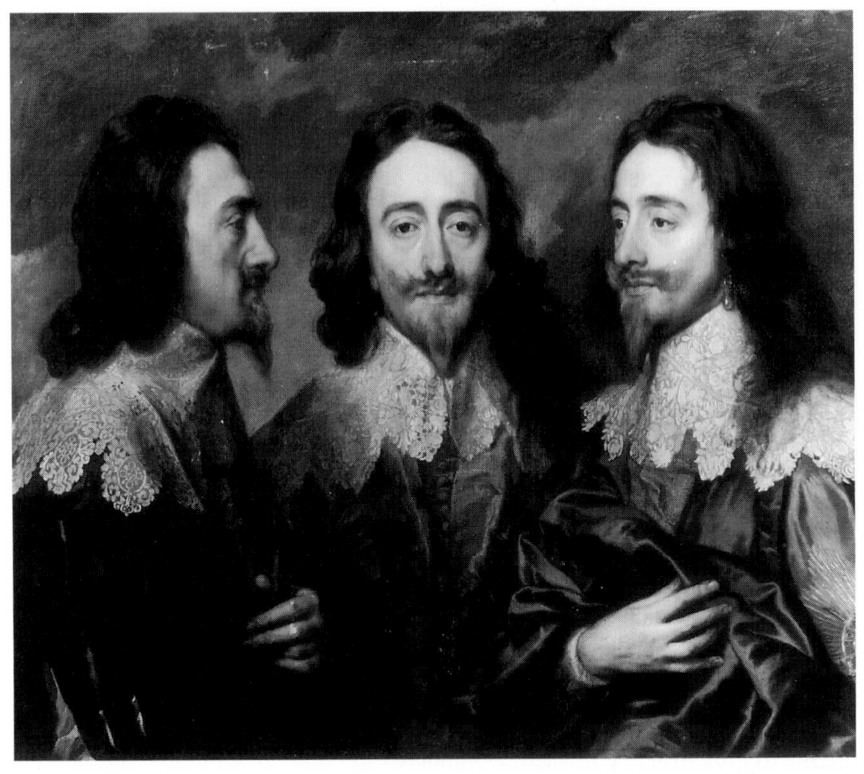

Sir Anthony Van Dyck, *Charles I in Three Positions*, 1635–6 (The Royal Collection)

Although the picture is the simplest of the series of Van Dycks of Charles I, it has the widest social and political ramifications. There is a political, even ecclesiastical dimension which makes it unique in the iconography of Charles. Bernini was commanded by Urban VIII to sculpt the bust, following a request from Henrietta Maria. Bernini was then at the height of his powers: a genius of legendary status whose works were sought after throughout Europe. Thus it was a mark of peculiar favour that the English court should have been granted 'permission'. But what made the project still more extraordinary was the involvement of Van Dyck. Naturally Bernini could not take a likeness from life. Therefore Van Dyck worked to give his collaborator all possible means to imagine the physiognomy. The two artists, unsurpassed in their day as portraitists on canvas and in marble, were commanded by the heads of two different faiths to collaborate. Much besides brilliant artistry however was intended to hang from those marble shoulders. Urban VIII and his diplomats in London thought the combination of the privilege granted in allowing a man with the canonical status of Bernini to take the portrait, together with the effect of the finished product itself, would actually help to bring England back to the Catholic faith. It is difficult to grasp that art could really be invested with such hopes but that was the case, as is clear from a letter which Cardinal Francesco Barberini wrote to Cardinal Mazarin about some unidentified statues which the Vatican was preparing for presentation to the English Crown:

> The statues go on prosperously nor shall I hesitate to rob Rome of her most valuable ornaments, if in exchange we might be so happy as to have the King of England's name among those princes who submit to the Apostolic See.[15]

To understand the significance of Urban VIII's gesture in allowing Bernini to take the head of Charles I, it is best to think of it as the equivalent to the presentation of an order of chivalry, which a head of state periodically presented to a brother ruler; as, for instance, Henry VII had presented Raphael's patron Guidobaldo of Urbino with the Garter.

Charles I in Three Positions is the simplest of the Van Dycks of the king; yet it is the richest historiographically because of the romantic legend which came to be associated with it. John Evelyn, that minute-taker of late Stuart culture, mentioned the painting briefly in his work on coins, *Numismata* (1697). Evelyn claimed, without documentary substantiation, that when the Van Dyck was unpacked by Bernini in Rome in the early summer of 1636, it had impressed the sculptor with 'something of funest and unhappy, which the Countenance of that Excellent Prince foreboded'.[16] Here then, just one year before a disastrous fire destroyed the bust and Whitehall Palace with it, was a powerful addition to the tragic romance which hung like an aureole around a martyr king; a cult which had long been promoted within High Church circles. What Evelyn was implying was that somehow Bernini had a premonition of disaster.

Legends are always reinforced by the disappearance of the cult object, and so from a short aside in a book designed for the erudite alone, support was given to the myth of Charles I as an unhappy, misunderstood and melancholic king. It was a myth which had sprung up within days of the execution of Charles I in primitive imagery startlingly dependent upon the iconography of Christ's Passion. A painting by an anonymous artist, now on loan to the National Portrait Gallery of Scotland, depicts the executioner holding up the severed head for the crowd. In the foreground a woman has fainted and is being helped by a bevy of attendants. It is a detail which the painter has taken from depictions of the Virgin at the foot of the cross. Although the dependency is all too obvious, that should not be taken as proof of the limitations of the artist since he almost certainly intended it to be recognised. It was after all propaganda. The belief that Charles I died for his people as Christ died for mankind had

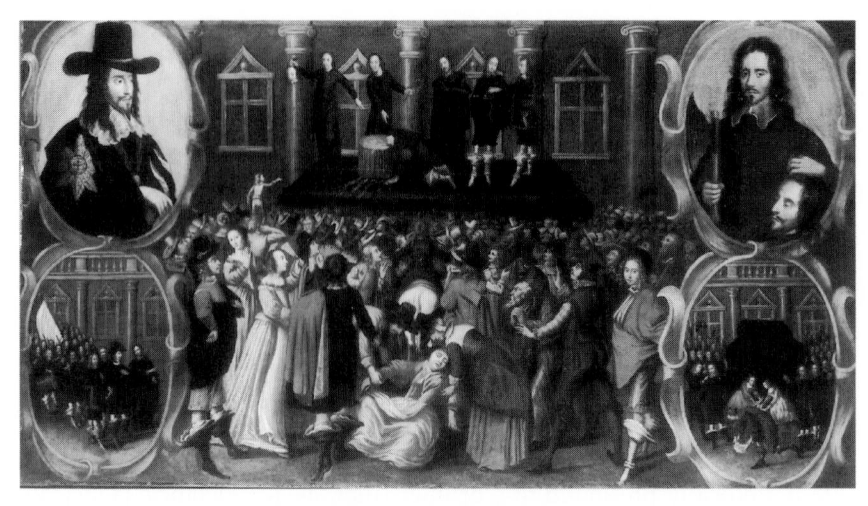

Anon., *Execution of Charles I*, 1649 (Collection of the Earl of Rosebery/on loan to the Scottish National Portrait Gallery)

taken hold, and the painter, whoever he may have been, was making his own contribution to that myth.

The frontispiece by William Marshall to the *Eikon Basilike* of 1649, shows Charles kneeling in a loggia, with a facial expression reminiscent of Christ during the Agony in the Garden. Charles looks up with the same agonised expression as Christ was conventionally depicted as displaying when he asked for the cup to be taken away. Charles kneels against a table, grasping a crown of thorns which is placed equidistant from his earthly crown which lies inscribed with the word 'vanitas', discarded on the ground, and a vision of a heavenly crown labelled: 'Beatam et Æternam', and 'Gloria'. The message is clear. It is only by grasping the crown of thorns that the martyr can aspire to the true crown. The frontispiece spells out the parallel between this earthly king and the King of Heaven; redemption came for both through suffering. In the far distance a rock of constancy is surrounded by a sea of turbulence as it is struck by flashes of lightning; an emblem which is explained thus:

> And as th'unmoved Rock *out-brave's*
> The boist'rous Windes *and rageing* Waves:
> So triumph I *And* shine more bright
> *In sad Affliction's Darksom night*

For some, such an explanation would have been redundant since these are theatrical effects which would have been recognised from the medal imagery of Elizabeth I. The reappearance of the rock in the turbulent

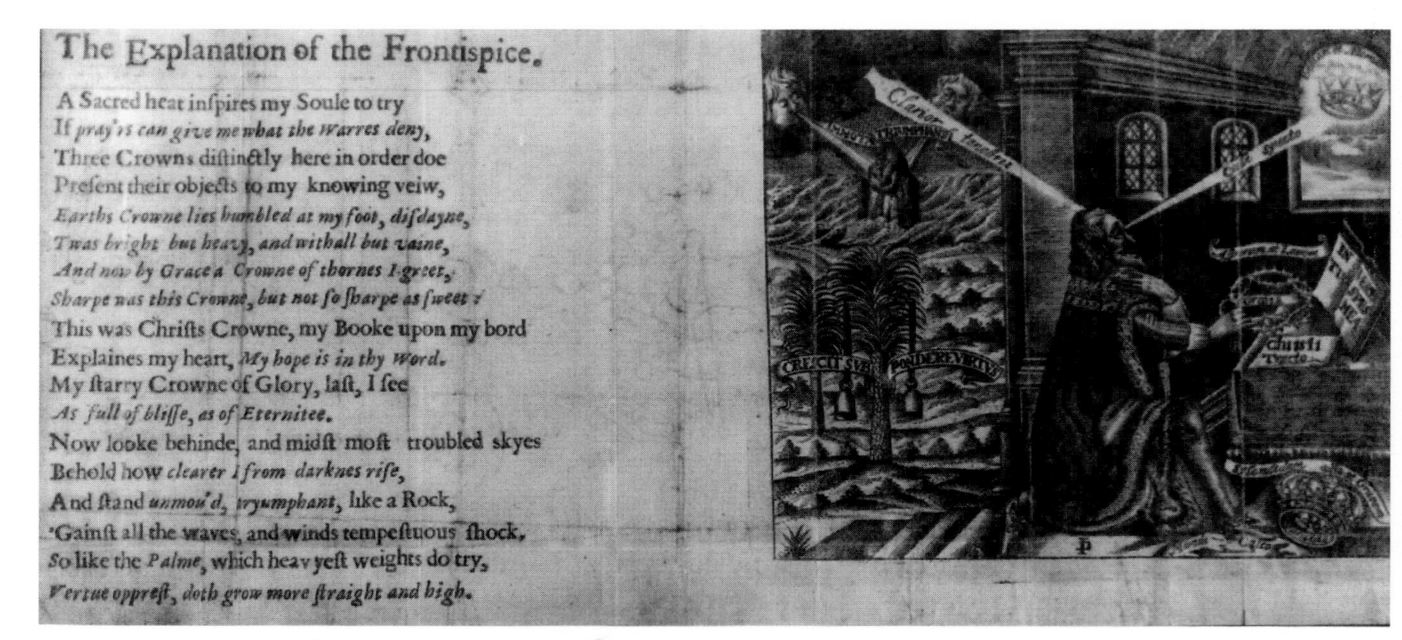

The Explanation of the Frontiſpice.

A Sacred heat inſpires my Soule to try
If pray'rs can give me what the Warres deny,
Three Crowns diſtinctly here in order doe
Preſent their objects to my knowing veiw,
Earths Crowne lies humbled at my foot, diſdayne,
Twas bright but heavy, and withall but vaine,
And now by Grace a Crowne of thornes I greet,
Sharpe was this Crowne, but not ſo ſharpe as ſweet:
This was Chriſts Crowne, my Booke upon my bord
Explaines my heart, *My hope is in thy Word.*
My ſtarry Crowne of Glory, laſt, I ſee
As full of bliſſe, as of Eternitee.
Now looke behinde, and midſt moſt troubled skyes
Behold how *clearer I from darknes riſe,*
And ſtand *unmov'd, tryumphant,* like a Rock,
'Gainſt all the waves, and winds tempeſtuous ſhock,
So like the *Palme,* which heav yeſt weights do try,
Vertue oppreſt, doth grow more ſtraight and high.

William Marshall, *Eikon Basilike*, 1649, frontispiece (Edinburgh University Library)

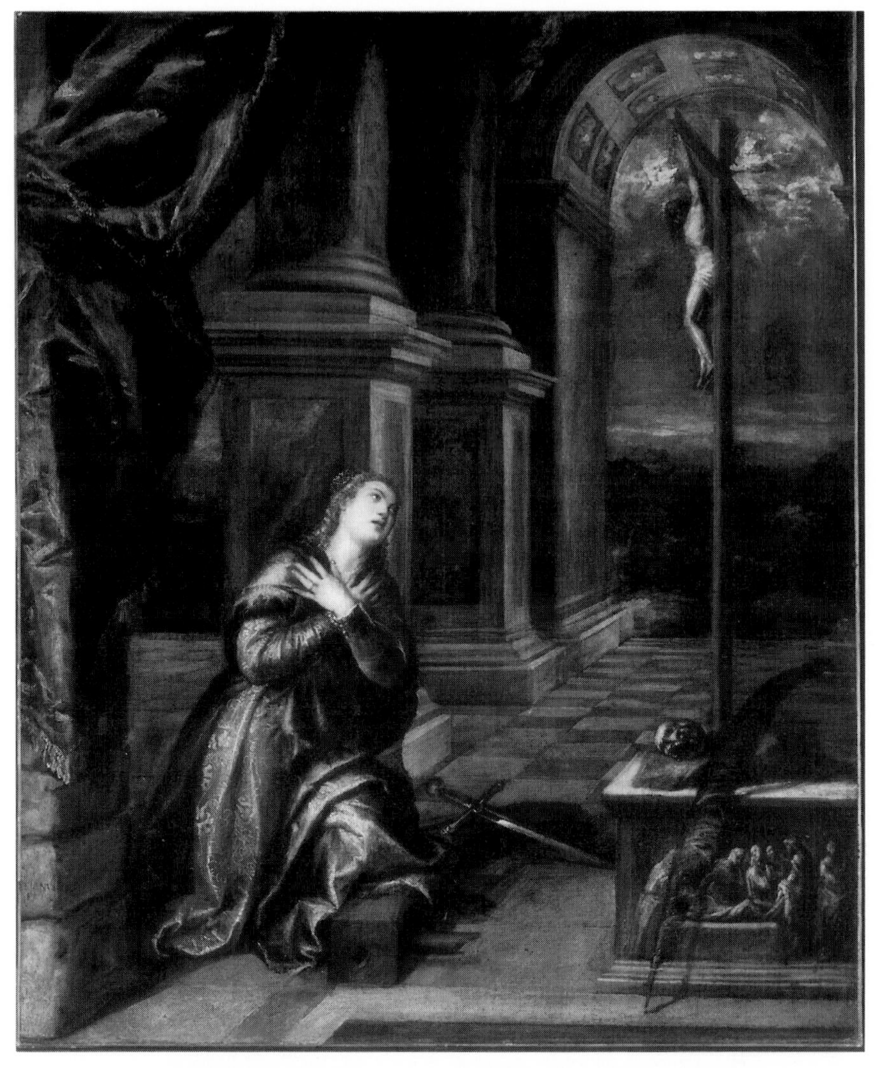

Titian studio, *St Catherine of Alexandria*, *c.* 1568 (The Museum of Fine Arts, Boston)

waters of Stuart politics is just one of many examples to illustrate how imagery was constantly being recycled throughout our world.

Although the Marshall print is not art, it shows a sophisticated awareness of what was required for a clear exposition. If the face of Charles is a Veronica's veil to remind the faithful of his Christ-like qualities, the whole image seems to have been formulated on a Titian studio work which Marshall could have studied in The Royal Collection.[17] There is a Titian studio picture entitled *St Catherine of Alexandria in Prayer* and it has been suggested that this may have been in the collection of Charles I. More certainly, there is a striking similarity between this Titian studio work and the Marshall print. St Catherine and St Charles the Martyr both kneel against the front plane, within a tunnel-like loggia seen in sharp perspective. The connection between the two images is one of many resonances which demonstrate how royal pictures in the Caroline age were actively used to defend either the institution of monarchy or republicanism. Pictures were an active constituent in political debate.

Contemporary images of the sufferings of King Charles the Martyr were enormously effective, far more persuasive than the written word. The nineteenth-century Frenchman Paul Delaroche had a very successful career painting melodramatic and wholly fictitious interpretations of history. He was much drawn to English themes and his *Charles I insulted by the Soldiers of Cromwell*, of 1836, is the most shameless association of Charles I and The Passion – specifically that stage known as The Mocking of Christ. The picture must rank as one of Delaroche's less happy essays in British history. The royal belly seems to anticipate the complacent girth of the great political economist Jeremy Bentham who at his death in 1832 had left himself to be set up in a glass case in the foyer of University College London. Faintly ridiculous as *Charles I insulted by the Soldiers of Cromwell* may seem, it was well pitched to appeal to the sentiments and mawkish sentimentality of the Victorians.

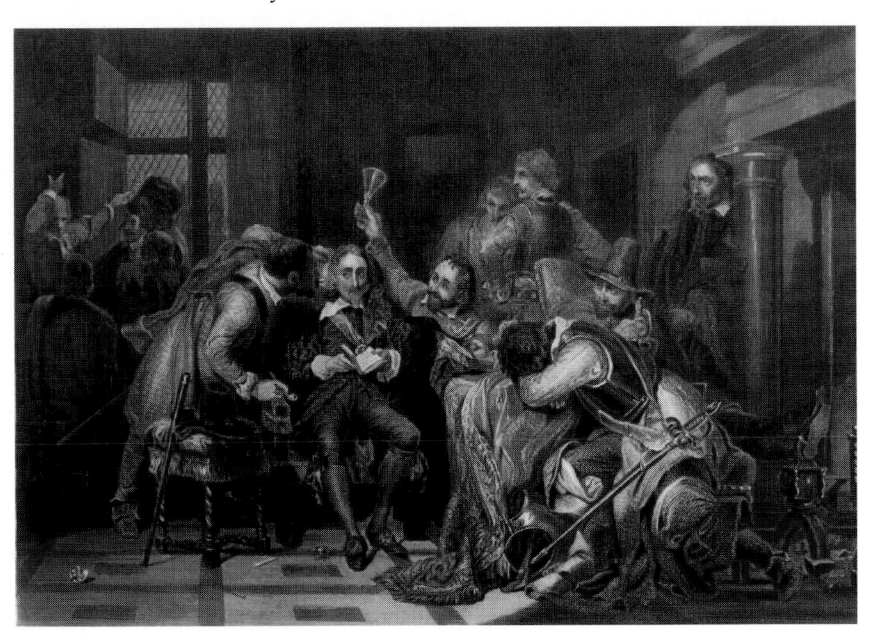

W. Hulland after Paul Delaroche, *Charles I in the Guardroom*, 1836, engraving (National Portrait Gallery, London)

Delaroche produced high drama not high art, but Bernini's bust of Charles I was the principal relic in the treasury. A faint and degenerate image of it exists in a marble bust after a cast from the original. It tells us what the Bernini looked like, but not what it felt like. For that, it is better to look for a parallel rather than a likeness, and turn to Bernini's bust of *Francesco d'Este, Duke of Modena*. Exuberantly asymmetrical like a splendid ormolu candelabra, *Francesco d'Este* is a supreme evocation of well-bred confidence. It is a vision of a man at the height of his powers, capable of carrying his subjects with him; surely indeed the message Van Dyck intended to convey to Bernini, rather than the doleful English martyr which Evelyn offered his readers. Evelyn's own temperament should be borne in mind here. His favourite portrait of himself, by Robert Walker (National Portrait Gallery, London), shows the diarist in the pose of Melancholia as codified by Dürer, and studying a skull. Evelyn loved to be despondent and the suspicion must be that Bernini's bust of Charles I set him off. The idea of Charles I as someone who lived in a state of clouded majesty, an idea that still prevails, stands not as a historical reality but as tribute to the power of imagery to rewrite history.

Kevin Sharpe has recently argued that Charles was at peace with himself as his subjects were with him. Things did go wrong – there was after all a Civil War – but that only began to happen in the autumn of 1637, after Bernini's bust arrived, and as a consequence of difficulties over religion with the Calvinist Scots. In Van Dyck's preparatory study for Bernini, the painter set out to echo the sentiments of a man whom he had come to serve not to defy. Charles declared that he was the happiest man on Earth and we should believe him as Van Dyck clearly did in this painting.

Bernini's 1637 bust of Charles I was the greatest of all free-standing sculptures of a British sovereign. Nothing to match its power had been created for the English monarchy since Henry VIII saw to the finishing of a tomb for his parents. In the next chapter we shall be examining the role of funerary sculpture and tombs in the creation of images of rule.

Chapter Five
The Tomb

Today it is hard to understand what a tomb meant in the sixteenth century, when few enter a church and none are buried within. The church has almost no place in our lives. It is one of the greatest single distinctions between the culture of the Renaissance and that of the late twentieth century. A real effort must be made to understand how much importance people attached to tombs in early modern England. Just as it was suggested that the medal meant more to an Elizabethan than the miniature, so tombs had more of an impact than painted portraits. Although many family monuments were reserved within private chapels, their splendour could still be felt through the screen of stone or metal which surrounded them. Most however were not enclosed and were therefore fully accessible to the community. Ordinary people were required to go to church but they were forbidden access to the Long Gallery and thus to family portraits. Accessibility has always mattered as much as the object itself when considering the impact of images.

Tombs have lasted, painted imagery much less so. When Michelangelo's *Pietà* was attacked, the assailant succeeded only in chipping the nose and severing an arm, damage which cannot now be detected with the group entombed in its bullet-proof box. By contrast, when more recently acid was poured over Rembrandt's *Danae* (St Petersburg), it was so severely damaged that the scars will always be visible. There was much to be said for the tank-like nature of the Renaissance tomb in an age of unprecedented religious turmoil. Those who orchestrated that turmoil, new families who were ennobled as a result of shaping the Tudor revolution in government, invested some of their wealth in tombs. They were looking to stabilise new-found power, and monuments to Norman or Angevin adventurers lying in dusty silence in a parish church provided reassurance and inspiration in the lethal world of the Tudor court.

Shrines had been singled out for destruction even before the iconoclasm of the Edwardian period, but provided tombs were not also shrines, they were usually left alone. Rood screens, stained glass, pulpits, fonts, lecterns, altars and vestments: all were subjected to mutilation or annihilation. The exception was the tomb and when the inviolability of the great seemed to be threatened, the Crown moved swiftly. Elizabeth issued a Proclamation within two years of her accession, forbidding people to desecrate tombs because in the words of John Weever, England's first historian of death, when commenting on Elizabethan attitudes, such vandalism tended to:

> the extinguishing of the honourable and good memory of sundry vertuous and noble persons deceased; but also the true understanding of divers Families in this Realme (who have descended of the bloud of the same persons deceased) is so darkened, as the true course of their inheritance may be hereafter interrupted, contrary to Justice.[1]

The Proclamation begins by reiterating an argument often found in the writings of antiquity where it was argued that tombs were an inspiration for the living; an argument which would be re-stated in the seventeenth century in that densely allusive text on the art of antiquity, Francis Junius' *The Painting of The Ancients*. Despite the title of a book which received the highest accolade when it appeared first in Latin in 1637, warmly praised by no less a person than Rubens, much space was given over to the efficacy of antique sculpture for the morals of the ancient world; sculpture which was often funerary in nature. Of more immediate concern to Elizabeth I in 1560, however, were material possessions not morals; the thinking that tomb-breaking threatened the stability of the social fabric by obscuring the rights of inheritance. John Weever reiterated Elizabeth's viewpoint about the defensive, protective function of the tomb when he published his *Antient funerall Monuments* in 1631. In that book Weever declared: 'And indeed these Funerall Monuments in foregoing ages, were very fittingly called muniments, in that they did defend and fence the corps of the defunct.'[2] For Weever the etymology of the word monument derived from muniment, the medieval Latin word *munimentum* meaning fortification; a word which when applied to a tomb, denoted the means of preserving the person, rights and dignity of the deceased. Nowadays muniments denote historical documents, which often include legal proof of descent or ownership of rights.

Elizabeth had to repeat her proclamation about tomb-breaking in 1571, but thereafter, outbreaks of vandalism seem to have ceased. Given the relative inefficiency of Elizabethan social controls, this success probably had more to do with an inherent respect for the tomb than with any direction from central government. Why was this so?

English iconoclasts were not social revolutionaries; indeed the most serious threats to the stability of the Crown were led by tomb-makers not tomb-breakers. Lord Darcy and Richard Aske, leaders of the Pilgrimage of Grace in 1536, wanted to restore Catholicism and had they not been executed as traitors, they would have expected tombs for their bodies and masses for their souls. These were the last people to encourage the rooting up of the old order and the destruction of its imagery. That had certainly happened in Germany during the 1520s where Lutheranism was fatally compromised by agrarian unrest. The contrast between the attitude to tombs in sixteenth-century England, and France in the age of Enlightenment, is also instructive. The French Revolutionary mob would systematically destroy royal tombs because they had destroyed the institution which these monuments helped to sustain.

Rites of passage were observed on a grand and public scale in Renaissance Britain. Internment required weeks of careful planning, while the obsequies themselves were second only to a coronation as public spectacle. The burial was orchestrated by officers of the College of Arms while an army of other dignitaries discharged a multitude of offices; the whole ritual one of the most complex anthropological expressions of the age. It was all very different from the discretion of the modern age, in which death is spirited away in a whispering limousine. We contrive to believe death does not exist and when forced to do so, regard it as an inexplicable frustration in a materialistic existence. In stark contrast to our present observances or lack of them, burial sometimes took place six weeks after death: the corpse embalmed and placed in a coffin with an effigy based upon a death mask resting above.

Funerals were of great social complexity because they expressed aspiration, not merely commemoration; they looked forward as well as backward. The splendour which accompanied men to their graves did not sink with them beneath the earth: it remained on the surface as tribute to the greatness of a house; a permanent recumbent effigy, replacing the temporary one created from the death mask. And yet for all the pomp of a funeral, the ordinary man could be affected more deeply by the rituals of death than by the imagery of life. Death was an intimate of every household; childhood usually included experiencing the death of a sibling and men began to make preparations for their departure once they were thirty. Morbid thoughts were not therefore an affectation upon the part of *précieux*, but an aspect of applied theology; metaphysical speculation made urgent in the light of the fact that few lived until fifty. For all classes therefore, the commemoration of the dead was a central tribal custom.

The sting of death was drawn by an emphasis on continuities; the event was often placed in a fixed three-dimensional perspective by the insertion of tombs within chapels already crowded with ancestors. The Beauchamp chapel in St Mary's, Warwick, is perhaps the finest; a wonderfully grandiloquent expression of family pride and, incidentally, a comprehensive account of medieval and Renaissance funerary art. The effect of looking at these mortuary chapels was to suggest the vigour of the line as much as the extinction of a particular person.

Death was mocked by a recumbent effigy, apparently alive and set about with as many armorial bearings as the family could decently muster. Thus the house was rendered immortal, whatever the fate of individuals. It was an expensive form of advertising. The product was the family, the logo: blazons, quarterings and crests, approved by those standards officers of the day in the College of Arms.

The possibility of coming to terms with if not overcoming death, was an incentive to spend large amounts of money on funerary monuments. but no less important was the social ambition which made the tomb as much an expression of getting on in this world as it had to do with getting out of it.

So much for the mental set which may help to explain the central place the tomb had during the English Renaissance. We turn now to specific examples to discover what they can tell us about the values of the age. We begin with the greatest of all; the double tomb of Henry VII and Elizabeth of York by Pietro Torrigiano in the mortuary chapel in Westminster Abbey; a chapel created for Henry VII and named after him. The tomb set the standard for high funerary art in Britain until the onset of the Baroque monument in the closing years of the seventeenth century.

Henry had intended to be buried at Windsor; a burial which was to have been preceded by the internment of the remains of his uncle Henry VI, to whom he was devoted, and about whose person an aura of sanctity had developed within a few years of what had probably been his murder in the Tower of London in 1471. But then Henry VII had abandoned the idea of locating their tombs at Windsor when persuaded by the Dean and Chapter of Westminster that it had been his uncle's intention to have himself laid to rest at Westminster. At Westminster therefore the project took form; influenced, it has been suggested, by the royal mausoleum at Cléry which had been built by Louis XI (d. 1483), or Margaret of Austria's memorial at Brou in Burgundy, erected to her husband Duke Philip of Savoy who had died in 1504.[3]

Henry VII pondered his death because it was a vital aspect of his future; the tomb was an elaborate form of autobiography. Among so many ambitious building projects, none was more important to Henry VII than his funerary chapel, which he eventually ordained was to be added to the east end of Westminster Abbey. When it was finally finished, *c.* 1520, that is to say, over ten years after Henry's death, it cost the enormous sum of £20,000; prodigious expenditure on a scale only matched by Henry's outlay on his uncle's chapel at King's College, Cambridge.

A sense of how much his tomb meant to Henry VII can be gauged from an extract of his will, nearly a quarter of which is taken up with ordaining minute details:

> AND if our said Chapel and Towmbe, and oure said wifs Ymages, grate and closure, be not fully accomplished and perfitely finished, according to the premisses, by us in our liftyme; we then wol, that not oonly the

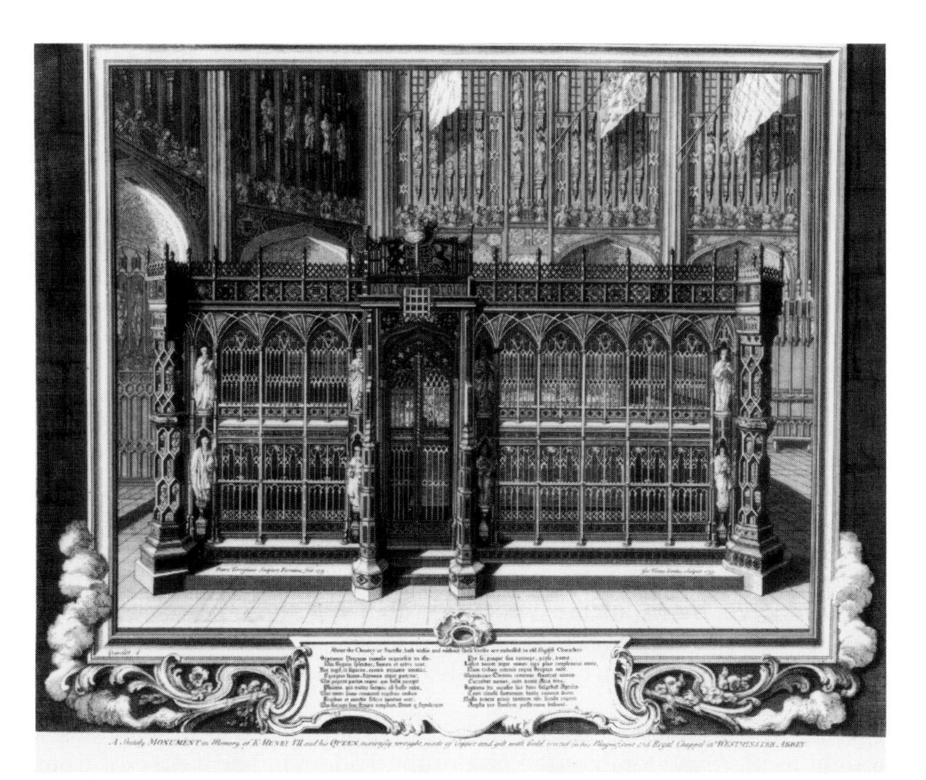

Pietro Torrigiano, *Tomb of Henry VII and Elizabeth of York*, 1512–19, Henry VII Chapel, Westminster Abbey (Society of Antiquaries of London)

> same Chapell, Tombe, Ymagies, Grate and Closure, and every of them, and al other thinges to them belonging, with al spede, and assone after our decease as goodly may be doon, bee by our Executours hooly and perfitely finished in every behalve, after the maner and fourme before rehersed, and sutingly to that that is begoune and doon of theim. But also that the said Chapell be deked, and the windowes of our said Chapell be glased, with Stores, Ymagies, Armes, Bagies and Cognoissaunts, as is by us redily divised, and in picture delivered to the Priour of Saunt Bartilmews besid Smythfeld, maistre of the works of our said Chapell; and that the Walles, Doores, Windows, Archies and Vaults, and Ymages of the same our Chapell, within and without, be painted, garnished and adorned, with our Armes, Bagies, Cognissaunts [cognisants], and other convenient painteng, in as goodly and riche maner as suche a work requireth, and as to a Kings work apperteigneth.[4]

The appearance of what had been intended at first for Windsor cannot now be reconstructed. Designs for that location were then followed by four separate schemes for Westminster: one for which we have no knowledge, and a second proposed by the Italian Guido Mazzoni. By 1507 Mazzoni had gone back to Italy and anyway his efforts were apparently 'misliked' by Henry VIII, who took over the direction of his father's tomb at his death in 1509. Meanwhile between the departure of Mazzoni for Italy in 1507, and the death of Henry VII in 1509, Henry VII enjoined his executors to provide a tomb which has been described as 'a monument of traditional Gothic character, apparently quite unaffected by either French or Italian influence'.[5] This in turn was rejected by Henry VIII and finally between 1512 and 1519, at the fourth attempt, Torrigiano went on to create the monument to be seen in the Abbey.

It was France and an Italian artist working there which had given Henry VII his second, rejected idea for his Westminster tomb. Guido Mazzoni or Paganino, a sculptor whom Charles VIII had brought back from Italy in 1495, suggested to Henry that he should appear on his tomb as a *priant* figure resting on a canopy; beneath which were to be recumbent cadavers of husband and wife. That idea was eventually replaced by something altogether more conventional by English standards. In the fourth, realised design, that is to say, Torrigiano's scheme, Henry and Elizabeth lie in their robes on top of the sepulchre; without a canopy, without kneeling figures, and without stone cadavers; all of which had been suggested at one stage or another during the tortured genesis of England's greatest Renaissance tomb.

What in the end was settled upon was a formula which consciously sought to place the tomb of the first of the Tudors in lineal descent from the monuments of the Angevin and Plantagenet kings located in the main body of the Abbey; for that is the basic matrix of the final realised scheme whatever quattrocento veneer may have been added by way of the classicising roundels and Verrocchio-like putti embellishing the basic structure. The rejection of Paganino's modish French designs, together with what had been suggested before and after his scheme, may have been dependent on the feeling that Henry's memory would be best served by having him cast in the image of those dynasties which had preceded the Tudors. The Tudors were after all new and they needed to be bedded into tradition.

But this does not wholly explain why Henry VIII rejected the idea of simulating the cadavers of his parents. It was not because such a schema was somehow 'medieval' and therefore outmoded. Bishop Foxe of Winchester, an executant of Henry VII's will and therefore an overseer of the tomb, was one of the most progressive educationalists of his day. Yet Foxe chose a horrifying suggestion of the corruption of his own body for his monument in Winchester Cathedral, which was housed in a splendid gothic chapel made to his own design. Foxe died in 1528: the year before Wolsey handed over Hampton Court to Henry VIII – that investiture, symbol of the coming of age of the Renaissance prince in England. There was therefore no easy identification between a progressive humanist and the new Italianate style in sepulchral design. In the case of the royal mortuary chapel at Westminster, perhaps Henry VIII changed the momentum of the project because he came to feel that uncomfortable reminders of bodily corruption would hardly enhance the image of the new dynasty. Instead we are confronted with triumph over death; the continuing presence of the life of the monarch who had given life to the Tudor dynasty. The same point would be made twenty years later in the Whitehall mural where Holbein suggests the abiding presence of Henry VII and Elizabeth of York. But before then however, and in the much more public context of a funerary monument, Henry and Elizabeth had already been remembered together as if still alive.

In Westminster Abbey the first of the Tudors and his consort lie awake and robed, hands piously clasped in prayer. It is a presentation which is in marked contrast to some of the most resplendent tombs of a century later, on which armoured figures lie with eyes closed in acknowledgement of the reality of death. Armour was frequently worn on ceremonial and formal occasions, and so its appearance on an early Stuart tomb cannot be seen as antiquated or anti-naturalistic. Nevertheless, its use militates against the realism, the eerie, threatening presence which the early Tudors favoured in their artists. Henry VII is sentient in death; though he may not be quite as alert as the fox portrayed in his celebrated bust attributed to Torrigiano.

The tomb of Henry VII was the most triumphant collaboration of the visual arts in the entire English Renaissance; with the possible exception of the Banqueting House on the feast day of St George, when the ceiling by Rubens framed within gilded caissons was complemented below by Mortlake tapestries copied from the Cartoons of Raphael.[6] In the Henry VII Chapel, Tudor dignitaries had known something very different but no less splendid. The gilt-bronze effigies of Henry and Elizabeth were placed behind but in alignment with the great columned high altar designed and executed by Torrigiano, probably in the winter of 1519–20, and destroyed by Parliament in 1644, while chapel walls rose like jewelled cliff faces; niche upon niche housing stone statuettes, not only of familiar evangelists and doctors of the church, but also remote Breton and Celtic saints to whom Henry had prayed in exile in France. Their features would have been difficult to pick out because the windows ran off in planes and angles; a faceted screen 'glased, with Stores, Ymagies, Armes, Bagies and Cognoissaunts [cognisants]' ablaze with colours of smalt and carbuncle.

The Henry VII Chapel now appears a mutilated but great national treasure. To the Renaissance it was an active constituent of royal propaganda. The point was made by the leading philosopher of early seventeenth-century England, Sir Francis Bacon. Bacon wrote a life of Henry VII; leaving the subject of his biography to live on through means of his tomb:

> he was born at Pembroke Castle, and lieth buried at Westminster in one of the stateliest and daintiest monuments of Europe, both for the chapel

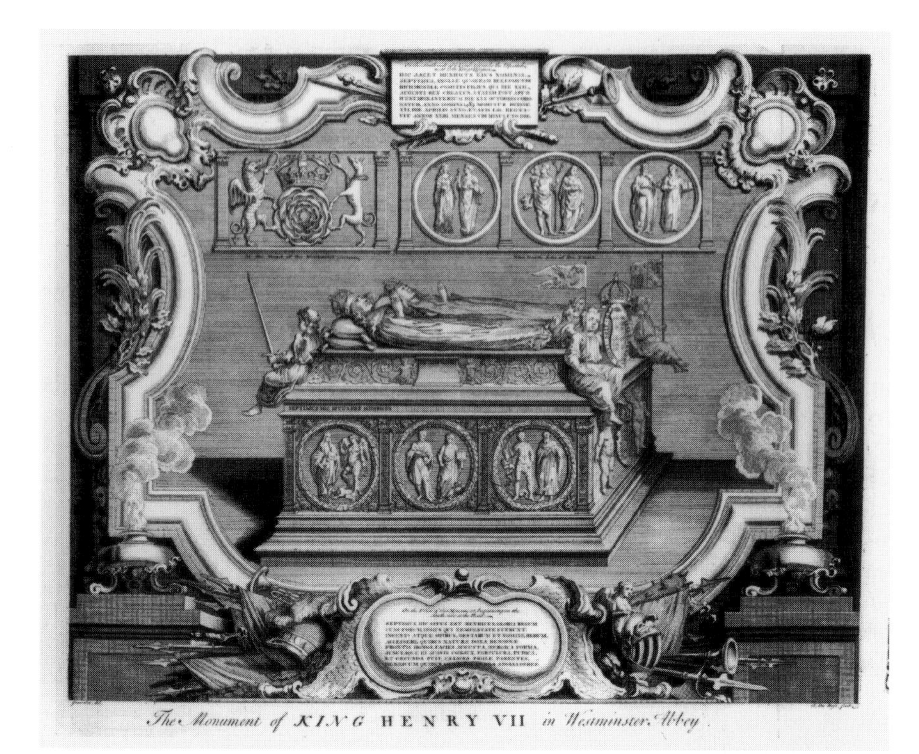

Detail of Pietro Torrigiano, *Tomb of Henry VII and Elizabeth of York*, 1512–19 (Society of Antiquaries of London)

> and for the sepulchre. So that he dwelleth more richly dead, in the monument of his tomb, than he did alive in Richmond or any of his palaces, I could wish he did the like in this monument of his fame.[7]

Shakespeare preferred print to marble as a means to eternity, but his contemporary Bacon, an exceptional mind if in a different sphere, evidently believed that the tomb was the key to a vital reputation.

Henry VIII was a monster of egotism and predictably he wanted a tomb of gargantuan proportions. Matters began within some bounds of decorum, but as the years passed, the project became swollen and corrupt like the body of the king himself. On 5 January 1519 a form of indenture was drawn up on behalf of Henry VIII and Torrigiano in which it was agreed Torrigiano would make a tomb of white marble and black touchstone with effigies of Henry and Catherine of Aragon. Torrigiano was to arrange to have a model delivered within a specified number of months. The tomb would be completed in less than four years and should not cost more than £2,000. Torrigiano would be told where it was to be placed.[8]

Although Henry VIII had clear ideas about what he wanted, Cardinal

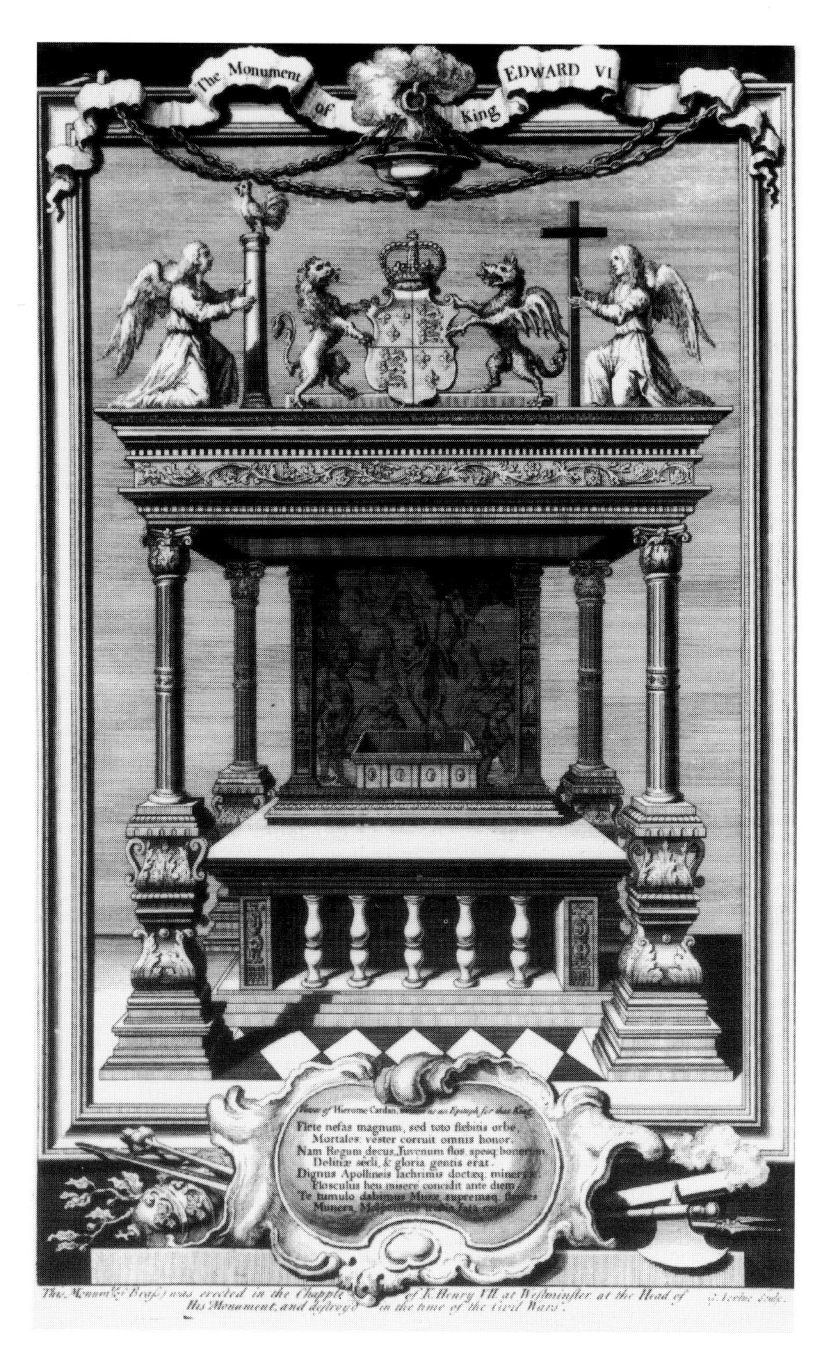

Pietro Torrigiano, *High altar, Henry VII Chapel, Westminster Abbey, c.* 1520–3; destroyed 1644 (Society of Antiquaries of London)

Wolsey was to act as surrogate patron: expected to interpret the wishes of the king to the artist, the difficulties of the artist to the king. Wolsey was by then at the climax of his career. He was responsible for bringing Europe to England to draw up a universal peace, The Treaty of London. Although that peace did not last, it then looked as if Wolsey had pulled off one of the greatest diplomatic triumphs of Renaissance Europe. He guided and manipulated the king in politics; it was natural therefore to entrust him with the posthumous reputation of his master through the creation of a suitable monument. As a member of the Curia, he might be expected to have had access to good advice about Italian style, and he was well on with his prodigious building programmes at Whitehall and Hampton Court; palaces which were to add immeasurably to the prestige of the monarchy. At this moment, the Roman Church in England appeared to many as an institution capable of reformation and Wolsey as the most splendid cardinal in its history. He was the obvious person to oversee the tomb of Henry VIII.

Henry VIII had his own views too; of which the most decided was a wish to better his father. Consequently it was specified that the tomb was to be 'one-fourth larger than that which he [Torrigiano] has already made for Henry VII'. Evidently competitiveness between father and son continued into the after-life; suggesting perhaps that Henry VIII may have been less concerned with his rivals Charles V and Francis I than with his father. Could it also be that the Holbein mural in Whitehall Palace may actually have been a challenge to some earlier, now vanished, wall-painting of Henry VII and perhaps Henry VI, whose memory the first of the Tudors had always revered?

Henry VIII wanted Torrigiano for his tomb but the sculptor left England to die in Spain in 1528. There then followed a move which provides one of the great ironies in the troubled history of Anglo-Papal relations. In November 1521 Pope Leo X was shown a model which he had commissioned from the sculptor Baccio Bandinelli as the basis for a tomb for Henry VIII; compliment and reward for Henry's appearance on the battlefield of religious controversy. Henry VIII had written against the Lutherans and so acquired the title 'Defender of The Faith' for his support of orthodoxy in the face of Martin Luther's attacks.

Bandinelli was second only to Michelangelo as a famous sculptor and what he envisaged for Henry was truly astonishing. For scale, allegory, symbolism and function, there would have been nothing to come near it in the whole history of English sculpture until the opening of the Albert Memorial in Hyde Park in 1872. Bandinelli intended one hundred and thirty-six statues, forty-four panels of bronze, and Henry himself triumphing over his own mortality mounted on a horse.

The Bandinelli project, like Michelangelo's celebrated tomb for Julius II, came to nothing; the only surviving evidence, a set of four giant bronze candlesticks bought by Ghent Cathedral at the sale of The Royal collection during the Commonwealth. However, it is possible to get a sense of the intended effect from a comment by John Speed, the famous map-maker. Speed noted various disembodied pieces of bronze lying about Elizabethan workshops like gigantic pieces of industrial machinery in a breaker's yard. Speed remarked that the King was to be recumbent, together with his Queen, 'not as death, but as persons sleeping, because to shew that famous Princes leauing behinde thm great fame, their names neuer doe die, and shall lie in roiall Apparels after the antique manner . . .'.[9] Speed suggests that the vision of life in death such as Henry VII procured and his son essayed was emphatically a vital ingredient in the posthumous fame of the monarchy.

Henry VII obtained a great tomb, Henry VIII aspired to a greater, but Elizabeth I was not interested in composing an autobiography in bronze. Her permanent commemoration had to wait until the arrival of a new dynasty and the accession of James I, who set about paying respects to the person to whom he owed his second crown as soon as he got it.

The combination of sarcophagus, effigy and *baldacchino* which James approved for Elizabeth I provoked the observation that 'truly, the monument is a permanent memorial of the funeral'. Permanency was a crucial aspect of the ritual of death. Death had to be mocked, life packaged as a triumph. This was sometimes achieved by making the recumbent effigy appear as if merely resting, as with Elizabeth I in Westminster Abbey, or better still, in heroic action as had been intended for Henry VIII at Windsor. The permanent celebration of the funeral through the creation of a 'living' portrait of the deceased, served to reinforce the legend surrounding the departed as it recalled the glories of one who could have provoked such a sumptuous ceremony of departure.

But why did Elizabeth I take little thought for the next world when she came to believe so wholeheartedly in her own propaganda and in her reign as peculiarly glorious? Surely there was every reason for her to have set about a great tomb for herself? We know of her neurotic fear of being painted as an ageing woman; perhaps then she could not face the prospect of her own extinction. She was too acutely aware that with her death, not only her own glories but the glories of her house would pass away. Quite simply she may have turned her back on these disturbing thoughts. She had too a fixed temperamental objection to spending money on lavish display; she contributed exceptionally little to the history of palace architecture in what was one of the longest reigns in English history. But whilst she took little thought for her bones while complimenting her flesh with a legendary wardrobe, she became deeply interested in some tombs of her Yorkist ancestors. These were royal tombs and they have a bearing on what the tomb meant to the Tudor mind.

In 1573 Elizabeth ordered new tombs for Yorkist ancestors at Fotheringhay where her cousin Mary, Queen of Scots, would be executed fourteen years later. The Fotheringhay tombs contained the bodies of Edward, 2nd

Duke of York, and his nephew Richard, 3rd Duke of York. The two had been buried in the choir of what had been one of the most splendid collegiate churches in England, founded by Edmund of Langley, Duke of York, at the beginning of the fifteenth century. Elizabeth had visited the site and noted the desecration of the tombs which had taken place during the iconoclastic scourge of her brother's reign. She ordered new tombs: though her habitual love of economy prevailed if William Camden is to be believed. Camden wrote in his *Britannia* of how the tombs 'are look'd upon as very mean, and unworthy such great Princes descended from Kings, and from whom the kings of England are descended'.[10] Whatever the limitations of the tombs themselves, what can be seen today in the truncated remains of a once great collegiate church, accords with Elizabeth's sentiments about respect for the dead.

Elizabeth's avowed respect for the dead does not however wholly account for why she became interested in clearing up the debris at Fotheringhay. In order to explain this it is necessary to look further back and into dealings between the English and the Scots in the Middle Ages. Long before Fotheringhay came to be favoured by Yorkists in the fifteenth century, it had been associated with the royal house of Scotland. David I, who became King of Scotland in 1124, had six hides of land at Fotheringhay, while the manor remained an asset of the Scots until Edward I seized the English lands of John Baliol in 1294. All this may seem arcane antiquarianism; hardly something with which Elizabeth I would have been concerned. However, at this juncture, the figure of Mary, Queen of Scots, enters the story and for Elizabeth, her cousin was a living threat not merely an interesting historical relict from a remote past.

A pedigree still exists 'tracing the descent of Mary Queen of Scots, now married to Lord Darnley, from Richard Plantagenet, Duke of York, and placing her in close proximity to the crown of England'.[11] It is dated 15 August 1565: a fortnight after Mary had married Darnley, and ten months before she gave birth to the future James VI and I. Could it be that the combination of the Scottish association with Fotheringhay, an association with that place older even than Elizabeth's Yorkist ancestors, Mary's rival kinship with the house of York and specifically with Richard, Duke of York, whose burial place was Fotheringhay, and finally her provocative if legitimate claim to proximity to the English crown through the Yorkist line, provided a strong incentive for Elizabeth to 'capture' a shrine for the English monarchy in defiance of a long-standing historical association with the royal house of Scotland? Could it also be that Fotheringhay was chosen as a prison for Mary because it lay at the centre of lands which had once belonged to the Scottish crown? By imprisoning Mary at the centre of what had been a significant holding of English land by the Scottish crown, Elizabeth hoped to negate symbolically the threat that her very existence presented to the stability of the Tudor regime.

There never was a grand tomb for James I; though the Banqueting

House was a kind of cenotaph. We should perhaps look on that chamber as a princely and magnificent funerary casket containing not the ashes, but the spirit of James, Prince of Peace, and God's Lieutenant upon Earth. The 1625 sets of proposals for allegories to be painted by Rubens for the ceiling, to which reference was made earlier, suggest that it was James' death in that year which gave new impetus to the project. The death of James I in March 1625 was a further stimulant for Charles I to use the world's greatest painter to extend the funerary rites of his father into permanent apotheosis. Surely there can never have been a more flattering tribute to past achievements nor a more optimistic prophecy of future happiness than Rubens' contribution to the passing of the first sovereign of the British Isles. Henry VII had exploited three dimensions in the devising of his own mortuary chapel, but Rubens succeeded in drawing heaven down to earth in tribute to a king who had thought himself divine in a way in which even Henry VIII would never have dared. The Banqueting House is the final solution to the burial of kings. Death has died. What is left is moral example of the timeless virtues of the monarch. These act as proof and evidence for the deification, if not sanctification, of a monarch whose ascent provides the final act of the drama, and the centrepiece of the architecture.

James I, like Elizabeth, gave no thought to his own tomb because his self-fashioning departure precluded it. James was careful to ensure that his corpse should be interred with that of Henry VII who lay with his wife Elizabeth of York.

Where precisely James was buried had been one of the great mysteries of the Abbey until its nineteenth-century historian, Dean Stanley, solved it on 11 February 1869. Stanley had obtained permission from the highest authorities to undertake the search. The Dean rifled through vaults and coffins under the Abbey floor to discover many famous men but not James alas, who still remained unaccounted for. Now there was only the vault of Henry VII itself. After some initial reluctance prompted by the thought of disturbing the tomb of the founder of the great royal mausoleum which towered above, Stanley set to work; accompanied by Sir Giles Gilbert Scott, architect to the Abbey and in Ruskin's view, architect of the destruction of the English Medieval heritage. Summoning up the sort of resolution encountered in *King Solomon's Mines*, Stanley and Scott broke through the wall into the final resting place of Henry Tudor.

The party found Elizabeth of York flanked by Henry VII to the right and James VI and I to the left. It was a sensational discovery. Important enough Stanley thought, to justify rushing out a third edition of his highly successful *Historical Memorials of Westminster Abbey*, which appeared in this same year of 1869. The odyssey, for so the discovery was, is recorded in the form of a gripping appendix of thirty-six pages. The story is made the more lugubrious by the inclusion of a print of the vault as it had appeared to the eyes of the Dean and his party on that February morning and which had stayed sealed since James had been deposited in it in 1625; the remains as the artist has taken them, look curiously like Henry Moore's bodies of Londoners sleeping in the Underground during the Blitz. Henry's body had been placed in a vault beneath and behind the actual Torrigiano monument and it was there the two kings came to rest. It is tempting to believe that James ordained this mortal encounter, because he was mindful that he, like his forebear with whom his ashes were to mingle, had preceded him in founding a new dynasty; though Henry was of course Welsh and he, James, of Scottish descent.

Bedding down with Henry VII meant that there could be no tomb for James without removing what had been ordained for the first Tudor king. That was not on, since Henry had created a new and splendid royal mausoleum which would be desecrated if its centrepiece – the tomb of the founder himself – was wantonly destroyed.

James VI and I was a shuttlecock; forever batted between personalities more dominant than his own. As a child he was carried from castle to castle; as a man, concerned to please not to command favourites. An early problem for James was how best to pay respects to his mother and also to her cousin Elizabeth I, who despite ordering Mary's death, had given him the English crown. It was a dilemma and it was typical of how James seemed fated to reconcile the irreconcilable. Faced with these circumstances, it comes as no surprise that James constantly played on that central theme of the Sermon on the Mount: 'Blessed are the Peacemakers'.

Westminster Abbey became the shroud to cover the horror of the execution of one sovereign by another. James I had always found the promise of the English crown more compelling than his disastrous mother, or a wasted homeland, and he set about the erection of a tomb to Elizabeth before turning to the rehabilitation of his mother's reputation. It was politic to honour the sovereign of a people in whose capital he had come to reside. Accordingly work on a tomb for Elizabeth began soon after she had died; Maximilian Colt, the designer, completing the eight-columned monument by 1606, at a price of £765. The tomb was engraved and through this means she came to be buried in parish churches all over the land; as the seventeenth-century historian of the English church Thomas Fuller pointed out in his *Church History* of 1655:

> of the lively draught of it, pictured in every London and in most country churches, every parish being proud of the shade of her tomb; and no wonder, when each loyal subject created a mournful monument for her in his heart.[12]

Thereafter it was the turn of Mary. Work began in January 1607 with instructions from James which spoke of 'our late deerest mother of famous memory'.[13] But since James had last set eyes on her when less than a year old, this was an exercise for public consumption, not an

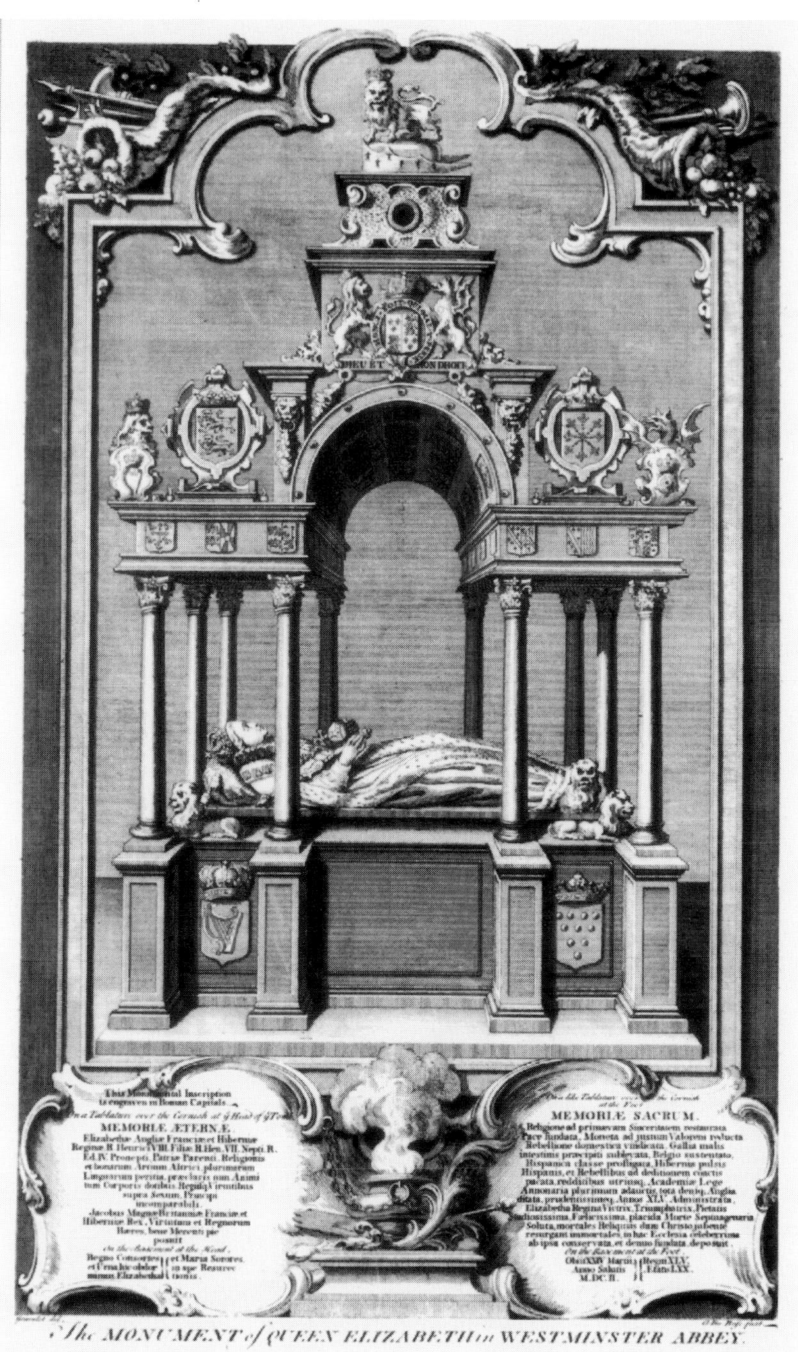

Maximilian Colt, *Tomb of Elizabeth I*, finished 1606, Henry VII Chapel, Westminster Abbey (Society of Antiquaries of London)

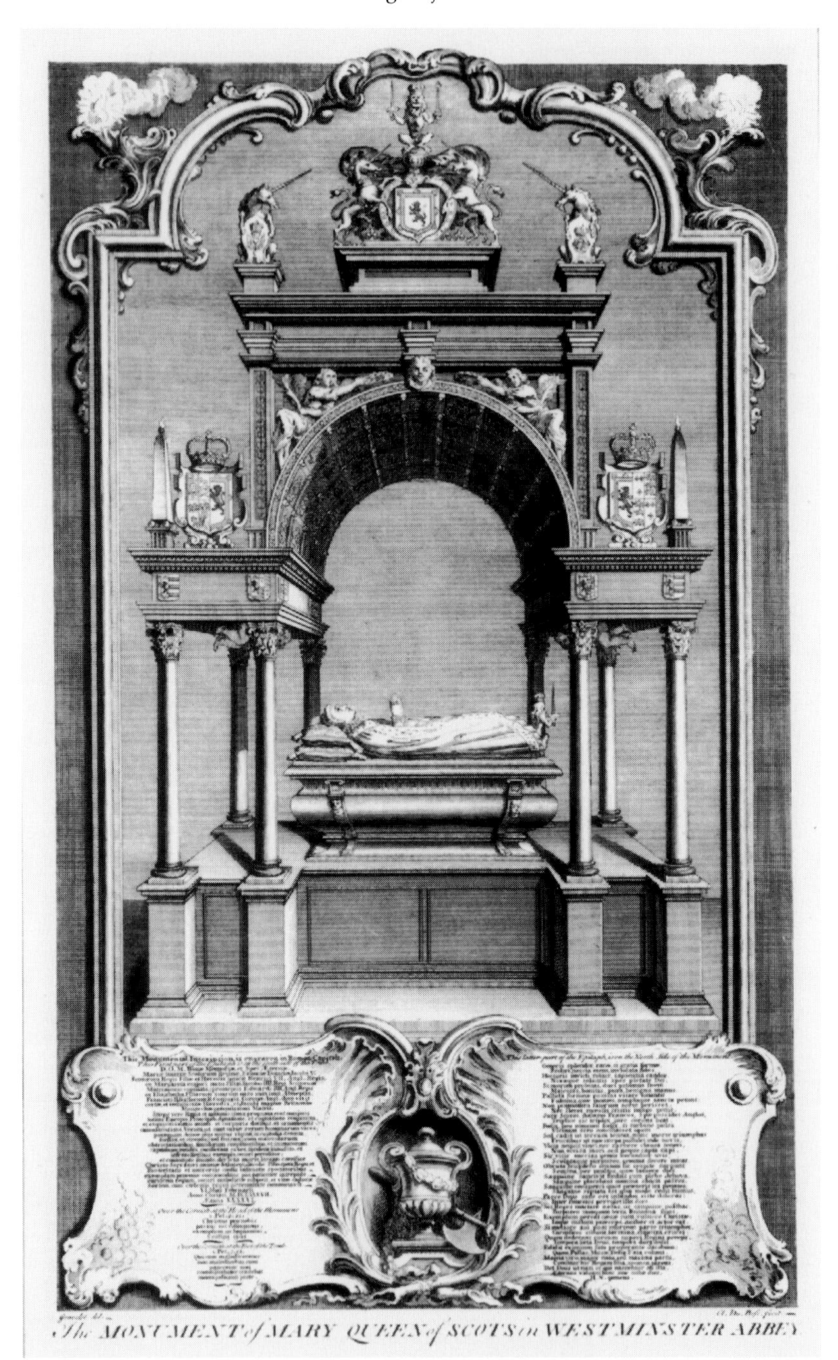

Cornelius Cure and William Cure II, *Tomb of Mary Queen of Scots*, 1607–12, Henry VII Chapel, Westminster Abbey (Society of Antiquaries of London)

expression of personal feeling. James used the translation of his mother's remains from Peterborough to make the point that killing the monarch was a bad thing. However, many English kings and queens were buried outside London. Peterborough may only have been an Henrician see, but William Rufus lay at Winchester, King John at Worcester. Thus a cathedral was a perfectly dignified setting for royalty. Therefore James cannot have been prompted to undertake the reburial of his mother because he felt the original location of her grave too mean. What James may have thought however, and no one had studied his Tudor credentials to the English throne more thoroughly than he, was that he would elevate the memory and reputation of his mother by having Mary Queen of Scots buried in Westminster Abbey, just as Henry VII, from whom his claim stemmed, had commemorated his own mother Lady Margaret Beaufort, with a most splendid Renaissance tomb by Torrigiano also in the Abbey.

Whatever James's thinking, his thoughts were transformed into the permanent façade of a great Renaissance tomb, moving in its sense of purity and peace. The recumbent effigy of Mary with her hands raised in prayer was carved in marble and set upon a black touchstone sarcophagus; the marble in its incandescent whiteness, seemingly illuminated from within; the whole body, not merely the head, emanating an aura of sanctity. Cornelius Cure, the contractor for the tomb, and his son William Cure II who appears to have accomplished most of it, played an ace. The Cures present Mary as a nun-like lady of purity and sanctity; helpless victim of forces beyond her control. It was a masterly readjustment and the means by which her reputation became as immoveable as the monument itself. Mary was duplicitous, volatile, sexually promiscuous, the centre of high political intrigue; equalled as a disaster among female rulers by her contemporary Catherine de' Medici. But whatever the reality, the truth has been of little effect on historians, painters or composers; all men and all seduced by a Scottish enchantress. The image of the helpless woman – of Andromeda clothed – became a favourite of the Victorian history painter in search of melodrama; the most famous, Robert Herdman's *Execution of Mary Queen of Scots* of 1867. A beautiful woman, long and elegant as the silver birch, glides noiselessly to her martyrdom as she is observed by the masculine world of the Tudor court disarmed by her Christian fortitude and it must be said, her physical charms. Herdman took the iconography of the *Presentation of the Virgin* as his starting point. That was an allusion which would have pleased Mary; though it was eloquent testament also to how myth substitutes for history in image-making; in her case, a myth begun by her son and his masterly sculptors, in Westminster Abbey twenty years after her death.

James laid ghosts as he laid Elizabeth and Mary in precise symmetry either side of the Henry VII Chapel. A Victorian historian of the Abbey pointed out that 'the tomb [of Mary] was raised opposite like [the tomb of Elizabeth], but on a grander scale, as if to indicate the superiority of the

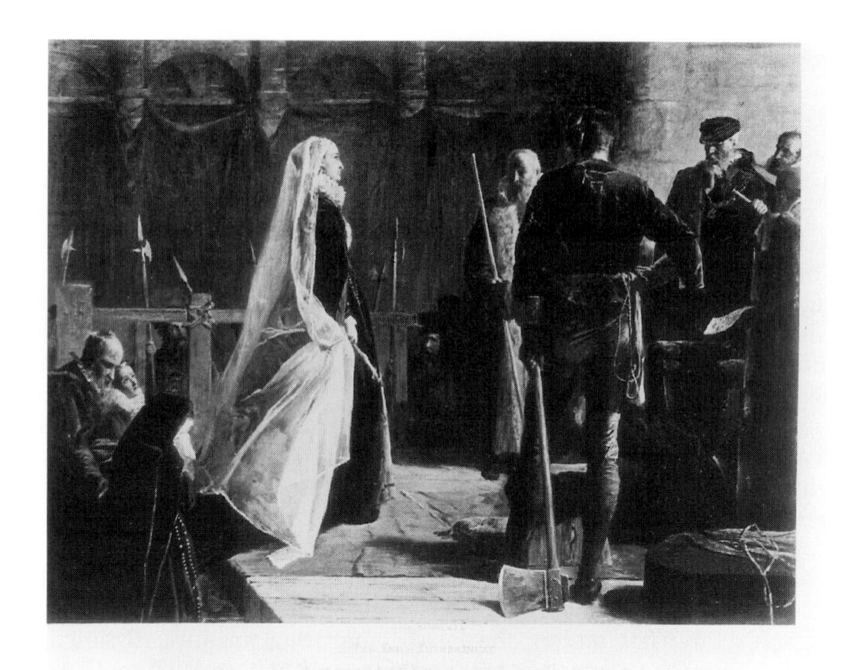

Robert Herdman, *Execution of Mary Queen of Scots*, 1867 (Joe Rock)

mother to the predecessor, of the victim to the vanquisher'.[14] Though the queens had never agreed during their lives, the new monarch made them lie close in the peace of death. It was the greatest diplomatic triumph in the history of the royal funerary monument. Such a reconciliation in marble which had evaded the cousins in their lifetime was symbol too of a larger reconciliation; of that miracle of abiding mutual toleration between the two nations since the union under James VI and I himself. Nowhere in Europe has there been a history in which the sovereign of one nation, judicially murdered by another, came to be rehabilitated so soon after the event in the country which had done her to death.

While the monument to Elizabeth was nearing completion, James ordered further monuments. These were to commemorate his daughters, the Princesses Sophia and Mary, who had died when three days and two years old respectively. Although James had already accorded the same honours to Robert, a son who had died in Scotland and had been interred in Dunfermline Abbey, the site of Royal burials in that kingdom, the making of tombs for the royal princesses at Westminster was part of the process of knocking on the door of the English royal burial chamber.

Writing of the tomb of Princess Sophia, Pevsner remarked on 'the questionable conceit of an alabaster cradle, accurately portrayed with its

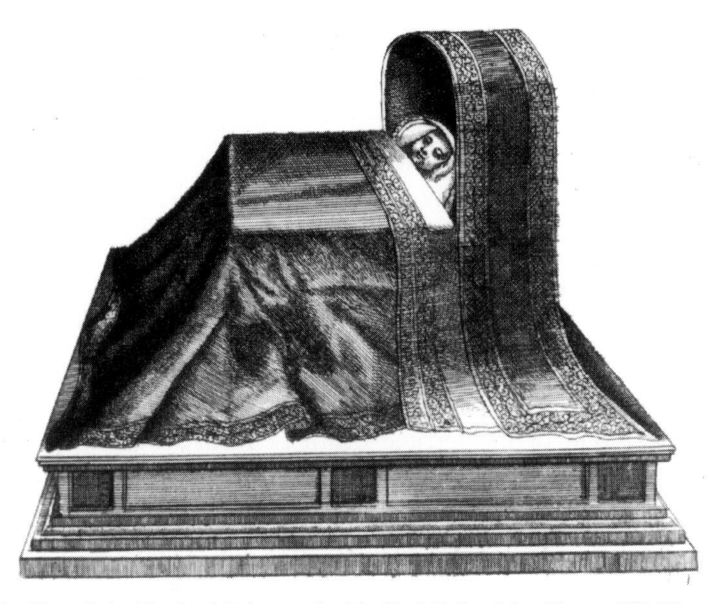

Maximilian Colt, *Tomb of Princess Sophia* (d. 1606), aisle, Henry VII Chapel, Westminster Abbey (Society of Antiquaries of London)

embroidered velvet cover'.[15] The visitor peeps into the arch of the cradle to see a pair of tiny hands laid out on an embroidered velvet coverlet, only to be startled seconds later by awareness of the puckered head of a child. It is a ghoulish intrusion from a palace nursery; not something to be expected in the mausoleum of kings. It is a premonition of a Victorian attitude to death, and indeed Jacobean taste would appeal powerfully to the Victorians whose fusion of their own style with that of the Jacobean evolved into the blowsy hybrid known as the 'Jacobethan'. But whatever impression the tomb of Princess Sophia made on the visitor to Westminster Abbey in 1610 – by then the building was a major tourist attraction, for the father of English historical studies William Camden had published the epitaphs in the Abbey in 1600[16] – its novelty gave it a significance out of all proportion to the personality and status of the child. James I wanted to leave his signature in the shrine of English kingship, early in the life of the new dynasty; a building in which to identify the new regime with the old; to reconcile former enemies by mingling the two houses of Tudor and Stuart in sleeping marble.

Such possibilities appear however to be flatly contradicted by James's failure to provide a permanent memorial to the life and death of his eldest surviving son. Henry, Prince of Wales, died in November 1612. The catastrophe was the greatest shock he had to bear.

Universal and engulfing grief was discharged over the hearse of the Prince during a prodigious funeral in the Abbey. It was a performance which left all profoundly moved. Sir Isaac Wake, a future Secretary of State, wrote to Lady Carleton:

> vnder that [canopy] laye the goodly image of that lovely prince clothed with the ritchest garments he had, which did so liuely represent his person, as that it did not onely draw teares from the severest beholder, but cawsed a fearefull outcrie among the people as if they felt at the present theire owne ruine in that loss. I must confess never to have seen such a sight of mortification in my life, nor neuer so iust a sorrowe so well expressed as in all the spectators whose streaming eyes made knowen howe much inwardly their harts did bleed.[17]

This is language of a religious experience: of an intensity anticipating Evelyn's description of the terrible death of Henry's younger brother Charles I, nearly forty years later. The high-pitched strain of Prince Henry's internment was perhaps all that James could cope with nervously and emotionally. Certainly the King was too overcome with grief to attend the funeral service, and the key to his feelings about how to come to terms with the thought of what might have been may lie in the epitaph by George Chapman attached to William Hole's engraving of the Prince's hearse. In a few condensed lines, Chapman offers tribute to a life well led, key to a bewildering death, and hope for the future:

> Whome all the vast fframe of the fixed Earth
> Shrunck under: now, a weake Herse stade beried
> His fatte he past in fact; in Hope his Birthe;
> His Youth ïn good life: & in Spirritt his Death

But although Prince Henry was never given a great tomb, the imagery of his catafalque lived on. Recently it has been demonstrated that the Hole engraving of the Prince's hearse was faithfully copied in 1646 for the exceptionally splendid ceremonial used in the funeral of Robert Devereux, 3rd Earl of Essex, Lord General of Parliament 1642–5.[18] The reason Parliamentarians turned to Henry's 1612 catafalque, it has been argued, was because Henry had been a martial type who would have dedicated himself to the defence of true religion if he had been spared. For his part, Essex, direct descendant of the famous Elizabethan scourge of the Spanish, had been the archetype of those who had gone to war to save the King from his enemies. A secondary reason for turning to a Jacobean model in the Commonwealth era was because 'Such archaic chivalric ritual was also an appeal to the imagination: to order and rationalise the traumatic and dislocated politics of 1646 by an act of relocation in the past; in the romanticised heroic age of Prince Henry.'[19]

Such resonances between the deaths of two heroes, one remembered through the promise of true Christian warfare, the other for its prosecution,

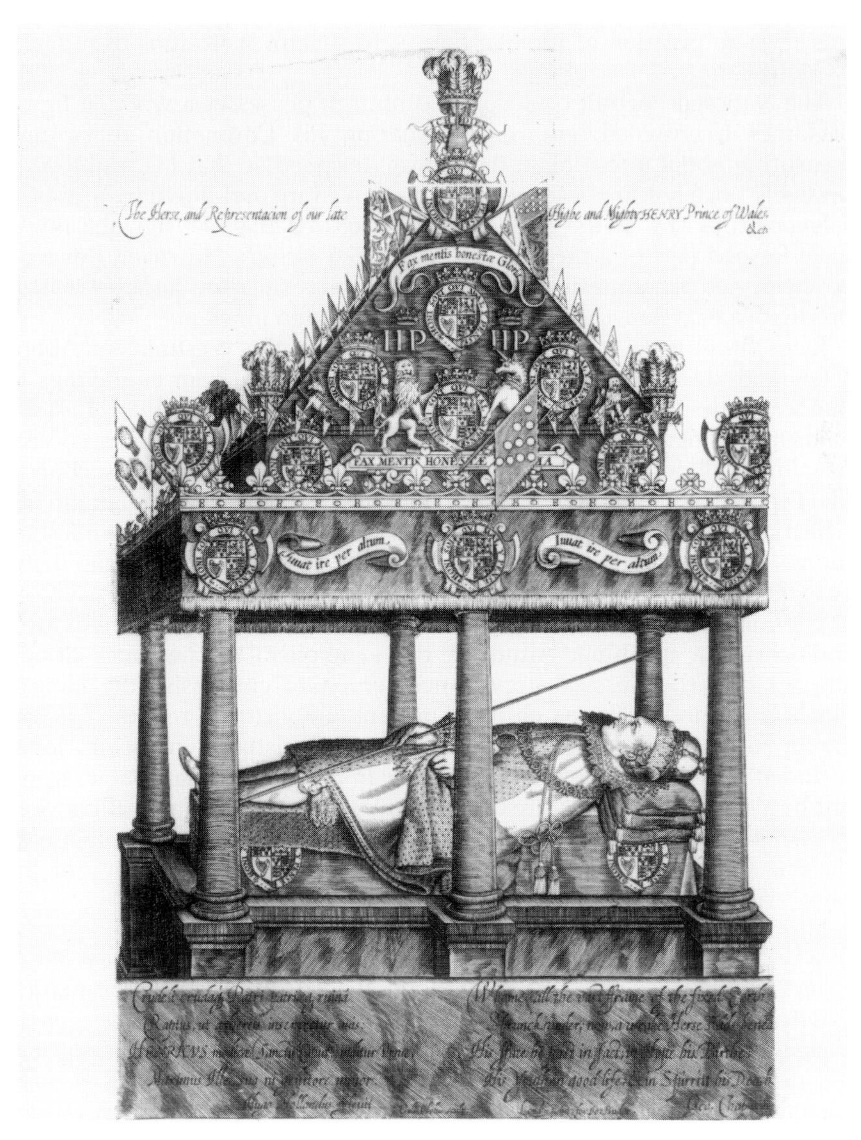

William Hole, *Hearse of Henry, Prince of Wales*, 1612–13 (British Museum)

shows the imagery of death to have been a versatile instrument. People looked to the dead for many reasons: to define their achievements; to locate themselves in history; to substitute for the invocation of the saints of the old Catholic world. Indeed there was much about the passage from this world to remind the Jacobean traveller of the sort of frumperies he often encountered at Loretto or Naples; Punch and Judy shows involving unseen manipulation of life-like figures to sustain the claims of miracle-working saints.

The National Portrait Gallery in Edinburgh possesses a wooden figure of James I, crowned, enthroned, wearing his Coronation robes, and measuring about a foot high; the figure 'designed so that his [right] arm, probably once holding a sceptre, can be moved up and down by means of a lever projecting at the back'. It is conjectured that the figurine might have formed part of a mechanical device like a clock. However, this may be connected in some way with the funerary rites for James. On that prodigious occasion, the Angel of Death was Inigo Jones.

Jones drew up a justly celebrated design for the Westminster Abbey catafalque, derived from a fusion of elements taken from engravings of the tempietto-catafalques of recently dead Popes: Sixtus V of 1591 by Domenico Fontana, and Sergio Venturi's for Paul V, of 1623. Fontana, Venturi, Jones, all depended on a common source: Palladio's reconstruction of the Temple of Vesta at Tivoli as illustrated in his *I Quattro Libri*.[20] But whilst the template may have been taken from the lost realm of antiquity, servers at the funeral would have been confronted not with a pagan deity, but with Colt's startling, staring effigy of James as if still alive.[21]

The contrivance was a subtle and complex interweaving of pagan form and Christian meaning. Although the symbolism of the Jones design stresses that the classical appearance served to emphasise the idea of James 'as a modern monarch in whom antique virtue is reborn',[22] it was also a subtle interplay between pagan and Christian symbolism. Jones included allegories of Religion and Peace in the guise of classical matrons, but he also gave the structure a theistic gloss. He drew a parallel between the tabernacle in which the host was reserved, and the royal catafalque; the one preserving the eucharist, the other presenting the effigy of the Lord's Anointed.

For that effigy, The Exchequer disbursed £56/3s/4d to:

> Maximilian Colte Carver for makeinge the body for the Representation wth severall Joynts in the Armes legges and body to be moved to severall postures, the face and hands thereof beinge curiously wroughte wth settinge upp the same in Westminster Abbey and for another Representation suddenly to serve at Denmark house wth a plate of Copper and an Inscription fastened to the brest of the leaden Coffin a Crowne of wood and a Lyon uppon it for his Ma^{te} Crest a Sheild wth his Ma^{te} Armes, a garter comptment and a Crowne uppon it, a Scepter and a Cloake a Crowne wth diverse Counterfett Stones uppon it and a better Crowne the former beinge broken wth often removeinge.[23]

An army of acolytes served this temple of death: Danyell Parke receiving £20 for 'twoe Periwiggs Beardes and eyebrowes for the Bodies the one at Denmark house and the other at the Abbey at Westminster'; the painter

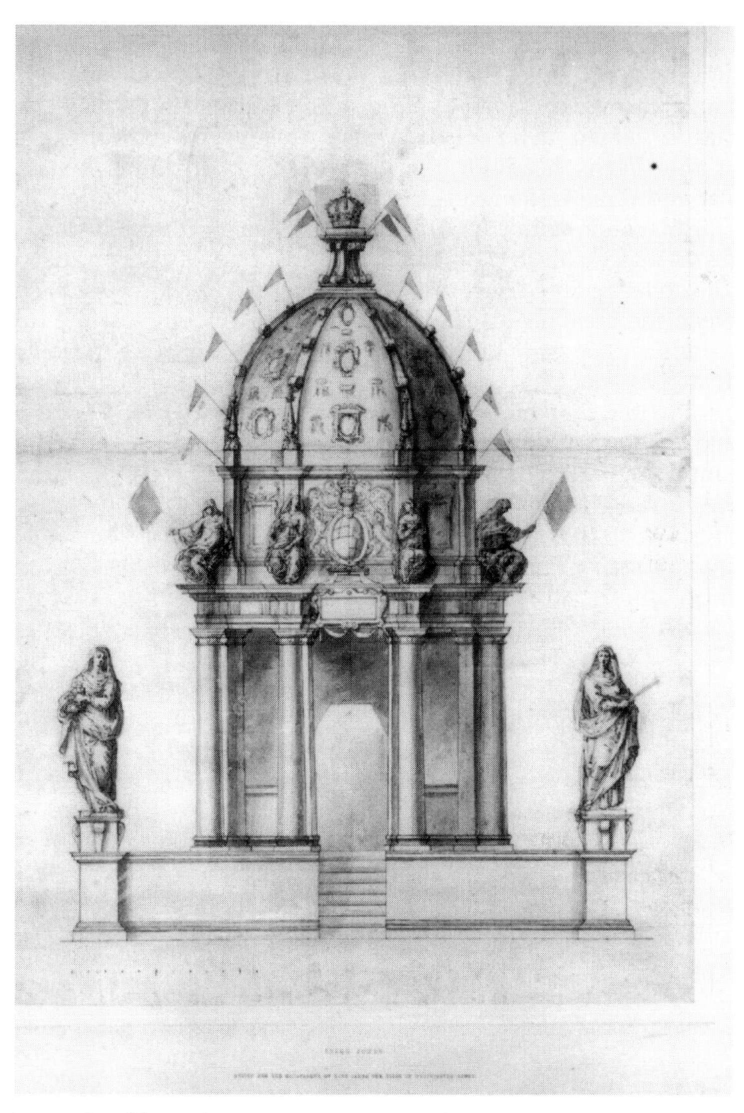

Inigo Jones, *Catafalque of James I*, 1625, pen and brown ink with grey wash over graphite and scorelines (Courtauld Institute of Art/The Provost and Fellows of Worcester College, Oxford)

Jan de Critz, £138/10s for painting and gilding 'a great hatchment for the gate at Denmark House' and 'The great Armes w[ch] hung over the Alter [of Westminster Abbey] bannerolles and Scutcheons burnishing helmet and gauntlets etc'.

Such illusionism now seems macabre and distasteful, but to the

Jacobean mourner it was a vital aspect of involvement. Provisions made for the funeral of James I were not unusual. Anne of Denmark had received an elaborate ceremony at her death in 1619 when Daniel Danbrooke was paid for taking 'diverse Parris heads and Attyres wth their furnitures viz for one Parris head for the Countesse of Arrundell beinge chief Mourner and three white heads for three Gentlewomen hir Attendants . . . Parris heads and so many Tippetts wth their furniture for so many Countesses and for their Gentlewomen attendinge'. It was an easy transition from collecting the finger of a saint to preserving the face of a Queen.[24]

Between the creation of the monument to Elizabeth and the death of James, there was an urge to freeze the action of a funeral in the stillness of a tomb; a permanent record of the gloriously transient, not in rolls of film as now, but on cushions of alabaster. Maximilian Colt, who probably designed the tomb of Sir Francis Vere in Westminster Abbey, could have been simulating an actual interlude in the funeral; for this is an action image. A robed effigy of Sir Francis lies beneath a bier supported by four kneeling knights whose burden is made heavier by sustaining armour formerly worn by Sir Francis in his profession of arms. Breast-plate, helmet, gauntlets, all lie disjointed like some monstrous, disembodied cockroach; anticipating the mechanistic arms from the effigy of James which Colt certainly assembled fifteen years later.

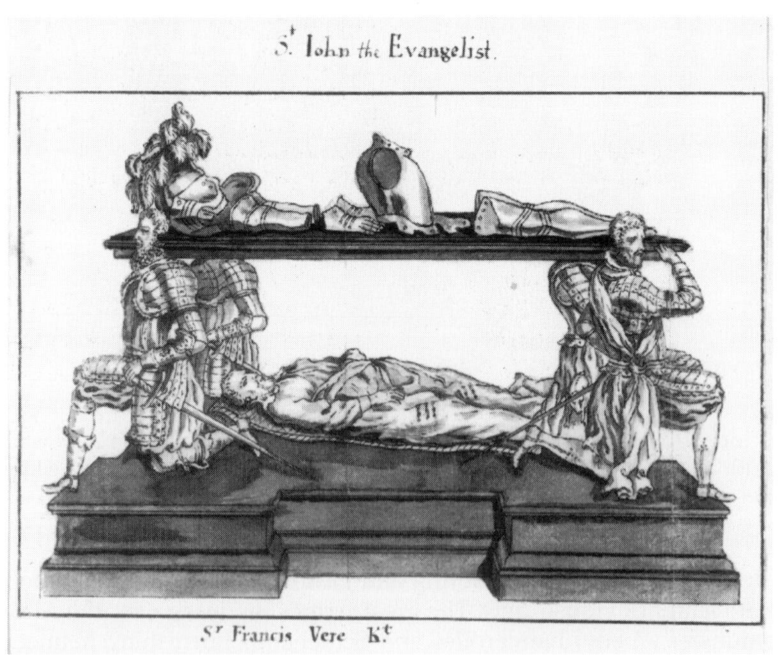

Maximilian Colt (attributed), *Tomb of Sir Francis Vere*, after 1609, Westminster Abbey (Society of Antiquaries of London)

The fantastic elaboration of state funerals suggests that if the staging was affecting enough, the building of a tomb was redundant. The coronation of a sovereign was not normally recorded for posterity; why should the burial, no less elaborate a ceremony, have had to be followed by a great tomb? No monuments arose from the obsequies of Prince Henry and James I; the most spectacular royal funerals of the century. With the former perhaps this was either because justice had been seen to have been done, or quite simply, the Exchequer was bankrupted in the process.

The funerals of Prince Henry and King James were profoundly moving and ruinously expensive. John Chamberlain, the most prolific Jacobean letter writer, relayed news of the funeral of James I to his correspondent of twenty years standing, Sir Dudley Carleton; shortly to be elevated to Secretary of State, but then marooned in the embassy at The Hague. Chamberlain wrote of how the funeral was 'the greatest indeed that ever was knowne in England, there beeing blacks distributed for above 9,000 persons, the herse likewise beeing the fairest and best fashioned that hath ben seen, wherin Inigo Jones the survayor did his part'. 'The whole charge', he added, 'is saide to arise above [£]50[,]000.'[25]

James could make no provision for a tomb and Charles seems to have had no interest in registering the fact that his father lay with the founder of the Tudor dynasty. Although it has already been remarked that James' decision as to what to do with himself precluded the possibility of a monument or cenatoph, he disappeared into the ground so effectively that his remains were only rediscovered in the nineteenth century. Charles's failure to signpost his father's mortal remains – the only practicable thing he could have done – may have had something to do with the fact that father and son had never been close. Possibly Charles I quickly became absorbed by the rather different commemoration of his father on the Banqueting House ceiling.

Whatever the truth, such a supposed dereliction of duty was commented upon unfavourably when Charles offered to pay for a tomb to commemorate Buckingham after his assassination in August 1628. Charles' advisers had to restrain him by arguing that what would appear to the world as the neglect of the one whilst promoting the other, would put the monarchy in a bad light.

Through exceptional gifts Buckingham had been able to make the seemingly impossible transition from lover of James I to inseparable companion of Charles I. No Englishman had managed to keep two kings enthralled as Buckingham had done. What Buckingham had meant to James I and Charles I, and his tragic end while preparing to put to sea in defence of England's honour, brought into being the grandest seventeenth-century tomb in England; comparable in size and ambition to the tomb of Henry VII which lay beyond its shadow.

Everything about the Buckingham tomb was exceptional. The Duchess of Buckingham was granted permission to have the tomb placed in

Henry VII's chapel. This was a unique privilege for one not of the blood royal, as John Weever reminded the court in his *Antient funerall Monuments*. Henry, so Charles I would have learned from Weever, had had confined views as to who was to have access to his sanctuary:

> [Henry built] that glorious fair chapel at Westminster, for an house of burial, for himself, his children, and such only of the blood royal, as should descend from his loins; forbidding that any other, of what degree or quality soever, should ever be interred in that sacred mould; as appears by his last will and testament.[26]

Could it be that Weever disapproved? Although Weever dedicated his book to Charles I, there was a well understood convention that a dedication did not preclude admonishment in any text which followed. The decision to put Buckingham within the royal mausoleum was not only a breach in the walls of the chapel, but a violation of the spirit of Henry VII's will and for this reason alone something Weever regretted. But then, in life Buckingham had broken into the reserved world not only of the Privy Chamber but even into the royal bed. Therefore there was a certain consistency that in death too, he should have his tomb thrust its way into the brittle vegetation of Henry VII's flamboyant Gothic mausoleum. Whether Weever was really admonishing the Crown it is impossible to say; though it is clear that Charles' closest advisers thought the issue a delicate one because Buckingham had been much hated by the time of his death.

Charles I intended to take charge of the Buckingham tomb but had been persuaded to leave off; not through any delicacy towards the feelings of a widow, but because he was advised people would murmur. Charles was told to abandon direct control by High Treasurer Portland, who would contrive a splendid tomb for himself in Winchester Cathedral a few years later. Portland 'told his majesty that not only our nation, but others, would talk of it, if he should make the duke a tomb, and not his father'.[27]

Before the king came to be persuaded to stay in the background, there had been an earlier tribute to Buckingham. This was the monument erected in St Peter's, Portsmouth; the church closest to the house where Buckingham had been assassinated in the summer of 1628. Buckingham's widow paid for a monument to the design of Nicholas Stone, formerly Master Mason at the Banqueting House, and the most talented sculptor then available in England. The heart was placed in the urn forming the centrepiece of the Stone monument, which was located at the east end of the church; traditionally the place of honour in any church because it was contingent to the altar and therefore to the administration of the Eucharist, the principal sacrament in Catholic and Protestant church alike.

The symbolism of the Portsmouth monument was enhanced at the same time with the placing of a bust of Charles I by Le Sueur on the Square Tower. The tower not only dominated the docks from which Buckingham had been about to sail when he was murdered, but also gave

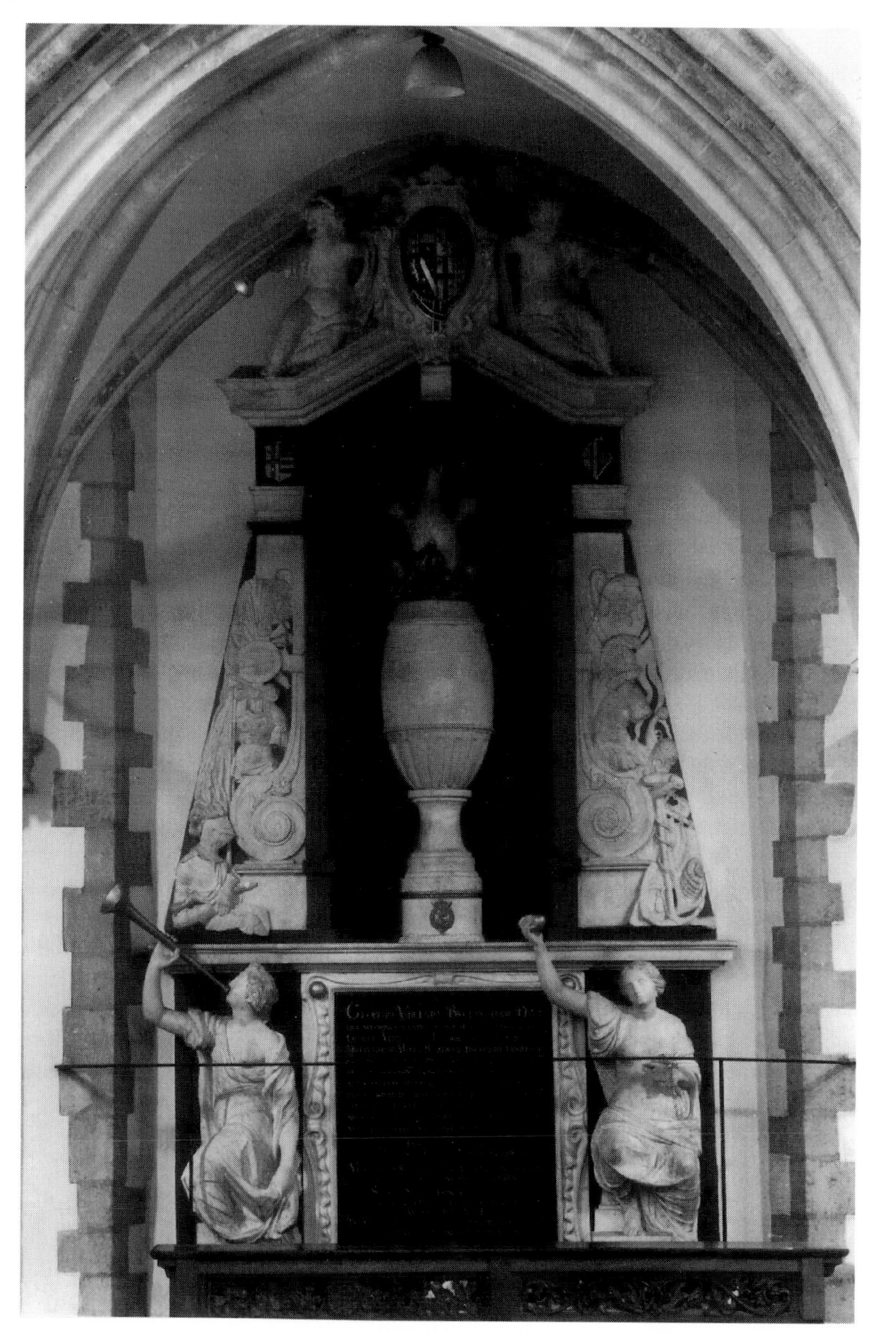

Nicholas Stone, *Monument to George Villiers, 1st Duke of Buckingham, c.* 1628–30, Portsmouth Cathedral (Courtauld Institute of Art)

a view onto the site of the assassination, and beyond to St Peter's itself. By placing his bust on a building with such a tragic perspective, Charles himself contemplated a *via dolorosa*; Charles became the constant companion of his friend, in death as he had been in life.[28] It will be recalled that images of sovereigns were taken as having summoned up the 'real presence'; the monarch was actually present in any particular location where his image rested. It was a point stressed in connection with the Portsmouth bust, by the military governor Viscount Wimbledon.

Charles also placed his bust on the Square Tower as a gesture of civic compliment to his most important garrison town. The Corporation were however, unwilling to make the necessary preparations for its honourable reception and so the installation went ahead without the presence of the civic dignitaries. But it appears that was not the end of friction. Five years later Wimbledon felt it necessary to give the town a stiff dressing-down for failing to respect the King's image. Wimbledon's peremptory letter merits transcription because it provides a unique insight into how people reacted to sculpture at the time:

> Mr Mayor and the rest of your brethen,
>
> Whereas at my last being in Portsmouth, I did recommend the beautifying of your streets by setting in the signs of your inns to the houses, as they are in all civilised towns, so now I must recommend it to you most earnestly in regard of his Majesties figure or statue, that it hath pleased his Majestie to honour your town with more than any others; so that those signs of your inns do not only obscure His Majestie's figure, but outface it, as you yourselfs may well perceive. Therefore I desire you all that you will see that such an inconveniency be not suffered, but that you will cause against the next spring that it be redressed, for that any disgrace offered His Majesties figure is as much as to himself. To which end I will and command all the officers and soldiers not to pass it without *putting off their hats*: I hope I shall need use no other authority to *make you do it*; for that it concerneth your obedience to have it done, especially now you are told of it by myself. Therefore I will say no more, but wish you all good health, and so rest your assured and loving friend.
>
> 22 October 1635 Wimbledon.[29]

It has recently been established that the tomb of the Duke and Duchess in Westminster Abbey was the collaborative effort of Hubert Le Sueur, who was responsible for the bronze work of the figural sculpture, and Isaac Besnier for the marble work, which consisted of sarcophagus, framing, inscriptions and subsidiary figures.[30] Something of its magnificence can be gauged from a splendid and unpublished drawing of it by the distinguished late seventeenth-century English artist Francis Barlow.

The skills of sculptor, herald, epigraphist, stage manager, and orator, all

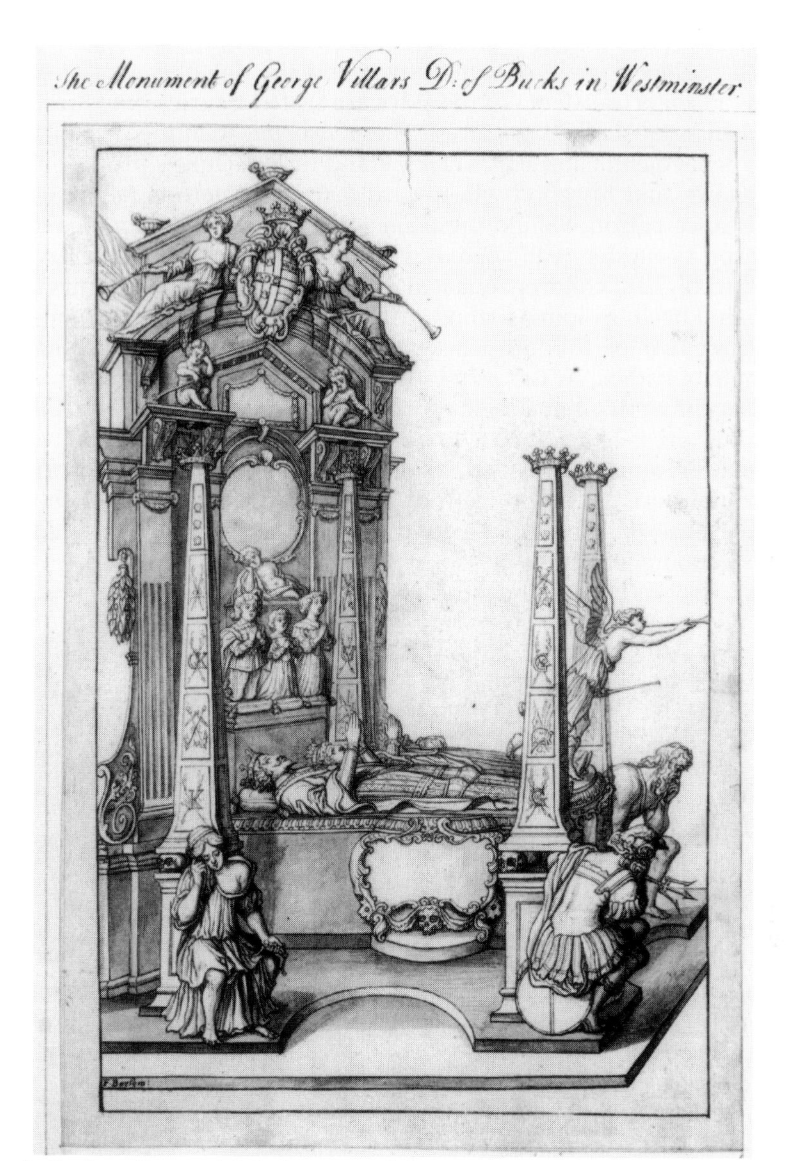

Francis Barlow, Pen and Ink drawing of the late 17th century, *Buckingham Tomb*, Henry VII Chapel, Westminster Abbey (design and marble carving by Isaac Besnier, bronze work by Hubert Le Sueur), 1630–4 (Society of Antiquaries of London)

were fused to make a monument as rich in allusions as it was in materials. The tomb consists of life-size effigies of the Duke and Duchess on a black touchstone sarcophagus bearing white marble tablets. At the corners, four obelisks rise; now less striking than before 'bronze ciphers and devices, as anchors, palm-branches, masks etc., in metal [were] stolen'. The obelisks rest on cushions made of skulls to remind the onlooker that at base all earthly glory is transient. To the sides are seated figures, heads resting on hands in grief-stricken gestures. These may be identified as: Neptune, Mars, Benevolentia and Pallas. They stand for the Duke's prowess in military affairs, and his good will toward learning; interests required of the Renaissance patron. Behind these allegorical figures rises an architectural backdrop as a tester over a bed. It is a proscenium arch for the entry of the four Buckingham children: one had died in infancy and he reclines behind his three kneeling siblings who stare out over the foot of the monument. Above are two tearful putti whose hackneyed gestures of mourning add a rare note of bathos. At the very top, beneath a gilded and flaming urn acting as a finial, two females support the Buckingham arms. But the most vibrant figure is Fame, who is to be located at the feet of Buckingham; the trumpet she once blew, now missing. She moves though her fourteen companions are asleep in death or as still as the grave. She is the quick and they are the dead. She sounds the achievements of the hero, she draws attention to him, but most importantly, she symbolises the last trump; that moment when the righteous shall be raised up. It is an authentically Baroque touch; implying that Buckingham is about to be woken from his sleep; an implication which would become a certainty in the mind of the onlooker, once he had been suitably edified by the recitation of the Duke's virtues. The honours and achievements of Buckingham were elaborately rehearsed in epitaphs possibly composed by a certain Monsieur St Giles with whom Buckingham's erstwhile factotum, Sir Balthazar Gerbier, seems to have been in contact after his elevation to the post of ambassador to the court at Brussels.[31] Although St Giles, about whom nothing is known, may have composed the epitaph, the whole exercise of epigraphical commemoration may have been orchestrated by Richard Mason, the Duke's old secretary.

Mason had been plucked by Buckingham from a Fellowship at St John's College, Cambridge; of which university Buckingham had been Chancellor. Mason retained a devotion to the memory of the Duke and the protection of the Duchess. Buckingham's sister Susan, Countess of Denbigh, wrote to her son, Lord Feilding, when he was touring the Continent in the late summer of 1631. She told of how the Portsmouth monument to Buckingham was finished and asked her son to commend her to Mason who was then acting as his tutor:

> remember me to Mr Mason and give him many thankes for his care hee has of you and tell him I have now finished the tombe of my deare brother and have sent a copy over with the inscription which I hope he will like being made of black and white marble.[32]

Justice has been done to the splendour and significance of the main Buckingham tomb in Westminster Abbey; though perhaps there remains something to add to Lightbown's richly suggestive account. There is surely an intimate connection between the Buckingham tomb and contemporary masque designs. The Buckingham monument borrows important elements from the theatre for a performance in stone and metal to match those of taffeta and egret's feathers which could be enjoyed in the royal masques which were then being performed a few hundred yards away in the Banqueting House.

In the Buckingham monument, Fame moving to the front of the stage introduces the performance, while the Buckingham children enter through an arch to enact a tableau of grief, filial devotion and piety. The principal actor is attended by a quartet of allegories, as the monarch was surrounded by representations of his most kingly virtues in the climax to the Jonesian masque.

A comparison of the Buckingham tomb with that of the Earl of Portland seems to confirm that this presentation of Buckingham was influenced by the masque. Portland, who took a close, not to say worried, interest in what was being done for Buckingham, ordered a tomb for himself in Winchester Cathedral. This too was a collaborative venture. Besnier again produced an overall design and carved the stone while Francesco Fanelli was probably responsible for the bronze effigy, and the now missing busts of children once in the separate niches above Portland's prostrate figure. Le Sueur was not asked to cast the bronzes; probably because he was too busy working on the Buckingham monument and the equestrian statue of Charles I, ordered by Portland himself for his garden at Roehampton and today in Trafalgar Square.

The Portland tomb is suaver if less magnificent than Buckingham's. The overall design has a lucidity which makes it easier to take in. This is hardly surprising since the designer was not inhibited by the impossibly restricted sight of the Buckingham tomb, which would have needed a Bernini to overcome. The Portland tomb is more reserved than the Buckingham, which runs to excess by comparison. Furthermore, it shows an awareness of ancient Roman funerary rites; a point which would be easier to grasp if the busts were still in their niches. Yet the Portland tomb is actually more traditional. It has more in common with those Tudor bishops propped on their lawn sleeves who line the walls of cathedrals like punts against a river bank. The reticence of the Portland monument is in marked contrast to the latent theatricality of the Buckingham tomb. The contrast expresses different ways of coming to terms with death. Tombs were the key in which composers wrote their symphonies. In front of Buckingham the onlooker is invited to beat his breast whereas decorous, reticent stoicism is demanded in the presence of Portland. They demand different responses because they have different antecedents: the Buckingham monument owes much to contemporary theatre; the Portland, to the art and archaeology of antiquity.

There is an irony that neither of the two kings who did most to make the English court were given decent tombs. Henry VIII intended to

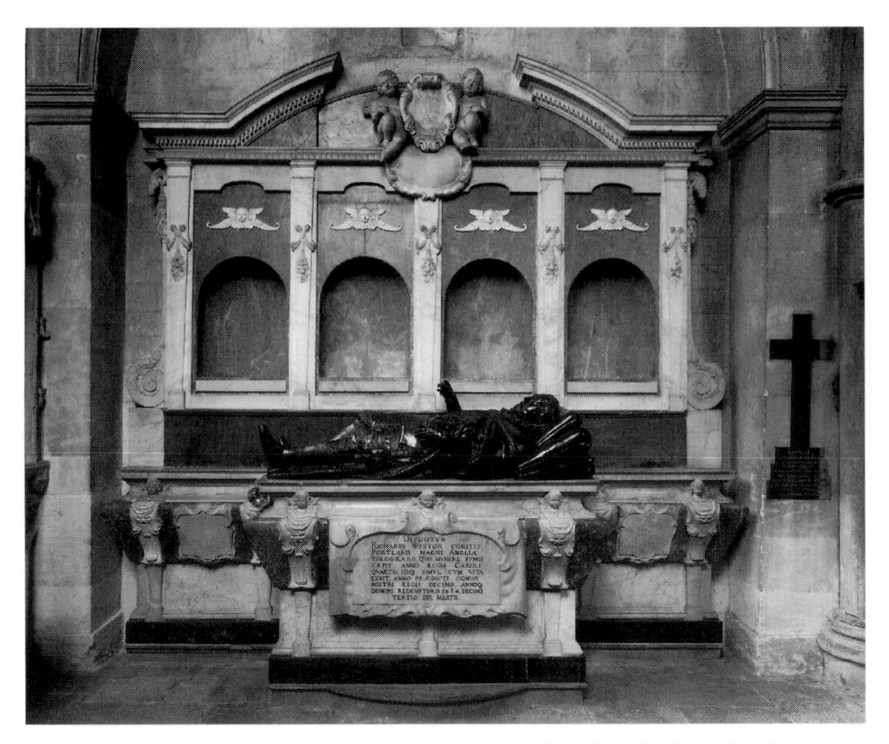

Isaac Besnier (design and marble carving) and either Hubert Le Sueur or Francesco Fanelli (sculptors of bronze work), *Tomb of Richard Weston, 1st Earl of Portland*, *c.* 1631–35, Winchester Cathedral (John Crook)

honour his own achievements, others wished to commemorate Charles I, a martyr king. But both visions faded into nothing. Nevertheless what is planned is often as influential as what is accomplished, and the projected mausoleum for Charles I has a place in any survey of royal tombs in Renaissance England.[33]

The mausoleum, which it was intended should be both tomb and larger monument to the Christ-like qualities of Charles I, arose in the late 1670s as a response to the gathering gloom of the Exclusion Crisis when loyal Protestants feared that Charles II was going to sell out to Catholicism. The great three-quarters columns proposed by the designer Sir Christopher Wren in 1679 were meant not only to support the drum of what would have been an English *Tempietto*, but to act as bulwark of an Anglican Settlement for which High Anglicans felt Charles I had laid down his life in 1649, and which Charles II threatened with Francophile, Catholic policies.

The immediate spur to the idea of re-interring Charles I had been the marriage of Princess Mary to William of Orange in 1677; a happy event which cast mens' minds back to the tragedy of 1649. It was remarked that

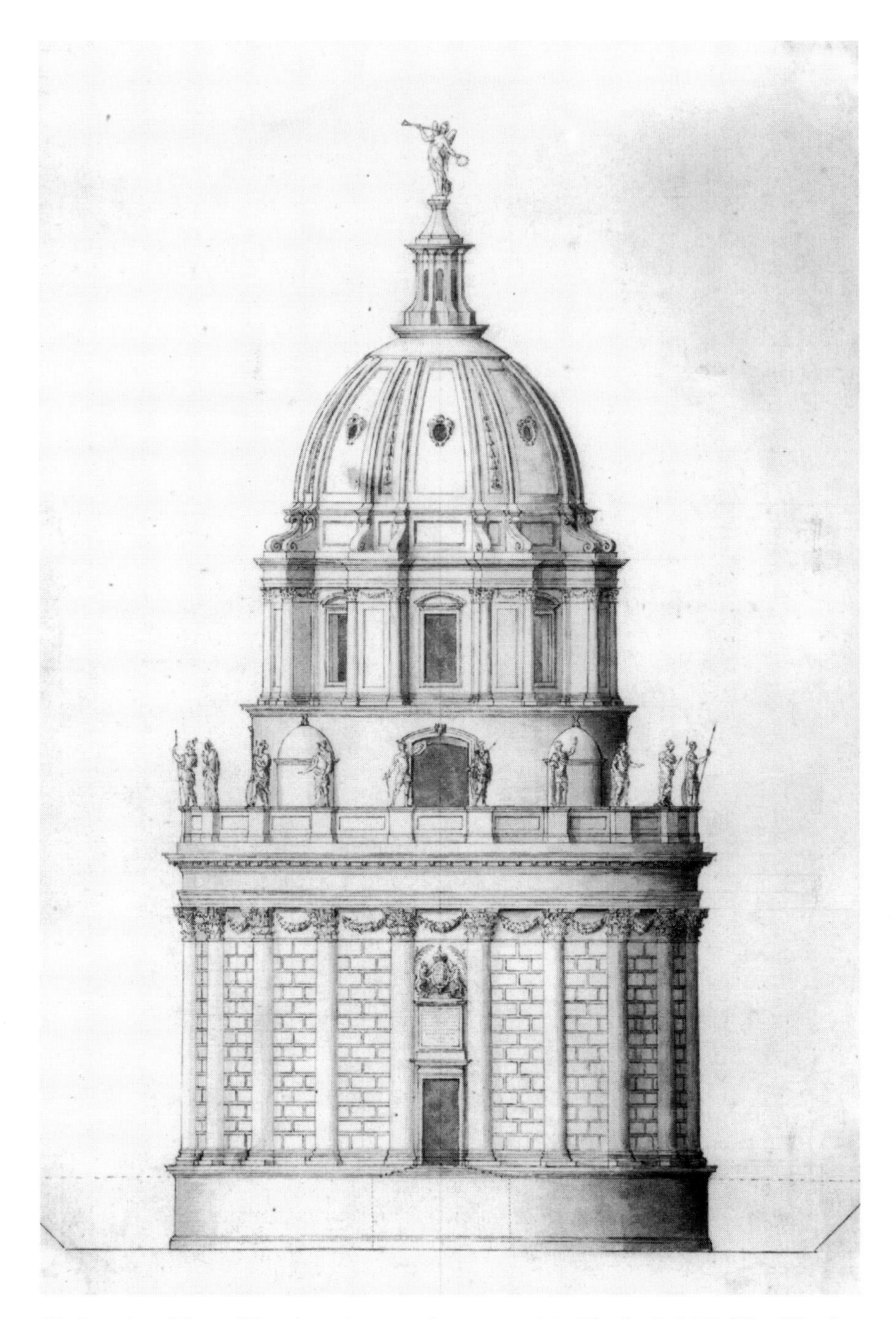

Christopher Wren, *Elevation of proposed monument to Charles I*, 1679 (The Warden and Fellows of All Souls College, Oxford)

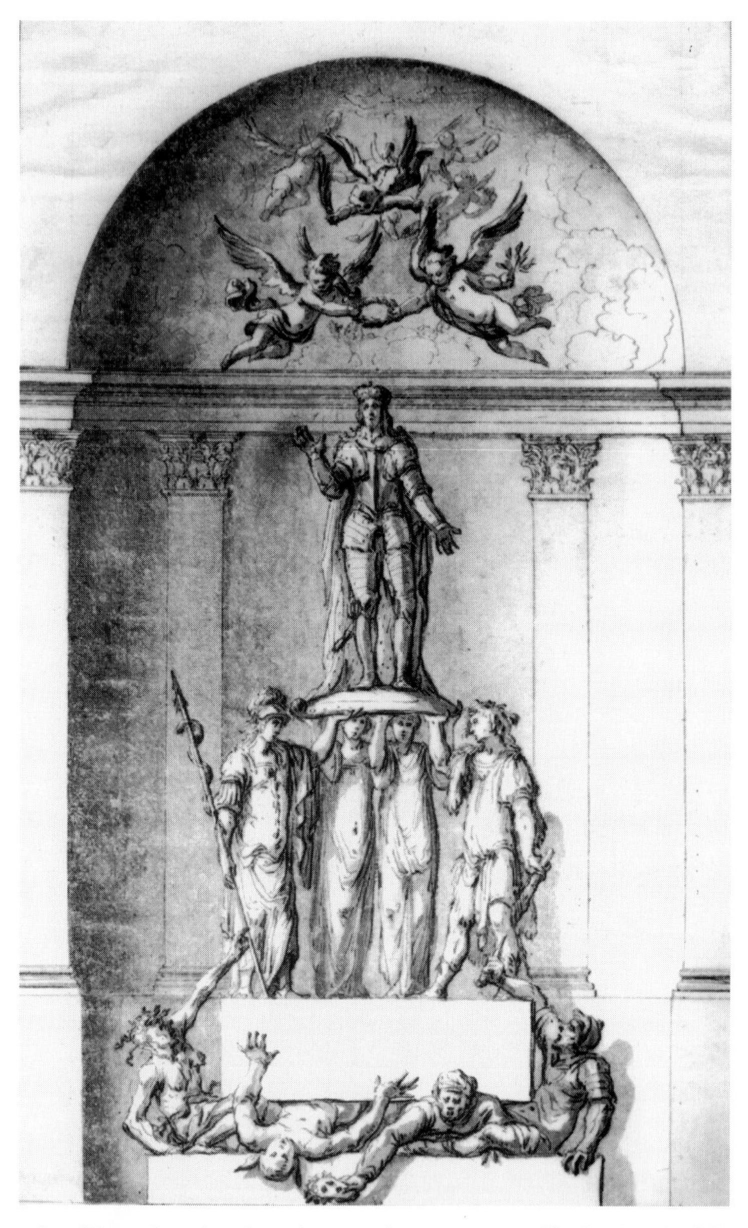

Christopher Wren, *Interior view of proposed monument to Charles I*, 1679 (The Warden and Fellows of All Souls College, Oxford)

the marriage united the 'Royal Blood and Kingly Virtues' of the 'Blessed Martyr'. The nuptials had represented something of a triumph for orthodox Anglicans but that was no more than a skirmish won in a long campaign against forces threatening what true Englishmen held, or should hold, most important.

Wren's monument to Charles I naturally demanded a long view; a perspective which hardly put Charles II in a flattering light. He professed himself supportive for what he described as the House of Commons' 'act of great piety' in forwarding the project of a mausoleum for his father. But although he appeared to unite with Parliament, some drew their own very different conclusions. In 1677 Francis Sandford had published his *Genealogical History of the Kings of England*, where he had pointed out how the Martyr King had been 'deposited in Silence and Sorrow' in a makeshift grave in St George's Chapel; whereas the King's grandfather James I had made splendid restitution to his mother by having raised 'a Magnificent Tomb . . . upon eight Corinthian Pillars, under the arch of which lies the Portraiture of the Queen'. Sandford was hardly being fair since no one was in any position to show respect to the dead Charles I for many years after his death. When the Restoration had come, it would not have been politic for Charles II to spend public funds in righting wrongs, when the situation cried out for the burial of old animosities not the reburial of a king. Nevertheless Sandford seems to have known his man, and Charles's *politique* attitude to the memory of his father had recently been exposed when he had given the honours many thought should have been reserved for his father to the Duke of Albemarle who had died in 1670, and who, as George Monck, had brought about the Restoration of the monarchy.

Whatever Charles II's private feelings about the death of his father, a Committee of the Whole House was constituted in 1678 and things went on briskly from there. Sir Thomas Meres suggested that the staggering sum of £70,000 should be allocated for the memorial to Charles I: half to be spent on the re-interment, half for what Wren would provide as the cover. No one seems to have thought such an amount excessive; though the difficulty of raising it was acknowledged by talk of the need to impose a land tax. Meres was quite clear. His intention was to 'perpetuate the memory' of 'him that died for the Protestant religion'. The Secretary of State followed with the long view; acting as mouthpiece of the King, he declared that the monument should be 'equal, if not superior to the late King's ancestors'.

Orders were at once given to Wren and he produced a very beautiful design; beautiful because of his conviction of the sanctity of the man to whom he was doing honour. His thoughts were on the King's table in a week; the speed with which they were delivered suggesting the project had really caught his imagination. What Wren envisaged, in collaboration with Grinling Gibbons who was to have been responsible for the statuary, provides a late seventeenth-century view of the Martyr King.

Wren broke with iconographic tradition by suggesting an upright figure of Charles I; never before had it been proposed that an English monarch should be presented standing over his own tomb. It was a daring break with tradition and one which needs further consideration. What were Wren and Gibbons thinking? A standing figure might have allowed for a more significant presence in what would have been a generous space; but this is not really a very convincing explanation when it is considered that Henry VII ended on his back in a larger mausoleum.

If however, the whole design is considered, certain explanations suggest themselves. One of a number of remarkable aspects of Wren's design is that Charles is not merely standing, but standing on a shield born aloft by the 'heroick Virtues': Prudence, Temperance, Justice and Fortitude. Here there may be a reminiscence of the *acclamatio* as practised, according to Tacitus, by the Germanic kings whose descendants became the Saxon kings of Dark Age England.[34] Tacitus' interest in this custom has been highlighted in a recent study of Dark Age shields where the authors write:

> Tacitus also high-lighted another symbolic function of the shield when he described how the Canninefates raised their new king on the shield: he called it a *mos gentis*. . . . Although there are no specific instances of this custom noted in Anglo-Saxon sources, the link between the shield and royal power is expressed in Beowulf (lines 427–8, 610, 1866, 1972) where kings are referred to as the shield of their people and warriors.[35]

The Restoration gentleman certainly knew his Tacitus and what is more, the ancient rites of the early English kings had begun to generate interest by this time. Ethnology and anthropology lay at the heart of the researches of the famous antiquary, naturalist and Garter King of Arms, Sir Elias Ashmole. Ashmole had a celebrated cabinet of curiosities which was something of an Ark of the Covenant for early students of the Dark Ages. Within just a few years of the Wren design, Ashmole's cabinet was to be transformed into Britain's first public museum. Ashmole offered his collections to the University of Oxford in 1675, and a purpose-built home for the exotica was then opened to the public by James II as Duke of York in 1683. Thus the mausoleum for Charles I was designed during the very years in which the Ashmolean was itself being conceived by Ashmole, Wren and their intimates in The Royal Society; a body whose obstruse proceedings included highly speculative, fanciful accounts of early English social customs.

But why should Wren have wished to make an arcane parallel between an obscure ceremony undertaken for kings in animal skins and this late king of blessed memory who had moved in rustling silk to worship beneath gilded beams?

The Windsor mausoleum was to have been a beacon amidst the gathering gloom of a Catholic revival which many Protestants believed, not without cause with the Catholic Duke of York waiting in the wings, would mean the extinction of ancient liberties. At the very time when Wren was designing the mausoleum for Charles I, a project which interested the Commons a great deal more than Charles II, fierce debate raged as to the place of Parliament in history. Polemicists and constitutional lawyers who argued that before the imposition of a 'Norman yoke' following the Conquest, the king had consulted with his people, and that therefore parliaments had always had a central place, would certainly have known their Tacitus. Following Tacitus' description of the custom of certain Germanic tribes of raising their chieftain on a shield to proclaim his rulership, they believed that the northern peoples, of which the Anglo-Saxons were one, had elected their monarchy.

The Wren design has both a constitutional and a sacerdotal frame of reference. Wren succeeds brilliantly in fusing two value systems which would in fact be exposed as irreconcilable by the Exclusion Crisis; though it had taken the entire century to understand that there could be no accommodation between them. On the one hand Wren flatters the pretentions of the Parliamentarians who saw this great project as a means to remind the king of his elective nature, on the other he offers succour to those who wished to see the hand of the monarchy strengthened. Charles I may depend for his support on the strength of others, but there is more than a reminiscence of the Christian martyr about his posture.

Wren employs a religious iconography for the statue of the king himself. Above and below the central tableau are details which may have struck a chord in those who could still remember the court of Charles I; Wren sets out to recollect two of the most magnificent creations of that reign. The first hovers perilously close to the ridiculous as the Virtues, standing on a massy block, crush the Four Vices: Envy, Heresy, Hypocrisy and Rebellion. Here Wren may have intended to link the design with Rubens' vision in the Banqueting House where Vices tumble out of the picture, thrust away from the Lord's Anointed.

Above the head of Charles, there is an aureole of seven angels bearing the palm and crown of martyrdom. This may have been intended as a reference to that great altarpiece which had been erected by François Dieussart for Somerset House chapel in 1636; a mount of piety which had scandalised the godly when it had first been unveiled. The design takes as its starting point the high altar of a church; the piers in the drawing acting like a screen to mark off the choir from the main body. The sacerdotal not to say deitistic element is confirmed by the very gesture of the king himself. The figure is based upon Christ from Michelangelo's *Last Judgement* where the raised left hand beckons to the elect, the lowered right, to the damned. Rubens had also looked to the Michelangelo for the gesture of James I in *The Benefits of the Reign* and thus there are further grounds for believing Wren was influenced by the most splendid of all monuments to the British Crown.

There is a certain irony about Wren's proposals which may have escaped men at the time but which should not go unremarked now. The mausoleum was to have been a weapon in the armoury of English Protestants, but its designers plundered the arsenal of Catholic visual weaponry; as indeed Elizabeth I had done when defending her role as Supreme Governor of the Church. Had the monument to Charles I been built, we should have had one of Sir Christopher Wren's most perfect classical essays. However, the comforts of equilibrium must have been threatened by discord; contradictions within a social system which allowed some to promote parliamentary government and others the divine right of kings.

It has been shown in this chapter that funerals and funerary monuments had a central part to play in the promotion of the monarchy in Renaissance England. Tombs contributed to the splendour of what was established, and gave authenticity to change. They bound the new to the old while suggesting the vigour of a ruling house. The first of the Tudors came to rest fox-like and sentient in the sanctuary of English kingship, while the first of the Stuarts ordained a tomb for the last of the Tudors. That act of obeisance on the part of one dynasty toward another helped in the legitimisation of what was new. Paying honour to the dead, or rehabilitating the despised, was both euphemism and expiation: King James I must have known that the translation of his mother's remains had more than a little in common with the translation of a saint's bones, while the reburial of Richard III by Henry VII clothed the brutality of *realpolitik* with a mysterious grace; providing absolution to a whole dynasty, not just to a man who had dared to snatch a crown in battle. When kings ordered tombs they became chroniclers in stone.

Chapter Six
Patrons of Power

There was an intimate, almost inseparable connection between rule and patronage of the arts in Renaissance England. Almost without exception, the great spent lavishly on appearances whatever their particular religious sympathies may have been. Attempts have been made to equate Catholicism and patronage of the arts but this cannot balance. Sensitivity to the arts and an awareness of their powers of persuasion had little to do with religious sympathies; the rabid iconoclast Protector Somerset destroyed the heritage of medieval decorative art while putting up the most 'progressive' building of the sixteenth century.

Distinctions were made between what a man might subscribe to in church and what he was prepared to hang on his walls; a disengagement between appearance and function which we make without even thinking. Today there are increasing numbers of gallery visitors who find themselves moved by a picture of a penitent St Francis without even being aware that he was a Christian saint. It may be thought that the beginnings of this divergence between appearance and meaning began, on the Continent at least, about 1500 when connoisseurs started to collect paintings because they were by a particular artist and not because they represented a new and more poignant interpretation of Christian history.[1] Such a capacity to disengage developed in England when Charles I made connoisseurship fashionable for the first time in our culture.

Philip, 4th Earl of Pembroke, combined Puritan sympathies with one of the grandest court offices. As Lord Chamberlain he was answerable to the king for the royal pictures since his office carried responsibility for the upkeep of the palaces. Privately Pembroke inclined towards the Puritans though he had no sympathy for their profound suspicion of sacred imagery; nor could it be said that such an inclination obliged him to rigorous observance of their strictures. His character was vicious and his personality devious, his tastes rich and his patronage lavish. He was second only to the King as patron to Van Dyck and there is no family more brilliantly painted in English history than the Herberts in their group portrait by Van Dyck, now in the Double Cube Room at Wilton but originally located in one of Pembroke's London residences (Plate 81, page 227). When Pembroke came to serve Parliament during the Civil War, he thought of transforming Durham House into a palace which would have pleased Louis XIV had the plans been realised.

Pembroke favoured Puritan lecturers in public whilst breaking most of the Commandments in private; he was 'soiled with physical excesses', as C. V. Wedgwood vividly expressed it. But with his great contemporary Thomas Wentworth, 1st Earl of Strafford, matters were reversed. Strafford bullied Puritans whilst inclining toward a strenuous regime of hard work and puritanical self-denial; or so he would have had enemies believe, who called him a 'Visier Basha', by which they referred to the imperious chief minister of the Sultan of Turkey. Strafford's patronage of the arts, the subject of this chapter, contributed to his reputation as a man of oriental magnificence. His building works were essentially political, and so recognised by those who saw them going up.

But architecture was no mere recreation for Strafford. It expressed a compulsion which he would come to share with his closest ally William Laud, Archbishop of Canterbury (1633–45); his 'ghostly father' as Strafford liked to call the divine. Both men came to believe that good architecture made for the seemly exercise of good government. Strafford undertook major works at Dublin Castle while Laud pressed on with the renovation of St Paul's Cathedral.

An account of Strafford as architectural patron must begin with a brief excursion to the principal family seat at Wentworth Woodhouse in South Yorkshire. There Strafford would temporarily retreat during the summers of the 1620s to recover from tumultuous opposition to the policies of the Crown and Buckingham. There too Strafford liked to play the ancient Roman, free from the toils of high politics in the capital. His epistles were coloured by a Ciceronian delight in the innocence of flowers and the countryside, though the extent to which his correspondence was studded with Latin tags suggests that he would have rapidly bored of playing the piping shepherd. He wrote to Sir George Calvert, the Secretary of State, on a spring day in 1623:

> Matter worthy your Trouble these Parts afford none, where our Objects and Thoughts are limited in looking upon a Tulip, hearing a Bird sing, a Rivulet murmuring, or some such petty, yet innocent Pastime, which for my Part I begin to feed myself in, having, I praise God, recovered more in a Day by an open Country Air, than in a Fortnight's Time in that smothering one of *London*. By my Troth I wish you, devested of the Importunity of Business, here for half a Dozen Hours, you should taste how free and fresh we breath, and *hos procul metic fruimur modestis opibus*, a wanting sometimes to Persons of greater Eminency in the Administration of Commonwealths.[2]

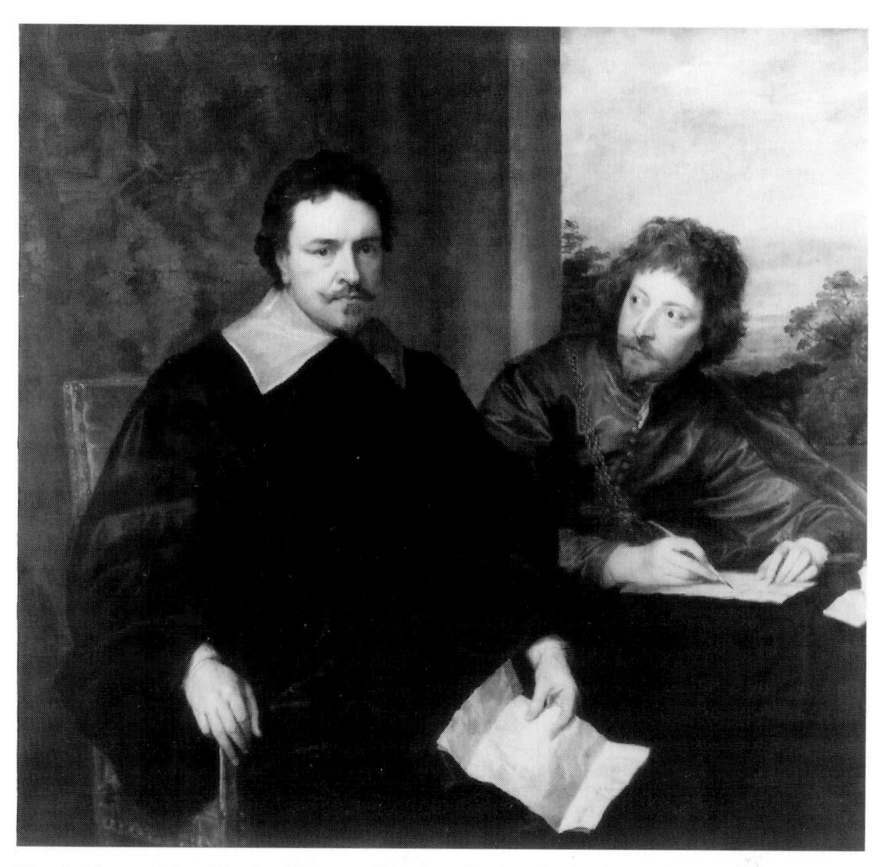

Sir Anthony Van Dyck, *Thomas Wentworth, 1st Earl of Strafford with Sir Philip Mainwaring*, 1636 (Trustees of the Rt Hon. Olive, Countess Fitzwilliams's Chattels Settlement, and Lady Juliet de Chair)

Retreat to a green shade, anticipating Lord Fairfax's life at nearby Appleton House, did not mean idleness however. Improvements at Wentworth and other properties had to do with the orbit of northern politics. The family were powerful in South Yorkshire, but then so were other families, and Strafford believed that it would help him to dominate the locality if he created the grandest house in the district. One eye was on the gentry of Yorkshire, the other on London. Strafford was always careful to keep in touch with those who mattered.

Buildings, parks and gardens, all were geared to the efficient running of a little world where greater ambitions were rehearsed: what was ordered and controlled at Wentworth Woodhouse, anticipated the running of the greater Estates of the realm which would preoccupy Strafford ten years later. Clarity and order, restoration and reclamation, centralisation and tidyness; all confirmed, for Strafford, the truth that architecture was a social, a political statement.

In the summer of 1628, Strafford's 'conversion' to the King's interest was followed by his appointment as Lord President of the Council of the North on Christmas Day of that year. What erstwhile friends in the Commons when he had led the opposition to Buckingham now came to call his 'apostasy', was thus complete. A grandiose title, the Lord Presidency was a position with great possibilities. It had been created by Henry VIII when he had felt the need for a reliable and powerful servant to watch lands which had proved fruitful recruiting ground for the Pilgrimage of Grace. Since English monarchs went beyond the Trent once a generation if that, the post gave vast powers. But the job required acute political antennae, huge energy, and administrative abilities of a very high order. All these Strafford could supply. But what he felt was missing was a sufficiently dignified setting, and this he began to rectify within weeks of taking up residence in The King's Manor; the official lodging of the Lord President, which was located within the ruins of St Mary's Abbey, outside the northern gate of York.

Strafford at The King's Manor was like the Christmas brothers, master carvers who would be summoned in 1637 to give splendour to Charles I's great new ship *The Sovereign of the Seas*, which emerged from its dock at Greenwich as the largest man of war to be built in seventeenth-century England. For *The Sovereign* the Christmases carved a figurehead, coat of arms, oriels in the stern, turned rails above living quarters. At The King's Manor in York, Strafford thrust classical door heads through plain Tudor masonry to frame exit and entrance in much the same spirit of embellishment rather than structural transformation. Although the appearance of doorcases was classical, their decoration looked back to the splendour of the Middle Ages. The King's arms and Strafford's coat shone like fish scales against the mulberry brick of York, dazzling those gentlemen come to pay homage to the King's representative in his northern court.

Much of Strafford's work at The King's Manor was surface decoration; only a small percentage of the ranges or rooms can be thought his: conceivably the 'New Hall' as it was called, and certainly a storey put over a ground-floor Long Gallery erected by Edmund, Lord Sheffield (President, 1603–19). The inventory of what Strafford built at The King's Manor suggests that he made less of an impact than either the Earl of Huntingdon (President, 1572–95), or Lord Sheffield. But Strafford would have done more had he not been appointed Lord Deputy General of Ireland at Christmas 1631. Nevertheless he continued Lord President while he was in Ireland and remarkably enough, continued a programme of building work in York throughout what he described as his 'pilgrimage' in Dublin; words he used to express his sense of exile throughout the long years of Personal Rule. In Dublin Strafford was unable to direct building in York at first hand, but although massively overburdened with Irish affairs,

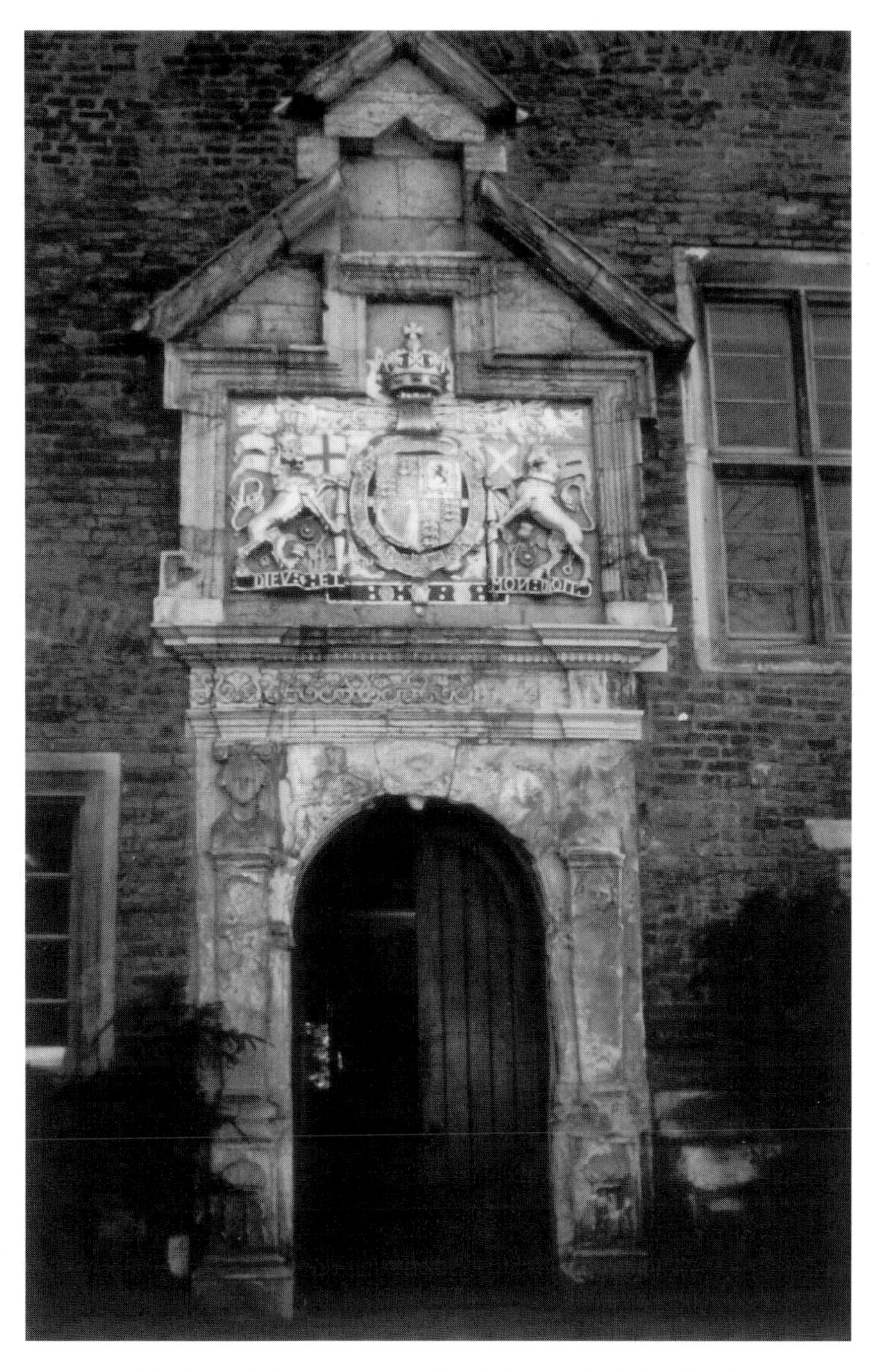

The Arms of Charles I, c. 1635, King's Manor, York (Joe Rock)

somehow found time to write as late as August 1639: '. . . there is a Gloria Patri sung at St. *Mary* Abbey, so as the Pillars in that Kitchen now may hope to have the Honour to become the Pillars again of a Church, as formerly they were'.[3] This has been interpreted as meaning that Strafford intended to convert the New Hall into a chapel; something he had always wanted for The King's Manor because of his fixed conviction that the secular sword should be wielded in defence of the ecclesiastical establishment. In 1633 Strafford had written from London to the Earl of Carlisle when his recipient was with Charles I at The King's Manor, as they prepared to travel to Edinburgh for the Scottish crowning: 'The House you will find much mended since my coming to it, and one thousand Pounds more to build a Gallery and Chapel in that Place where you may perceive I intend it, will make it very commodious.'[4]

Charles I was much impressed by what he saw as he stopped at York bound for Scotland, and his encouragement helped persuade Strafford to press on with his building programme: £1,712 was allowed for building work in 1634 out of compositions in distraint of knighthood, and by 1637 the North Riding had been at 'a great charge in leading timber and other materials for his Majesty's house at York'.[5] Building went on intermittently for a decade; suggesting perhaps that Strafford contributed rather more to the splendour of The King's Manor than has been allowed. This however we shall never know because of the destruction of much seventeenth-century work during later building campaigns, and the blowing up of St Mary's Tower adjacent to The King's Manor by the Parliamentary Earl of Manchester during the siege of York in 1644, and with it, the records of the Council of the North.

Buildings and grounds belonging to The King's Manor included the royal hunting forest of Galtres ten miles to the north. Here Strafford was anxious to ensure that others should not be seen to pursue field sports with more magnificence. He set about reasserting the claims of the Crown, claims which had been neglected by his predecessors and encroached upon by magnates like Sir John Bourchier of Beningbrough; a local grandee whom Strafford regarded as stark mad. Strafford threw Bourchier off the royal demesne and then proceeded to mete out a severe punishment; a method of humiliating equals or superiors which would become familiar in Ireland and vitally contribute to his desertion by his peers when he was impeached by the Commons in November 1640.

Hunting was enormously important as a social gesture in the seventeenth century. Nobody knew this better than Rubens, since portraiture aside, scenes of the chase constitute his most important secular genre; some of which ended up in the collections of Jacobean courtiers. Even a superficial acquaintance with the life of James I makes it abundantly clear that he spent days on end charging across Royston Down or Newmarket Heath in pursuit of animals; admittedly not with the ferocity with which Rubens' hunters launch themselves at hippopotamuses, but with hardly less enthusiasm. Hunting was much more than recreation in the seventeenth century. Through the pursuit of an elaborate social ritual, the ruler showed himself to his people; rearranged favourites on the chess board of court intrigue; suggested wealth by marking boundaries of Royal Forests, and implied a capacity for military command by the vigorous pursuit of the beast. It was a tribal custom which evolved into the Edwardian shooting party at Sandringham, and now the company golf tournament at Sunningdale.

Strafford's pursuit of the stag involved the displacement of grandees who had exploited the Royal Forests of the north where their encroachments had grown into unchallenged custom. Strafford reasserted Crown control but he used an axe to do it; a powerful but crude weapon which sent shivers through roots of social dominance and dependence. Men not only lost good hunting but status, and this they never forgot.

Wherever he represented the King, Strafford had set aims. One was to ensure the Crown obtained restitution of alienated lands. This was not always easy and favourable judgement in the courts was often not the end of the story. But in the case of Galtres, where Strafford did triumph, he felt the need for permanent physical expression of restored ownership. He built New Parks, a hunting lodge at Huby which stands to this day as a farm.

It was reported after the death of Charles I that he had said: 'I looked upon my lord of Strafford as a gentleman whose great abilities might make a prince rather afraid than ashamed to employ him in the greatest affairs of state.'[6] Strafford would have had distinctly mixed feelings had he heard of this verdict on what was always their complicated, uneasy relationship. Strafford was full of paradoxes: he was the most domineering of the king's servants, but one of the most doubting. Despite a genius for executive office, and no one was more aware of it than he, he was always doubtful of where he stood with his master. He would importune the king with embarrassingly open requests for an earldom. These were motivated in part by *raison d'état*: Strafford's stated belief that it would allow him to exercise the King's command more effectively in the face of a phalanx of Irish earls ranged against him. But there was more to it. Strafford craved an earldom because he craved reassurance. Not even he could have doubted Charles respected him, but what was hardly less important was the nagging question, did his master like him? It was something which tormented a tumultuously emotional man. The devotion Strafford offered Charles I, and which Charles only accepted without reserve when in desperate trouble with the Scots, was a devotion Strafford wished to see publicly reciprocated. He believed that this could only be expressed and assured by his elevation to the highest levels of the peerage.

The verdict of Charles I on Strafford, whether actually said or not, has a ring of truth. It mirrors Charles' contradictory feelings toward Strafford for it contains compliment and reservation in equal measure. Fear was exactly what Strafford induced as he presided over the Vice-Regal court in Ireland where he used the visual arts to frame that threatening greatness caught so memorably by Van Dyck in his portraits. Strafford had a terrible bearing which made him the most formidable and the most awesome of all who have tried to pluck order out of the endemic chaos of Ireland.

Strafford lost no time in making his presence felt in Dublin. He had been chosen as Lord Deputy by 1631, but despite an impatient temperament which made it difficult for him to hold back, he did not actually arrive until July 1633. The interval had been spent in reading books to read the minds of those he was being sent to control.

Don Nicolaldi, the Spanish ambassador in London, appreciated an absolutist monarchy when he saw one and was moved to congratulate Strafford within six weeks of his taking up residence in Dublin Castle:

> your . . . Success in that Government, in which I hear you are become already like a *Spanish* Vice-Roy in what is befitting the Greatness of the Lieutenant of his Majesty, and the Honour of so eminent a Dignity, which being the sole, which we find in the Way of Government of this Crown, your Predecessors, it seems, have not so well attended to set it in the Esteem it deserves.[7]

The tone was set but it was a tone which Strafford believed needed permanent expression in a programme of building works, furnishing, and reordering of court protocol which would involve much thought over the eight years he was to dominate Irish affairs.

The King's Deputy wrote to Sir John Coke, one of the two Secretaries of State, about the decay of Dublin Castle in October 1633, three months after his arrival. Strafford found the Castle as much in need of repair as The King's Manor had been when he had taken that over. He told Coke of how tragedy had been narrowly averted; a tower had crashed down during an interval in the games which the children of the Irish Lord Chancellor, Viscount Loftus, liked to play on the Castle lawns. Strafford had the tower demolished and, on a more constructive note, informed Coke that he had at once begun building a new stable to accommodate thirty-six horses for his bodyguard. Coke was told that hereafter, the Horse was to play a more prominent role in the passage of the Lord Deputy through the streets. A church which had acted as the Castle stable would now revert to its former use, and the new stable, already two yards high, would be ready by June 1634.

As he took down the dangerous parts of the Castle, Strafford started to dismantle the pretentions of the nobility. There was a messianic quality about his urge to contain and regularise the life of the Irish aristocracy: something admirable if foolhardy in his refusal to spare anyone however grand. The most dangerous he chose to pluck down was Richard Boyle, 1st Earl of Cork, Lord Treasurer of Ireland. Cork was an English Protestant whose family had come from Kent during the Elizabethan period and done uniquely well. The 1st Earl was inordinately rich and he headed what is known as the 'New English' interest in Ireland – Protestants well supplied with lands near Dublin, and the complacent recipients of government perks; distinct from 'Old English', who tended to be Catholic aristocratic families whose Irish peerages dated from the Middle Ages. But Cork and his like were also distinct from the Planters; usually Presbyterian Scots who had colonised Ulster following encouragement given to Plantations by James I from 1608 onwards. Cork headed the natural party of dominance in Irish affairs because he was very able and he was richer than anyone else. Strafford's actions against him were therefore ill-advised; the more so since Cork had run affairs with Viscount Loftus between the departure of the last Lord Deputy, Viscount Falkland, and the arrival of Strafford himself. Only a man with a fixed conviction of his own rectitude would have taken on Cork. Cork represented and would have continued to represent a real threat, but the manner in which Strafford cut him down to size undermined the foundations of the structure of government which he was trying to build.

Strafford was easily scandalised. His Yorkshire steward Richard Marris, who was entrusted with all the building work at The King's Manor when Strafford had moved to Ireland, got hopelessly drunk one night, fell off his horse, and drowned in a puddle; Strafford was upset to loose a trusty servant, but far more concerned that such painful evidence of gluttony might reflect unfavourably on himself. A year or two before the wet end of poor Richard Marris, a more public scandal had affronted Strafford in Ireland. Strafford was shocked to discover that the Earl of Cork was building a massive tomb for his wife in Dublin Cathedral where the high altar should have been. He ordered its immediate removal. Eventually Cork complied though with an ill grace; understandably, given the money spent and the demolition of family pride.

In a certain sense Strafford could not be faulted: he was starting as he meant to go on; demanding dignity on behalf of an established but beleaguered church which would rise or fall according to the respect given to the monarchy of which Strafford was representative. None the less, what was right was not what was *politique*; something to which Strafford was always fatally blind.

The quarrel with Cork was relished by Strafford for the exultant sense of power which came with victory. From the discreet confines of his intimate correspondence with Laud, there is a sense of the enjoyment Strafford gained from the sweet sensations of humiliating one who had patronised him. Strafford wrote to Laud about the final removal of the Cork monument in a way which mocked a wounded but far from disabled enemy:

> The Earl of *Corke's* Tomb is now quite removed; how he means to dispose it I know not: But up it is put in Boxes, as if it were Marchpanes

and Banquetting Stuffs, going down to the Christening of my young Master in the Country. The Wall is closed again, and so soon as it is dry and fit to be wrought upon, it shall be decently adorned, or else – it costs me at least one fifty Pounds for my Share.[8]

The priority Strafford gave to building is suggested by his renovations within the Castle and in the city beyond. Others before him had seen the importance of such things, though none had had that passion for building which he seems to have possessed; not even his immediate predecessor Lord Falkland who wrote to him surely not entirely seriously, asking for thanks for making his successor a great deal more comfortable than he had been:

My Lord,

I Pray your Lordship's Leave to congratulate your safe Arrival at *Dublin*, which is but the Effect of my good Wishes to you: And now I have performed thus much of my Part, I take the Boldness to put you in mind of thus much of your own, which is the Performance of your Promise you made me, that when you found how much less a Prison the Castle was, through the Benefit of the Gallery I built, not more for the King's Honour than for your Ease and Delight, you would acknowledge, that you did owe my Act Commendation and me Thanks for the Service, both which I make humble Claim unto, and expect your Accomplishment of.[9]

Falkland was not being altogether serious but he makes the point that buildings were regarded as monuments to the achievement of past rulers. Strafford took great pride in what he was to build and what he encouraged others to build; a pride which lay at the root of bad relations with Inigo Jones, the King's Surveyor.

The basis of the quarrel between Strafford and Jones, a sequel in Jones' life to the much more famous strife between himself and Ben Jonson, lay in the seriousness with which Strafford took himself as an architect. Both men were proud and abrasive: Jones later to be accused of wanting to be sole monarch in any project, Strafford never one to receive favours graciously. The quarrel is worth following because it shows how much interest public building generated within the court of Charles I.

Trouble began when Strafford decided that he would apply in Dublin, London regulations for the erection of new buildings. These stemmed from the Commission for New Buildings which James I had established in 1618; a body whose work was being driven forward with increased momentum by Jones, just as Strafford had first arrived in Dublin. The spade-work of the London Commission was presided over by Jones himself and spade-work is what it was. It all added up to extremely paternalistic control; just what Strafford felt Dublin needed, given his urge to order every aspect of public life. Accordingly Strafford reminded Coke:

> You will be pleased to remember the Proclamations, Orders and Decrees concerning Buildings, which you here mention, that they may be sent us over; for undoubtedly they will cause a great Reformation in this Town.[10]

Unfortunately Strafford failed to ask Coke to thank Jones; something he would have been careful to do for a higher-born servant of the king. Bad manners was then compounded by provocation, as Strafford made the mistake of suggesting that he could order a city as well if not better than Jones himself:

> The Money allowed for the Repair of this Castle is, I assure you, of absolute Necessity; I will be as good a Husband of it, as possibly I can, and trust to prove as thrifty a Surveyor as the best; nay, without offence to Mr *Jones*, or Pride in myself be it spoken, I take myself to be a very pretty Architect too.[11]

Coke proceeded to annotate this passage 'In the Reparations your Husbandry will be acceptable, your Architecture commends itself.'

That however was not how Jones came to see things and surely he was right since it is indeed extraordinary that Strafford perceived himself as rival of the man who had designed the Prince's Lodgings at Newmarket, and was then designing the Queen's House, Greenwich. It was a grotesque claim and no wonder it made Jones so angry. Yet Strafford's great Irish country house at Naas, fourteen miles south-west of Dublin in the rich county of Wicklow, was much admired. Jigginstown, as the palace was called, was begun to Strafford's own designs soon after his arrival in Ireland. It was broadly modelled on the Palazzo del Té, the summer pleasure dome created for the Dukes of Mantua by Giulio Romano in the 1520s. Mantua may have been surrounded by water but the Wicklow hills are covered with it. Thus to create an Italian palace in such a location was something of a quixotic gesture. Nevertheless Strafford's creation was admired by votaries of classicism until the building was reduced to open cellars by the mid-nineteenth century. Strafford was not a Lord Burlington; still less one of the unrecognised masters of classical architecture. But while he was no match for Jones as a designer, he was his equal as a visionary of how architecture might express kingship.[12]

Strafford was a uniquely energetic vice-regal builder; a ruler who came to understand, well before Wren, how buildings express and inspire nationhood. Strafford's buildings, and his efforts to get the Irish to build for themselves, constituted a conscious 'programme' which paralleled and complemented more obvious policy initiatives: law courts, parliamentary acts, proclamations of the Irish Privy Council.

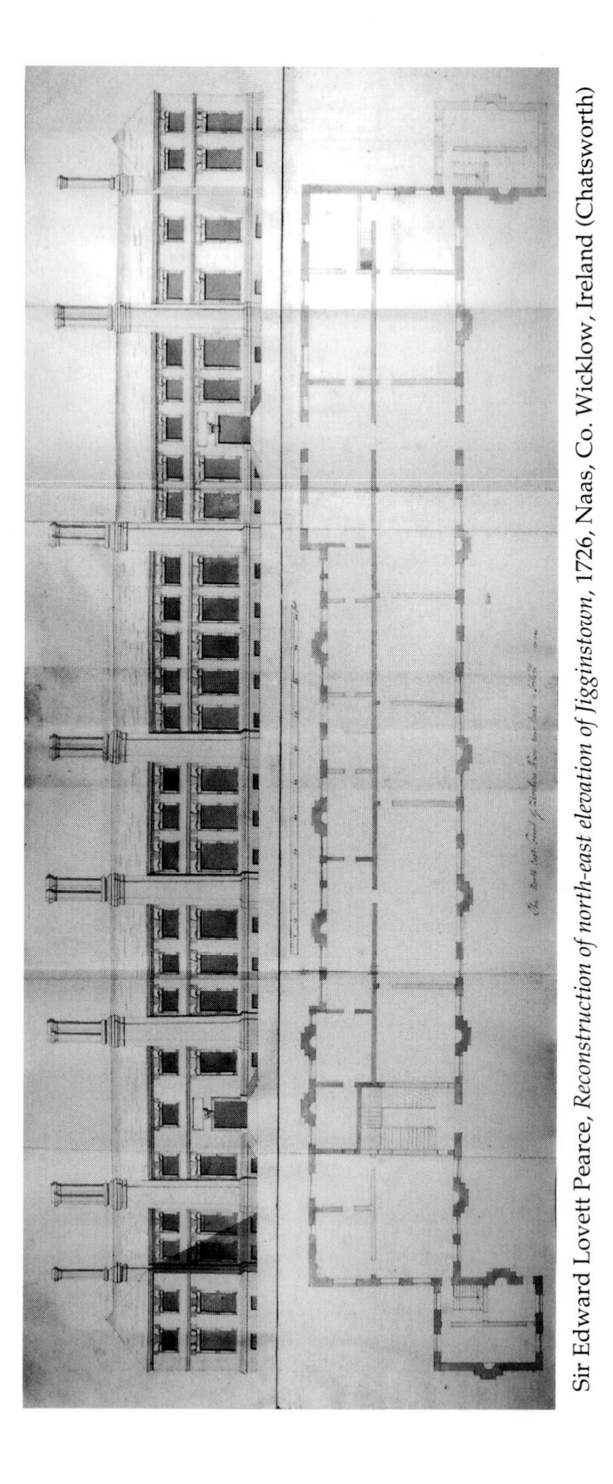

Sir Edward Lovett Pearce, *Reconstruction of north-east elevation of Jigginstown*, 1726, Naas, Co. Wicklow, Ireland (Chatsworth)

A measure of Strafford's passion for architecture cannot be taken by looking at his buildings. They have disappeared. But their number and variety constituted a rich inventory: besides Jigginstown, there was continuous and extensive work on Dublin Castle; the creation of new stables for the Lord Deputy's mounted bodyguard; the restoration of old churches; the laying out of parks and hunting boxes; the encouragement of masques, that inventive type of temporary architecture, and the opening of marble quarries. Strafford shared the philosophy of the Medici and the Barberini that public architecture should be a permanent, persuasive civic proclamation. Strafford was rare among his English contemporaries in holding this view and his unusual response to the potential of building helps to account for the feeling among those who hated him that he was bent upon trying to introduce a Continental type of absolutism. It was only the absolutist states of Europe which properly understood the propaganda value of architecture.

Coke was commanded by Charles I to inform Strafford how much the King approved of:

> all the Works and Reparations you take in Hand about the Castle of *Dublin*; and especially he is well pleased with your pious Restitution to the Parish of that decayed Church. . . . He is also well satisfied with the new Building of a Stable to contain your whole Troop of horse; and commandeth your noble Resolution to make your own Troop so complete with brave and Serviceable Horses, that you may, with Confidence, press others to do the like . . .[13]

On Christmas Eve 1633 Strafford had written something unusual, a rare tactful letter; induced perhaps by the imminence of the season of good will. It was addressed to the Earl of Leicester and couched in the kind of terms which had they been used with Inigo Jones, would have avoided much bad blood. Strafford had found it necessary to take down an inscription which had to do with Leicester's grandfather Sir Henry Sidney, who in 1567 had 'caused the old ruinous castle there to be re-edified'. Strafford may have regarded the inscription as something of a relic since it was commonly held that Sidney had been the ablest of the Elizabethan Lord Deputies. He told Leicester of how he had been careful to reposition it:

> *My very good Lord,*
>
> I confess I made a Fault against your noble Grandfather, by pulling down an old Gate within this Castle, wherein was set an Inscription of his in Verses, but I did so far contemplate him again in his Grandchild as to give him the best Reparation I could, by setting up the very same Stone, carefully taken down, over the new one, which one Day your Lordship may chance to read, and remember both him and me by that Token.[14]

A month later Strafford was assailing Coke with a memorandum of great interest for what it reveals of the elaborate court ritual which he promoted in Dublin Castle. The memorandum deserves scrutiny as the most eloquent of all testaments to Strafford's love of ceremony, decorum and good order:

> [Paragraph] 32. The Rooms of this House are almost become common, every ordinary Gentleman thinking it a Disparagement to stay any where but in the Drawing-Chamber, which indeed is occasioned in part, by suffering the Presence [Chamber] to be so familiar, that for the most Part it is filled with their Servants, whilst their Masters are within. Lest therefore the King's Greatness, albeit but in the Type, become less reverenced than truly it ought to be, I pray to receive the like Command; that upon Days of Meeting none but Noblemen come further than the Drawing-Chamber; the Gallery only free for those that be of the Council, and that all their Servants stay in the great Chamber, where they and all others are to be bare, as well as in the Presence, there being there a State as well as in the other.
>
> [Paragraph] 33. Then the Gentlemen-Ushers to the Chancellor and Treasurer do always come before their Lords as far as to the Gallery Door; and the Purse-Bearer (albeit the Seals are never there) comes into the Gallery, and there stands amongst the Counsellors, which is not altogether so comely, where I conceive their Gentleman-Ushers should leave them at the Door of the Presence (my Servants being there ready to do them all Respect and Service belonging to their Places) and the Chancellor to take the Purse at the Presence-Door, and carry it himself when he comes into the more inward Rooms, it being no ways below his Honour to bear the Purse there himself.
>
> [Paragraph] 34. I confess I might, without more, do these Things, but where I may seem to take any Thing to myself, I am naturally modest, and should be extream unwilling to be held supercilious or imperious amongst them; so as I cannot do therein as I both could and would, where I were commanded. Therefore, if these be held Duties fit to be paid to his Majesty's Greatness, which is alike operative, and to be reverenced thorough every Part of his Dominions, I crave such a Direction in these as in the other; that so, they may know it to be his Pleasure; otherwise I shall be well content they may be spared, having, in Truth, no such Vanity in myself as to be delighted with any of these Observances.[15]

Strafford valued ritual highly; though he claimed to do so only in his capacity as a 'Type' of the King. That was probably fair because Charles I promoted dignity and decorum to disperse the Bacchic train of his father's court. Thereby he created an aura of majesty but also a dank mist: cold, remote and obscuring.

Strafford was punctilious about protocol and he was fascinated by court entertainments. He loved to hear about masques and pastorals which garlanded the court year in London. For Strafford the masque was a type of court ceremony; set to more continuous music than a stately parade through public rooms, and expressed through dance rather than careful filtering of officials, but a recognisable relation, nevertheless, of those rituals which Strafford himself was recommending to Charles I in the memorandum transcribed above.

Less than a month after Strafford burdened Coke with the rituals of life in Dublin Castle, the great collector, the Earl of Arundel, wrote a letter full of what the gay blades of the court in London had recognised as Jones' most successful masque, *The Triumph of Peace*. This was enacted as a peace offering by the Inns of Court for the embarrassment caused by William Prynne, a Lincoln's Inn lawyer, who had denounced the Queen's delight in acting. Strafford must have been fascinated by what Arundel had to tell him:

> Though we have been here, in a long vacancy of hearing from you in Ireland, yet we hope you are well and in good health. For us we are as well and merry, as the brava Cavallata of the Innes of Court, with their Antemasques and Triumphal Chariots could make us, by seeing it in the street first, and after danced in the Banqueting House. . . . This masque was again rehearsed both in riding through London, and Dancing at Merchant Tailors Hall, where their Majesties did them the honour to see them again and to dance in person before the good citizens. But his Majesty on Shrove Tuesday last far surpassed it not only in dancing but in the scene wherein Mr Surveyor did his masterpiece.[16]

Strafford came to rely on one man to tell him about London entertainments. The Reverend George Garrard became Strafford's eyes and ears at a court to which he had access: first as chaplain to the Earl of Northumberland, and later as Master of the Charterhouse; a dignified position which gave status but also leisure for the penning of long gossipy letters. Garrard knew to be careful to include mention of the latest masque and the Commission for New Buildings; high priorities for his recipient in Ireland.

In April 1634 Garrard conveyed bad news about Strafford's close ally Lord Cottington, an ardent hispanophile who appears to have been largely instrumental in obtaining Strafford's appointment to Ireland three years earlier. Cottington's house, Hanworth, one of the most lavish of its day, had been destroyed by fire. Up went all the costly furnishing and decoration about which Cottington had enjoyed writing to Strafford as the house was being built. In June 1634 Strafford heard from Garrard of how the Earl of Bedford was running into trouble with the Commission for New Buildings over his new development at Covent Garden.

In the following September Strafford wrote to the King: '. . . if I might before our Meeting again in Parliament receive so great a mark of your Favour as to have this Family honoured with an Earldom'.[17] The King's precise response is not recorded; though the crudity of the appeal was not so disarming as to make Charles surrender to the request. The Parliament was the Irish Parliament of 1634, which turned out to be a great deal less amenable to bullying than Strafford had anticipated. It was perhaps feelings of exhaustion after its dissolution, coupled with disappointment at not obtaining the earldom, which induced Strafford to write that autumn to his Yorkshire neighbour Sir Edward Stanhope in response to news of his gardens at Wentworth Woodhouse:

> Next you mention my Garden at *Woodhouse*, and I thank you for the Visit, and as prosperous as you conceive his Majesty's Affairs go here, and indeed inprosperous, I praise God, they have not been hitherto, yet could I possess myself with more Satisfaction and Repose under that Roof, than with all the Preferment and Power a Crown can communicate of her Grace and Favour.[18]

Strafford did not remain despondent long. In October 1634 he was once again getting at the hapless Coke, complaining that 'the Castle is in mighty ruin', and adding that he was going to lay forth £2,000 on repairs 'with some additions for Stable and Gardens'. With those plans in train, he then took Coke into Dublin to complain of how:

> There is a great Want of good Houses in this Kingdom, which may be an Occasion they take not that Delight in their Abodes in the Country, as otherwise I am persuaded they would, found they at home a Decency and Handsomness to entertain them. I confess this must be redeemed by Time and Degrees, yet if there were some strict Course used to bring them in this Town to a good Order in Building, the Example might stir up an Emulation through the whole Kingdom to intend and accommodate their own Dwellings, much more than now they do. Certainly, the Proclamation you have in *England* might be of good Use here, so as I desire you would cause the same to be sent me, with all the Orders of the Council-Board in that Business, and a Copy of some Sentences passed in the *Star-Chamber* against the Contemners thereof, where-unto we shall conform ourselves as near as we can, and I am very hopeful it will be a Means in few Years to beautify this City exceedingly.[19]

It is a richly suggestive document: 'delight', 'decency', 'handsomness', 'utility'; words brought into the English repertoire of architectural description by Sir Henry Wotton, but applied by Strafford in an Irish context, to carry a sense of moral approbation to the building of the state as columns support a pediment.

Coke appears to have passed on Strafford's concerns to Arundel, who seems to have mediated the rivalry between Strafford and Jones by virtue of being friend to both. Arundel wrote to Strafford to tell him how everyone, Jones especially, liked Strafford's Proclamation for New Buildings. However, there was a sting in the tail because Arundel then added that while Jones approved of Strafford's policy of improving standards of building, he 'hopes yr Lop will one day acknowledge him to be ye better architect'.[20] Strafford wrote complaining that he had not actually received Jones's own Proclamation, to which Arundel replied:

> . . . for the Proclamacion for buildings Inigo told me longe agaoe he had sente it unto yr Lop and so sayeth still, wch he avowes he did out of his duty and to propagate the Artes but not to begge ye suffrage for his abilitye in his owne profession, wch he understandes soe well, as though he be not worthy to looke upon yr Lops abiltyes in all thinges els yet in this particular he would be sorry yr Lops skill should presume to enter ye listes wth his.[21]

Strafford in turn responded sardonically:

> . . . I desire peace wth ye great and good genius of Architecture Mr Inigoe Jones, Soe as it may be wthout negelect to us ye lesser Intelligences in yt high and noble art, and thus I shall be willing to borrow from and acknowledge his Authority. But if he look big and disdainfully upon us, I shall not forbear to tell him, I have built a better stable for ye King here in Ireland than ever he did in England. That a worm if trodden on will turn again.[22]

A new venture for Strafford began in the autumn of 1635 when he found himself a somewhat reluctant promoter of marble quarries; induced to do so by Arundel who had significant economic interests in Ireland. However, the shipment of marble and building stone may have had some significance for the Irish economy long before Strafford became involved. Twenty years before Strafford began quarrying, Donogh O'Brien, 4th Earl of Thomond, described laconically in Burke's *Extinct Peerage* as the 'great earl,' had been in correspondence with Christian IV of Denmark. Thomond had written to Christian from Limerick on 3 October 1616 that 'his ship is laden with grey marble, according to his desire; if he will send again next year, a cargo of red marble shall be provided'.[23] History does not tell us about the red marble but we may speculate that the consignment of grey might have been for Fredericksborg Castle, the great Danish palace built on three islands in Copenhagen Sound. Fredericksborg had been begun in 1599 and was topped out *c.* 1620 with the installation of the celebrated Neptune fountain, commissioned from the international court artist Adrien de Vries; a *Speculum regale* allegorising Christian as master of the Baltic and the North Seas.[24]

Strafford could have done without the extra burden of dealing with dubious profiteers in the building trade and he suspected that although a public servant, he was going to be used to supervise private gain. He did not like it. Nevertheless the enterprise was successful. Irish stone was supplied both for the steps of the giant portico at Old St Paul's and for the Queen's House, Greenwich, where work had begun again after the death of Anne of Denmark seventeen years earlier.

On 14 September 1635 Strafford wrote to Arundel:

> By your L^{ps} of ye 14 of August you recommend unto me Mr Page to whom I will wth all my hart doe ye best respects I can, I wish your trade for marbles may succeed, for I like all things that may be still a mean to breed a greater commerce and familiarity betwixt ye two nations, every day more than another. Certainly I am persuaded they will find very good black and mingled with white about Gallway, and in some part of Munster excellent good white and red, I will be bold to harken after them, hoping that I may get a barque lading to send about to Hull and so into Yorkshire, to make me a chimney piece or two at Woodhouse.[25]

Strafford managed to get leave to return to London for an extended period in 1636 and it was then that he sat to Van Dyck for at least four separate portrait types: two different full-length presentations, a half-length, and a double portrait (Plate 74, page 193). Strafford was one of Van Dyck's most ardent admirers and it was to his unique capacity to flatter that Strafford turned when he wanted a public face.

Strafford's dealings with Van Dyck have been very fully discussed by Oliver Millar.[26] The published letters not only give a rare glimpse of the thoughts of a patron when faced with the bills of his painter, but they also dispel the assumption that Van Dyck was director and his clients his actors. Earlier I suggested that Charles I, not Van Dyck, would have ordained how he was to appear in his own portraits, and Strafford too had decided views for himself. Each of the single portraits of Strafford shows a profound debt to Titian's imagery. This in itself was hardly unusual; almost all Van Dyck's English portraits did that. But it is interesting that in two out of the four types, Van Dyck has looked to famous figures of Habsburg history. The full-length of Strafford with hunting dog depends upon Titian's *Charles V*, which was then in The Royal Collection; one of the consolation prizes from Charles' failed mission to Madrid of 1623. The three-quarter length has Strafford presented within the iconography of the *adlocutio*; the convention for the Roman Emperor addressing his troops. It depends on Titian's portrait of the *Marquis del Vasto* who had been a celebrated general in Habsburg service. Thus it may be that there was a 'Habsburg' and not merely a Titianesque inspiration behind the single portraits, and that this owed something to Strafford's temperamental sympathy with Spain. Who can say that Strafford took a biographical rather than a merely visual interest in the Titians which he saw in London? It is however a distinct possibility. What we take to be the right priorities in looking at a Van Dyck portrait were inverted by his sitters. We care about brushwork; Caroline courtiers more for the supposed identity of the sitter. Whatever the exact nature of Strafford's dealings with Van Dyck, he had a perception of the manipulative potential of portraiture which may have been unusual in England in his day.

After Strafford returned to Dublin and life was becoming increasingly difficult, he wrote to Laud to take heart in their joint crusade to pursue the business of the King's government with all possible thoroughness. The best Strafford could do was to suggest that the Archbishop take a brush from Van Dyck's palette:

> And seeing that all Beauties take not all Affections, one Man judging that a Deformity, which another considers as a Perfection or a Grace; this methinks convinceth the certain Incertainy of Rewards and Punishments: Howsoever he is the wisest commonly, the greatest, and happiest Man, and shall surely draw the fairest Table of his Life, that understands with *Vandike*, how to dispose of these Shadows, best, to make up his own Comeliness and Advantage.[27]

Strafford was given to rather exhausting and contrived parallels and this was one of many which fell flat. Laud was learned and though a most distinguished patron of architecture, unmoved by pictures. All he could do was to tell Strafford he would be better off if he 'read over the short Book of *Ecclesiastes*, [where] . . . you will see a better Disposition of these Things, and the Vanity of all their Shadows, than is to be found in any Anagrams of Dr *Donne's*, or any Designs of *Vandike*'; so to the Lines there drawn I leave you'.[28]

Besides having a series of portraits painted by Van Dyck, Strafford studied the great collections while on leave in London in 1636. He had dealings too with his admirer the Spanish ambassador, who organised a shipment of Brussels tapestries. Acquisition of de luxe objects was an investment; part of a strategy to make Strafford's presence in Dublin more effective. Fine portraits clad in armour, a bust of Charles I by Le Sueur presented by the king himself,[29] tapestries heavy with gold and silver thread;[30] all made a fresh impact in those rooms the use of which Strafford had so carefully ordained before he left for London. The Earl of Cork may have been richer and better supported within Irish society, but he lacked Strafford's sense of presentation.

The year 1637 was important because it was then that Jigginstown began to attract adverse criticism. It was a political folly on a monumental scale; had it been an architectural one only, it would have been of no consequence. Jigginstown was as disastrous for Strafford as Ceausescu's palace in Romania. It cost £22,000; much of it milked from the revenues, or so enemies liked to suggest. It was significantly longer than either Hatfield or Longleat; though the cost was also due to craftsmanship of a high order.[31] It had two entrances with grand flights of stairs; so arranged, Strafford claimed, because he intended half the house for the King and the rest for himself. The *piano nobile* appears to have been on the grandest possible scale: twenty-four stone windows 25 feet in height and 6 across, set against brickwork consisting of four different colours worked together on the same façade and all greatly admired for virtuosity. There were marble columns and floors, but by 1656, the date of the survey in which the cost of the building is revealed, the lead had been removed for ammunition, the house deserted and left open to the skies.

Strafford was well aware of what was being said about Jigginstown. The stories that it was going up out of profits from office, Strafford tried to refute in a characteristically long and self-justificatory letter. It was addressed to Laud at the end of September 1637 and in it Strafford wrote:

> I have good Advertisement that some, who sure find I serve the Crown too entirely for their Purpose, do yet endeavour to persuade his Majesty, that I serve myself too well in this Place, so to bring me into Suspicion with My master, and thorough that open a Way to my Prejudice.
>
> Their first Charge is, that I have two or three and twenty thousand Pounds a Year coming in . . .
>
> Next they say I build up to the Sky. I acknowledge that were myself only considered in what I build, it were not only to Excess, but even to Folly, having already Houses moderate for my Condition in *Yorkshire*: But His Majesty will justify me, that at my last being in *England*, I acquainted him with a Purpose I had to build him a House at the *Naas*, it being uncomely his Majesty should not have one here of his own, capable to lodge him with moderate Conveniency (which in Truth as yet he hath not) in case he might be pleased sometimes hereafter to look upon this Kingdom; and that it was necessary in a Manner for the Dignity of this Place, and the Health of his Deputy and Family that there should be one removing House of fresh Air, for want whereof I assure your Lordship, I have felt no small inconvenience, since my coming hither; that when it was built, if liked by his Majesty it should be his, paying me as it cost; if disliked, *a suo damno*, I was content to keep it and smart for my Folly. His Majesty seemed to be pleased with all, whereupon I proceeded and have in a Manner finished it, and so contrived it for the Rooms of State and other Accommodations which I have observed in his Majesty's Houses, as I had indeed been stark mad, ever to have cast it so for a private Family. Another Frame of Wood I have given order to set up in a Park I have in the County of *Wickloe*. And

gnash the Tooth of these Gallants never so hard, I will by God's Leave go on with it, . . .

Yet lest these magnificent Structures might be thought those of *Nebuchaedunezzar*, the plain Truth is, that at the *Naas* with the most may stand in six thousand Pounds, that in the Park at twelve hundred; Faith, at worst methinks, they should not judge it very much for a Person of my great *Hazienda* to case away twelve hundred Pounds upon his own Fancy;[32]

Each phase of Strafford's Irish building campaign threatened a complacent and corrupt community. While Jigginstown cast a long shadow over the Wicklow countryside and the social standing of men with grander titles than the Lord Deputy, Strafford's renovation of the physical assets of the Irish Church hardly endeared him to the clerical estate. The Church in Ireland included distinguished divines like James Ussher, Archbishop of Armagh, whom Strafford effectively ignored, but it was largely peopled by the venal and the supine.

Strafford had begun his attack on the Church in December 1633; in much the same abrasive and impolitic way as he was then handling the business of the Cork monument. He told Laud that he intended to 'trounce a Bishop or two in the Castle Chamber'; he was determined to make an example of those who had alienated or sold off lands belonging to the Church. But the net effect of such a policy towards the Church was destabilisation. Although he saw to the appointment of a number of able careerist churchmen, by the time the regime was brought down with his own impeachment in 1640, their reach exceeded their grasp.

It has been suggested that the problem with the Personal Rule was that it was too efficient; those who sustained it interfered too much with the autonomy of local communities. So too in Ireland, Strafford goaded and irritated those who wanted to enjoy the fruits of an undemanding office. He cast the money lenders from the Temple. He was appalled to discover that the under-croft of Christ Church Cathedral, Dublin, was used as an ale house. While Laud was provoked into tackling the renovation of Old St Paul's partly because of the scandalous uses to which the Cathedral was put, so in Dublin, it was the misuse of Christ Church which goaded Strafford into writing to Laud:

There being divers buildings erected upon the fabric of *Christ-Church*, and the Vaults underneath the Church itself turned all to Alehouses and Tobacco Shops, where they are pouring either in or out their Drink-Offerings and Incense, whilst we above are serving the high God. I have taken Order for the removing of them, granted a Commission to the Archbishop of *Dublin* and others to view and certify, settled and published these Orders for the Service there, which I send your Grace here inclosed, whereof not one was observed before.[33]

Repairs and removal of buildings which abutted onto Christ Church served to give the Cathedral that dignity Strafford wanted. His task seems to have been easier than Laud's, for he does not seem to have met the same obstructions, in the forced removal of those who nested in the lean-tos which abutted Christ Church, as dogged Laud and Jones at St Gregory's. Strafford did not stop at restoration and restitution however. He extended the capacities of the Church by erecting new buildings. He began a new cathedral at Downe, which disrupted and inconvenienced the lives of those who administered that diocese; serving only to make him enemies in that quarter.

Strafford found Ireland profoundly uncongenial but there were pleasurable interludes. After stretching himself on the wheel of interminable correspondence, a torture made worse by continuous justification of his own actions, he liked to relax by watching theatricals.

Strafford had probably approached James Shirley the playwright and composer of texts for masques, when Strafford had been sitting to Van Dyck during his period of leave in 1636. Whether it was Strafford himself or his deputy is not known, but by whatever means, Shirley was invited to Dublin to oversee vice-regal masques and plays. The invitation was probably made on the strength of the popular success Shirley's plays like *Hyde Park* enjoyed, and the reputation Shirley had made for himself as a composer of masques, with his *Triumph of Peace*. That, it may be recalled, had been described in unusually long and enthusiastic detail by Arundel when writing to Strafford a year or two earlier. Shirley duly went to Ireland, though it has been suggested, only induced to do so because of the closure of London theatres with a severe outbreak of plague in 1636.[34] Anyway whatever Shirley's motives may have been, he established the first professional playhouse in Ireland, under the patronage of Strafford, in Werburgh Street in Dublin. It was at the Werburgh Street theatre that Shirley's most ambitious Irish creation, *St Patrick for Ireland*, was performed. The play contained some of the same kind of moveable devices which had been familiar for the last twenty years to anyone attending a London masque: fantastic costumes, moving statues, flames behind an altar, and a burning house.

However, perhaps because of the ambition and sophistication of the play, it was not a success. Nor for that matter were the four years Shirley spent at the vice-regal court before he departed Ireland for good in April 1640; sailing in the same boat as Strafford who was returning to what would be his trial and execution the following spring.

Strafford relaxed by enjoying the company of a select band of devoted subordinates; more disciples than companions but enormously important nevertheless, to this intense and lonely man. There is a vivid picture of Strafford on what he declared a resoundingly successful progress through the south and west of Ireland in the summer of 1637, when a series of triumphal entries were enjoyed and endured in equal measure. Of these he wrote good humouredly to his old friend Lord Conway:

Hither are we come through a country upon my faith if as well husbanded, built, and peopled as are you in England, would show itself not much inferior to the very best you have there. . . . They have all along to the uttermost of their skill and breeding give[n] me very great expressions of their esteem and affection. . . .

Oratory hath abundantly magnified itself through those excellent pieces we have heard, one at Caterlaghe, three at Kilkenny, two very deadly long ones at Clonmel, four not of the shortest here at Limerick.

Architecture and invention not asleep, as appeared in their archtriumphals, with their ornaments and inscriptions; the ingenuous accomodation of their Cupids, their Apollo, their ancient genii, their laureat poets, and such like; here, *pour la bonne bouche* (as the French say), we saw all the seven planets in a very spericall and heavenly motion, and heard each of them utter in harmony several verses in our praise, telling is [us] thereby upon my knowledge rather what we ought to be than what we were (the common case, you will say, of all painters and orators), and the sun, the King of Planets, over and above all the rest did instead of his indulgent heat benignly squirt of his sweet waters upon us forth of a seringe, my hopes being all the whilst the instrument was new, and had not been used before.[35]

Strafford also enjoyed antiquarian studies in these rare moments of relaxation; one of the few interests he shared with Archbishop Ussher, pre-eminent student of Irish history. Strafford was deeply fascinated in archaeological finds turned up by the passing plough in an Irish bog. On 6 January 1639, just months before he went down in the morass of Scottish politics, he wrote to Charles I:

Some Years past there was found in the Ground a Silver Seal of one of the Kings of *Connaght*, which I then sent your Majesty. Now as it seems one of their Bits of Gold, weighing ten Ounces, was in like Sort chanced upon lately in the county of *Gallway*, which I herewith present your Majesty with. I have sent to dig there again, in case any more of the Furniture thereto belonging might be found.[36]

Strafford also became interested in setting up a tapestry manufactory in Ireland; his opportunity, the death in 1636 of Sir Francis Crane, the first director of the Mortlake Tapestry Works in London. Strafford tried to persuade Jan Benoot, one of the Mortlake weavers, to set up a manufactory in Dublin. It came to nothing though negotiations got to the point at which Benoot laid down what he would require by way of wages, equipment and manpower. Benoot's letter suggests that both parties took the project seriously.[37]

Strafford was a melancholic who hid despondency by constant hurry, constant activity. It took the form of a phrenetic urge to set up a multitude of business ventures. He found these reassuring as they gave him the illusion that something was being done to ameliorate the indolence and chaos he thought he saw all about him.

'Thoroughness' and 'efficiency' are words commonly used to describe Strafford's regime in Ireland. But no less a priority for Strafford was dignity in the exercise of his office, which meant the dignity of that majesty for which he deputised. Strafford's own abrasiveness was certainly met by an equal force of harshness when he came to face his peers during his trial for High Treason at the bar of the House of Lords on 22 March 1641. Strafford conducted his own defence for the next six weeks and it was his remarkable dignity in adversity which affected some of those who had been his most voluble critics. One of these was George Digby, later Earl of Bristol. Digby was brave enough to state in the Lords on 20 April that he could not reconcile himself to the judicial murder of the plaintiff. In what was one of many moments of high drama not to say pathos, Digby rose to declare:

> Let every man lay his hand upon his heart and sadly consider what we are going to do with a breath, either justice or murder. . . . I do, before God, discharge myself, to the uttermost of my power, and do with a clear conscience wash my hands of this man's blood, by this solemn protestation, that my vote goes not to the taking of the Earl of Strafford's life.[38]

Another observer of these remarkable events was Sir John Denham, a poet of real and lasting distinction who would eventually become Surveyor of the King's Works at the Restoration. His poetic masterpiece *Cooper's Hill* was written at that time of turbulence when Strafford was tried and executed.

Like Digby, Denham too had begun with a fixed hostility to Strafford, but also came to see remarkable qualities in what Strafford's enemies framed as this 'enemy of the people'. In what is known as 'Text III' of *Cooper's Hill*, Denham deplores the King's weakness in not saving Strafford. The poet refers to Strafford's famous letter sent to the King in which Strafford absolved his recipient from his promise not to let him die, which the King had made in one of his own letters to Strafford. Denham does this by likening Strafford to a stag at bay which is being hunted on 'Egham Meade', a royal hunting ground which was visible from Cooper's Hill and near Windsor Castle. Denham suggests that the stag encourages the King himself to deliver the fatal blow:

> As some brave *Hero*, whom his baser foes
> In troops surround, now these assaile, now those,
> Though prodigall of life, disdaines to die

By vulgar hands, but if he can descry
Some Nobler foe's approach, to him he cals
And begs his fate, and then contented fals:
So the tall Stagge, amids the lesser hounds
Repels their force, and wounds returnes for wounds,
Till *Charles* from his unerring hand lets flie
A mortall shaft, then glad and proud to dye
By such a wound, he fals, the Christall floud
Dying he dies, and purples with his blood:[39]

Castle, cathedral, palace, hunting lodge, mint, law court, record office, houses of restitution, state portraits, quarries, tapestries, antiquities; all built, altered, planned or acquired because Strafford thought they promoted him as a 'Type' of the King. It was much the same attitude as Leonardo had betrayed when he had written to Giuliano de' Medici to describe a 'political town plan' and the philosophy which lay behind it. 'Give me authority', Leonardo had written, 'and all regions shall obey their governors at no cost to yourself. . . . Your fame will last forever . . . all the inhabitants will have to obey . . . and their governors will be bound to their lord in two ways: through ties of blood, when their sons, like hostages, offer a pledge of unfailing loyalty, and through justice, when you have one or two houses built for each of them in your city and each receives a certain revenue from them.'[40]

For Strafford, buildings were necessary for the dignity of a state invested in the Lord Deputy who passionately believed in the persuasive powers of the visual arts. It was a point Strafford made to Charles I when he was raised to that earldom he had craved for so long, just six months before his execution. Strafford gave thanks for the honour, adding: 'It is acknowledged with Reverence and Truth, that Kings on the Throne are sacred Pictures of Divine Majesty.'[41] He might have added that in Ireland he had tried to make a persuasive if not a sacred picture of the King's government.

How Strafford used the visual arts has been overlooked by historians of the seventeenth century; with the single exception, that is, of the greatest of them all: Edward Hyde, Earl of Clarendon. In his *Short View of the State and Condition of Ireland*, published posthumously in 1719, Clarendon castigated what he considered a hapless race for throwing away all the benefits which Strafford had brought them:

They now have leisure enough, and I hope spirits better prepared to revolve the wonderful plenty, peace and security they enjoyed till the year 1641, when they wantonly and disdainfully flung those blessings from them; the increase of traffic, the improvement of land, the erection of buildings, and whatsoever might be profitable and pleasant to a people.[42]

Clarendon may not be objective history but an important perception emerges through the haze of his invective. It is that great Renaissance patrons saw high political purpose in the visual arts. Strafford, like Wolsey, Northumberland, Burghley and Buckingham before him, understood that ministers of the Crown needed a sustained programme and exposition of visual splendour.

Chapter Seven
Collecting: Patronage and Display

The early seventeenth century in England has been described as the golden age of the arts; more splendid than the eras of Henry VIII or the Prince Regent. Some of the world's greatest artists came to London in the reign of Charles I where a colony grew up around St Martin's Lane, the talents and output of which made London, for an interval at least, outshine Paris as a centre of the arts. Cleyn, Dieussart, Fanelli, Orazio Gentileschi and his daughter Artemisia, Honthorst, Jones, Keirincx, Lievens, Le Sueur, Lely possibly, Mytens, Petitot, Poelenburgh, Rubens, Van Dyck and Christian van Vianen were some of the painters, sculptors and silversmiths who visited or came to live in London. Bernini, Jordaens, Rembrandt, Reni, and a host of others, some of whose identity and output still remains to be defined, had their work displayed in The Royal Collection. It is an astonishing group including many of the best talents of the Baroque age. It gave the kingdom a reputation as an elysium of the arts. The purpose of this chapter is to look at what might be termed 'itinerant' works of art and to consider why collecting became fashionable.

The portraits of Elizabeth I were sometimes 'itinerant'; an unlicensed image might appear in a town hall anywhere; as Elizabeth herself was acutely aware. Royal portraiture has been the subject of earlier chapters and here we shall be concerned with easel or cabinet paintings, which were more often moved from one location to another; relatively small pictures without overt propagandist elements, collected ostensibly for the fame of the artist, quality of workmanship, or the attraction of subject matter. Here it will be argued that there were other less obvious motives which made them much sought after by the Jacobean and Caroline grandee; motives it will be our purpose to uncover.

But we begin at the Tudor period, not at the end of the story. What then of the place of Holbein at the court of Henry VIII? He came to London in December 1526, encouraged by Erasmus and with what may have been distinctly naive expectations. Sir Thomas More, into whose household he was received, responded by replying to Erasmus:

> Your painter, dearest Erasmus, is a remarkable artist; but I am afraid he will not find England as fertile and fruitful as he expected. Still, I shall do my best to see that he does not find it altogether barren.[1]

More's assumption proved right. Although Holbein painted his group portrait of the More household at Chelsea, a picture celebrating a palace of the intellect, matching in ambition Mantegna's Gonzaga family in the Ducal Palace at Mantua of half a century earlier, never again would Holbein be called upon to orchestrate a portrait of such complexity. English patrons were not interested in making demands on that scale. What Holbein left behind in Basle was far superior in ambition to anything he accomplished either on his first London visit of 1526–8, or when he came to settle between 1532 and his death in 1543.

There is a compelling parallel between the English career of Holbein and that of Van Dyck of exactly one hundred years later. The *Family of Sir Thomas More* stands with *The Pembroke Family* as two of the greatest group portraits in Western painting. But they are among a small group of pictures accomplished by these artists in England which can bear comparison with what Holbein left in Basle, and Van Dyck in Antwerp.

When Holbein was at Chelsea, More was in daily contact with Wolsey. Yet there is no evidence that Wolsey took that close interest in the portraitist which he certainly expressed in Nicholas Kratzer, the royal astronomer. Wolsey appointed Kratzer one of his lecturers at Corpus Christi College, Oxford. Corpus, Bishop Richard Foxe's foundation of 1516, had become a centre of humanist students and a nursery for the schoolroom of Cardinal College (now Christ Church), Wolsey's great foundation which it was intended should surpass Wykeham's New College and Waynflete's Magdalen, to become the greatest monument of learning not only in Oxford, but in all England.

Holbein and Kratzer worked together in orchestrating the iconography for the Banqueting House at Greenwich in 1527. But that was transient splendour. Both Wolsey and Henry VIII liked it enough to have what were temporary buildings run up to receive French ambassadors, opened to the public for two days. But it cannot be said that Holbein became The King's Painter as Van Dyck would become to Charles I.

It has been argued that Holbein's most sympathetic patron was not the king but Anne Boleyn.[2] She was the most attractive and vivacious of Henry's wives, and superior too in having a real understanding of how to make good use of artists. For Anne, Holbein designed jewellery and, most spectacularly of all, the Parnassus pageant of 1533, which caused Charles V's ambassador Chapuys grave offence. He thought Parnassus was crowned by the Imperial eagle. That was an heraldic device to which

Catherine of Aragon, the late cast-off of the king, would have been entitled, but Anne Boleyn assuredly not. However, Chapuys was wrong. What he was looking at and complaining about was the white eagle of the Boleyns.

Holbein came to England when conservatives felt the ship of state was turning turtle after baggage and ballast had been thrown overboard. It may well be that the hazardous nature of court life under Henry VIII partially explains why Holbein was never intimately associated with the king. At first glance this seems wide of the mark: Holbein's image of Henry VIII as a colossus astride the world is every bit as impressive as any portrait of Charles I by Van Dyck. However, Holbein's repertoire of Henrician imagery is much more confined than Van Dyck's of Charles I.

Henry appears to have been well aware of Holbein's extraordinary talent, but patronage has always been a two-way affair, and Holbein never identified with the values of the Tudor court as Van Dyck became absorbed with the Whitehall world of the 1630s. The double portrait was a genre well within the grasp of Holbein since during his first visit to London he painted, in 1528, *Sir John Godsalve and his Father*. However, no double portrait exists of himself with an English friend such as Van Dyck created in his double portrait with Endymion Porter; a suave image in which it is impossible to know who is the Flemish painter and who the 'compleat gentleman', as Porter was described by the popular author Henry Peacham at the time. Holbein's self-portraits suggest the independent, stubborn artisan of powerful convictions: that double portrait by Van Dyck, a socially ambitious neurotic.

We have already seen how Henry VIII used Holbein as an ambassador. The analogy is a real one: twice Holbein was required to go abroad to make portraits of prospective brides. Although both missions embroiled the artist in difficulties, the end results were two of his most beautiful portraits: *Christina of Denmark* (National Gallery, London) and *Anne of Cleves* (The Louvre). With Anne of Cleves, Holbein triumphed as artist only to fail as a servant of the Crown. During these foreign missions, Holbein was required to work rapidly since, as always with Henry, what was required was wanted at once. Holbein's second, disastrous excursion into the genre of bridal portraiture signalled the end of what seems to have been, in any event, a remote working partnership between the king and his painter. Not only had Holbein failed on an important diplomatic mission, it has been suggested that his very style was beginning to appear rather old fashioned by 1540; in the last five years of his life, Holbein was 'the living embodiment of an earlier era', so Strong believed; though to accept such an argument requires giving rather more credit to the percipience of the Tudor patron than he deserved.[3]

Nevertheless whatever the tensions and difficulties which may have subsisted between Henry VIII and Holbein, Holbein himself contributed to English culture in a decisive and lasting way: not only with royal portraiture, but in the much humbler sphere of the popular print. Holbein

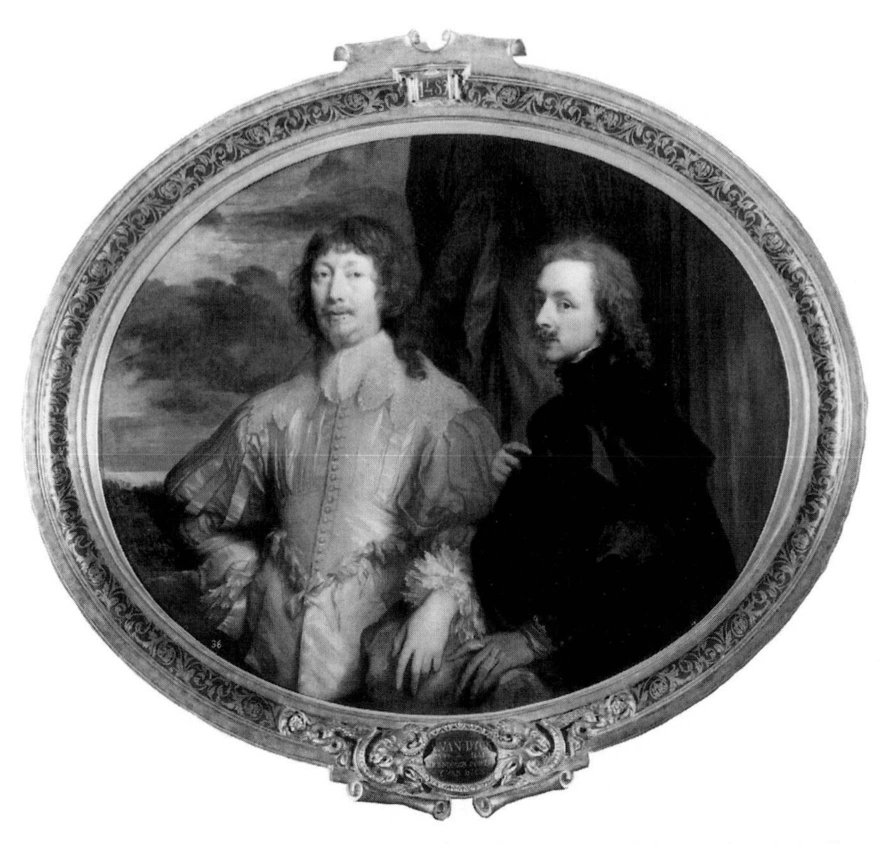

Sir Anthony Van Dyck, *Self-portrait with Endymion Porter* (The Prado, Madrid)

affected the development of the English church as fundamentally as he conditioned the pattern of English portraiture. It is, then, to the ecclesiastical realm as well as the secular that we have to turn to understand the English years of Holbein in their true light.

Holbein made a personal commitment to the country of his adoption through the medium of the cheap print. Print-making demanded very different talents from those deployed as a pensioned court official. Holbein naturally exerted himself in painting frescoes at Whitehall – how else would an ambitious artist have reacted to a commission of such importance? – but he did so as an artist with a European reputation. What engaged him with prints was the opportunity they gave for personal expression of religious loyalties. Religion was something central to Holbein's inner life and it was his perception that England was a more sympathetic environment for the safe exercise of his beliefs which may have decided him to settle permanently in 1532.

Holbein's most famous contribution in England to the printing press was his frontispiece to Coverdale's Bible of 1535. It was a frontispiece in more ways than one. It stands as a landmark in the dissemination of visual propaganda in England; the effects of which came to be far more widespread than any image of Henry VIII.

Images of Henry derived from the 'Great Picture' by Holbein were necessarily confined. No prints of the original were issued. Although copies were certainly distributed, they were limited in number; confined to some well favoured colleges like Henry's own foundation of Trinity, Cambridge, or the houses of courtiers. Copies had their effects on what might be termed the 'converted': literate undergraduates, pages in noble households, lawyers at the Inns of Court, rising stars in Cromwell's bureaucracy. But these hardly needed persuading that Henry VIII was a good thing.

By contrast, the Coverdale frontispiece came to be scrutinised in parish churches from Carlisle to Chichester, working its effects on those who could read, but perhaps more importantly on those who could not. The frontispiece announced the new and revolutionary relationship between the secular and ecclesiastical swords; drawing attention to issues which men cared about passionately and which were the weekly subject of exposition from the parish pulpit. Henry VIII regarded the vernacular Bible with the gravest suspicion. But the truth was out. Or perhaps it should be said, the opportunity to argue as to what the truth was now lay at the disposal of Piers Ploughman should he learn to read. There was no going back after the appearance of an English Bible. It was a turning point in social history; a revolution in accessibility with incalculable consequences.

Thomas Cromwell made the Bible accessible to the laity as both architect and builder of the English revolution. The personal commitment of Holbein to those changes, a commitment he never felt to Henry VIII, is suggested by the probability that it was Cromwell, not the king, who provided Holbein with encouragement and understanding after the death of Anne Boleyn.

Holbein gave the impetus to bible illustration; others followed its implications. Much of what followed can be traced back to Holbein's output, or to that of the 'school' of graphic designers which emerged as a result of his inspiration in the last years of Henry VIII's reign. These anonymous printmakers, the followers of Holbein, were inspired not only by the Coverdale frontispiece, but by Holbein's justly celebrated plates: *The Dance of Death* and *The Old Testament*.

Two separate series, the first moralistic, the second merely illustrative, both were designed *c*. 1520–26, but only published separately in Lyons in 1538. *The Old Testament* was uncontroversial. But that could not be said of *The Dance of Death*, where in one plate, a porcine Cardinal with beretta dishes out an indulgence with its seals of authenticity, whilst the pilgrim to whom it is being handed fumbles in his pocket for cash and skeletal Death creeps upon the unseeing churchman.

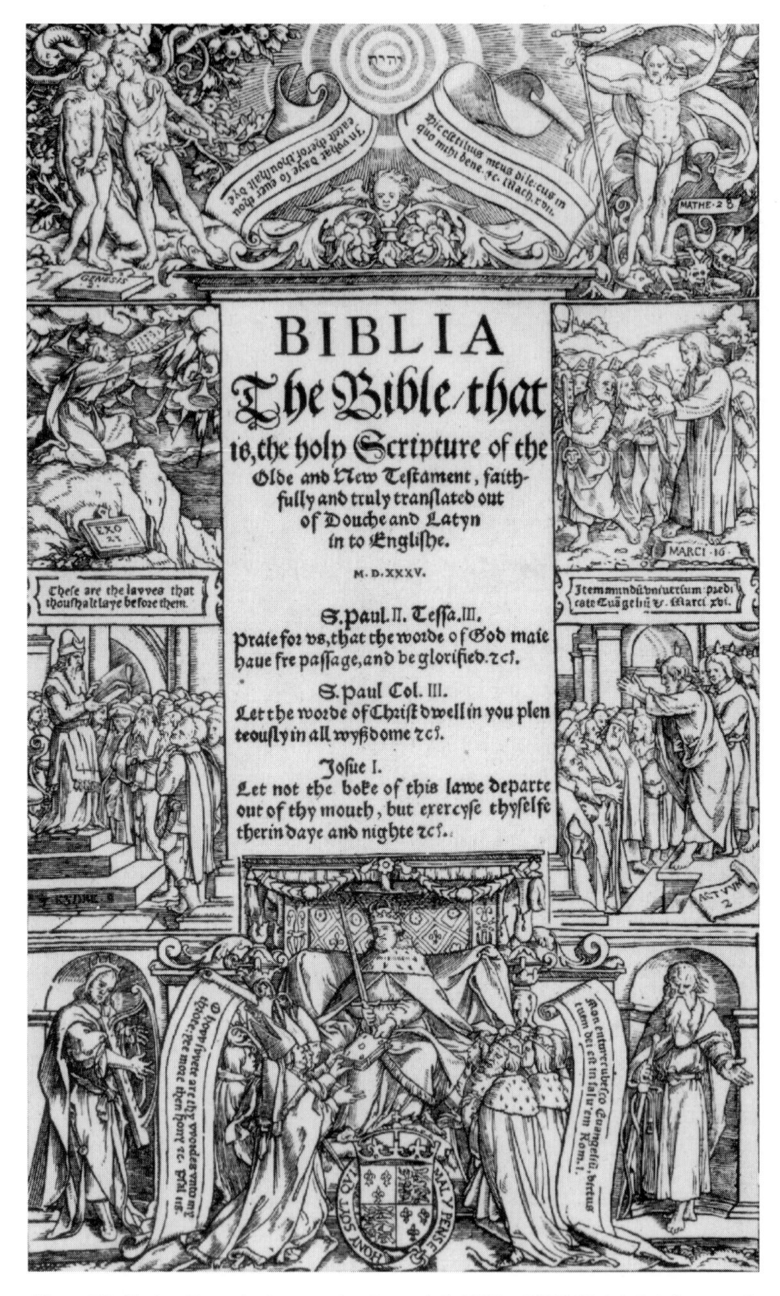

BIBLIA
The Bible/that
is, the holy Scripture of the
Olde and New Testament, faithfully and truly translated out
of Douche and Latyn
in to Englishe.

M.D.XXXV.

S.Paul.II. Tessa.III.
Praie for vs, that the worde of God maie
haue fre passage, and be glorified. ꝛc.

S.Paul Col. III.
Let the worde of Christ dwell in you plen
teously in all wysdome ꝛc.

Josue I.
Let not the boke of this lawe departe
out of thy mouth, but exercyse thyselfe
therin daye and nighte ꝛc.

These are the lawes that thou shalt laye before them.

GENESIS

MATHE·28

MARCI·16

Hans Holbein, *Frontispiece to the Coverdale Bible*, 1535 (British Museum)

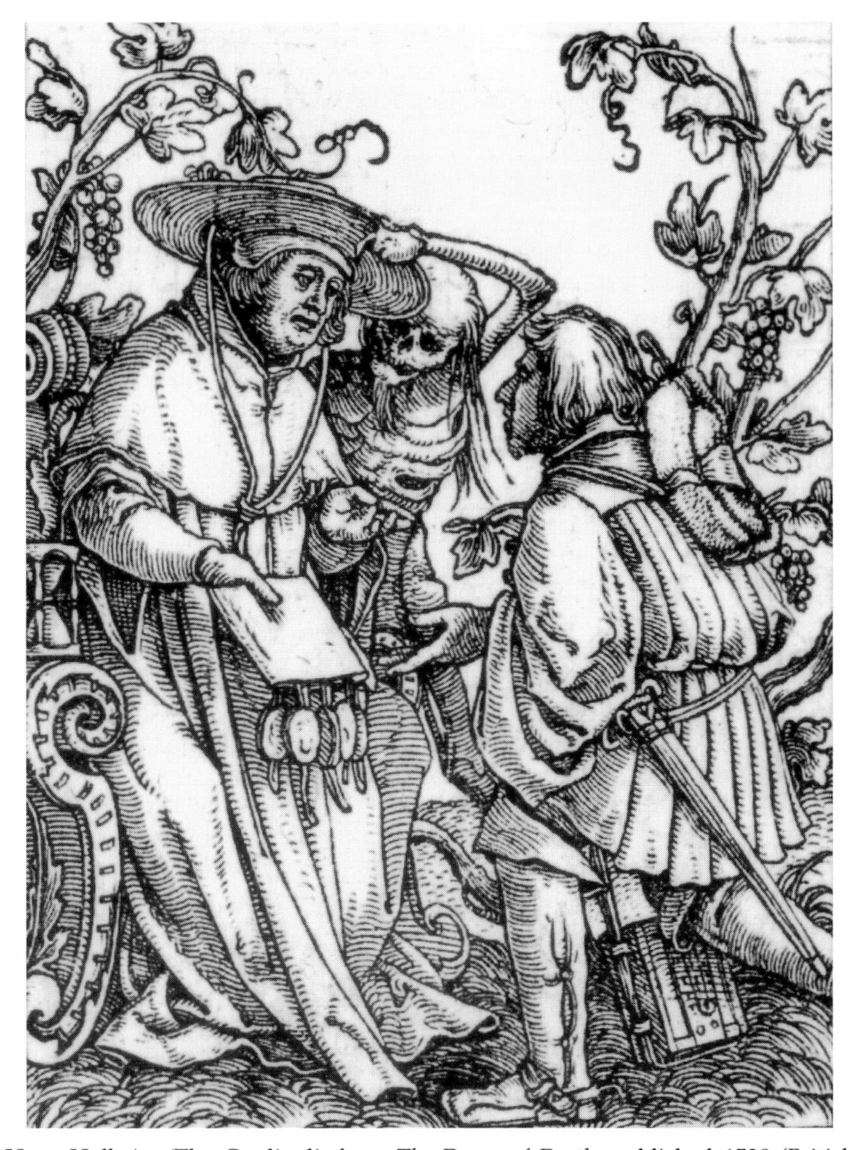

Hans Holbein, 'The Cardinal', from *The Dance of Death*, published 1538 (British Museum)

The 26 cuts for Archbishop Cranmer's so-called *Catechism* some regard as by Holbein, some not. What is certain however is that they owe their inspiration to Holbein. It is from just such a work that the immensely influential illustrations to Foxe's *Book of Martyrs* derives. Foxe's book was one of the most powerful instruments of ecclesiastical propaganda to emerge in sixteenth-century Europe. It is hard to assess whether it was more effective in creating a demonology of Catholicism, or a consciousness of Election for English Calvinists. The illustrated text was one of the most formidable weapons in the arsenal of religious warfare at the disposal of Tudor controversialists. It had been Holbein who had taught them how to use it.

What Holbein did to add to the controversies of religious debate in the English Church, Dürer had already done for German reformers. With the appearance of a whole encyclopaedia of illustrations from the New Testament by Dürer, and Holbein's *Dance of Death*, it was no longer possible to confine curiosity about religion, or indeed religious differences, within leather boards. Prints were sold individually and at a price which made them accessible to a vast market. The effect must have been like the revolution in cable television today. People worry now about the exposure of the vulnerable to that intrusion, just as the Tudors saw the undermining of ecclesiastical order as a consequence of the accessibility of the Bible.

The interest Henry VIII took in Holbein appears to have been confined to direct rather than elliptical expressions of kingship. It may be significant that Holbein seems to have been called upon in London to create multi-figured allegories, not usually by Englishmen but by the merchants of the Hanseatic League. The Steelyard, the trading house of the Hanseatic merchants, was decorated in much the same way as their Venetian business partners at the Fondaco dei Tedeschi had embellished theirs thirty years earlier with the allegories of Giorgione and Titian.

Painters working at the court of Elizabeth were highly articulate; quite capable of making persuasive imagery in defence of a new religion or an old Queen. The Elizabethan artist was at his most effective as a cartoonist to judge from *Edward VI and the Pope*; not the cartoon understood as the careful preparatory drawing by a Renaissance master, but a newspaper cartoon. Unfortunately, too few Elizabethan allegories or history pictures have survived to see how they added to the currency of topical debate. It is therefore to the era of Van Dyck that the historian must turn to discover ways in which images were used to comment on current affairs.

The first is a double portrait identified only recently and still the subject of heated scholarly debate; neither the attribution to Van Dyck, nor the identity of the sitter, nor even the precise nature of the allegory it contains, have been universally agreed. In the 1991 Washington Van Dyck exhibition the picture was 'unveiled' after its discovery and subsequent cleaning; described in the catalogue as *Sir George Villiers and Lady Katherine Manners as Adonis and Venus*; a complicated title suggesting the confused, provisional assessment of the picture as then prevailed.[4]

There are still unanswered questions, theories which half fit appearances about the picture, which make it certainly a controversial work. I would suggest that the painting was created to celebrate the marriage of

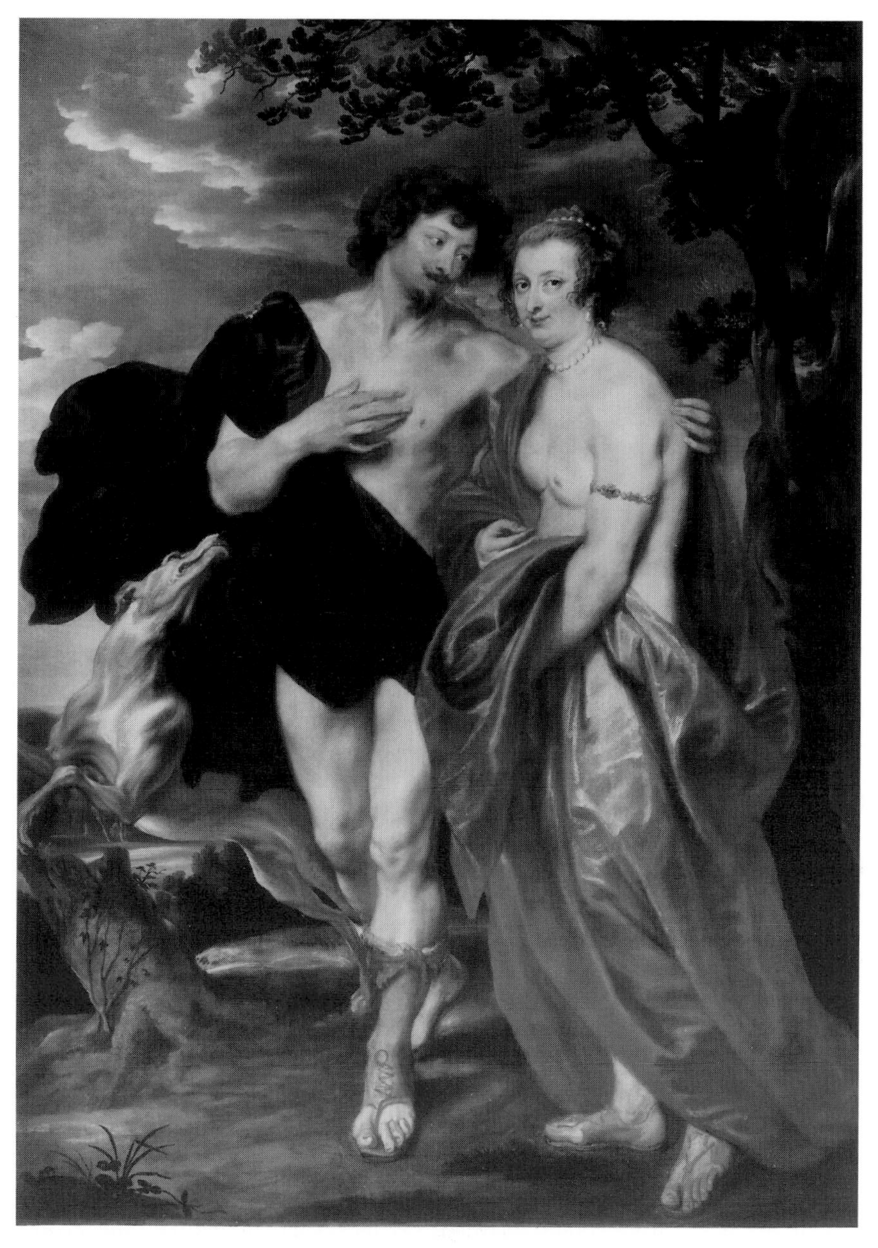

Sir Anthony Van Dyck, *Adonis and Venus* (The Duke and Duchess of Buckingham), 1620–1 (Harari & Johns, London)

the Duke of Buckingham to Lady Katherine Manners in May 1620 – perhaps as an accompaniment or complement to a Hymen masque celebrating the happy union in verse and music.[5] If this was the case, and the idea is pure conjecture, it would make unlikely the suggestion that what is admittedly a startling celebration of the pleasures of the flesh must have been for the eyes of bride and groom only; that the picture was painted for the ducal bedchamber at York House.[6] Whether painted in connection with a masque or not, there is no need to apply Victorian standards of prudery to the mores of the Jacobean court as did the compilers of the Washington catalogue. Semi-nudity was quite acceptable in public in the early seventeenth century, as the costume designs of Inigo Jones make startlingly clear. It remained so for much longer in France. During the *Directoire* ladies would attend the theatre effectively bare-breasted.

Why did Van Dyck paint the Duke and Duchess of Buckingham as Adonis and Venus? Adonis had met a violent death because he had persisted in disregarding the warning of Venus not to go hunting when she was absent. Here, however, Adonis–Buckingham – and everyone agreed that the Duke was an extraordinarily good-looking man – has been tamed by his Duchess; the Stuart Venus was superior to her mythical prototype because this goddess of beauty could tame her Adonis, which the goddess of antiquity could never do.

The painting is less an image of rule than an invitation to love. Nevertheless it was a commission from the man who would shortly become England's chief minister. The muscular body of George Villiers, the golden wire of the Duchess's hair and her ample, exposed breasts, suggest fecundity and thus the promise of felicity.

Marriage paintings were enormously important. They represented the proclamation of a treaty between great powers: it was a genre which by implying vitality, promoted the vigour of those houses whose unions the artist celebrated. Many of the greatest paintings of the epoch were devoted to an exposition of the importance of marriage; the most important of all social gestures at a court. As has been remarked in an earlier chapter, no less than four of the Marie de' Medici cycle, in a fable told by Rubens, were devoted to that state and its consequences. As Rubens well knew, the union of Valois with Medici might shift the balance of power in Europe. Van Dyck was not a political observer of the acuity of Rubens, but those who saw the *Adonis and Venus* were aware of the possibility that the marriage of a Villiers and a Manners might re-align factions within the English court in a similarly decisive way. Marriage was a political not a private act when undertaken at this level; as the greatest surviving group portrait by Van Dyck theatrically demonstrates.

The Pembroke Family (Wilton House) by Van Dyck was brought into being by a marriage which it had been expected would have saved the fortunes of the Pembrokes in a very literal way. Pembroke was fast approaching a major financial crisis when he succeeded in manipulating a

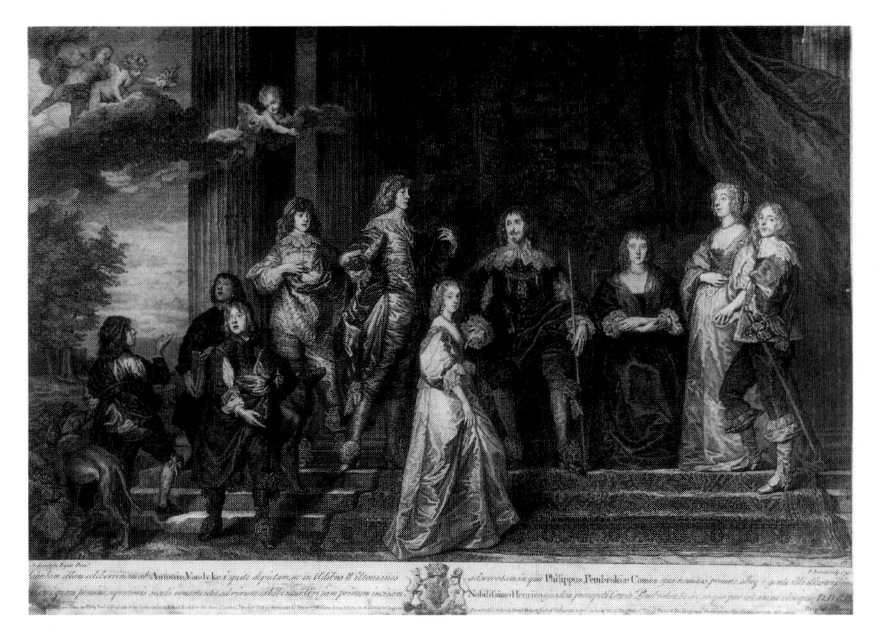

Bernard Baron, engraving of 1740 after Van Dyck, *The Pembroke Family, c.* 1637 (National Galleries of Scotland)

great union. He persuaded Buckingham's widow to give her daughter, Lady Mary Villiers, to his eldest son Charles, Lord Herbert, and more to the point, a £10,000 dowry. Unfortunately the son died in Italy soon after the betrothal. He had gone to join the army of the Grand Duke of Tuscany. The dowry had to be returned.

The painting is presided over by Pembroke who sits beneath the Herbert arms, which glow like a rose window. Pembroke points to Lady Mary who looks back proudly but with an expression of apprehensive farewell to a world she is leaving. Her future father-in-law glances in the direction of his eldest son, Lord Herbert. Herbert adopts a strutting posture, his red satin cloak flowing behind like the tail feathers of a cock on a farmyard wall. To Pembroke's left a woman sits huddled in black. It has come to be assumed that her tense, sullen isolation indicates Pembroke's second wife, Lady Anne Clifford, with whom Pembroke had contracted a loveless marriage (see plate 43, page 118). However, this woman, whoever she may be, is shrouded in black, hands folded on stomach as was conventional in recumbent effigies of the dead, and it was presumably these features which made O'Donoghue in his catalogue of British portrait prints in the British Museum, suggest that this disconsolate creature is in fact a posthumous likeness of Pembroke's first wife, Lady Susan Vere.[7] This is surely right. The picture is not about death but the celebration of the living and the hope of future progeny. Therefore it was entirely appropriate that Van Dyck should have included the mother of Pembroke's children. The spirit of the 4th Earl's first wife thus complements the presence of Lady Mary Villiers, by whom Pembroke himself expected to be provided with grandchildren to make that rose window shine with yet more splendid and refulgent colours.

Marital alignment and its defence formed the kernel of the portrait by Van Dyck of *Lord George Stuart Sieur d'Aubigny*. Lord George was a blood relation of Charles I and in 1638 declared his intention of marrying Lady Katherine Howard, daughter of the 2nd Earl of Suffolk. This was against the express wishes of the king, who was furious.

The auguries for a Stuart–Howard alliance were certainly not auspicious. Early in 1626, Lord Maltravers, eldest son of the collector Earl of Arundel, had secretly married Lady Elizabeth Stuart, daughter of Esmé, 2nd Duke of Lennox. On this occasion too Charles I had been greatly displeased. He had wished to see Lady Elizabeth married off to Lord Lorne, the son of the Earl of Argyll, to heal old wounds between Stuarts and Campbells. The consequences of defiance had been serious indeed; as again, they threatened to be for Lord George in 1638. When Charles had come to hear of Maltravers' defiance, the very next morning he had sent four royal guards to take Arundel to the Tower. There he had languished while a major constitutional row blew up in the Lords. The Lords saw the precipitate action of the king as a serious threat to their privileges. Arundel was eventually let out but the whole episode contributed significantly to the estrangement between Charles I and Arundel, which lasted until after the assassination of Buckingham.

Twelve years later however, Lord George Stuart could not help himself; or so he proclaimed by getting Van Dyck to paint 'Me Firmior Amor' (Love is stronger than Me), as if carved on the rock against which he props himself in fashionable langour, but actually, with a lover's adamantine determination. Emblem books would have told Lord George's contemporaries of how the rock was a symbol of constancy; though they would hardly have needed to refer to a book since the rock had been one of the favourite devices of Elizabeth I. By such means, Lord George tells us, as he told Charles I, that his love for Lady Katherine was stronger than his constancy to his master. In fact that was not altogether true. Lord George belonged to a branch of the Stuarts who would prove themselves exceptionally loyal to the Royalist cause: he was to die for the King in the Civil War, as his two brothers Lord John and Lord Bernard would also; young men in the prime of life who themselves had been painted by Van Dyck in what must rank as one of the most supercilious of all English double portraits.

The portrait of Lord George Stuart ranks as the quintessence of the romantic cavalier who appears to have escaped from the world. However, as a recent essay on the meaning of the painting demonstrates, the actual event which gave rise to the portrait placed the sitter at the centre of

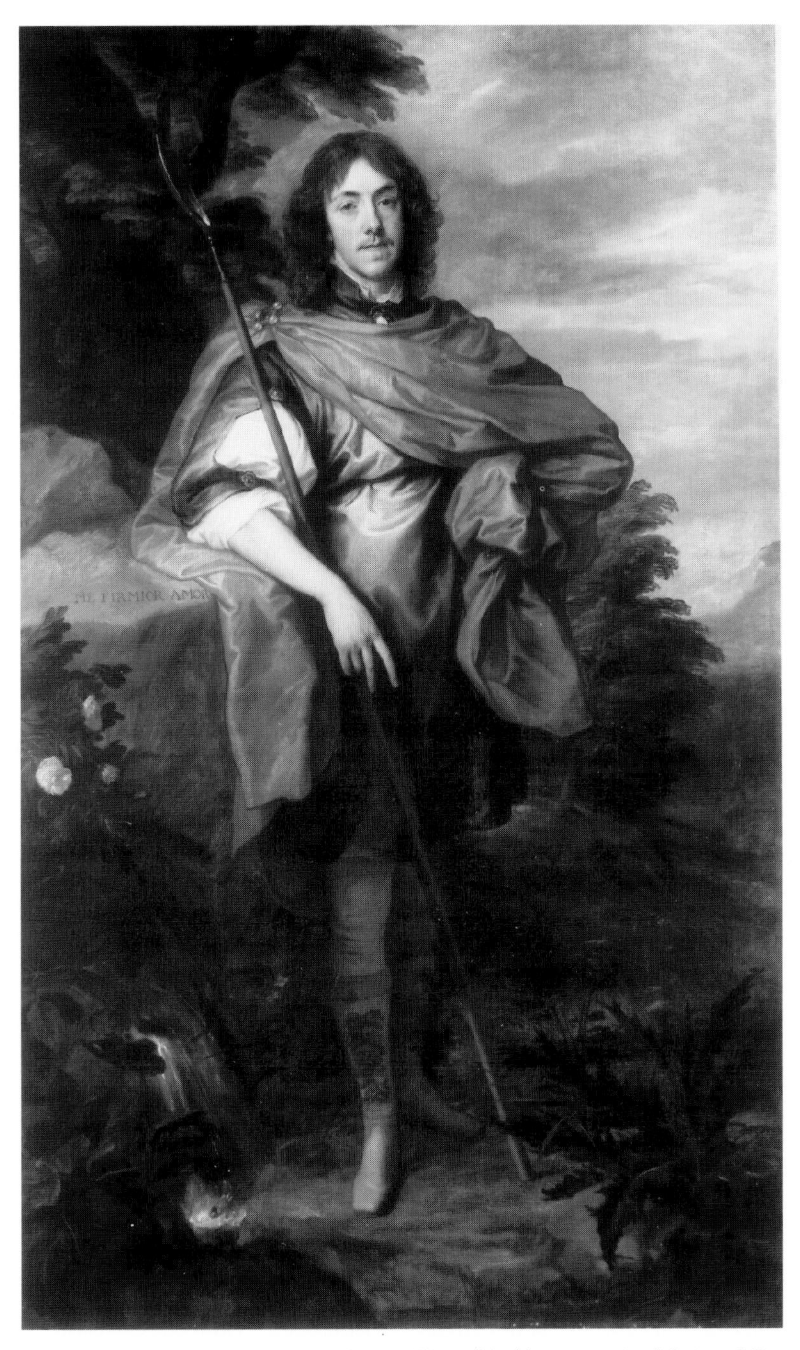

Sir Anthony Van Dyck, *Lord George Stuart, Sieur d'Aubigny, c.* 1638 (National Portrait Gallery, London)

another crisis in what was a very worldly court.[8] Lord George may appear as if he has just stepped out of one of the interminable pastorals concocted for Henrietta Maria by Walter Montagu and Inigo Jones, but cloak and blue leather bootees, probably borrowed for the occasion from Van Dyck's fancy dress wardrobe, should not encourage us to see the portrait as an escapist image. Beautiful and romantic as the painting may be, what mattered most was that it should be a sophisticated, densely argued apologia. It was a defence of a position adopted at a competitive court where the wrong marriage could mean the wrong turn down a palace corridor leading nowhere.

Here, not only words but weeds speak in defence of defiance. It is suggested that the presence of the thistle in the bottom right of the picture, symbol of the Scottish Stuarts, was also part of the sitter's gallant attempt to reconcile his difficulties. Essentially these revolved round the wish to compliment his master, whose commands the sitter was willing to obey in all other things except in his compulsion to marry Lady Katherine Howard.

Recent scholarship concerned with the English work of Van Dyck suggests that his portraits are much more than they used to seem. The imagery of Van Dyck has tended to be taken as the most visually alluring proof of that world of fantasy to which courtiers were supposed to have escaped prior to the Civil War; an abnegation of responsibility which defined a doomed and decadent cause – or so it has been argued. Incapacity through the pursuit of hopeless love might fit as a description of Watteau's Cythera but not of the Fortunate Isles to which Van Dyck had brought his talents. Van Dyck painted men who had a firm and competitive hold in society.

While Van Dyck seems to have subscribed to the king's estimation of himself, his sitters differed as much in political and religious outlook as they did in the poses Van Dyck made them adopt. Philip, Lord Wharton, probably had more Van Dycks than any other peer and he became a notable supporter of Parliament in the Civil War. Many of the grandest aristocrats took their colours into the Parliamentary army when it came to push of pike. No one on either side appears more strikingly the cavalier grandee than Robert Rich, 2nd Earl of Warwick, in his voluptuous portrait in the Metropolitan Museum in New York. Warwick commanded the Parliamentary navy, but before then, chose to have himself immortalised by Van Dyck with a luxuriant sumptuousness which would not be surpassed even by John Singer Sargent in his imagery of the Edwardian plutocracy.

Warwick may never have been the plutocrat which the Edwardian 'red' Countess of Warwick became, but like her he was full of engaging contradictions. The latter, the subject of a luscious portrait by John Singer Sargent, gave a ball when her husband inherited Warwick Castle in 1895, the extravagance of which caused something of a public scandal. Thereafter, as a result of newspaper disapproval, and in the laconic words of

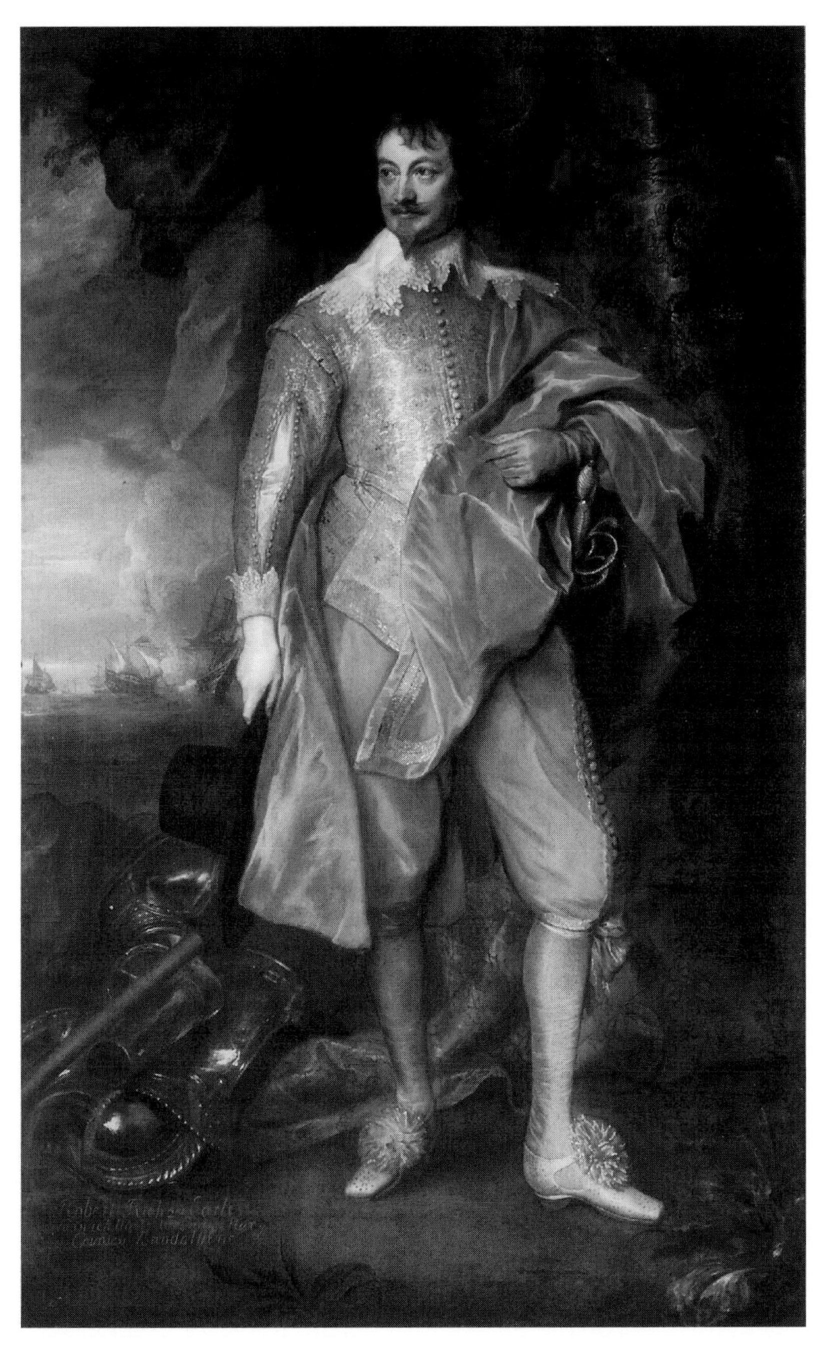

Sir Anthony Van Dyck, *The Earl of Warwick*,? 1636 (The Metropolitan Museum of Art, New York)

The Dictionary of National Biography, 'her devotion to the cause of labour was as complete as her early conquests in society'.

Much before then and in the seventeenth century, the 2nd Earl of Warwick had combined Puritan sympathies in matters of worship with a fondness for making money in much the same way as his spiritual ally, that other great Puritan grandee of the reign of Charles I, Francis Russell, 4th Earl of Bedford, with whom we shall make a brief acquaintance in the last chapter. Warwick would appear to have divided the best part of his time before the Civil War between encouraging Puritan lecturers in denouncing Mammon whilst he got on with exploiting the riches of the Americas.

Warwick's portrait by Van Dyck is not dated. The sea battle going on in the background refers to a modest naval flotilla which Warwick had led against the Spaniards in 1628. But that had happened four years before Van Dyck was settled in England and anyway brushwork suggests a mid-thirties date. All in all it seems more likely that the portrait was connected with Warwick's involvement with the New World.

Warwick was one of the most zealous members of the company of Old Providence (modern-day Nicaragua), and in 1636 he had declared his intention of going there as Governor. Thus it may well be that the portrait represents a prospectus for a new enterprise which was to have entailed the English under the leadership of Warwick grasping central America firmly by the neck of its isthmus; with the same forthright confidence with which Van Dyck has placed his sitter amidst blasted rock and smoking battle. If it is correct to see the image of Warwick as what might be termed one of Van Dyck's 'colonial' portraits, then it comes after his unsurpassed portrait, the *William Feilding, 1st Earl of Denbigh* (*c.* 1633, The National Gallery, London), but before the *Madagascar Portrait* (1639, Arundel Castle), which shows the Earl and Countess of Arundel poised to run off to Madagascar to avoid their creditors.

In the event only the portrait of Denbigh can be regarded as 'biographical' since he did indeed wander through the Indian jungle in a pair of pyjamas as he is depicted in the canvas, whereas neither Warwick nor the Earl and Countess of Arundel waded ashore in Nicaragua or Madagascar. But although the Old Providence enterprise, if that is indeed what is here alluded to, may have vanished into thin air, the portrait of Warwick did not. One hundred and twenty years later Warwick's ghost still haunts a great Reynolds naval exercise such as his *Commodore Keppel* (1752, National Maritime Museum, Greenwich).

The portraits of Van Dyck were no more escapist than the masques of Inigo Jones. The very success of both artists was due to their involvement in the lives and personalities of courtiers to whom the King made frequent but ineffectual appeals to abandon the social round of London for the exercise of their natural social function: the nurturing of rural estates and the round of county administration. Portraits and masques reflected the demands of an articulate clientele who looked to such means to promote a wealth of causes and a multitude of values.

So much for patronage. We turn now to collecting. Patronage and collecting is a diptych in the Stuart period at least. What was ordered from the living, and the quality of old master paintings acquired by the early Stuarts, reached unprecedented levels of scale and ambition; though neither patronage nor collecting were new interests as was the case with the New World and colonisation. There had been collector–patrons on the grandest possible scale before.

Wolsey had spent vast sums on art of all kinds; a prodigality which would not be matched again for a hundred years. Sir Christopher Hatton and Lord Burghley were arguably the most lavish patrons of the Elizabethan age but neither can be compared with Wolsey in terms of their palaces, tapestries and gardens.

Wolsey owed a double allegiance and that is central to understanding the inordinate scale of his patronage.[9] He was beholden to two masters: to Henry VIII but also to the Papacy in his capacity as a cardinal and as legate *a latere*. Wolsey was a member of the Curia which served Popes Leo X and Clement VII, two of the greatest Italian Renaissance patrons. He was ambitious to be thought a Renaissance Prince of the Church and surely interested too in hearing of Leo X's programme of Papal works in Rome; a programme whose director was the Pope's occasional dining companion Raphael. Clement VII followed the austere Dutchman Adrian VI, whose elevation Vasari had seen as a dark day for the art world. By contrast to Adrian, Clement had commissioned Raphael to build the Villa Madama; the purest Renaissance evocation of a Plinian villa.

Wolsey did not commission Raphael; still less ever look at a Raphael palace plan. But he had a conception of princely magnificence which would not be surpassed by either Henry VIII or Charles I. As for Hatton and Burghley in the next generation, they seem never to have encountered an artist of more significance than Nicholas Hilliard, while the ornamentation of their houses derived from Flemish pattern books, not from the excavations of the Golden House of Nero, as with Italian villas of princely cardinals.

Henry VIII became a phrenetic, competitive patron of the arts but only when he had learned how to do it from Wolsey. The 1530s saw the great expansion of Henry's role as a royal builder; his palaces the secular equivalent to his father's pious works, which had coloured the autumn of medieval building in England. But although Henry acquired, added to, or built more than fifty royal houses, he treated them like an Emir with his tents in the desert.

The pattern of use for the Henrician palace militated against the assembly of a Royal Collection as it might be understood today. Hampton Court was more an encampment than a group of buildings with fixed, set parameters. It was a plastic, flexible context which frequently expanded to meet the new priorities of a court going through a period of exceptional change. Henry spent much time at Hampton Court after Wolsey had disgorged it, but then chose to move from palace to palace and to create new buildings. Constant change does not suit pictures. It was easier and more effective to roll up the tapestries and move on to Woodstock, than to hump wooden crates of heavy framed pictures over rutted muddy roads. Logistical problems of this nature account in large part for the woollen and metal character of The Royal Collection in the early Tudor period. Of easel pictures little is seen in the surviving inventories. But the combination of Burgundian tapestries winking with gold and silver, table ornaments studded with rubies, and merman clocks as tall as greyhounds, made the Crown holdings of moveables a rich if not a very subtle affair.

Once Wolsey fell, and with him his stained glass windows, Henry had nothing to fear from rival magnificence; no courtier dared to vie with what the Royal palaces contained. Whether collecting and the momentum of patronage was continued into the reigns of Edward and Mary is difficult to establish. It must be doubtful. Mary's chief hope for the restoration of Catholicism, Cardinal Reginald Pole, had been painted by Sebastiano del Piombo, who had been entrusted with turning Michelangelo's ideas into paint before sloth and a fat papal appointment rendered him useless. But such brief, flitting encounters with the greatest work Italy could produce hardly provided much inspiration for the post-Henrician generation.

The danger of visiting Rome whilst it was being presided over by the great Counter-Reformation Popes was not merely an indulgence but a dangerous folly for the Elizabethan gentleman. In a more northern sphere, the Antwerp Mannerists were producing work which was admired and collected well beyond the confines of the Spanish Netherlands. But that was something of a miracle since the country was awash with blood during the regime of the Regent Alva. Antwerp in the 1560s was hardly a place to round off a young man's education. The glories of Elizabethan culture have always been seen as bookish and surely that is right. Sir Philip Sidney was painted by Veronese when in Venice in February 1574 but that isolated triumph for the art of painting has to be compared with the scores of Englishmen who came to have their portraits taken in the city fifty years later by Domenico Tintoretto, the talented son of the more famous Jacopo.

Large houses always need to be filled, but in the reign of Elizabeth, this was with fixed not pendant decoration. The Long Gallery at Hardwick, built by the Countess of Shrewsbury in the 1590s, ostensibly in the hope of attracting the Queen, but actually to nurse the vanity of an impossible woman, was decorated with what an estate agent would describe as fixtures and fittings. Theoretically, tapestries were moveable but they were often treated as wallpaper, cut to fit walls and corridors. Sculpture at Hardwick took the form of elaborate narrative friezes and deeply cut panelling; painting was portraiture and as much a filing cabinet of family relations as a pleasing display for the eye. Hardwick had a famous collection of needlework, but however skilled the samplers, they were homely in every sense; artefacts which reflected the tedious round of female imprisonment in these great houses and certainly not something for which there was a competitive collectors' market.

Collecting as we understand it, did not exist in late Tudor England. The Queen's spy-master, Sir Francis Walsingham, owned some interesting curios which might be considered the rudiments of a *wunder-kammer*; rarities, natural and artificial, of which the Princes of the Empire were especially fond.[10] However, the nearest to what could be considered a mixed collection of fine art belonged to John, Lord Lumley.

Lumley assembled the finest of all Elizabethan portrait collections, interspersed with choice statues and busts which provided a medley of ancient and modern heroes. But Lumley came to own the portrait of Christina of Denmark because it represented an interesting historical personality, not because it was by Holbein.

By the early years of the new century, all this began to change. Neither Wolsey nor Henry VIII could remotely be described as connoisseurs in the sense in which that term can begin to be applied to the Jacobean grandees. Appreciation of art amongst Tudor patrons had extended to a relish for the luxurious and 'curious work'; the intricate sundials and mechanical contraptions devised by Henry VIII's instrument maker Nicholas Kratzer. By contrast, the courtiers of James I began to appreciate the hand of an artist and to make recognisably modern distinctions between a master and his assistants.

James I opened Britain to Europe. He established permanent embassies where none had existed or where they had been abandoned years before. The embassy in Venice soon became a stopping place for English travellers. When presided over by the art connoisseur Sir Henry Wotton, it was not merely a free pensione for the well connected, but an academy of polite accomplishments. Justice has yet to be done to the educative influence of Wotton, who was a metaphysical poet, authority on classical architecture, purveyor of fine pictures to the British nobility and, in his years of retirement when Provost of Eton, charged by the King with writing a history of England. This was never accomplished.

It would help our understanding of the growth in collecting, if we knew more of Wotton as educator to a well-travelled generation which suddenly found itself with exhilarating access to the art markets of Europe. Wotton was the first to collect sixteenth-century architectural drawings; he seems to have supplied Salisbury with Palladio drawings, and he got excited by the possibility of acquiring drawings of the Villa Farnese – Mannerist masterpiece of Antonio da Sangallo and the rural retreat of the Neapolitan family who dominated mid-century Papal Rome. Sadly however, much of what Wotton had acquired over many years in Italy would appear to have been destroyed towards the end of his diplomatic career, as William Trumbull, Wotton's correspondent and colleague in Brussels, was informed in a letter of February 1619:

> haveing made a great and sumptious feast, for the Principall of that place, had by the negligence of his servants, the moste and best part of his howse burned downe and little of the goods saved.[11]

What was destroyed might have constituted a very effective study collection for some of the well-born who would be collectors in London twenty years later. Wotton much enjoyed showing the sights of Venice and supplying rich patrons in England with portraits and mythologies by Palma Giovane and Domenico Tintoretto. Wotton loved painting and would clearly do his best to encourage an eye amongst schoolboys when he came to live out his days as Provost of Eton. But none of this was disinterested. Wotton helped the development of other people's collections because he hoped to curry favour or make money. He sent Salisbury the recipient's portrait in mosaic; accompanying the present with a characteristically fawning letter expressing the hope that such a thing might find a place at Hatfield. But what Wotton really hoped for was promotion from the man who held the key to preferment.

Wotton knew Italy better than any other Englishman, but even he remained decidedly defensive about aspects of its culture. In 1618 he gave his backing to an idea of setting up Protestant seminaries in Italy 'so wishing it may prove that mustard seed wherein the birds of heaven did afterwards build their nest'.[12] He had always been suspicious of a newly invigorated Papacy and quickly penetrated what he believed to be the subterfuge of Rome. He made this clear in a letter to Salisbury of 18 August 1605, in which he surveyed a shift in Papal policy during the previous decade:

> Sixtus Quintus carried all things, and even the matters of religion violently; . . . Clement VIII [was] generally moderate. . . . For whereas before the English Protestant that came in fear to Rome, either lived disguisedly, or craved at his first coming the protection of Cardinal Alen, obliging himself to depart within a day or two, when he had seen the antiquities . . . under Clement VIII (*mutatis artibus*), began not only permission and connivency, but invitation and allurement of all nations promiscuously . . .[13]

Rome was a scene of enduring fascination for Shakespeare and Jonson, Jones and the incorruptible Milton. Yet the Low Countries affected English taste more than Italy in the early years of the new century. The point can be made by comparing the voluminous correspondence of Wotton with that of William Trumbull, who resided in Brussels as English Agent to the court of the Archdukes between 1609 and 1625.

Trumbull was in Brussels long after Wotton had finally left Venice and Trumbull's private correspondence covers the years when collecting in England suddenly took off. It confirms that the high-heeled spent lavishly on: tapestries; fireplaces; flowers and trees to transform the English garden under the careful nurturing of the Tradescants, plantsmen to Salisbury and later to Buckingham. The riches Trumbull supplied to his English clients calls to mind Dutch still-lifes where a monkey plays with a nautilus cup, striped tulips cascade upon a rich Turkey carpet and oranges lie in a silver dish like glowing coals. What Trumbull provided were luxuries; reflecting a diversity of interests which went beyond merely civilising the English interior, to broaden the horizons of what had been an insular nation.

In time Trumbull was asked to provide something new and much more exciting in the judgement of history: the paintings of Rubens, the world's leading artist. Trumbull was more interested in print than in paintings. So in the challenging not to say awesome business of dealing with Rubens, he came to rely to a significant extent on the judgement of Sir Dudley Carleton.

Carleton had been appointed to the United Provinces having followed Wotton at the embassy in Venice where he had acquired an exceptional eye for a picture. For Carleton too, paintings were a commodity to be traded for advantage. Carleton had acquired a large collection of antiquities in

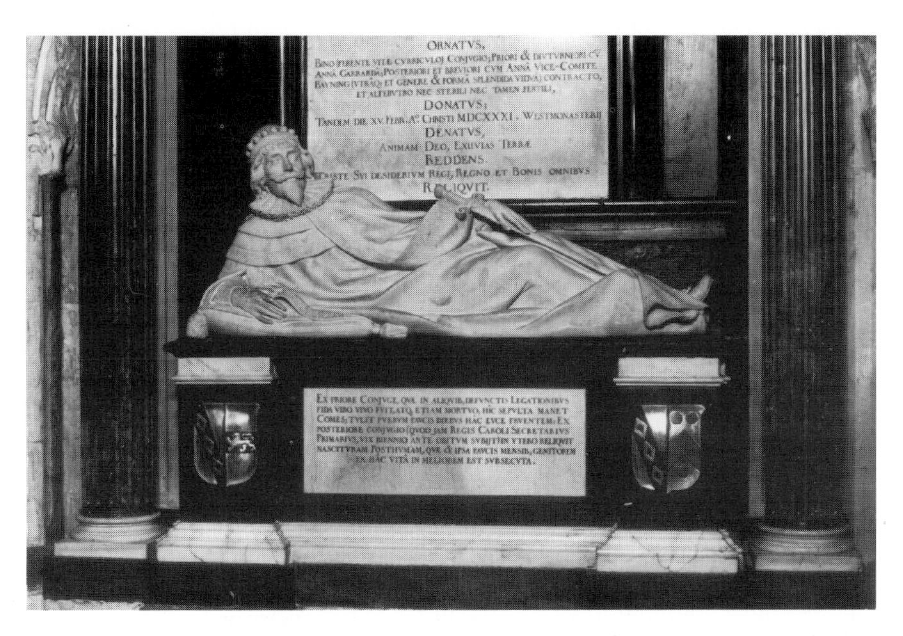

Nicholas Stone, *Tomb of Dudley Carleton, Viscount Dorchester*, 1640, Chapel of St Paul, Westminster Abbey (Courtauld Institute of Art)

Venice; remarkable for their number though not for their intrinsic distinction as sculpture. These he had intended to sell on to the Earl of Somerset, favourite of James I. But Somerset had been disgraced and Carleton was left with them on his hands. When he arrived in The Hague he had been able to sell them to Rubens; indeed the artist was so impressed that he acquired them in exchange for nine of his own paintings, including such masterpieces as the *Prometheus* (Philadelphia, Museum of Art).

Carleton certainly appreciated his Rubens collection. Yet they remained valuable assets to be disposed of when they could promote his career. When Carleton first arrived at his new posting in The Hague, Buckingham was then beginning his ascendancy. By 1625 he was dominant while Carleton was desperate to be recalled to London and a more central place in affairs. Carleton had long made it his business to keep on good terms with Buckingham, and Buckingham repayed his client handsomely if Clarendon is to be believed when he wrote:

> As soon as he [Carleton] returned from Holland, he was called to the Privy Council; and the making him Secretary of State, and a peer of the realm, when his estate was scarce visible, was the last piece of workmanship the duke of Buckingham lived to finish, who seldom satisfied himself with conferring a single obligation.[14]

Carleton got to the top whereas Wotton had to be content with the consolation prize of the Provostship of Eton. Now it would be over-stressing the significance of collecting to suggest that Carleton gained the highest office because he was able to seduce Buckingham with the ample charms of Rubens' *Susannah*, whereas Wotton was not able to offer the favourite comparable riches. The important point is that Carleton was percipient and circumspect, acknowledged indeed to be the finest diplomat of his generation. More than this, Carleton was someone of real significance to the culture of Europe. Carleton brought Sir Constantijn Huygens (1596–1687) to London where Huygens became intimate with John Donne for whose poetry he developed a huge regard and where in 1622 he was knighted by James I. Thereafter Huygens became secretary to the Stadholder of Holland, Henry Frederick, as well as the greatest luminary of seventeenth century Dutch culture; distinctions which owed much to Carleton's shrewd capacity to spot brilliant young talent. In 1619 Huygens had been with Carleton amongst the English contingent at the Synod of Dort which swung the Dutch church away from the complexities and compromises of Arminianism towards in implacable Calvinism. In March 1623 Carleton had provided Huygens with a letter of recommendation to enable him to travel to the splendid court of Christian IV of Denmark, then the most ebullient in all Europe north of the Alps.[15]

In some senses there was much in common between Carleton and Wotton since both were notable promoters of young and exceptional

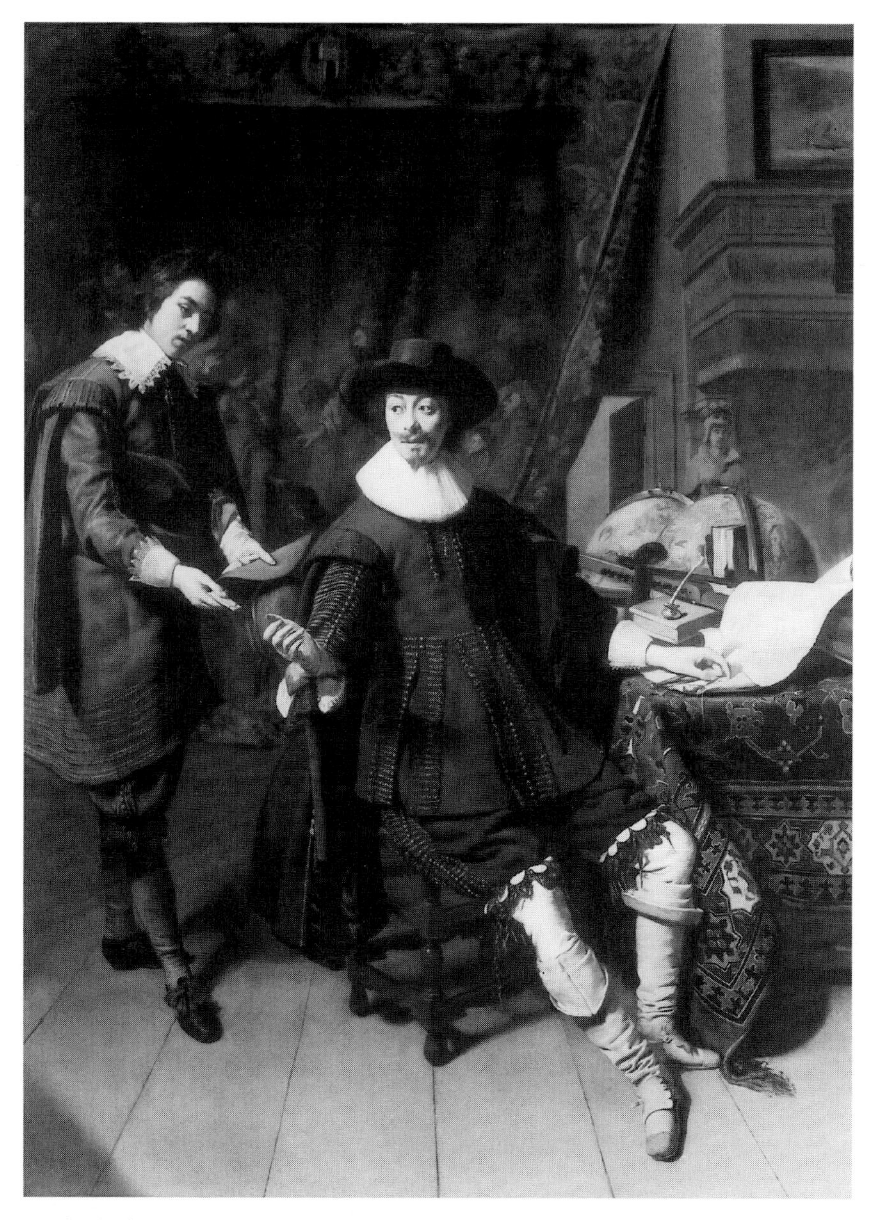

Hendrick de Keyser, *Constantijn Huygens and Companion*, 1627 (National Gallery, London)

talent. However, there were crucial contrasts between the two great Jacobean diplomats. By contrast to Carleton, Wotton was devious and indiscreet; his second term in Venice ended quite disastrously when he equivocated about taking decisive action to clear Lady Arundel's name after a major scandal engulfed her when staying in the city in 1622. Nevertheless, there were a number of others whose claims to the Secretaryship were at least as serious as Carleton's, and it is possible to suggest that it was the hard work Carleton had put in to supplying Buckingham with wonderful pictures which may have given him the edge over rivals.

Warnke, in his important study of the role of the court artist, and when writing about sixteenth-century Italy, has made the claim that the surviving documentary evidence points to the conclusion that 'the principal task of ambassadors in Venice and Rome seems to have been the recruitment of artists'. Knowledge of painters and paintings on the part of those like Carleton who were ambitious to move from a diplomatic out-station to the centre of affairs, may have been a vastly more important qualification than we realise.[16]

Taking a more circumscribed view of the scene than Warnke, a broad and generous study of the cultural role of the English ambassador in early modern Britain is long overdue. We need it to try to understand how Britain had succeeded in breaking down its cultural isolation by the reign of Charles I.

Today the fist grasping the pommel on an Augsburg blade has been replaced by a limp wrist resting upon a pile of faxes in the ambassadorial portrait. But had Van Dyck followed Holbein to paint his own *Ambassadors*, his image would have been no less rich than Holbein's depiction of Jean de Vinteville and Georges de Selve, the subjects of his great double portrait now in the National Gallery in London.

Van Dyck would surely have had Carleton and Wotton presiding over chests of architectural drawings with Mercator's atlases propped to one side; the sharp perspective of the black and white tiles set off with 'rare wynde instruements' made by Italian craftsmen in England and sold from embassy premises abroad.[17] An ebonised cabinet adorned with Ovid's *Metamorphoses* in silver by Paul Van Vianen of Utrecht, a favourite artist of Charles I, might have contained those famous English miniatures so greatly prized by connoisseurs from Copenhagen to Rome. The miniatures of Hilliard were indeed exquisite works of art but only the size of raindrops when compared with the exhausting dimensions of a Rubens' bottom such as Carleton liked to order, but which he confessed to Rubens 'ought to be beautiful to enamour even the Elders', as he directed the artist when asking for a second version of the painter's *Susannah and the Elders*.[18]

Behind the heads of Carleton and Wotton there could have been a Mortlake tapestry entwined about a marble column; such as were to be found in the princely courts of India by the end of the 1620s. Instead of the great hunting dog which Van Dyck favoured as the appendage to great men, here high culture might have been mocked by the inclusion of 'two birds of paradise, the best that can be gotten . . . one extraordinary fair' which a certain Abraham Williams, a contact of Trumbull's at The Hague, had gone to much trouble to acquire for the otherwise colourless Secretary of State Sir Ralph Winwood, back in 1610.[19]

Carleton has an immensely distinguished place in the history of collecting. He had more paintings by Rubens than any other person in Europe when the artist's work was virtually unknown in London. Nevertheless the credit for creating a taste for Rubens in England does not belong to diplomats exclusively. There were the soldiers too.

Sir Henry Danvers, later to be elevated to the peerage as 1st Earl of Danby, Sir Edward Cecil and Lord Vere of Tilbury were mercenaries who had found their swords rusting under the less than heroic James I. They had needed to go abroad to find a living and had picked up an acquaintance with north European art. They started buying tapestries, tiles, whole fireplaces even, but then began to commission their own portraits by fashionable if dull artists like the Dutchman Michiel van Miereveld.

It was due to these military men, much addicted to horsemanship and the chase, that a taste developed for the series of great hunting pieces which Rubens was then producing in such numbers; vast canvases the size of tapestries, and ferocious expressions of the union of man and beast. A Rubens hunting piece seems to have had an especial appeal to English mercenaries, who liked nothing more than the pursuit of a quarry, whether human or animal. Danvers and his fellows always enjoyed a close encounter and relished the sight of oriental warriors being disembowelled in a Rubens *Lion Hunt*.

Danvers was much taken with Carleton's *Daniel in the Lions' Den* (National Gallery, Washington); one of the pictures Carleton had acquired from Rubens in exchange for statues. Here Rubens captures a latent fury which not even Géricault could match; a *terribilità* which clearly appealed to Danvers, who had fled to France for killing a man during a reign of terror he had conducted in his native Wiltshire when young. Danvers wrote from London in the summer of 1619, to Carleton, then at The Hague:

> . . . geve me leave to accept against soum such of his workes, as ar made to be sett at great distance for our roumes ar littell in this cold cuntrye of England, and pleasing peeces to stand ten fowte hye sutes best wth our clime; even such an on as yr Lo: Daniell wth thoes bewtifull lions in the den would well satisfye my desire, and now I have sayed for that matter.[20]

Danvers became one of the most important and demanding patrons of Rubens and he gave Charles I the chance to acquire his first great picture by the artist. Charles, then Prince of Wales, already possessed an indifferent work by Rubens, when Danvers learned he was keen to acquire something to do justice to artist and Royal Collection alike. What Charles got was nothing less than a *Self-Portrait*, which is still one of the greatest treasures of the Royal Collection. Through an elaborate series of subterfuges to ensure that Rubens would not know who his painting was destined for, and thereby the price would not be inflated, Danvers persuaded Rubens to part with something which was very precious; in the *Self-Portrait*, he wears the gold chain given by the Archdukes when they had made him their court painter.

I have suggested that the *Self-Portrait* had started life as a *modello* for an engraved frontispiece to Rubens' book *I Palazzi di Genova*.[21] The folio had just appeared in 1622 with handsome, engraved plates of the façades and ground plans of the major Genoese palaces. Genoa was the spiritual home of Rubens. It was presided over by a merchant patriciate. A world ruled by commerce appealed to Rubens. He had built his own palace amongst the silk merchants of Antwerp. But there was a difference between Genoa and Antwerp. The Balbis and Lomellinis, vastly rich ruling families in Genoa, had a swagger which appealed to a man who had stood in Florence Cathedral representing the Dukes of Mantua at the marriage of France and Tuscany. Furthermore the Genoese silk prince enjoyed one great advantage over the guildsman of Antwerp. He looked out across the gulf of Liguria and not the herring fleet bouncing about on the inky waves of the Scheldt as Rubens had chosen to do.

Danvers wrote to Carleton on 18 December 1622:

> but yet being very desirous that the Prince his gallerie should contayne some excellent peece of his to paragon those workes that are there of many famous men I must with all manner of earnestnesse crave y^{ur} uttermoste endeavo^{r} and his favour for his owne picture made originall and every part of it wrought with his owne hand; Ffor the price I will not lymitte wh^{ch} shalbe readily payed to any merchant heere by his own assignment. Lastly lett me intreate you to take care for the sending over of this much requested picture wch I hear hee hath made alreadie . . .[22]

The information that the picture was 'made already' is important. The sending or the exchange of pictures carried much more significance than it does now. Erasmus and Pieter Gillis, the Town Clerk of Antwerp, sent Sir Thomas More their double portrait by Quentin Matsys.[23] It came with a letter in which it was declared that in sending it, the three friends actually meet again. Much of the point of dispatching portraits in the Renaissance was precisely so that donor and recipient should be able to discourse together; in much the same way as famous letter writers like Erasmus himself used their correspondence to defy international borders and continental wars.

The presentation of a self-portrait to a social superior was a hazardous business. Painters and princes were not equals; however, often the hoary

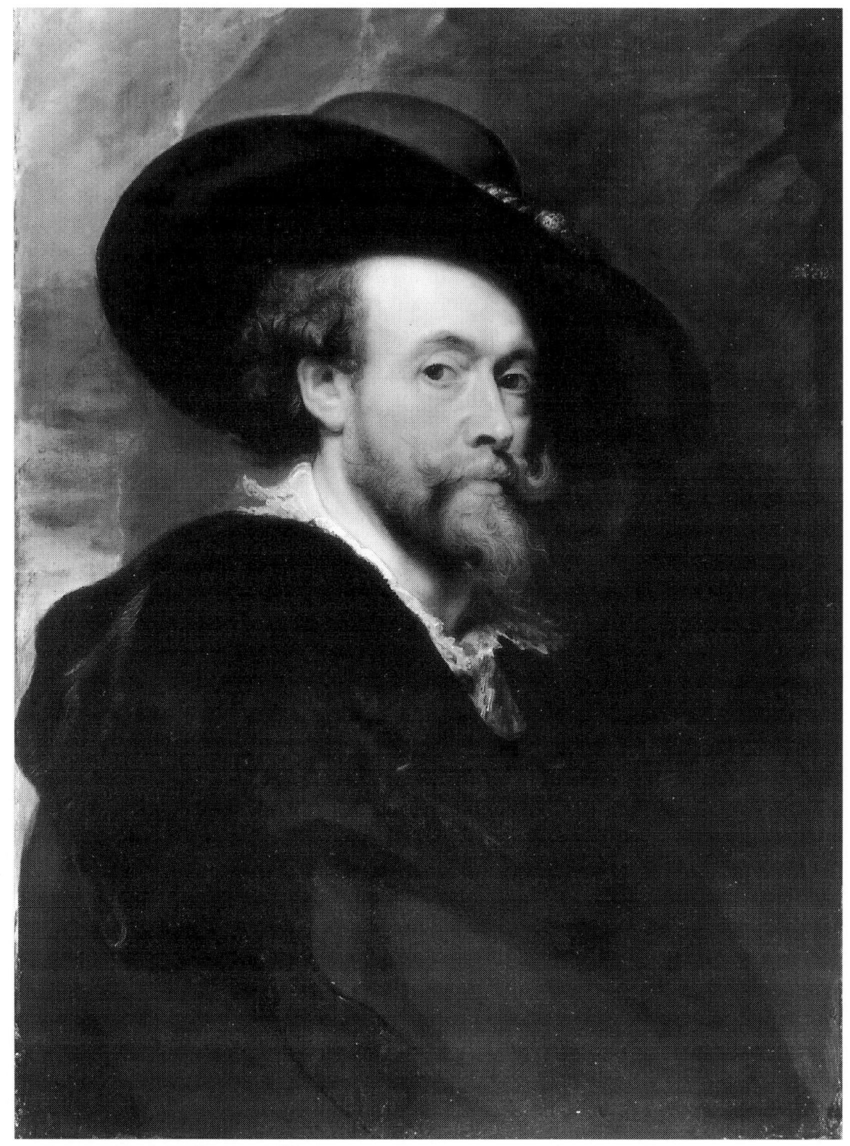

Sir Peter Paul Rubens, *Self-portrait*, presented to Charles I in 1623 (The Royal Collection)

old anecdote about Alexander picking up the brushes of Apelles was repeated in the literature on art. Thus it is inconceivable that Rubens would have intended his *Self-Portrait* for Charles I *ab initio*. The painting was a gesture of compliment reluctantly extracted from its creator by Danvers; reluctantly, because as no one knew better than Rubens with his twenty years of diplomatic and conciliar experience, it was a compliment which protocol demanded should have had the sitter bare-headed. The first gesture of obeisance which ambassadors made when entering the Banqueting House in London, was to take off their hats. This they would then do twice more as they made their processional way, before the royal hand was proffered for them to kiss. That was how a fully accredited ambassador behaved and they were invested with significantly more status than Rubens, the most public of painters in the whole history of art. Since presentation made presence, Rubens stood before Charles I in the Windsor *Self-Portrait*. He would never have chosen to remain covered before the English prince if the choice had been his.

Ambassadors and mercenaries were important but they were go-betweens. They were the crucial middle men; running between the fashionable painter in his studio and the great Officers of State in London. Put in another way, Carleton and Trumbull were partners in a firm. They fixed the deals and they kept the most important clients happy. But they did not normally attend sales or go into the studio to criticise and encourage as a modern dealer might. That side of things was left to agents like George Gage, who sometimes, as most obviously he did, immeasurably improved their prospects thereby.

Carleton and Trumbull had to look on paintings as assets not treasures to be added to the family stock of greatness. Permanent ambassadors like themselves were gentry never aristocracy. They had careers, and a career in Jacobean England meant salary arrears and the pursuit of back pay by any means available.

Carleton was not in the same league as great hereditary peers of the realm like the Earls of Arundel and Pembroke, Buckingham and Carlisle. They were fortunate recipients of court office, incomes from monopolies and vast landed rents; a combination which gave ample opportunity for expenditure on a prodigious scale. However, although Carleton acquired pictures to trade them for promotion, the great also made strategic gifts of their pictures; in their cases, for self-promotion, to patch up a quarrel, or to reinforce a petition.

Arundel had puffed his own reputation with a gift which he knew would be noticed abroad and not merely at home. In September 1620 Cosimo II had written asking for one of his celebrated Holbein portraits; a request Arundel could hardly have refused since he had stayed at the Palazzo Vecchio when he had been in Florence in 1614. Accordingly he presented Cosimo with *Sir Richard Southwell*. It was one of the finest portraits from a collection of the painter's work which, the recipient had assured the donor, was second to none. There was, however, some delay while the picture was given a new frame designed to hold four silver badges: two for the Howard and the Medici arms respectively, and two to tell the story of the gift.[24]

It is unfortunate that such exemplary documentation was so rare, since

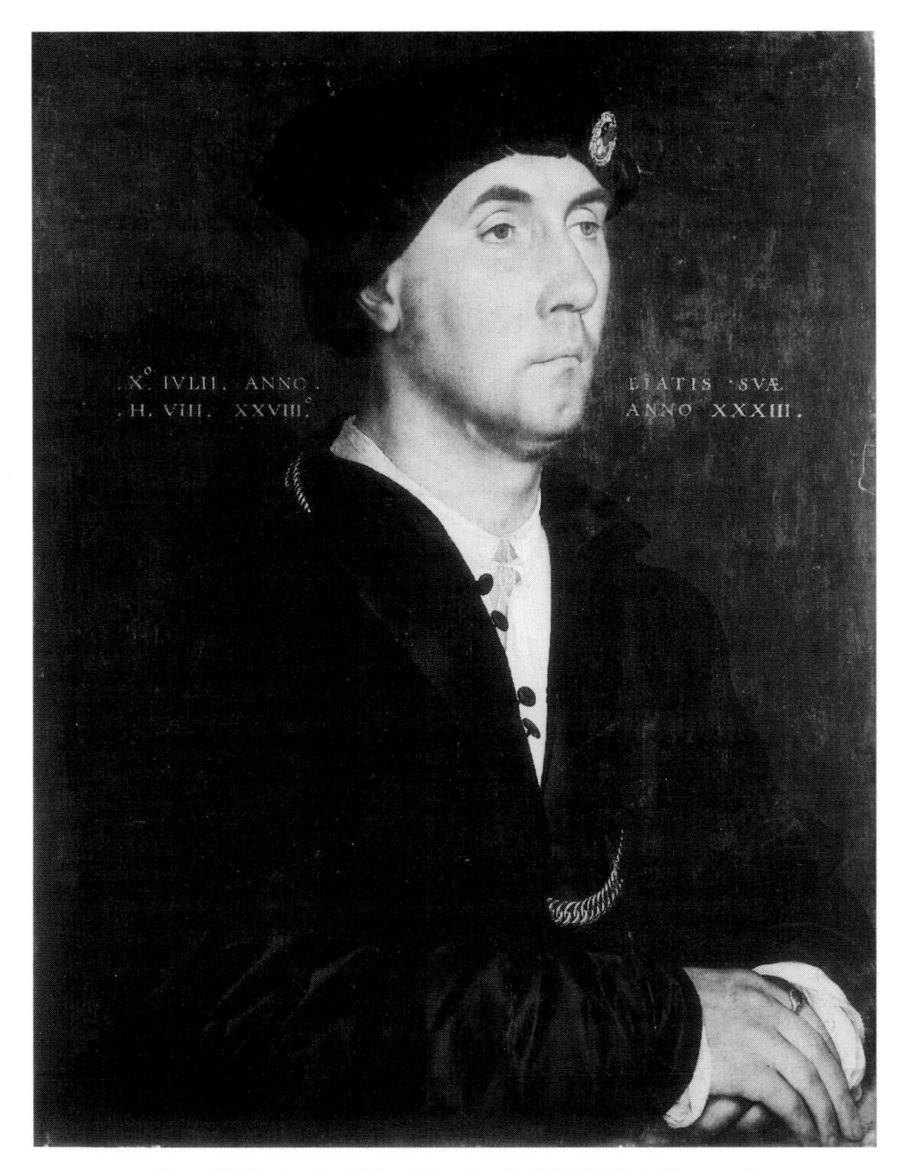

Hans Holbein, *Sir Richard Southwell*, 1536 (Uffizi, Florence)

we should know much more about the exchange of high-prestige gifts were that not so. But it is hardly less unfortunate that the taste of a later age demanded the dismantling of the frame which Arundel had contrived for the presentation of his portrait of Sir Richard Southwell. What is now in the Uffizi is still a great painting but a much impoverished image. The dismantling was doubtless done in the same tiresome quest for stylistic

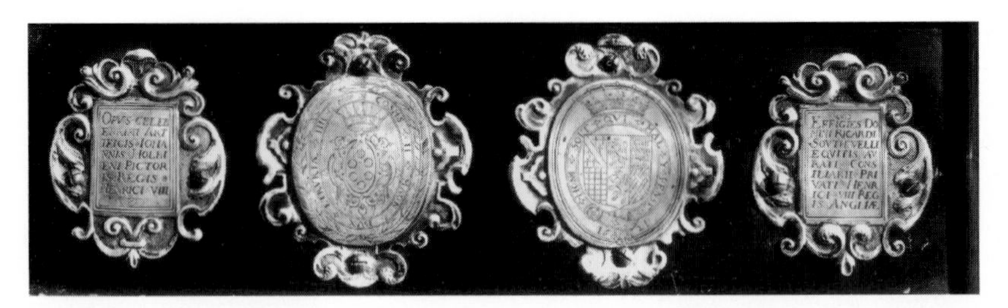

Anon., Silver badges for the Southwell Portrait, 1621 (Uffizi, Florence)

integrity which once made the Italians strip the churches of Ravenna to 'return' to the evangelical simplicity of the early Christian basilicas beneath, or made the National Gallery in London wipe off the *trompe-l'oeil* label or *cartellino* which Lumley had had painted on his Holbein of *Christina of Denmark*. The National Gallery removed it because it had not been put there by Holbein.

Although there were rare occasions when the great London collectors gave things away, they tended to hang on to what they had because they saw their galleries in the long perspective. They expected them to remain as heirlooms for ever. It is again Arundel who suggests this. He acquired a very important collection of Greek inscriptions in 1628. It included the Parian chronicle, still the earliest stone inscription about the Greek City States. The inscriptions were published by John Selden under the title *Marmora Arundelliana*. Selden was the great latinist of his generation and the learned world was immensely excited.

But then so was Arundel. He made the 'Warden and Commonality of the mistery of Fishmongers of the City of London' trustees of a settlement created by Act of Parliament to ensure that the fabric and contents of Arundel House and Arundel Castle would be maintained in good repair. The Fishmongers were to be paid £210 a year to carry out an annual inspection to ensure that 'those furnitures and ornaments which the now Earl of Arundel with . . . great charge hath provided and gathered together may so remain as ornament to this house. . . . That all and every such plate, jewels, hangings, pictures, household stuff, statues, inscriptions, stones unfinished, and ancient monuments of marble or of any other matter whatsoever and all and every books, arms, armour' as might appear in inventories to be deposited in the Court of Chancery, were to be annually apprised by the Company, who were also to see to the good repair of House and Castle.[25]

Arundel saw his treasures as an asset which should descend from generation to generation. It is therefore ironical that the only collection to be hedged about by an Act of Parliament and planted upon a rampart of the Law Courts, was the first to fall to the onslaught of Civil War. Arundel was essentially bankrupted before the Civil War. Much of the contents of both Arundel House and Arundel Castle was sold off well before Parliamentary Commissioners got their hands on the Royal Collection following the execution of Charles I in 1649.

Much can turn on a preposition. In the contract between Arundel and the Fishmongers, the use of the word 'to' rather than 'of' in the phrase 'ornament to this house' is revealing. It suggests that what was one of the most famous collections in early modern Europe, was regarded as a timeless ornament to a dynasty, not merely decoration of a house with a small 'h'. The vast amount Arundel spent on his collections was seen by him, if not by all, as an investment. Not investment as we now understand it, but as something which would add to the fame of the Howard family; something as inalienable as the very Howard titles themselves. Arundel saw more than material splendour in his objects; frames emphasised magnificence as well as Mantegnas; plinths supported immortality not only inscriptions.

Many questions arise in trying to understand the social significance of collecting in early Stuart England. They are hard to answer but worth asking if we are to get an inkling of what these objects really meant to people at the time. Some which suggest themselves might be: How much choice did great collectors have? Why did collecting become fashionable? Why were people prepared to spend large amounts on painting? How many pictures were given away and to whom?

The Rubens *Self-Portrait* arrived in 1623; the year Charles and Buckingham went to Spain and saw Titian at his best. From Spain Charles sent orders to the Privy Council back in London to acquire Raphael's Cartoons for the Sistine Tapestries. Charles' order may well have been prompted by the Countess of Arundel who was then in Genoa and thus well placed to discover that the cartoons were for sale. Whether she did indeed play a central role we cannot be certain though her movements and the chronology of acquisitions certainly suggest so. As it was she was anxious to curry favour with Charles because she wanted to come over to Madrid to accompany the Infanta to England and thus steal a march on the Duchess of Buckingham, with whom she was then competing for the role of the first lady at court.[26]

In the event Lady Arundel never made it to Spain but Charles and Buckingham returned with Giambologna's *Samson and the Philistine*; one of the most celebrated pieces of Renaissance sculpture, which Buckingham then mounted in his garden at York House where it was recognised as playing the same kind of role in enhancing the status of the owner as his coat of arms. That famous group, now in the Victoria and Albert Museum, gained many admirers very soon after its shipment to England, where, known as *Cain and Abel*, it soon became a tourist attraction.

When the Giambologna first arrived, Buckingham was employing Sir Balthazar Gerbier as Keeper of York House, who would succeed Trumbull as Agent in Brussels. With indecent haste, Gerbier built up an astonishing collection in which the paintings of Veronese and Rubens were pre-eminent. No less indecent however was Gerbier's boast of how he had bought in the space of a few years what it would have taken others a lifetime to acquire. It was true but immodest. Under the overall control of Gerbier, the Buckingham collection rapidly came to include some of the great masterpieces of European painting: Titian's *Ecce Homo* (Kunsthistoriches Museum, Vienna) among them; for which, tradition had it, Arundel offered Buckingham the staggering sum of £7,000.

Gerbier's famous remark can be taken too readily to mean that the Whitehall collectors paid much to understand little; that Buckingham no more knew how Titian laid on his paint than how his tailor made his clothes. That is too simplistic. It ignores the very wide experience of pictures which came with the grand life. Many of the great London collectors travelled abroad extensively. Dukes and earls ventured abroad in their capacity as the King's representatives. They would be given not only privileged access to the finest collections of France, Italy and Spain, but choice examples too. That was an education in itself. Furthermore, London possessed an astonishing range of great art with ample opportunity to train the eye. What was to be seen at Arundel House or York House in 1635 was therefore a partnership between the owners and their agents.

This is suggested from the surviving letters sent by Arundel, his wife and children to the Reverend William Petty, principal agent of their collection for approximately twenty years. The spring of any given year might find Petty in Samos; the autumn, moving from Venice to Rome. But wherever Petty went, he would find letters waiting with the English consul. The letters came with specific responses to suggestions about purchases.

Ideas put forward by agents were frequently rejected by the London collectors. Where collectors' letters survive, it is abundantly clear that patrons knew what they liked, to use a notorious phrase. When the benighted Sir Thomas Roe, English ambassador in Constantinople, tried to serve up Buckingham with a collection of battered rarities from archaeological sites in Asia Minor, he was very firmly told that things of that nature would not do.

Precisely the same kind of tight controls were exercised by collectors over their agents digging at Ephesus as were dispatched by the Directors of the East India Company to their factors in Madras. Thus the answer to the first question is that the London collectors were able to exercise considerable initiative and wide choice.

Rivalry between Buckingham and Arundel over acquisition of the *Ecce Homo* by Titian, for example, suggests that collecting became fashionable as a reflection of the whole competitive ambience of the court. But it was not simply the issue of lateral rivalries; Arundel was Earl Marshal, which made him head of the nobility and thus a match for Buckingham, who took precedence by virtue of his Dukedom. There was also, however, the need to have a place in the sun; to keep above younger growth which may have had shallower roots but was thrusting through from below. It is surely no coincidence that people started to collect at the same time as James I had begun to upset the equilibrium of honours, that relatively set social hierarchy which Elizabeth had established and Charles would re-impose.

'Older' families complained about James I's policy of expanding the honours system. James had created the order of knights banneret, or baronets, in 1611. Although Sir Robert Cotton had written in support by arguing that bannerets merely represented a revival of a vestigial medieval order, this was mere sophistry. For Arundel and his like, things were evidently slipping. Baronets were mere shooting stars and they hardly represented a threat to planetary figures revolving round the sun king, but they were worrying none the less. Furthermore they were created at a time when James was also increasing earldoms. Those who enjoyed titles of respectable antiquity felt uneasy.

Part of the problem had been that James had needed to satisfy the demands of his Scots cronies whilst making sure that he did not offend the English nobility by appearing to favour those from north of the Border. The solution, and it was typical of James, had been to try to keep everyone sweet by prodigally dispensing titles. Ennoblement made what was always a competitive environment still more so. Therefore it may well be that courtiers began to collect to be ahead in the race.

Combatants at Renaissance courts had to live well. In England they came to possess a good collection of pictures, a splendidly carved barge, and a villa in the Thames valley. Today company trusts create an art foundation while the directors drive Mercedes and own a farmhouse in France. The equivalent to taking a prominent box at Covent Garden as might happen now, was to appear in a court entertainment. Buckingham's wife may be in just such a guise in the *Adonis and Venus*, in what is perhaps a record of a wedding masque in which those to whom the masque was dedicated were themselves the principal performers.

After the assassination of Buckingham, his sister Susan who was married to William, 1st Earl of Denbigh, wrote to her son Basil who as Lord Feilding and ambassador to Venice, was to supply the King and his friends with some of their best Venetian pictures. Feilding was then abroad, assiduously acquiring that *politesse* which would qualify him for his posting to Italy. The Countess of Denbigh confided to her son how she felt that:

> a fitter time for you and more convenient, to present your servis to the King, and wth all to apeare in the perfexions of those qualitys wch I hope you have by your travelles gained and therfore I would have you stay till the time of dansing and masking are in season, for if you should come now you would be stalle before fit time weare to advanse your selfe in those exercises, and lose all that you have gained in your travells.[27]

High office and conspicuous display went together: indeed the connection is so close that the exception proves the rule. Sir John Coke stands apart. Sir John was Charles I's longest-serving Secretary of State; an office he held from 1625 to 1639. He was the unglamorous but dependable bureaucrat of the Personal Rule. Coke was conscientious, skilled, and diligent, but about as far from Van Dyck's image of the romantic cavalier as it was possible to get. No great portrait survives, and although those alternative schemes for Rubens to use in the Banqueting House were recently discovered among his papers, he appears to have remained quite unmoved by contact with the artist.

By contrast to such stolid indifference on the part of Sir John, a whole succession of James's favourites had bought pictures to enhance status and to conceal a modest start. Robert Carr, 1st Earl of Somerset, James Hay, 1st Earl of Carlisle, George Villiers, 1st Duke of Buckingham; each the first to hold his title, were all enthusiastic patrons and collectors.

A taste for collecting grew. It became as necessary for the ambitious to discourse knowledgeably about pictures as it had been for Elizabethans to appear in ever more elaborate disguise for the Accession Day tilt. Elizabeth would graciously condescend to receive an emblematic shield from a triumphant Essex, as Charles I later came to accept a fine Rubens from Buckingham.

While Buckingham kept relations with Charles I good by presenting well chosen pictures, he created as much as followed fashion. His development as a connoisseur preceded that of Charles I though it followed Arundel's. The love of pictures and mutual encouragement of taste formed one of the many indissoluble bonds between Charles and Buckingham. It had been hugely stimulated by their unforgettable experience of Spain. In Madrid they had enjoyed Titian together, they were both presented with masterpieces, and Charles sat to Velazquez who had been brought from Seville a year or two earlier by Buckingham's arch rival on the European stage, the Duke of Olivares.

Buckingham had more effect on the development of Charles I's taste than anyone. He had a flair for pictures, and an irresistible personality. But Arundel had more than a flair. He had a profound feel for art in all its manifestations; he knew more, much more than Buckingham. But his character prevented him from influencing the king to the same extent. He was grand, aloof and intense, and Charles I recognised too much of himself in Arundel to accept him easily as a tutor. The king found relief in the friendship of the irresistible Buckingham. Arundel was only to become close after the assassination of Buckingham in 1628, but by then the metal had cooled, the contours of the king's taste had emerged from the mould.

The manner of Buckingham's going to France was of a refulgent splendour matched as a joyous public spectacle only some ten years later when the Inns of Court would parade through London by way of an opening to the most grandiose of all early Stuart masques, *The Triumph of Peace*.

Buckingham is described as leaving London on 31 March 1625 in terms which make *The Twelve Days of Christmas* seem positively parsimonious: 'Twenty Privy Gentlemen; seven Grooms of his chamber; thirty Chief Yeomen; two Master Cooks . . . Twelve Pages, three rich suits a-piece; . . . eight-score musicians richly suited; twenty-two watermen, suited in sky-coloured taffety, all gilded with anchors, and my Lord's arms; all these to row in one barge of my Lord's . . .' (see Appendix I).

The parallels between Buckingham's departure for Paris and that lawyers' masque of 1634 are indeed close. The description of the clothes worn by the Buckingham entourage of 1625 suggests that they formed a band of strolling masquers, anticipating *The Triumph of Peace* in their fusion of high politics and dazzling symbolism. Buckingham's train left London like some fabulous bejewelled chimera departing a masque in the Banqueting House to journey to a far country.

The description of who wore what on the road to Paris, reinforces Smuts' argument that historians of English culture, and art historians in particular, have woefully neglected ephemera like dress as a cultural signifier in favour of paintings, by which the late twentieth century sets such great store.

The extent to which Buckingham's progress to Notre Dame was itself a kind of masque, also serves to reinforce an argument I have offered in another context. I have tried to suggest that we should see the masque proper as germane to politics in a more intimate way than some have allowed.[29] The audience to whom a masque was addressed were themselves performers on the stage of politics and for that matter, often performers in the very Banqueting House itself. However fey the masque may seem now to all but the revivalists of authentic performance on Radio Three, it must be recognised that it was an *engaged* expression of achievement and aspiration, compromise and the rewriting of events; all wrapped within a fantastic gauze which was, and this is important, osmotic.

Buckingham went to Paris to accompany Henrietta Maria to London after her marriage by proxy to Charles I in Notre Dame in May 1625. There Buckingham saw Rubens' Marie de' Medici cycle, met the artist, from whom he had commissioned what would turn out to be the greatest of all Baroque portraits of an English sitter, and was presented with enviable presents. Although exactly what Buckingham got is not known, the gifts must have been remarkable if one of Trumbull's correspondents is to be believed. Joseph Rumny wrote to Trumbull from Paris on 5 June describing how Buckingham had been fêted. The occasion was the first grand reception held in the gallery, which had just been decorated by Rubens with scenes from the life of a disastrous queen:

> The King [of France] presented the Duke (from his own hand) w^{t} a hat-band of Diamonds soe ponderouslye rich, that hee excusd the not wear-

> ing of y^t more then one daye because of the waite thereof. The Queene and Princes of the Court have emptied their Cabinetts of all rich pictures and Statues to bestow upon him. But that whereof hee may most triumph is that he had the Maydenhead of the Queen Mother's new howse. Whether being invited by her Matie to a banquet, none but the thre Queenes, the Kings brother, and the Duke sate at table. They are now all togeather upon their Royall March to conduct our Queene.[30]

Buckingham told Charles of the fabulous hospitality he had received in Paris. It may well be, therefore, that when Charles saw what Buckingham had been given, he determined that he too should acquire a still more famous collection. It may be no coincidence then that the negotiations for the Gonzaga collection really began in earnest just after Buckingham returned from Paris.

History was repeating itself. A hundred years earlier, Henry VIII had been spurred on by awareness of the visual splendour of the courts of Francis I and Charles V. And so in 1627, at the onset of a new reign requiring a new means toward regal splendour, Charles bought the Gonzaga collection; having seen in Madrid and heard from Paris of the value his 'cousins' of France and Spain placed upon art.

The arrival of the Mantuan horde gave new impetus to collecting in England. The Gonzaga holdings had been surpassed by the Vatican and equalled only by the Medici amongst Italian Renaissance collections. By the end of the 1620s when everything from Mantua had finally arrived, Charles I had given the English Crown not only great pictures by Titian, Giulio Romano, Mantegna and others, but a repertoire of visual propaganda which lent the Stuarts the same prestige as the Habsburgs and the Valois already possessed.

Charles I had mixed motives for spending what has been calculated as £18,000 on the Gonzaga collection; money which Filippo Burlamachi, the harrassed royal money lender, considered could have been spent more usefully on victualling the English army at war with France.

One motive which hardly requires explanation was Charles I's love of paintings pure and simple. He had a capacity to appreciate great art regardless of what it might do to enhance the image of the monarchy. Vicarious evidence, however, suggests that competition with France also spurred him on.

Charles had found himself bidding against Cardinal Richelieu for some of the finest Gonzaga treasures. Although Charles certainly came away with the best and the most, Cardinal Richelieu, chief minister to the minor Louis XIII, had already managed to siphon off a number of spectacularly fine pieces including Mantegna's *Parnassus* and *Pallas expelling the Vices*; choice pictures from what had been the inner sanctum of Isabella D'Este's collection, the studiolo of the Ducal Palace in Mantua.[31] But the most decisive evidence to suggest that the acquisition of the Mantuan collection had to do with more than a love of pictures comes from the chronology of the Banqueting House ceiling.

It will be recalled that Rubens had been approached in September 1621 and matters had then stalled because of the intervention of the Marie de' Medici cycle. The commission was then revived; brought into life by the death of James I. But was that the whole story? There is, I believe, another dimension.

In the standard work on the Banqueting House, it is suggested that the central oval was originally to have been a depiction of *Psyche received into Olympus*, but that idea was then abandoned in favour of what we have now: *The Apotheosis of James I*.[32] Perhaps we need look no further for the substitution of the one by the other, given the prodigious lamentation which followed James to the grave. However, it could be that the decision to move from a mythological to an earthly kingdom, to abandon Cupid and Psyche for James I and True Religion, may have had something to do with the unveiling of the Marie de' Medici cycle with its inflated claims for the greatness of Henri IV.

At this juncture Lord Danvers returns to the scene. We recall that on 19 May 1625 he wrote to Trumbull: 'His Majesty is now upon a design of building at Whitehall which plot once resolved will give me the measure for Rubens' picture.'[33] This must surely be a reference to the Banqueting House project. It was written less than three weeks before Buckingham sat down to dinner under the Marie de' Medici cycle. What therefore it is tempting to believe is that it was not just the death of James I in March of that year which got Charles I thinking more urgently of the ceiling, but reports by word of Buckingham's mouth as to what Rubens had achieved for the French Crown in Paris. Buckingham returned from Paris full of the splendours of a court which had flattered him in a hundred ways. Thus it may have been what Buckingham had to say about Paris and its new splendours which vicariously provided Rubens with new ideas to work on.

The Whitehall ceiling was conditioned therefore, by awareness among those close to Charles I of the skilfull exploitation of Rubens' talents in support of a monarchy much less securely placed than their own. The purchase of the Mantuan collection and the revival of the Whitehall ceiling proposals were interests which absorbed Charles I during the first summer of his reign because they were seen as powerful weapons in an international war of propaganda.

All this is conjectural. With the establishment of the Mortlake Tapestry Works we find ourselves on much firmer ground. The Mortlake works once set up, proved to be the single most successful entrepreneurial art venture ever undertaken by the Crown in the history of the English monarchy. Within a very few years of the factory being set up, it was producing the finest tapestries in the world. They soon came to be exported. The reign of Charles I proved to be the great period for the factory, even though it remained in production until the early eighteenth century.

James I actually established the business. The Privy Council instructed a committee to proceed with setting up the factory in a proclamation in which the influence of France was openly acknowledged:

> [The King] hath been pleased of late to cast his princely cogitation upon that excellent art of making tapestry, and finding that our neighbouring countries . . . have attained already to so great a perfection therein [the King] is not without hopes that the same be established also in this kingdom . . . we have sent you a copy of an edict made some years since by the late French King when this art was by himself established in France, from which you may take some light . . .[34]

What had turned cogitation into action was James's purchase of the remarkable series of tapestries designed by Cornelius Vroom which depicted the Armada. These had been acquired in 1616 for £1,628 and they immediately established themselves as one of the greatest treasures of the Royal Collection. In August 1619 Sir Francis Crane, the first director of the works, bought properties in Mortlake; the next year fifty Flemish weavers were imported and work began.

So much for how James looked at Henri IV, but how did his subjects look at one another? What distinctions were there between the great London collections? Characterisation of early Stuart collections is not easily done, but it is possible to make some generalisations. The first to be noticed must be Arundel's. It was the earliest, the most idiosyncratic and the most varied in what it contained.

The more that is learned about Arundel's tastes, the more they seem to have been informed by the devotion Arundel himself felt for his family past and present. The Tudor era had been a century of unparalleled drama in the history of the family; a history more bloody than a Webster tragedy. There were continuities in what was a story of hubris and nemesis unique in English history. The Howards not only had a character permanently on the stage of Tudor politics, but each generation contributed in distinguished ways to the culture of the English Renaissance. The Howards did as much to promote humanism as the monarchy itself.

Thomas, 2nd Duke of Norfolk, had destroyed the Scottish Renaissance at Flodden, only to nurture the English with his encouragement of important writers: Alexander Barclay and John Skelton, the most prominent poet at the court of Henry VII, both worked for him. Henry Howard, 'the Poet Surrey' was one of the most distinguished literati of the century. Surrey's translations of the second and fourth Books of the Aeneid was the first English blank verse, while Surrey shared with Sir Thomas Wyatt the distinction of introducing the Petrarchan sonnet into English. Surrey's poetry was immensely popular: within a year of the publication of his poems in 1557, there were no less than four impressions, and the collection was reprinted seven times within the next thirty years. Surrey and his father, the 3rd Duke of Norfolk, were major patrons of Holbein and they attracted a number of distinguished men of letters amongst whom was the poet Thomas Churchyard. Thomas Howard, 4th Duke of Norfolk, son of the poet, was first tutored by Hadrianus Junius, second only to Erasmus among Dutch humanist luminaries. After the execution of the 4th Duke's father in 1547, his education had been rounded off by John Foxe: author of the *Actes and Monumentes,* and the greatest apologist for the Reformed religion in England. Thereafter the 4th Duke became a great patron of architecture, converting the Charterhouse into one of the most important houses in London.

While Thomas, 4th Duke of Norfolk, sat at the feet of the martyrologist Foxe, his son Philip, father of the collector, became a Catholic martyr through the auspices of St Edmund Campion. He was canonised in 1970.

Henry Howard, 1st Earl of Northampton, uncle to St Philip Howard, and great uncle of the collector Earl, was taken to be one of the most learned of the nobility. He was a prominent aristocratic patron of the Society of Antiquaries, keenly interested in mathematics, philosophy, and architecture; to the extent indeed that by the middle of the seventeenth century he was considered to have been the architect of Audley End. Laud's chaplain Peter Heylyn wrote in 1650: 'He [Northampton] assisted his nephew the Earl of Suffolk by his designing and large contribution, to that excellent *Fabrick Audley End*. He built the *Noble structure at Charing-Crosse,* from the Ground, Northampton House and presented it a New-years-gift to the Lord Walden, Suffolkes eldest Sonne, and now called Suffolk House . . .'.[35] Audley End was the last of the prodigy houses to have been built and one of the few to have survived to this day, built for Northampton's nephew, the Earl of Suffolk, a venal Lord Treasurer in an age outstanding for corruption.

The story of the Howards in the sixteenth century was indeed remarkable and Arundel was acutely, not to say tediously, aware of it. His perception of himself as a patron and his ambition to be a dominant figure in the Stuart age, was profoundly shaped by wanting to rival ancestors. This is why he developed what he described, in a rare moment of self-deprecation, as his 'foolish curiosity in enquiringe for the peeces of Holbein'. It may have been foolish but it made him famous. Joachim Sandrart whose *Teutsche Akademie* (1675) provided a German approximation to Vasari, singled out Arundel House for especial praise because it was there that Holbein 'held the master's place' and visitors could admire scores of works by Holbein in the form of portraits on panel, as drawings, sketch books, and in the form of his prints.[36] The Holbein collection at Arundel House must have made something of the impact the Clore Gallery at the Tate now has on admirers of Turner.

Nearly all of the people in the Arundel Holbein portraits constituted the *dramatis personae* of Henry VIII's court. Fascination with Tudor ancestors was also why the Holbein portraits of the 3rd Duke of Norfolk and the

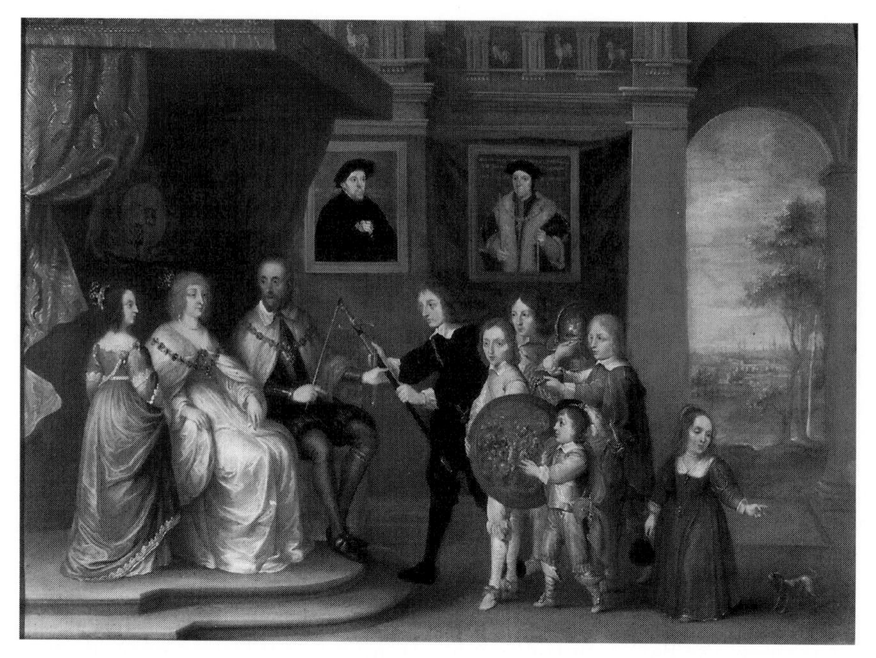

Philip Fruytiers, *Arundel Family* (after Van Dyck), *c.* 1642 (His Grace The Duke of Norfolk, Arundel Castle)

Poet Surrey hover so prominently above Arundel in the record of a Van Dyck design for a large family portrait which, had it been painted, would have rivalled *The Pembroke Family*. Images within an image, these likenesses are recognisably Holbein but also tutelary saints, or the lares of an ancient Roman family.

Arundel's over-developed cult of family history probably accounts for why he did not envisage a great new palace as Buckingham seems to have done for York House, and Pembroke would want at Durham House during the Civil War. Arundel built a two-storey gallery running down to the Thames for paintings and statues, and a small free-standing house in the inner courtyard which, it has been suggested, may have housed what Arundel himself described as 'o^{r} Rome [room] for Designes',[37] created *c.* 1635 for the legendary Arundel drawings and possibly by Inigo Jones: Leonardos, Michelangelos, Raphaels, Dürers and Holbeins, were just some of the artists represented. A smattering of this legendary collection of drawings would later be copied by Hollar and carefully inscribed 'ex collectione Arundelliana' so that all the world would know that the originals came from that famous collection. But what Arundel never seems to have contemplated was sweeping away the Tudor ranges of the chapel and Great Hall; perhaps because picturesque accretions to what had started as the medieval inn of the Bishops of Bath and Wells reminded the owner of the great days of the family. If that is correct then it answers John Evelyn who questioned why Arundel was always 'inciting' others to build though he built little himself.[38]

Arundel was familiar with illumination in his capacity as Earl Marshal; an office in which he was served by the College of Arms. The College had to register and examine titles, and issue coats of arms. Much of the evidence for such claims took the form of old manuscripts, many of which contained illuminated pages. One of the officers who served under Arundel was Henry Lilly, Rouge Dragon Pursuivant. Lilly was a talented manuscript illuminator, and in 1638, Arundel commissioned from him an illuminated family history, described on the title page as a 'Genealogie of the Princelie familie of the Howards exactly deduced in a right line from the XVth yeere of the raign of King Edgar . . . to this present XIIIth yeere of the raign of ar Dread Soveraigne Charles', the book consists of an illuminated family tree as thick as a King James Bible, with 110 painted shields and numerous miniatures of tombs, stained glass windows and other artefacts; the whole consisting of an illustrated biography of the Howards. The book is perhaps the last great illuminated manuscript to have been produced in England.

The frontispiece of Lilly's manuscript takes the form of a triumphal arch, flanked by two elongated porphyry Corinthian columns, with four niches to left and right containing portraits of members of the Howard dynasty, including Arundel himself. Above is what appears to be a personification of the English monarchy seated under a cloth of state. The frontispiece is a distinct anachronism like the manuscript itself. Here was an artist working in a tradition which went back beyond Edward the Confessor when Van Dyck was painting his last royal portraits.

Lilly's book is, though, more typical of its age than it appears. The emphasis on dignity and decorum was something Charles I consistently promoted at his court, whilst the frontispiece is like much Caroline architecture in retaining distinctly gothic detail within a classical framework. Such a 'bastard' style was by no means confined to frontispieces. Ten years before Lilly was gilding the Howards, the west front of Peterhouse Chapel in Cambridge had been begun under the Mastership of Matthew Wren, that most conservative of the Caroline bishops (Plate 2, page 17). The chapel and its arcades, now no longer 'posthumously Gothic' as Pevsner described them, because classically rebuilt in 1709, gave prominent public expression to the same fusion of the classical and gothic; a fusion of two streams creating eddies which defy attempts at canalisation by architectural historians; a style so distinct that it is tempting to christen it 'Carogothic' in the same spirit as the revival of interest in Jacobean architecture in the early nineteenth century has come to be called 'Jacobethan'.[39]

Arundel commissioned a golden legend from Henry Lilly, lovingly restored family tombs in Framlingham church, and put a roof back on the

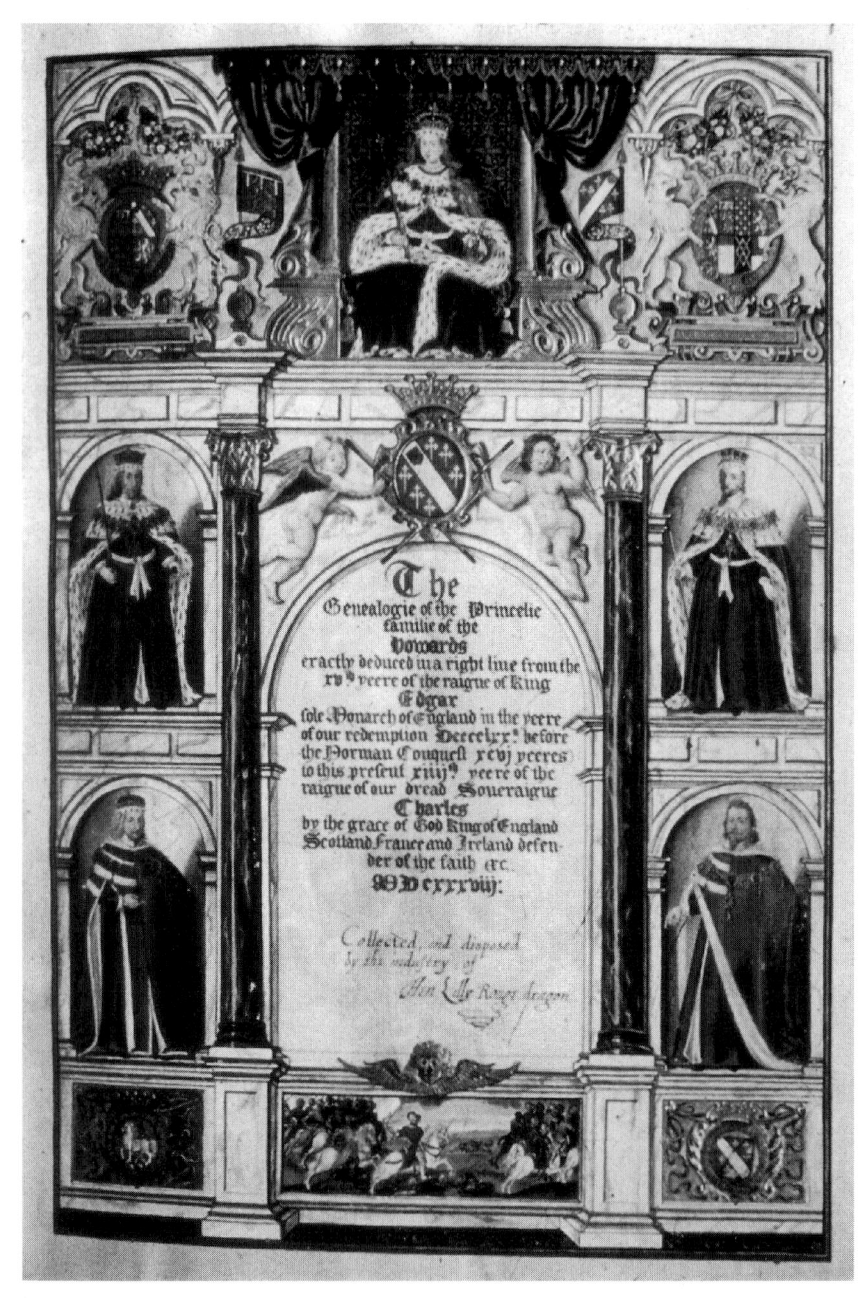

Henry Lilly, *Genealogie of the Princelie familie of the Howards*, 1638 (His Grace The Duke of Norfolk, Arundel Castle)

Mortuary Chapel near King's Lynn where the mortal remains of the first Howard had been buried. All these were acts of familial piety. But they were acts of policy too. They commemorated the family, while they sustained the reputation of Arundel at a court where stakes had been much enhanced since Charles had dispensed with Parliament.

Arundel's dealings with *savants* were, too, just another aspect of reliving the glory of the Howards. Arundel appointed the internationally respected Dutch philologist Francis Junius as his librarian. He made William Oughtred vicar of Albury, a Surrey parish. In that parish Arundel had his villa, with its sandy grotts where he liked to preside over his learned circle like some Athenian philosopher in his stoa. Oughtred was a conscientious vicar but an outstanding mathematician who would later be described by Newton as the best of those who had come before him. Oughtred was also tutor to the Arundel children. William Harvey, whose *De Mortu Cordis* appeared in 1628 and gave the world the principle of the circulation of the blood, was Arundel's doctor. The legendary collection of inscriptions, 'misshapen stones' as Buckingham called these sorts of things, Arundel valued because they gained him reputation as a learned man.

Arundel was a pioneer of taste. He was the first Englishman to collect classical inscriptions in a systematic way, the first person in Europe to put engravers to reproducing his drawings. But in other respects he cultivated the past to an affected extent. His dress was years out of date because he identified himself with previous generations of his own family. As head of the College of Arms it was his job to be aware of nice distinctions of social rank, but his rigid insistence on protocol made him an awkward and sometimes embarrassing figure at court.

The Arundel Collection, more demanding than that of Buckingham, was no less concerned with self-promotion than what could be admired at York House. It was simply the difference between intellectual conceit and visual pride; Arundel was gratified by the praise lavished on him by the *savants* of Europe, Buckingham elevated by the visual splendour of his galleries. His were certainly more spectacular than the 'world of learned lectures' which a visitor to Arundel House was likely to get from the mounted inscriptions.

The 1639–40 inventory of the Royal Collection suggests how often courtiers made presentations. Important work remains to be done to establish who gave what, when and why. Until then however, we have to rely on the motives of one late-comer to the collecting scene in trying to value the currency of art at the early Stuart court.

The most naked manipulation of art for political ends concerns James, 3rd Marquess and 1st Duke of Hamilton.[40] The unfinished Mytens of Hamilton (National Portrait Gallery of Scotland) is the finest English portrait by that artist; though it was painted several years before the sitter made his mark as a collector. That happened largely through accident.

Hamilton's brother-in-law, Basil, Lord Feilding, was made ambassador to Venice. Hamilton saw his chance. He began to speculate in a futures market in much the same way as Carleton had played the Venetian and Antwerp exchanges twenty years earlier.

Hamilton was, however, better placed than Carleton had been. He was extremely well connected and he was already in London. Faction fighting at court was rife in the 1630s when, with no Parliaments to share in the dispensation of patronage and office, the prizes were richer. Hamilton decided that he could help to maintain himself as the leading voice on Scottish affairs by plying Charles I with pictures. The inventory of The Royal Collection covers only a limited number of royal palaces and therefore provides an incomplete list of pictures and gifts. Nevertheless it suggests that Hamilton presented more paintings to Charles I in the five years that he was an active collector than Arundel had presented in thirty.

While Hamilton was busy bribing the King, he was promoting himself by being associated with a fine collection of Renaissance masters. His correspondence with his brother-in-law provides the most direct evidence we have of the spasms of furious jealousy which collecting could provoke at this time. Hamilton was determined to beat Arundel to one acquisition because if his rival were to get it 'the truth is, my Lord of Arundel's jesting will trouble me more than the costing double their value'.[41]

Charles I used to be thought of as an escapist: as one who retreated from the tedious, painful business of governing to the masque rehearsal or the serenity of the coin room. However, Sharpe's compendious study of the years of Personal Rule suggests that Charles I maintained not only a detailed grasp but control of the administration too. What this chapter has attempted to do is to add a gloss to Sharpe's account. It suggests that patronage and collecting were important to the tensions of court life which Sharpe has brilliantly illuminated. The buying of pictures was part of the currency of rivalry: pursuits which defined and inflamed jealousies, promoted forgotten careers, recorded distinctions of rank, and illuminated moments of glory. Collecting was a very public and social act at the court of Charles I.

In the final chapter we end by looking at the writings of contemporaries to discover how Tudor poet and Stuart gossip saw the buildings, the portraits, the tombs and the paintings which have been the concern of this book.

Chapter Eight
Writers and Critics

The ceremonial with which Cardinal Wolsey surrounded himself was a work of art in itself. The Chancellor of England would proceed from his palace of York Place to the Law Courts, dressed in full panoply with pages walking before, carrying silver staffs of office. When Wolsey said Mass he conducted a ritual which had more to do with emphasising the earthly glory of the celebrant than with recalling the principal means to salvation. As Wolsey raised the host, a brace of Dukes held basin and towel.

The purpose of this chapter is to consider how Tudor and Stuart writers responded to visual magnificence. The Italians called it *superbia*; a term which encapsulates the colossal appetite for self-expression which helped to make Wolsey known not only as the English Cardinal, but as the leading statesman of Europe during the negotiations which led up to the Treaty of London of 1520. *Superbia* could be applied equally well to the Duke of Buckingham, who matched the Cardinal's prodigality and flamboyance a century later.

How then did observers react to the sight of Wolsey as Chancellor of England processing through the streets of London, or the Senate of Cambridge University receiving Buckingham as its Chancellor? Did onlookers see rituals and ceremony, banquets and portraits as seemly, or rather as something which alienated those who both consoled and provoked themselves with the thought that the Cardinal had begun life as the son of an Ipswich butcher, and the Duke as the issue of a modest Leicestershire gentleman?

The most famous account of Wolsey is 'the life of . . . the rich and triumphant legate and Cardinal of England' written by his gentleman usher, George Cavendish. Cavendish entered Wolsey's service in 1522 and his biography is the witness of a man who came to know his subject more intimately than many; though only when his days of glory were waning. The book is much heavier at one end than the other: the years up to the divorce of Henry VIII constitute less than half, while Cavendish concentrates on the last year of his subject's life. Nor is it a contemporary account. Begun in the winter of 1554, it was finished in the summer of 1558. None the less it provides us with the most vivid evidence we have of Wolsey's display; the decade 1514–25 between the acquisition of York Place and when Wolsey felt it politic to offer Hampton Court to Henry VIII.

Cavendish offers a very positive account of Wolsey as a patron. There is no suggestion that Wolsey damaged himself through the Byzantine splendour of his ritual or the extravagance of his recreation. Cavendish implies that it would be wrong to imagine Henry VIII sulking at the feast while Wolsey took pride in the inventive richness of entertainments laid on for his master. On the contrary lavish display was a vital ingredient of their mutual regard.

Peter Gwyn, the most recent biographer of Wolsey, cites the famous description by Cavendish of an entertainment put on by Wolsey for Henry, probably sometime after 1526, to argue: 'it . . . may serve to capture a vital aspect of their mutual attraction: a shared delight in the good things of life, an enormous vitality and animal energy, and a feeling that together they could set the world alight'.[1]

Cavendish is a somewhat uncritical witness of Wolsey but surely he was broadly correct to suggest that Wolsey's patronage was much admired; at least by most of those who stayed within the perimeters of orthodox Catholicism. Cavendish wrote of how:

> it pleased the King's majesty for his recreation to repair unto the cardinal's house (as he did divers times in the year); at which time there wanted no preparations or goodly furniture with viands of the finest sort that might be provided for money or friendship. Such pleasures were then devised for the king's comfort and consolation as might be invented or by man's wit imagined. The banquets were set forth with masques and mummeries in so gorgeous a sort and costly manner that it was an heaven to behold.[2]

In a world of Christian Aid, we feel instinctively uneasy about material splendour in the church. We would surely feel a lot happier about Wolsey had he worn his hair shirts more often. Understandably he preferred to dress in 'crimson satin, taffeta, damask or caffa' with 'a tippet of fine sables'. But we cannot assume that magnificence was found as provocative in the Renaissance as some find it now. Sixteenth-century prelates were men of immense political importance; indeed they were princes. The Church was the First Estate of the Realm; a bishop took precedence in state ceremonials over the officers of the king's household. Therefore it was impossible for Wolsey to have lived the life of an ascetic. If he had not maintained a massive household he would have been severely censured.

Wolsey was merely the most splendidly feathered bird in an exotic aviary. The Henrician bishops lived in great style whether they liked it or not. Most did. William Warham, Archbishop of Canterbury during Wolsey's years of dominance, was one of the first of Henry's courtiers to have his portrait painted by Holbein. He was alleged to have spent £33,000 on doing up the archiepiscopal palace of Otford. That must be an exaggeration surely, but whatever sums were dispersed, the money spent represented an extravagance when it is appreciated that Otford was within easy horse ride of Knole, another archiepiscopal palace which had only recently been modernised by Warham's predecessors Bourchier and Morton. The courtyard at Otford was larger than the equivalent at Hampton Court. And yet for all this, Warham is never cited on charges of corruption or unworldliness. Furthermore, it is questionable whether improvements at Otford were such an extravagance when considered against the priorities of the time and the station of the patron. If Warham was indeed a prince, and his tenure of the see of Canterbury represented an ecclesiastical regime which had very considerable independence from the Crown prior to the Reformation, then just as secular princes developed their own programme of self-glorification so too could an archbishop.

Wolsey was criticised for the splendour with which he liked to surround himself, but none of those who levelled accusations can be regarded as objective; not that objectivity seems to have been within the grasp of a Tudor observer before Camden published his *Britannia* and the writing of history as opposed to chronicles had its first beginnings. None the less whatever capacities were available to the Tudor historian, Wolsey certainly provoked strong reactions which people were prepared to publish after he was safely dead. These we must consider briefly in the light of the partiality of Cavendish.

John Skelton was allied to the Howards who manoeuvred against Wolsey; Edward Hall had markedly Protestant sympathies which made him try to discredit the old Church and its most provocative representative in his *The Union of the Two Noble and Illustre Famelies of York and Lancaster* (1542). The Italian chronicler Polydore Vergil hated Wolsey for the revenge Wolsey had taken on him when Vergil, on a visit to Rome, had spread critical stories of the Cardinal. In all cases therefore, what was written represents something no more satisfactory than Cavendish.

Skelton had been poet laureate to Henry VII and tutor to Henry VIII and was therefore a man of considerable influence. Skelton's gifts as a poet, combined with his influence within courtly circles, ensured that what he wrote became something of an orthodoxy. Skelton was responsible for creating the myth that in building Hampton Court, Wolsey was making himself into what Gwyn has neatly described as an *alter rex*. Two poems in particular encapsulated the venomous feelings Skelton reserved for Wolsey: *Speke Parrott* and *Whyt come ye nat to Courte?* In the latter

Skelton asks himself the question which forms the title of the poem and then provides his own reply as the verse unfolds:

> To whyche court?
> To the kynges courte?
> Or to Hampton Court?
> Nay, to the kynges court!
> The kynges courte
> Shulde have the excellence;
> But Hampton Court
> Hath the preemynence![3]

It must be doubtful however whether Henry felt irritated by the size and splendour of palaces owned by Wolsey. The accidental survival of Hampton Court has given Wolsey's suburban residence and his role as a patron more prominence than it would merit if Nonsuch, for example, had survived. We should not forget that the Henrician palaces vastly outnumbered what Wolsey could muster. In reality there was no competition between the King and his Chancellor in the stakes of splendour.

Wolsey always kept a steady eye on the European scene and so should we in trying to understand what response he provoked. The chief ministers of Francis I and Charles V behaved in exactly the same way. They would not have kept their jobs if they had not maintained princely households; Wolsey could not have been the great impresario of The Field of the Cloth of Gold if he had not already transformed York Place.

It is one of the ironies of English cultural history that Wolsey was the most conspicuous and energetic patron of the English Renaissance and yet so much about him is opaque. There is not a shred of evidence from Wolsey himself of his likes and dislikes in the arts; so little of his personal life remains that we do not even know the colour of his hair. The famous portrait in the National Portrait Gallery in London is not life-like in any meaningful sense, while some contemporary commentators describe him as fat, others as thin.

No trace remains of what Wolsey thought he was doing in spending a vast income on treasure. Paradoxically however this is very telling. Wolsey was not only the sole English Cardinal, but the only great English stateman of his generation who really seems to have delighted in art. There were of course peers and commoners who well understood the importance of shows. There is, too, much evidence that tapestries were greatly valued for their richness and the intricacies of their designs. But there was no one besides Wolsey whom it might be supposed would have taken a close interest in the careers of great artists had they been available in London. Torrigiano had been in England for a decade but we know nothing of his relations with his royal patrons as we know at least something of Charles I's encouragement and nurturing of Le Sueur. With

Wolsey alone in the Tudor era is it possible to imagine a Giulio Romano or even a Cellini sustaining a long creative partnership, such as Giulio had begun to enjoy with Federigo Gonzaga at the court of Mantua during the last years of Wolsey's life. The Englishman Lord Morley had his portrait taken by Dürer in watercolours, but Dürer is the only great artist working in Europe who can be associated with a Henrician figure; and then only through the accident of foreign travel and in the form of one solitary watercolour.

The complete absence of inventories and letters of commission to artists in Wolsey's papers surely reflects the priorities of that age; the selective survival of Wolsey's personal papers. Wolsey himself had no legitimate heirs to preserve the archive and thus what has survived represents what Tudor antiquarians and historians of later ages thought history was about. Inventories of palaces, or, say, instructions to artists, must have been discarded because history, since its invention, has had to do with treaties not tapestries.

A reading of Sir Thomas Elyot's *The Boke named The Gouernour* provides vicarious evidence for such a view. *The Gouernour* appeared in 1531, very shortly after the death of Wolsey. What Elyot has to say about the place of the visual arts at the English court confirms the impression that painting and its associated activities had to justify itself.

Elyot, the subject of one of the most beautiful Holbein portrait drawings, had been a client of Wolsey, and until 1530, looked destined for a promising career at court. In that year however he was dismissed from the clerkship of the Council, and though he was later to be sent as ambassador to Germany, he devoted his later life to literary pursuits and most famously to writing. *The Gouernour* is about how to educate the sons of gentlemen. Prior observation of the great, qualified Elyot to suggest what needed to be done to bring the education of future administrators into line with progressive developments in humanist education in Europe.

Elyot's principal contribution was to urge greater use of the vernacular and a broadening of the educational curriculum. Here he was following the arguments of Vives in Spain, whose *De tradendis disciplinis*, of 1523, constituted a plea for the use of Spanish in schooling. This had then been followed in Italy by Pietro Bembo, patron of Bellini and Titian, whose *Della Volgar Lingua* said the same thing, but in Italian rather than Latin, as with Vives. Elyot owed much to their encouragement.

Elyot has interesting things to say in *The Gouernour* about the place of the visual arts, but they constitute a series of apologetics. It is clear from Elyot's tone that 'portraiture', which for Elyot meant every aspect of the graphic arts, was remote to his readership.

Chapter VIII is devoted to 'Painting and Carving'. Elyot begins by rebutting the 'enuious reder' who 'hereof apprehende occasion to scorne me' for trying 'to make of a noble man a mason or peynter'. He then goes on to suggest the many ways in which painting can be useful to the man

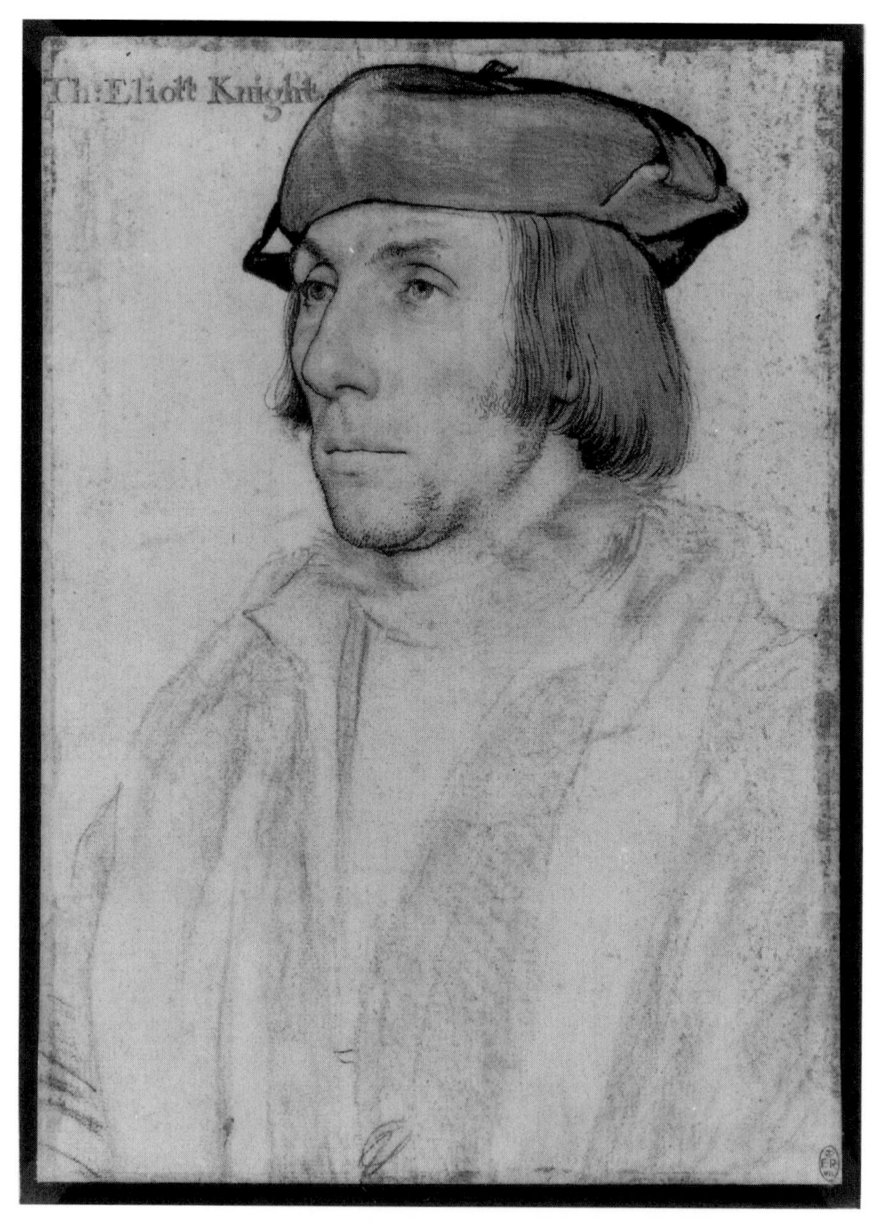

Hans Holbein, *Sir Thomas Elyot*, c. 1532 (The Royal Collection)

of affairs. He cites Roman Emperors who actually took to drawing and painting:

> suche were Claudius, Titus, the sonne of Vaspasian, Hadriane, both Antonines, and diuers other emperours and noble princes: whose warkes of longe tyme remayned in Rome and other cities, in such places where all men mought beholde them: as monuments of their excellent wittes and vertuous occupation in eschewynge of idelnes.[4]

The most ambitious claim Elyot makes for imagery was not however the citation of Roman emperors, but its capacity to enhance memory; that is to say, the art of mnemonics, as it came to be called. The memory was best developed by the visual arts not the printed word. It was an ambitious claim which would influence English writers on the visual arts for a hundred years and more.

> And where the liuely spirite, and that whiche is called the grace of the thyng, is perfectly expressed, that thinge more persuadeth and stereth the beholder, and soner istructeth hym, than the declaration in writynge or speakynge doth the reder or hearer.[5]

Elyot's book helped English education put out more leaves. It is justly famous for the contribution it made to humanist studies. What, however, the book entirely lacks is any reference to a pre-existing visual culture. There is no sense in which Elyot seems to be addressing an educated elite who looked at pictures as they were used to reading Virgil. Indeed the impact of the book owes much to the fact that Elyot was introducing his peers to a whole range of exciting new possibilities, one of which was to see the various ways in which 'the feate of portraiture or payntyng' could be turned to good account. Elyot was deploying persuasive and probably quite successful arguments to make men see just what the visual arts could offer.

But not even Elyot, the enlightened civil servant, dared go so far as to suggest that the 'delight' which he acknowledges to be readily derived from a picture, needed no apology, no further comment. It is only when 'delight' is awarded the apple in the reign of Charles I that it can really be said England had a visual culture akin to what had long existed in the courts of Europe.

There is some evidence that the Elizabethans began to take an interest in exploring the nature and function of painting after the influx of Low Country artists in the 1570s. A debate began as to the relative merits of painting and writing which would grow in volume until the Civil War. Arguments as to the efficacy or otherwise of the visual arts, entered the bloodstream of educational debate through the writings of Elyot. But they were given a transfusion by John Lyly, the distinguished Elizabethan grammarian; a life-saving transfusion after the damage sustained during the years of iconoclasm.

Lyly made a further range of classical allusions to painting readily accessible in his book *Euphues* (*c.* 1578); though the novelty of discussing the topic at all may account for why Lyly could never decide whether he approved or disapproved of art. Lyly was not alone in feeling confused; there is a larger problem for the historian of today in understanding what exactly the Elizabethans felt about the position of painting in society. There are many stray references to the analogy between painting and poetry and much on the educational purposes to which painting might be put. But it is impossible to nail writers down; theorists do not take the reader to a painting which can be identified and so bring the slide into focus. Interest in actual paintings is minimal if not non-existent. By contrast, the Elizabethans were intrigued by ekphrastic pictures: paintings which survive only through written descriptions in antique literature.

Lucy Gent, who has provided the fullest account of Elizabethans on painting, makes that point herself before going on to suggest two other reasons which may account for our confusion.[6] For Gent the memory of the great Edwardian scourges of iconoclasm made it dangerous to write about actual pictures.[7] She then argues that the vocabulary to discuss contemporary issues of style and artistic progress simply did not exist; that is to say, by inference, that the absence of an appropriate language, so to speak, closed up the whole issue.[8] Both points seem doubtful.

If the controversies which surrounded royal portraiture could induce the drafting of not one but two royal proclamations in the reign of Elizabeth, then people must have discussed actual pictures. Secondly, where there is an interest, the means of expressing it follow at once. A dictionary could now be compiled to cover the world of the computer, though most of the words will have entered the language in the last twenty years. An exact and expressive vocabulary for describing real as opposed to ekphrastic pictures did not exist because wide-ranging collections did not exist either; the Elizabethan was interested only in portraiture or the emblematic expression of rule.

There is no corpus of Elizabethan writing on the nature of art. The visual arts get a good if rather a thin press. Shakespeare's famous claim for the immortality his love would gain through the printed sonnet is contrasted by the poet with the futility of pursuing the same through means of 'unswept stone, besmear'd with sluttish time'.[9] Paper may have been more durable than marble for Shakespeare, but his thoughts as to the best method of arriving at immortality were not views shared by a popular and much read contributor from the later Elizabethan era: the sonneteer Samuel Daniel.

Today the name Daniel means nothing beyond the confines of English literary scholarship, but he was a very successful writer at the time. Daniel urges his dedicatee in sonnet 34 of *Delia* to 'take this picture which

I heere present thee. . . . This may remain your lasting monument.' Daniel aimed to please the lover and appeal to the teacher. He repeated Elyot's old argument that pictures were an excellent method of mnemonics.

It is no accident that arguments for painting based upon its utility as a teaching aid were revived just as the first illustrated emblem books began to be produced in England. Before then, the emblem was often presented in words alone without accompanying diagrams to reinforce the moral. Emblem pictures which accompany Daniel's own *The Woorthy Tract of Paulus Jovius* (1585), and Whitney's *A Choice of Emblemes* (1586) (Plate 47, page 130), reinforced what was one of the most formative aspects of late Elizabethan culture. To the extent that word and image came to hold hands, it helped claims that the image deserved to be considered comparable with the printed word. Poetry and painting had become cousins if not yet sisters. But there were Elizabethan critics of painting as well. The Muses had emerged dishevelled from the thickets of Edwardian controversy and iconoclasm. The grove echoed with discordant not to say contradictory voices, as Gent has pointed out.[10]

But whatever the standpoint of educational and literary theorists may have been, debates as to the place of painting and the allied arts in contemporary culture have a disengaged and theoretical quality which characterises the late Tudor response. The achievements and limitations of the visual arts were discussed more fully than before, but it was not until 1598 that the work of Lomazzo, a major Italian art theorist, was translated. Discussion as to the true nature of painting lacked the urgent social or political dimension which it would gradually gain under the Stuarts, and it is to this we now turn.

The most celebrated debate on the power of art during the reign of Charles I was the bitter, irreconcilable quarrel of 1631 between Ben Jonson and Inigo Jones, following years of competitive tension between them. They fell out over the question of whether poet or architect deserved most credit for the success of the masque. That success derived from the synthesis of all the arts inherent within the masque; poetry, painting, architecture, dance, song and costume design. The arch which sustained them all was illusionism. The rest of this chapter will be concerned with my argument that it was Puritan attacks on the deceit of illusionism which led to the adoption of a defensive posture amongst apologists of the arts in the years before the Civil War.

In 1633 William Prynne published *Histrio-mastix*. The book changed the nature of the debate about art and morals which had been an aspect of cultural discourse since the publication of *The Gouernour*. Prynne differed from earlier writers who had been concerned to point up the deceitfulness of art. Whereas previous discussion had been pitched at an abstract not to say abstruse level, Prynne's was levelled specifically at the court. Prynne threw a cat amongst court doves. *Histrio-mastix* proved to be the most controversial book about Caroline culture to be published during the years of Personal Rule. *Histrio-mastix* saw the inception of a debate about the morality of acting, the masque, building and painting, which grew in stridency until it degenerated into an outbreak of iconoclasm as public order broke down just before Charles I left London for Oxford in January 1642.

Prior to the appearance of the book, it is difficult to see that patronage and collecting provoked any interest beyond the court itself; though there had been the isolated episode which suggests that occasionally art had complicated policy. In the autumn of 1627 Charles's Italian Protestant banker Filippo Burlamachi had complained of difficulties in victualling the army whilst meeting bills for Charles's purchase of the collections of the Dukes of Mantua. Burlamachi was being expected to underwrite not only a great art purchase, but also the British expeditionary force sent to La Rochelle to help Protestants besieged by the French royal armies. In a letter received from Nicholas Lanier, Burlamachi added a marginal comment of frustration not to say desperation at the way the king was muddling royal finances:

> I praie lett me know his Matie pleaseur, but above all where monie shall be found to pay this great somme [for the Mantuan collections]. Iff it where for 2 or 3000£ it could be borne, but for 15000£, besides the other Engagements for his Ma^{ts} service, it will utterli put me out off ani possibilite to doe ani think in those provisions w^{che} are so necessari for M^{i} Lord Ducks relieve.[11]

Evidently the interest the king took in art did sometimes create awkward choices. Burlamachi's letter suggests that perhaps to some, Charles I appeared willing to put first things last and last things first. By diverting money which should have gone to buying pikes, towards pictures, Charles may have been perceived to be sacrificing the Protestant cause for trifles. Though there were still relatively few in London in 1627 who cared about pictures, there were a great many who felt passionately about the defence of their Protestant brethren in France. Consequently Charles's decision to send the Duke of Buckingham at the head of an English army had been a high moment of popularity for him but one which he then mishandled by starving it of funds.

A year later Buckingham faced impeachment by the House of Commons.[12] Sir John Eliot who led the prosecution in the Commons compared Buckingham with 'the beast called by the ancients Stellionatus: a beast so blurred, so spotted, so full of foul lines that they knew not what to make of it'. Buckingham, according to Eliot, had used crown revenue to satisfy his lusts and others' luxuries. He had, too, received vast sums, far exceeding the value of supplies voted by Parliament, which he had then proceeded to spend on 'costly furniture, sumptuous feasting and magnificent building, the visible evidences of the express exhausting of the state'. He

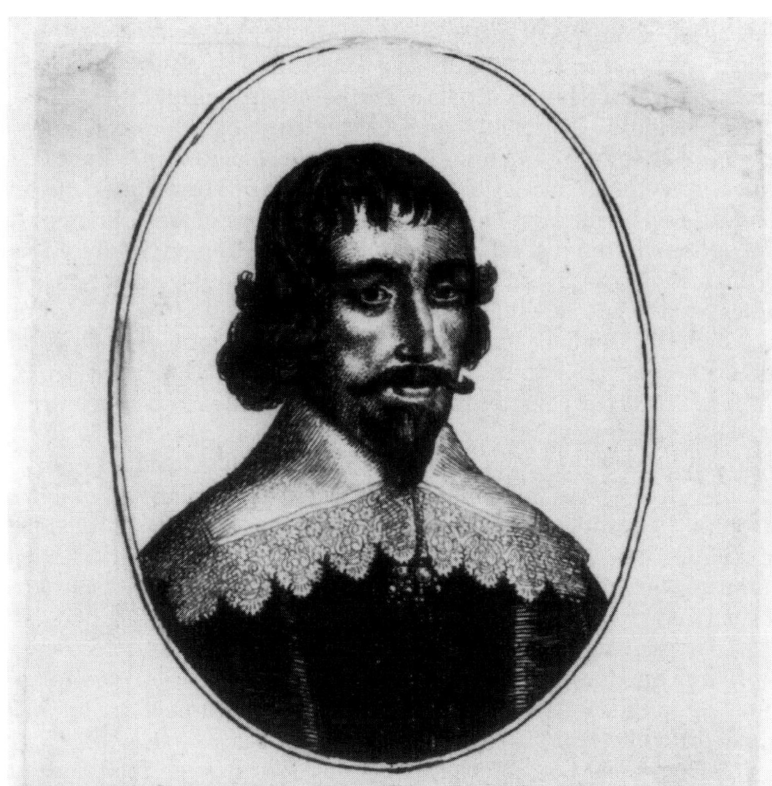

Wenceslaus Hollar, *William Prynne* (Ashmolean Museum, Oxford)

was, so Eliot went on, a canker which ate the king's treasure; a moth which consumed the goodness of the kingdom. His power made it only possible to compare him with Sejanus, the unscrupulous favourite of the Emperor Tiberius. Opponents of Buckingham, of which the most intemperate was unquestionably Eliot himself, calculated that Buckingham had made powerful enemies with his rebuilding of York House and lavish expenditure on its interior. High politics and Buckingham's dominant role in that sphere, in the ten years prior to his impeachment, mattered vastly more than his activities as an art patron. Yet there is a clear sense from reading what went on in Parliament that all those painted visions of Ovid which Buckingham had bought so recklessly, certainly helped in his metamorphosis from Adonis to Sejanus.

Although the extravagance of collecting does seem to have contributed to periodic embarrassment for the Crown, in no sense was it anything other than of occasional concern to critics of the court during the 1620s. At the time Prynne's book appeared in 1633, Charles was enjoying all that he had bought in Mantua. There is no evidence that the ever-more splendid royal palaces provoked hostile criticism. *Histrio-mastix* changed all this. Its appearance concentrated the minds of Puritans upon the offensive content of palaces and chapels.

Histrio-mastix is about the sinfulness of the stage, not the deceitful illusion of painting. Nevertheless the relevance of the book to painting will become apparent when Prynne's method of argument is taken into account; difficult though that is, as Milton was the first to observe. He wrote that he needed 'other arguments to be perswaded the good health of a sound answer, than the gout and dropsy of a big margent, litter'd and overlaid with crude and huddl'd quotations'.[13] What irritated Milton was the method Prynne first adopted with *Histrio-mastix* and which became his habit as a controversialist. He would express an argument briefly in his own words and then support it, not only with hugely long quotations from the Church Fathers and other recondite sources, but with his own printed interjections in the margin. It was as if he was conducting a dialogue with himself.

Milton was embarrassed by Prynne's excesses and doubtless *Histrio-mastix* would have been forgotten, but for a few famous words which were only inserted into the book at proof stage. Late in the day, Prynne had added to the index the entry 'Women actors, notorious whores'. His life was never to be the same again. Once that phrase was noticed by the court, it was taken as an offensive reference to Henrietta Maria; she was a devotee of the masque, in which she liked to dance, and even an occasional attender at plays in the public theatres of London.

Martin Butler has recently argued that neither Charles I nor Henrietta Maria had been particularly incensed by Prynne's notorious reference. Butler turns to the Puritan lawyer and theatre impresario Bulstrode Whitelocke to point out how Whitelocke claimed that the king and his consort had merely been 'exasperated' by *Histrio-mastix* but 'did direct nothing against [Prynne]'. It was Laud not the king who orchestrated the counter-attack against Prynne. This was because of Prynne's previous attacks on Arminianism and because Laud believed that the book went far beyond the London theatre, to attack fundamental aspects of church and state. Laud got his chaplain Peter Heylyn 'to peruse *Prynne's* books and to collect the scandalous points out of them'. It was Laud not the Crown who insisted on Prynne's prosecution at the Star Chamber.[14]

Laud brought a successful case but it was a pyrrhic victory and one which succeeded only in doing Prynne a service by underscoring the connection between art and religion which Prynne had been trying to establish in *Histrio-mastix*. Characteristically Laud had managed to undermine the very position he had set out to defend. The Star Chamber proceedings gave Prynne a public platform which he would never have achieved from *Histrio-mastix* alone; the merits of which were increasingly difficult to find in a thousand pages of denunciation of all that made a court a civilised environment.

Much of Prynne's trial turned on whether it had been his intention to slander the Queen.[15] He denied it. His inquisitors were incredulous. Surely they were right to be so. There are good grounds for thinking that Prynne knew all along that his reference to actresses as whores would be taken in the worst possible light.

Prynne's technique in *Histrio-mastix* was to throw everything at his opponent in the belief that something would stick; a technique which was both the source of Milton's contempt, and the leading characteristic of his monument of intemperance. Prynne identifies what he sees as a whole school of vice, going far beyond stage actors to condemn fashionable pursuits of the court wholesale. Thus what had begun as an attempt to reform manners which Prynne believed could be seen to be corrupt from observation of the London stage, both public and private, ended as a root and branch attack on many of the social values of the court.

Prynne's ambition was nothing less than a radical reformation of society as a whole. This is clear from a consideration of the preface addressed 'To the Christian Reader':

> . . . *there are several passages in this Discourse, which* prima facie *may seeme heterogeneous to the present subject, as those* concerning Dancing, Musicke, Apparell, Effeminacy, Lascivious Songs, Laughter, Adultery, obscene Pictures, Bonefires, New yeares gifts, Grand Christmasses, Health-drinking, Long haire, Lords-dayes, Dicing, with sundry Pagan customes *here refelled: but if you consider them as they are here applied, you shall finde them all materially pertinent to the theame in question; they being either the concomitants of Stage-playes, or having such neare affinity with them, that the unlawfulnesse of the one are necessary* mediums *to evince the sinfulnesse of the other.*[16]

The case against Prynne arguably did more damage to the Queen than it did to the man who stood condemned. The judges made the fatal mistake of injecting into the public mind the perception that the book was an attack on Henrietta Maria. Puritans began to identify the Queen with much else that Prynne denounced. It was in this way therefore that royal pictures and buildings, which Prynne includes in his attack by inference, first came to be viewed with suspicion.

Prynne was not against all plays, nor against the principle of putting on a court masque. He argued that respectable performances are permissible on certain occasions. His objection to the stage was that the better sort of plays were being performed too frequently and in front of the wrong people:

> for if Stage-playes be meet ornaments for Princes pallaces at times of greatest state and royallest entertainment, great reason is there to suppresse their daily acting, and to appropriate them to such times, such places, such purposes as these, *for feare their assiduity, their comonnes should make them despicably base and altogether unmeet for such sublime occasions.* Extraordinary royall occasions, persons, entertainments will not suite with common prostituted Enterludes, which every tinker, cobler, foot-boy, whore or rascall may resort to at their pleasure, as they doe unto our Stage-playes;[17]

Such distinctions serve to draw attention to an important point. Prynne had been part of the Establishment; he had been Recorder of Bath. Though he was to be stripped of that office, he remained a conservative radical. He was certainly no millenarian leveller. Prynne would always claim that he revered both the office and the person of the King. He saw himself as sent to save Charles I from evil counsellors and vicious habits. In adopting such a standpoint, he anticipated one of the major justifications used by Parliament during the Civil War.

Although Prynne's animus is largely directed at the stage, he was deeply suspicious of painting. Specifically he points the contrast between what he claimed were the mores of the Jacobean court and those of the Caroline. It was a comparison which was much to the disadvantage of the latter. The historian of today may have difficulty with this but there can be little doubt that criticism of life at Whitehall damaged the court in the eyes of some:

> since our late renowned *Soveraigne King James*, and our owne *Homilies, against the perill of Idolatry* . . . doe absolutely condemne, *as sinfull, idolatrous, and abominable the making of any Image or Picture of God the Father, Son, and Holy Ghost* or of the Sacred *Trinity, and the erecting of them, of Crucifixes, or, such like Pictures in Churches*, which like the *Emperor Adrians Temples built for Christ, should be without all Images, or Saints Pictures.* So

> they, likewise codemned the very *art of making Pictures and Images, as the occasion of Idolatory*, together with all Stage-portraitures, Images, Vizards, or representations of Heathen Idols, etc as grosse Idolatry, *as Josephus witnesseth.*[18]

This is an important passage: one which not only condemns painting but turns it into idolatry by identifying it with religion. If John Morrill is right to have identified differences about religion as the most important single cause of the Civil War, then Prynne's association of religion with art was critical. Prynne connected the arts with something which had long been of passionate concern right across the social spectrum.

Prynne also succeeded in associating a love of the arts with Roman Catholicism. That was important too. Important because even those otherwise well-disposed to the king himself, had long expressed considerable disquiet about the undue influence enjoyed by favoured Catholics during the reign of Charles I.

The proximity of Catholics to the crown was a theme which Prynne would return to with relish in his book *Romes Master-Peece*, published in 1643 after the downfall of Archbishop Laud. In *Histrio-mastix* he writes about 'all our Roman Catholiques, (who are much devoted to these Theatrical spectacles,)'.[19] Thus early in his career as a court scourge, Prynne saw an enthusiasm for theatre, music and painting, as something which had a particular appeal to English Catholics. Now Catholics were the one group above all feared by Puritans. Thus through the identity of Catholics with collecting, collecting began to be perceived as something alien, even threatening. As it happens, collecting was not a 'Catholic' activity; though there were enough high-profile courtiers who bought pictures and were of that religious persuasion to allow Prynne to contrive a connection. Once the association was made in the minds of the paranoid, it was comparatively easy to frame picture-collecting as an alien and threatening pursuit.

The affable Portland for example, whose tomb at Winchester was discussed in an earlier chapter, was an ebullient patron. His appointment to the Treasurership had been broadly popular, but Clarendon believed the skies then clouded over:

> That which first exposed him to the public jealousy, which is always attended with public reproach, was the concurrent suspicion of his religion . . . his domestic conversation and dependants, with whom only he used entire freedom, were all known Catholics, and were believed to be agents of the rest.[20]

Portland was just the sort of great officer of state who fitted the scenario depicted by Prynne. Clarendon and Prynne actually shared something in common; hard to believe though that may be, given where their loyalties would eventually come to rest, and their literary styles, which could not have been more different. The mind of Clarendon was tinged by an uneasy suspicion of a conspiracy to promote Catholics at court, that of Prynne wholly obsessed by the belief. But while the one may have deplored what the other denounced, both were profoundly antithetical to the king's Catholic subjects.

Sir Francis Cottington became a close confidant of the king during the years of Personal Rule, in part because he had formerly been secretary to Charles when Prince of Wales. A figure of 'great and long experience . . . in business of all kinds', he eventually rose to become Chancellor of the Exchequer;[21] not quite the job it is now but nevertheless one which made him central to the councils of the king. But whereas Cottington's public career followed a predictable path, his religious loyalties were wildly confused; sometimes he was a Catholic, sometimes a Protestant. But at whichever altar Cottington may have temporarily worshipped, he had been ambassador to Spain for an unusually long period and that had served to damn him in the minds of the Puritans.

Cottington, like Portland, was a patron of the arts. But he compounded his faults in the eyes of his critics by conspicuous promotion of the Hispanophile party at court. This was as a consequence of his years of service at Madrid. The pro-Spanish party grew in importance with the passing of the years; much to the consternation of more extreme Protestants.

Portland paid for Le Sueur's statue of Charles I. Cottington built Hanworth in Middlesex, one of the major houses of the period. In connection with it, Cottington was much given to corresponding with Sir Arthur Hopton, English ambassador in Madrid, about pictures, and with Strafford in Ireland about the progress of his works. A number of Cottington's letters to Hopton are about how best to direct the King's painter Michael Cross, who had been sent to Madrid to copy the Titians; including perhaps, the high altarpiece in the royal chapel of the Escorial, *The Martyrdom of St Lawrence*: a piece of idolatry nicely calculated to scandalise the godly.[22]

The court was not only damaged in the eyes of Puritans by the association they saw between art and Catholicism at the most elevated levels. There were lesser men whose backstairs influence more than countered an absence of outward rank. The Jesuit George Gage, to whom reference was made earlier, was just such a person. Predictably enough he became a target for Prynne's invective.

Gage was a scandal to his calling by standards other than those of Prynne. Although he had been ordained priest by the famous Cardinal Bellarmine in Rome in 1614, he never went near an altar except to decorate it. He spent his time mixing art and international diplomacy; combining informal and clandestine diplomacy of an extremely important order, with the acquisition of Italian pictures for the chapels of his wealthy Catholic patrons in London. In addition he played a major part in the monopolies, lotteries and projects which were to be savagely lampooned on the London stage.

Gage was entrusted with the soap monopoly, which was an attempt by Charles I to raise money by persuading sceptical laundresses that royal soap was superior to all else. The project was a resounding failure; one which Butler describes as perhaps 'Charles's most inglorious hour'.

Monopolies were unquestionably a major source of friction between the king and the City of London during the Eleven Years Rule, though Gage's 'soap business' was farcical rather than seriously damaging. Prior to Gage's involvement in soap he had a great stake in the London lottery, and was too, heavily engaged in an early attempt to privatise London water. He had been a director of a proposal to build an aqueduct which was to have brought clean water to the City from Hoddesdon in Hertfordshire. Today lotteries and the privatisation of public utilities are controversial issues, and so they were in the seventeenth century. But before all that, Father Gage had been encouraged to take initiatives over major aspects of foreign policy and this was altogether more serious business.

It will be recalled that Gage was employed running between London, Madrid and Rome, to obtain the necessary dispensation to allow the marriage between Charles and the Spanish Infanta. Gage had been entrusted with responsibilities which bore directly on the central issues of international affairs; responsibilities it appeared he had been given not because of any prior experience as a diplomat, but because of his ability to talk knowledgeably about pictures, architecture and music. He was certainly exceptionally well travelled for an Englishman and was, too, a superlative linguist. It was surely sensible to send a Catholic to talk to the Pope. There were therefore good reasons for giving him such a remit. But the important point was that these arguments were clear only to the king and his close advisers. To those who were not a party to such thinking, why he was chosen was baffling; unless, some thought, it was because he was a Jesuit priest and secretly the king favoured them. Now if there was one person Prynne abominated above all others, it was a Jesuit, and the access which Gage had had to the highest councils during those marriage negotiations of the 1620s seemed a gross affront. Prynne was to make much, much too much of the influence Catholics enjoyed at court but it was not just alienated fanatics who felt affronted. At the time Gage was travelling Europe in search of a Catholic marriage for a Protestant prince, the king's official ambassadors had felt outmanoeuvred by this suave but untrustworthy priest. Futhermore there was a strong current of anti-Catholic feeling running in London while the Spanish marriage hung in the balance, as Gage himself remarked when writing from Rome to Trumbull in Brussels:

> I can tell you no newse from hence, but that lately the Congregation of Cardinals . . . have come to a resolution amongst themselves, and

> whereas wee expected now their answeare they dimurre upo newse of arming and intended persecutions by the Parliament in England and such like.[23]

Violence did not ensue although one worried commentator observing the scene in London in 1623 wrote: 'But the truth is that Priests and Jesuits swarme here extraordinarilie.'[24] Some of these Jesuits were in London to effect discreet conversions, but others had a more public and provocative role. On 30 May 1623 John Wolley, who looked after the London end of Trumbull's business affairs, wrote about the chapel which Inigo Jones had designed to receive the Infanta. It is an early reference to a building which would gain great notoriety as a symbol of what men came to hate and would eventually attack not only with books and pamphlets, but with bars and bricks:

> The Chappell wch is abilding at St Jameses for the Princes, goeth forwarde apace, the Spanish Amb haveing the last weeke, wth all solemnity, layed the first stone, and the Earle of Arundel the second (as I have heard).[25]

Prynne had an easy job persuading a gullible readership of a Catholic conspiracy in many London palaces of the 1630s and it comes as no surprise to discover that Gage was identified as the prime mover. Prynne alleged that Gage, who had died in 1638, had directed operations from his own establishment in Queen Street, one of the most fashionable streets in the newly developed West End and where Gage's 'palace', as Prynne described it, was adorned with a golden statue of Henrietta Maria. Prynne wrote:

> *The President of the aforesaid Society was my Lord Gage, a Jesuite Priest, dead above three yeares since. Hee had a palace adorned with lascivious pictures, which counterfeited prophanenesse in the house, but with them was palliated a Monastery, wherein forty Nunnes were maintained, hid in so great a Palace.*[26]

Prynne also attacked Arundel, claiming that he had maintained a 'feminine School . . . which otherwise is a Monastery of Nunnes' in one of his properties at Greenwich. The young girls of the Greenwich establishment had been sent 'hither and thither into foraine Monasteries beyond the Seas'. In one of those marginalia which so irritated Milton, Prynne then made the gratuitous comment: 'No wonder the Earles debts be so great. A Schoole of Nunnes.'[27] There is not a shred of evidence that Arundel ever maintained such an establishment. Ironically Arundel was actually coldly indifferent to religion, and his debts, which were indeed colossal, had more to do with buying pictures than paying for nuns. What Prynne had to say about the Greenwich nunnery was wholly fantastic but that did not matter since it was easy enough to frame Arundel as the father of the most prominent English Catholic family and the son of an exceptional witness to the old faith.

Prynne had been a successful barrister but he was unsurpassed as a truffler for conspiracies. This was why Parliament appointed him to read the private correspondence of Laud by way of preparation for his trial. Accuracy never troubled Prynne. For him, the sand of supposition could be mixed with the lime of fantasy to construct an edifice of Catholic conspirators; all busy subverting the king who, would he only attend to what Prynne had to say, could yet be saved from his friends who in truth were enemies not only to the king, but to his kingdom.

Prynne directed his reader to what he regarded as an intimate connection between catholicism and a love of court recreations. He was the first English writer to argue for a connection between art and society and to see it as political.

When *Histrio-mastix* appeared it did not create a sensation. However, Prynne's trial gave it vicarious publicity, whilst his punishment for subsequent behaviour ensured that *Histrio-mastix* became a text of Puritanism.

There is a real sense in which Prynne's enemies did his work for him. Just as Laud had over-reacted to the appearance of *Histrio-mastix* in the first place, so the punishment which was meted out to Prynne in 1637 for his abuse of the Anglican Church made him a martyr. *Histrio-mastix* had a delayed fuse which only went off some years after its first appearance.

Butler has made the point that *Histrio-mastix* was not followed by a torrent of publications attacking the theatre. In the light of this we must be cautious in overestimating its impact. But it was the man not his work which mattered. By July 1637 the authorities had had enough of Prynne's torrent of abuse and he was punished with abominable savagery. The common hangman cut off his ears, and his forehead was branded with the letters 'D.D'; mocking reference to his doctorate in divinity.

Prynne's horrific mutilation was supposed to be a public warning to others not to step beyond the bounds of acceptable criticism. However, what that punishment achieved was to make the victim a popular hero, and best-sellers out of his dismal books. The consequences were disastrous for the court as it tried to immunise itself from further criticism.

Sir Kenelm Digby was a cosmopolitan gentleman of the type Prynne suspected of favouring Popery. His comments on the treatment of Prynne suggest that Puritanism was given a significant impetus by the unspeakable cruelty of his punishment. Digby's description of Prynne's public humiliation, and the way he saw an analogy with the Stations of the Cross when describing Prynne's journey to his distant prison after torture, though ironical in the light of the victim's religious allegiances, suggest how even those well disposed to the court were aware of what damage was being done to the image of the king. Digby wrote to Viscount Conway on 27 July 1637:

> The King and Queen will be in London on Thursday to assist at the Duke's marriage; but I believe there will not be so great flocking of the people to see it, as was this last week to accompany Mr Prynne and Mr Burton's pilgrimage to their stations in the country, nor be kept with such venerations as the Puritans keep the bloody sponges and handkerchiefs that did the hangman service in the cutting off their ears. You may see how nature leads men to respect relics of martyrs.[28]

Digby's comment was not an isolated one. The memory of Prynne's bloody stumps lived with those who had witnessed his punishment. Indeed such was Prynne's notoriety after the events of July 1637 that anything he wrote was assured of a good market. Digby was by no means alone in thinking that what had been done to Prynne was a mistake. In the Civil War a Royalist was to remark that Prynne's books were more prevalent than ministers' sermons, while a Cavalier journal complained in 1648 that fighting might have been averted if the punishment of Prynne had not been so maladroitly handled.

There were other reactions to Prynne's writings which were of a somewhat fuller and more measured nature than thoughts confided to private letters or paraded in weekly news-letters. Two books appeared after the publication of *Histrio-mastix* the inception or re-issuing of which should, I believe, be understood in the light of the controversies which Prynne had provoked. The third edition of Henry Peacham's *The Compleat Gentleman* appeared in 1634, just a year after Prynne. It included, for the first time, a chapter on Drawing and Limning. Peacham's book, together with *The Painting of the Ancients*, the 1638 translation of the *De Pictura Veterum* of 1637 by the Dutch philologist Francis Junius, were quite possibly intended as a riposte to Puritan criticism of 'licentious images'. Peacham was aimed at a popular audience, Junius at a learned one.

Peacham has an easy, conversational style which precludes a very profound exposition of his case. Yet the facility with which he writes was doubtless as effective an apologia in its own sphere as the earnest moralising of Junius, which was aimed at the well-read man.

There are distinct echoes of Elyot about what Peacham has to say in a chapter 'of Drawing, Limning, and Painting, with the Lives of the Famous Italian Painters'. With a title such as this, the reader is alerted to what promises to be an exciting and ambitious survey. However, it transpires that the lives are simply forgotten, and after just a few pages, Peacham moves on to his next theme, the Blazon of Arms.

Peacham's main defence of art is its utility: the prince needs it for warfare, just as the traveller requires it to master cosmography. There then follows the familiar citation of famous Roman families who had not been ashamed to proclaim themselves as painters. Peacham writes:

> In no less honour and esteem was it held among the Romans, as we find in Pliny and many others, who everywhere advance the professors, and the dignity of the practice thereof, nothing base or servile, since one of the most nobel families in Rome, the Fabii, thought themselves much honoured by the addition of that surname *Pictor*. For the first of that name . . . after with his own hand he had painted the temple at Salus round about within and finished his work, he wrote in fair letters in an eminent place *Quintius Fabius pinxi*.[29]

A few lines before alluding to Pliny, Peacham associated painting with the Christian God. Having suggested to the reader the multiple ways in which painting and drawing can be an effective way of absorbing all the new experiences flooding in upon the traveller abroad, Peacham continues:

> And since it is only the imitation of the surface of nature, by it as in a book of golden and rare-limned letters, the chief end of it, we read a continual lecture of the wisdom of the Almighty Creator by beholding even in the feather of a peacock a miracle, as Aristotle saith.[30]

Francis Junius was an intimate if intermittent member of the Arundel circle from 1621 when he became librarian at Arundel House until Arundel retired to Italy in 1642, overwhelmed by the troubles which had descended on England. Junius owed his important appointment as keeper of one of the great libraries of Europe, a library which would become greater still under his custodianship, to introductions to Arundel from Lancelot Andrewes and William Laud. From time to time Junius and Arundel would quarrel; Junius would leave Arundel House but always return. Clearly this was a stormy relationship, but Junius was to be associated with the larger Howard family for over thirty years.

Junius' book, entitled in its Latin edition of 1637, *De Pictura Veterum*, is a compilation of all the references to painting in classical literature which the author had been able to discover with his vast learning. Such may have been its primary purpose but it was not its sole one. Junius had been urged by Arundel himself to compose the *De Pictura Veterum* in consequence of the *éclat* which had greeted the publication of John Selden's much acclaimed work on the Arundel marbles: the *Marmora Arundelliana*, which had appeared in 1628. Junius told his relation Gerhard Johann Vossius that he was at first engaged on a *catalogus artificium*, an encyclopaedia of classical artists, which he was doing 'ut ardentissimo Arundelliae Comitis desiderio satisfacerem'.[31] From a letter of 1634 it appears that the project had developed larger ambitions. The book was no longer simply to be an encyclopaedia, but would approach the arts of painting and sculpture in antiquity through the writings of classical authors. As it was, however, the digest of passages in antique literature on the arts appeared first in Latin in 1637 and then in an English translation

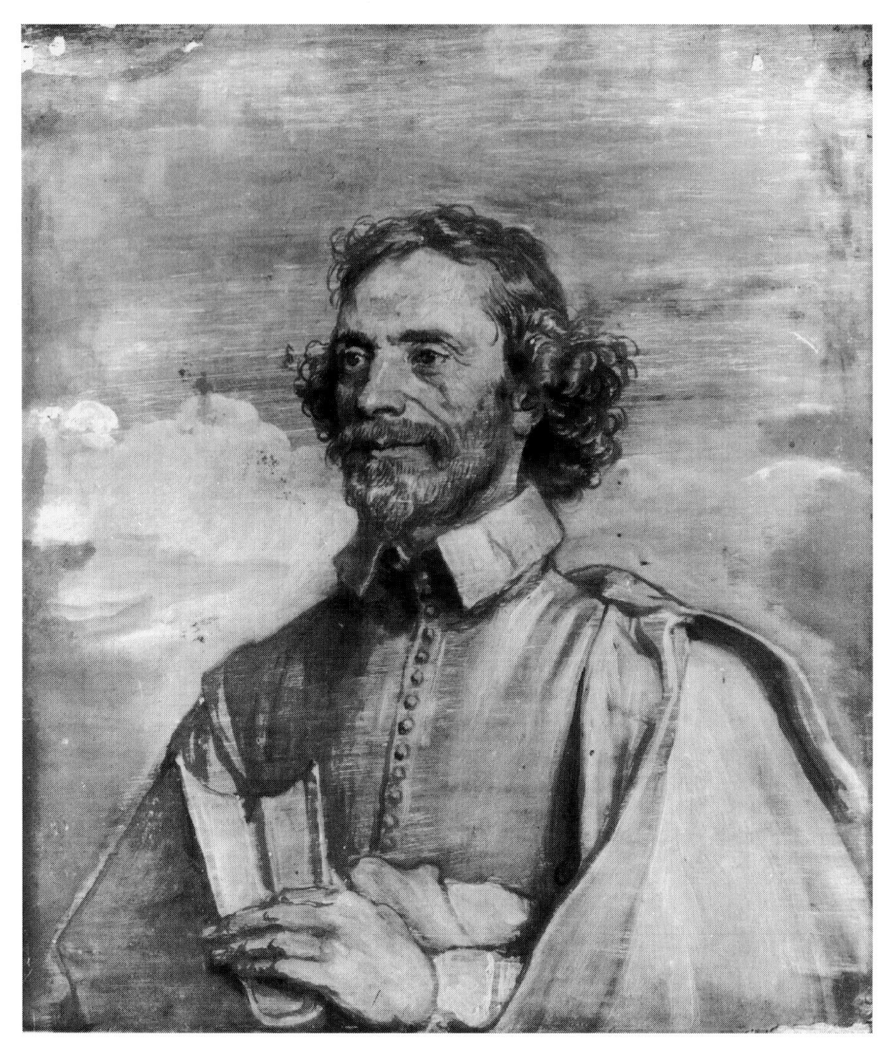

Sir Anthony Van Dyck (attributed), *Francis Junius, c.* 1640 (Bodleian Library, Oxford)

in 1638, whereas the lexicon, or *catalogus artificium* of artists and their works, was only to appear in 1694, nearly twenty years after the death of Junius.

While Junius worked on classical texts for the *De Pictura Veterum* and its companion volume, the *catalogus*, Petty, the principal picture agent for the Arundel collection, seems to have been working in parallel on a 'dictionary' of Renaissance artists; though whether Junius and Petty were intending to complement each other or they were quite independent, is not known.[32] It was not easy to compose a work of scholarship on fishing boats plying between the Greek Islands, and to add to his distractions, Petty went to Italy in 1634, where he remained for four years, wholly absorbed in pursuing treasures for the Arundel collection. Petty's 'dictionary', which would have anticipated by some one hundred and seventy years the first of its type in English, was never to be completed because Petty died in the summer of 1638.[33]

Allan Ellenius has analysed the genesis of the *De Pictura Veterum* and concluded that both the Latin edition of 1637, and the English version of 1638, *The Painting of the Ancients*, had a 'private character': both Latin and English versions were intended for the edification of the Earl and Countess of Arundel and their circle of connoisseurs. Ellenius argues by reference to Junius' contribution to the question of optics and perspective:

> when he [Junius] describes perspective he starts from problems of literary style and descriptions of antique paintings. The extreme abstraction of this approach clearly shows how remote he is from works of art; this shows yet again the fundamental shortcomings of *De Pictura Veterum* as a piece of practical pedagogy.[34]

That however is not the view of the editors of the recent, definitive edition of *The Painting of the Ancients* and the much later *Catalogus*.[35] Here it is argued: 'In Junius' work before us the Renaissance apology of painting and sculpture – the arts which by their palpably sensuous nature are most open to censure – steps forward in its most comprehensive effort to meet the challenge.'[36] It is suggested that the *De Pictura Veterum* immediately found a place at the centre of European culture because it was recognised as a peerless defence of the timeless connection between art and morality. It was not the first English attempt to defend the arts from philistines, since the text of *The Painting of the Ancients* reveals Junius' debt to and admiration of Sidney's *Defence of Poesie*. Moreover, in *The Painting of the Ancients* Junius took up the challenge thrown down by Sir Henry Wotton in his *Elements of Architecture* when, metaphorically speaking, Wotton carved over the entrance way to that book: 'Ab abuti ad non uti, negatur consequentia'; a tag which appears in Wotton and translates: 'We reject the argument from the abuse [of art] to the denial of its use.'[37]

It is easy to underestimate the accessibility even of the Latin edition of Junius, as has been done so often. Take for example Junius' dedication to Charles I. Junius praises Charles I's patronage of the arts, viewing the matter partly from an ethical standpoint. In Junius' opinion, royal initiatives are nothing less than an attempt to reform society in the light of the contemporary state of morals.

Junius' dedication provides a critical clue to an aspect of his writing which has been overlooked even in the definitive edition of his work. Junius's book is a tract for the times and specifically, for the state of English court culture, of which Junius had had fifteen years' experience when *De Pictura Veterum* came out. The book enters the lists against those who would abuse the values of the court; exemplified in what critics perceived to be the court's extravagant and opulent patronage of painting, sculpture and architecture.

The Painting of the Ancients, that is to say the English edition of *De Pictura Veterum*, is addressing itself to a wider readership than those who could read Pliny's *Natural History* and other classical texts which contain famous anecdotes of painters. The English version of Junius is full of earnest and often strained moralising; naturally enough, it might seem, when it is discovered that the writer's father was the pupil of Calvin and Beza in that Renaissance City of God, Geneva.[38]

The Painting of the Ancients is far more than simply an arid compilation of classical texts in translation; a hand-me-down for the pedant to pass himself off as learned in classical literature. At an early stage Junius establishes the serious moral purpose which underlies his text. He infers that what he is to address is far from those vices which some might identify as attractive to the court. Junius does so with phrases stacked one upon another – a technique reminiscent of the style Prynne had adopted in *Histrio-mastix*. At one point Junius writes:

> besides that stage-playes, banquets, cards and dice, unnecessary journeys, the immoderate care of our pampered carkasses, rob us also of a good deale of time that might be better husbanded: not to speak of wanton lusts, drunkenesse, and other such like beastly vices, by the which our distempered bodies waxe altogether unfit to make good use of so small a remnant of our time.[39]

Once Junius has established that a love of painting is not to be associated with 'beastly vices', he then becomes ambitious to establish the dignity of painting. He argues that she is a sister to Clio, the Muse of History: 'he is the best Historian that can adorne his Narration with such forcible figures and lively colours of Rhetoricke, as to make it like unto a picture'.[40] To establish parity between painting and the Muses of poetry, Junius cites Simonides' famous epithet of how: 'Picture is a silent Poesie, as Poesie is a speaking Picture'.

These are ambitious claims and they stem from what may have been a feeling within the Arundel circle that a further apologia was needed to support the rather more familiar defence of painting which Peacham had offered in his *The Compleat Gentleman* of three years earlier.

Ellenius points out that *The Painting of the Ancients* does not contain a single reference to a specific work of modern art. However, in no sense did that preclude the book from being topical. Junius mentions the famous Arundel drawings which its owner is to exhibit. 'in the Accademie at Arundell house'. It is that establishment Junius surely has in mind when he praises those who allow people to enjoy their riches.[41]

Junius believed that patrons were to be congratulated for their liberality. For Junius the admiration of pictures and statuary was not primarily a pleasurable but a moral activity. The visitor to Arundel House, for example, could contemplate the *deus artifex*; the beneficent architect whose handiwork, observed in the beauties of the natural and artificial world, served to reassure the Christian soul of a benign creative force at work.

In the same passage in which Junius draws attention to a creative deity, he also suggests that the contemplation of great art, Orpheus-like, assuages the passions of the soul:

> for how can that same contemplation deserve the opinion of an unfruitful and idle exercise, by whose means wee doe understand the true beautie of created bodies, a ready way to the consideration of our Glorious Creator? besides that this same exercise, like a most sweet Musick to the eye, doth cleare up all heavinesse and sullen drownsinesse of the mind; it worketh in us also, by the examples of things past, a perfect love of innocence; it doth bridle the most violent passions of love and anger.[42]

Although *The Painting of the Ancients* is cast in the mould of a theoretical, literary, and historical discussion, and it is certainly in no sense a reaction to trends in what were contemporary artistic styles, the richness of the text is lost unless it is understood against its social and cultural background. Junius writes at length about statues in antiquity; what they meant to their creators, the occasions when they were erected, and where they were placed. These were issues which were of lively concern to the early Stuart monarchy.

In an earlier book I have suggested that Charles I had his own very private reasons for erecting his bust on the Square Tower at Portsmouth. Writing on Charles I's abiding interest in sculpture, I argued that the king had his statue placed before 'the main doors of Inigo Jones' St Paul Covent Garden, because he wanted parishioners to recall that he was head of both church and state; an affirmation which had particular significance in front of the first church to be erected in the capital since the Reformation'.[43] I also suggested that the bust by Le Sueur which was erected on the market cross at Chichester, and for which payment may have been made in 1637,[44] symbolised the return of order to the cathedral city after a particularly acrimonious dispute between the notorious Arminian bishop Richard Montague, and the mayor and corporation, over who should have precedent within the cathedral. Charles had intervened personally to settle the matter and he may have had his bust erected to symbolise the return of good government to a troubled community.[45] Thus in the light of what may be termed a 'political' dimension to Charles I's patronage, it is of interest to note two separate passages in *The Painting of the Ancients* which express attitudes the king would have found sympathetic. Junius writes of how images of the dead in private houses 'doe very much asswage our griefe'; claiming 'how much more shall those images bring that to passe, which in a place of great resorte do not only show their shape and countenance, but their honour and glory also'.[46] Junius adds a further comment about the motives the ancients had in erecting statues; motives which the great patrons of Caroline art would have readily understood:

> statues were erected upon severall occasions, yet was this always the chiefest motive, That generous spirits seeing Vertue so much honoured, should likewise be provoked unto Vertuous actions.[47]

The Painting of the Ancients operates on three levels. It is a work of scholarship, since the dense weft and web of classical quotation is addressed to a learned and international audience. The book also sets up a debate with other art forms so that Junius finds support for arguing that painting should be regarded as equal if not superior to poetry, history and music: aspects of culture which the majority of Junius' readership still regarded as superior to painting – then still considered a mechanical trade and not a humane pursuit. However, it is the third strand in Junius' book which has gone unremarked hitherto. This is its moralising vein, which in part accounts for its appeal to English writers from Shaftesbury to Ruskin who have written on the relationship between art and society. The defensiveness of Junius' text, a marked aspect of the commentary which accompanies the endless citations from classical authors, is not only a means to climb Parnassus, but surely too, a rebuttal of Puritan critics like William Prynne who had put the painter's world on the defensive for the first time.

The most conspicuous and indeed controversial aspect of royal patronage of the arts to attract criticism was not 'lascivious pictures' as Prynne termed them, but the building and decoration of chapels at Somerset House and St James's; a theme which has already been discussed at some length in a previous chapter. Even members of the court well disposed to the Queen, for whom the chapels were primarily intended, raised an eyebrow at what they felt was the all too public demonstration of fervent piety which accompanied their dedication and inauguration. The furnishing of a Catholic chapel provoked widespread disquiet and not merely among Puritans. But what is perhaps more surprising is the unpopularity of government policy towards civic building in London; something which featured quite largely on the London stage of the 1630s.

The reputation of the Caroline playwright Richard Brome just about lasted into the twentieth century; T. S. Eliot tried to revive it in an essay. Nobody now reads a Brome play, still less sees one. But both Brome and the much less acerbic James Shirley were enormously popular in the 1630s. This had less to do with their intrinsic merits as dramatists than with the popularity of the public theatre during the years of Personal

Rule. Butler has argued that the theatre was far from the emasculated affair which theatre historians had hitherto always assumed; much hard-hitting criticism of life at Whitehall passed the pen of the Master of the Revels Sir Henry Herbert to be heard at Blackfriars and Southwark.

Brome's plays enjoyed long runs and huge audiences. Thus what Brome identified as social abuses got a very good airing. Furthermore, his work and that of rival playwrights like Shirley, Nabbes and Davenant, attracted a wide social mix. Plays were cheap and whilst it has been recognised that the Jacobean audience was a broadly heterogeneous social mix, even as late as 1632 Jonson could still refer in *The Magnetic Lady* to 'the sinful sixpenny mechanics' who came to Blackfriars. Evidently ordinary Londoners went to the theatre during the years of Personal Rule.[48]

The popular theatre of the 1630s was a powerful, critical force which weakened the court. This can be demonstrated by a consideration of Brome's *The Weeding of The Covent-Garden*, which contains much hard-hitting satire directed at court builders. Architecture promoted by the Crown and its officers may have been important in a growing perception that the court was adopting values which some found unsympathetic and repellent.

The piazza of Covent Garden was the civic masterpiece of Inigo Jones. To the more sophisticated observer, perhaps a gentleman who had sailed into Livorno for a journey through Italy, it constituted an impressive reminder of the main square of that gracious city. However, to those who never travelled anywhere, Jones' development seemed the product of the contentious paternalistic Commission for New Building.

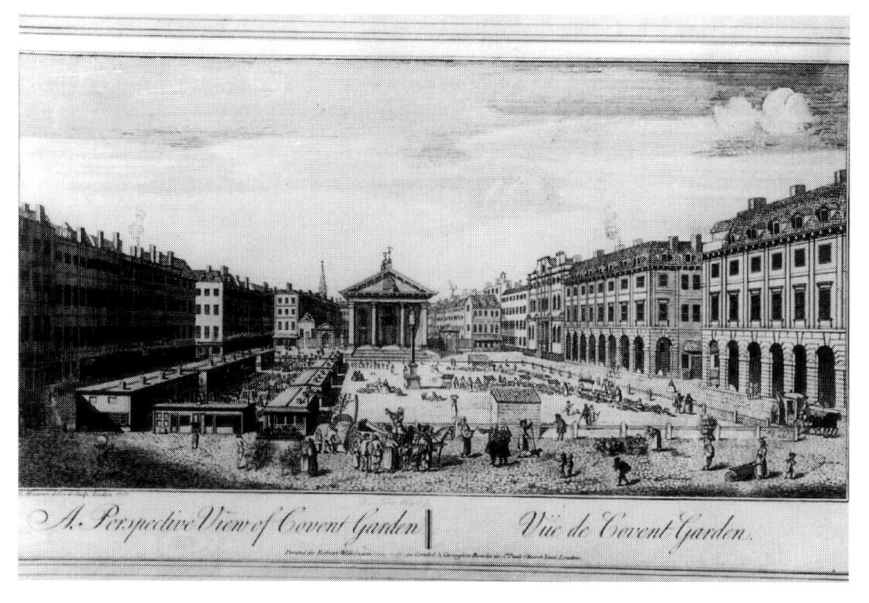

J. Maurer, *A perspective view of Covent Garden*, 1751 (British Museum)

By the time Brome was writing, the Commission had developed into a very significant means of raising revenue and a constant irritant to the speculative builder who came to resent its officious interference with his life. It became a much resented aspect of Charles I's conciliar government and therefore a rich seam for satirists.

Brome's popular comedy *The Weeding of The Covent-Garden* was probably first performed between 1632 and 1634; as Jones was heavily engaged in the development of the Covent Garden site. That Jones was the target for what the play's title-page describes as 'A *Facetious* Comedy' is hardly in doubt since the play had an alternative title. It was described as 'The Weeding of The Covent-Garden Or the *Middlesex* – Justice of Peace'. Jones was a J.P. for Middlesex.

The first scene of the play reveals Cockbrain, a Justice of the Peace, complimenting Rooksbill, a surveyor, on the wonderful buildings which Rooksbill has just designed. The rascals represent the two public faces of Inigo Jones in the capital: Surveyor of The King's Buildings and Justice of the Peace for Middlesex.

The opening dialogue begins:

> *Cockbrain*: Marry Sir! This is something like! These appear like Buildings! Here's Architecture exprest indeed! It is a most sightly scituation, and fit for Gentry and Nobility.
> *Rooksbill*: When it is all finished, doubtlesse it will be handsome.
> *Cockbrain*: It will be glorious: and yond magnificent Peece, the *Piazzo*, will excel that at *Venice*, by hearsay, (I ne're travell'd). A hearty blessing on their braines, honours, and wealths, that are Projectors, Furtherers, and Performers of such great works. And now I come to you Mr *Rookesbill*: I like your Rowe of houses most incomparably. Your money never shone so on your Counting-boards, as in those Structures.[49]

Rooksbill reacts to such fulsome compliments not by talking of his creation in terms of its distinction as architecture, but by saying how rich it will make him. It is Cockbrain 'a Justice of peace, the Weeder of the Garden', not Rooksbill 'a great Builder in *Covent-Garden*' as he is described in the *dramatis personae*, who judges the Covent Garden development by the criteria of good architecture. Cockbrain is not as stupid as his name suggests since he has read his Wotton, as he reveals by declaring how Rooksbill 'has wedded strength too beauty; state to uniformity; commodiousnesse with perspicuity!'[50]

There then follows a discussion of what sort of people might be expected to take up the leases of the tenements which were a notable feature of the whole development. Cockbrain declares that 'the lewdest blades, and naughty-packs' will settle there, but assures Rooksbill that in time the better sort will be attracted; reinforcing his point with a metaphor from husbandry: 'do we not soile or dung our lands, before we sowe or plant any thing that's good in 'hem?'[51]

For Brome the Covent Garden scheme, in which Charles I took the closest interest, was nothing more than a stratagem for architects and rapacious patrons to make a large amount of money with no thought for the social consequences.[52] The emphasis in the play on the way in which Covent Garden would encourage the evils of gaming and prostitution without bringing any social benefits, suggests that Brome saw speculative building as a burden no less onerous than the scourge of monopolies. For Brome, as no doubt for his audience, speculative building and monopolies were impositions placed upon London society by a fundamentally irresponsible court.

Rooksbill is no better than a monopolist. Cockbrain associates Rooksbill with those 'Projectors, Furtherers, and Performers of such great works'.[53] Here the use of the word 'projectors' is significant since many of the most burdensome monopolies were then referred to as 'projects'.

Brome gives his surveyor an offensive name, while Cockbrain, the unjust Justice, is only interested in the value of leases. Cockbrain congratulates Rooksbill for having the good sense to let out money on 'red and white, then upon black and white'.[54] Here Brome refers to the dressed white stone quoins, which contrasted with the red brick of Jones's houses framing the Piazza; colours contrasted in the play with the black and white squares of the gaming tables which had been Rooksbill's expedient until he had hit upon building as a more efficient way of making money. Rooksbill abandoned the gaming tables not because of any moral reformation but merely on the grounds of expediency. The inference of the play was that the Covent Garden area, which had always had an evil reputation, would now simply get worse.

It may be that this bitter attack on Jones had to do with partisanship; *Covent Garden* was put on shortly after Jonson had quarrelled irreconcilably with Jones, and Brome had owed much to Jonson. However, although the Jonson–Jones quarrel may have given a barbed attack a sharper tip, there is evidence throughout the play to suggest that Brome was preoccupied with a much larger issue.

Brome chose to attack the Covent Garden scheme because he was concerned to demonstrate how such a project showed that the King's government was more concerned to extract than to succour, to exploit than to exercise benevolent paternalism. The evidence that Brome is aiming at a larger target than merely Jones comes a scene or two after the opening conversation between Rooksbill and Cockbrain with which the play opens.

Master Gabriel, the son of Crossewill, a dyspeptic who has abandoned the social obligations of being a country gentleman to become a lodger in one of Rooksbill's new houses, is suddenly struck with amazement as he takes us on a topographical tour of the neighbourhood. Crossewill sees his son Gabriel rooted to the ground. He assumes that his son has been staggered to see the crucifix on Rooksbill's new church, which is, of course, Jones's St Paul Covent Garden.

Crossewill pauses to tell the audience that Gabriel 'is at defiance with it' and crosses himself. He does this because 'My name is *Will. Croswill*, and I will have my humour'; adding that if, in doing this, he shocks certain people, so be it.[55] Here Brome may be taking a dig at what some felt was the Popish adornment of Anglican churches under the regime of Laud, who remained Bishop of London until 1633. If so, there is an irony implicit since Bedford, who financed the development, was an austere Puritan, and his church of St Paul, notable for its rough-hewn simplicity.

The situation is richly humorous because Crossewill is at cross purposes with his son, who is certainly no pious Arminian of the Andrewes school. Gabriel is mesmerised not by a cross but by a prostitute who, in a reversal of roles with Don Giovanni, stands on a balcony to seduce her customers. She elects to play the lute after she regales them in stentorian tones:

> Whilst I fly out in brave rebellion;
> And offer at the least, to break these shackles
> That holds our legs together: And begin
> A fashion, which pursu'd by Cyprian Dames,
> May perswade Justice to allow our Games.
> Who knows? I'le try. Francisca bring my Lute.[56]

Is it too far fetched to suggest that Francisca, described as 'a Punk' in the *dramatis personae*, may be a play on the Christian name of the patron who gave Jones the chance to sing his song; that is to say, to design the greatest urban development yet seen in London? Francis Russell, 4th Earl of Bedford, put up the money for Covent Garden. According to the late seventeenth-century antiquary John Bagford, the first historian of the British printing press, the balcony which 'Country folks were wont much to gaze on' was first introduced in Chandos Street in Covent Garden in about 1632.[57] Bagford's claim comes in a four-folio manuscript biography of Jones compiled in the course of extensive researches devoted to the history of London.[58]

The Commissioners of New Building certainly welcomed the arrival of the balcony as a gracious addition to the London façade. It was they who had promoted the fashion in response to James I's declared ambition:

> that we found our Citie and suburbs of stickes, and left them of bricke, being a material farre more durable, safe from fire and beautiful and magnificent.[59]

Now it may be thought that such references to innovations in the building trade were somewhat arcane for Brome's audience; especially since many who sat through the performance had no hope of ever owning a dwelling of any sort, let alone building one. However, that would be to underestimate both the acute crisis of accommodation which had existed in London since the late 1570s, and the extent to which government initiatives on housing directly interfered with people's lives. Both pressures made for awareness of metropolitan building and its social consequences.

Other plays by Richard Brome offered a powerful critique of royal policy during the Personal Rule. The popular theatre played a part in developing something of a hostile attitude to the rarefied Whitehall world of the masque and the collectors' gallery. *The Weeding of Covent Garden* suggests surprisingly forcefully that art and architecture may have contributed to a growing loss of sympathy with the court and its values.

Richard Brome's Crossewill is a type who is encountered not only in the theatre but in the literature of manners. During the Personal Rule, Charles I became increasingly preoccupied with the problem of getting peers and gentry to take their county responsibilities seriously; a number of proclamations were issued which forbade those upon whom the King relied for the proper running of local administration, to stay in London for the season. These were fairly ineffectual but they point to an issue which concerned not only the government but those who wrote about what was wrong with society.

One of the most influential of these was Richard Brathwaite. He was a Westmorland gentleman of some substance: Recorder of Kendal, Deputy Lieutenant of the county, and Justice of the Peace. He was of the same social class as Prynne, who had been Recorder of Bath before he had fallen foul of the Establishment. They had other things in common. John Aubrey tells of how when Prynne was in the mood for writing: 'About every three hours his man was to bring him a roll and a pot of ale to refocillate his wasted spirits. So he studied and drank and munched some bread.'[60] Brathwaite too was a famous drinker. Brathwaite, also like Prynne, was immensely prolific. His works were enormously successful because they described contemporary fears and prejudices, as was the case with Prynne.

Brathwaite enjoyed considerable success with his two books *The English Gentleman* and *The English Gentlewoman*. The first was published in 1630, reprinted in 1641, and then again in 1652. The second book appeared in 1631 and was issued in a new edition in 1641.

Analysis of the second editions of each book suggests that Brathwaite had made a close study not only of Prynne but of Peacham and Junius. This was because Brathwaite was concerned with many of the same issues: especially the effect court fashions had on the morals of the nation.

Little of what Brathwaite writes is new; though mercifully he is a much better stylist than Prynne. In *The English Gentleman* Brathwaite laments the passing of old English hospitality; a theme Ben Jonson had given wings to in *Penshurst*. Brathwaite deplores the drying up of that spring; sentiments with which Charles I would have concurred. However, where Brathwaite and Charles must have parted company was over the attack Brathwaite made on the pride of conspicuous display to be seen in great country houses. Brathwaite objected not only to vain-glorious building but also to the way in which country houses were no sooner put up than deserted for the seductions of the London season. Charles I was concerned about the absence of the right sort of people to run county administration, but he thoroughly approved of those who built great mansions in the counties because at least some patrons were likely to use them. Brathwaite writes:

> . . . let me speake a word or two touching this neglect of *Hospitalitie*, which may be observed in most places throughout this Kingdome. What the reason may seeme to be I know not, unlesse riot and prodigalitie, the very *Gulfes* which swallow up much *Gentrie*: why do many sumptuous and goodly *Buildings*, whose faire Frontispice, promise much comfort to the wearied *Traveller*, should want their *Masters* . . . so their *Store-House* being made so strait, and their *Gates* so broad, I much feare me, that *Provision* (the life of *Hospitalitie*) hath run out at their *gates*, leaving vast penurious houses apt enough to receive, but unprovided to releve. But indeed, the reason why this defect of noble *Hospitalitie* hath so generally possessed this Realme, is their love to the *Court*. This moved his *Highnesse* of late, to declare his gracious pleasure to our *Gentry*: that all persons of ranke and quality should retire from the Citty, and returne to their Countrey; where they might bestowe that on Hospitality, which the liberty of the time; too much besotted with fashion and forraine imitation, useth to disgorge on vanity.[61]

Brathwaite's critique remained firmly within acceptable criticism unlike the animadversions of Prynne. *The English Gentlewoman* is dedicated to Lady Anne Clifford, whose family portrait by Van Dyck we have already looked at.

The message of *The English Gentlewoman* is much the same as that of its companion volume. Brathwaite exhorts his ladies to see through the folly of monuments; though his advice seems to have been entirely ignored by his dedicatee, who littered the north of England with pillars and inscriptions to the greatness of her family. Lady Anne Clifford's famous campaign happened after *The English Gentlewoman* came out, however; after, that was, a hopeful author had appealed to Lady Anne and her friends:

> When the subtill Spider shall weave her curious web over your Monuments; when those beauteous structures of yours shall [b]ee dissolved; when all your titular glory shall bee obscured; when those fading *honours*, on which you relyed, and with which you stood surprized, shall bee estranged; and you from this goodly low Theatre of earth translated; it shall bee then demanded of you, not how eminent you were in *greatnesse*, but how fervent in acts of *goodnesse* . . .[62]

Brathwaite devoted much ink to the corrupting nature of fashions – pictures, houses, dress, stage performances and masques – and his books were widely read. What is more, Brathwaite was a well respected member of his county, as a prominent representative of the King's government in the north-west. To judge therefore from the status of this author and the impact of his writings, doubts about the morality of Caroline culture were being expressed from within the governmental class and not merely by crazed bigots like Prynne whose abusive denunciations led to mutilation and imprisonment. This is not however to suggest that anyone was persuaded to fight against the King because they disapproved of his taste for pictures; art has never been something to die for. All that I would claim though is that images of rule began to be noticed in ways they had not before.

There is no easy equation between the visual arts and religious and social loyalties in the reign of Charles I. Lady Anne Clifford not only ignored what Brathwaite had to say about the deplorable habit of putting up monuments; she ordered not one, but two painted family groups which are larger than the Ghent altarpiece.[63] The Earl of Bedford, for whom Jones worked at Covent Garden, would nowadays have had a page to himself in *Private Eye*, but in 1630 he escaped criticism for commissioning the largest urban development in London before the Civil War. Bedford liked his rental income while he maintained a strict religion and a conspicuous hostility to a court from which ostentatiously he absented himself. But then Lady Anne was also an austere lady who maintained an exemplary habit of bible reading and the promotion of Puritan divines.

Puritans and Philistines were not necessarily fighting on the same side at Edgehill. What can safely be said from this brief survey of literature on the visual arts during the English Renaissance is that images had come to mean a great deal more to educated people in 1642 than they had done in 1442. Images became controversial by the reign of Charles I in a way which could not have been said of them under a Yorkist or Tudor monarchy: in the Henrician era they had either elicited a positive response, or not been noticed at all; by the end of the years of Personal Rule they had acquired the capacity to be divisive.

The aim of this chapter has been to trace the slow process whereby visual imagery became a much more central aspect of social relations. Just as the paintings which were bought by English patrons had become more sophisticated by the middle of the seventeenth century, so too the messages which they gave out were more articulate. Responses of popular writers to the place of the visual arts suggest that the arts themselves were not only increasingly valued as a method of self-promotion, but had become an eloquent means of expression. Men may not have been prepared to die for a picture, but they were willing to go to war for the values which pictures, architecture and monuments had come to express more eloquently than ever before. Collectors in seventeenth-century Britain had acquired a whole range of wonderful objects, but they had also acquired a new language of expression. Perhaps Sir Thomas Elyot's hopes had been realised: pictures had indeed become no less powerful a medium of communication than the printed word. That may or may not be true. What is certain is that the fine arts had been politicised in ways which were quite new in the cultural history of the British Isles. One might end by suggesting that effectively the English monarchy, and those who served it most closely, had come to perceive the wisdom of Bernini's advice given to Louis XIV's great minister Colbert that 'Even if the king lacks any profound understanding of artists and scholarly talents, he must be sure to attract them because of the reputation it gives him in the world.'[64]

Appendix I

ACCOUNT OF THE VASTLY RICH CLOATHS OF THE DUKE OF BUCKINGHAM, THE NUMBER OF HIS SERVANTS AND OF THE NOBLE PERSONAGES IN HIS TRAIN, WHEN HE WENT TO PARIS, A.D. 1625, TO BRING OVER QUEEN HENRIETTA MARIA.
(From the Harleian Collection.)

[This is a singular specimen of the luxurious magnificence of that great favourite.]

My Lord Duke is intended to take his journey towards Paris, on Wednesday the 31st of March.

His Grace hath for his body, twenty-seven rich suits embroidered, and laced with silk and silver plushes; besides one rich white satin uncut velvet suit, set all over, both suit and cloak, with diamonds, the value whereof is thought to be worth fourscore thousand pounds, besides a feather made with great diamonds; with sword, girdle, hatband and spurs with diamonds, which suit His Grace intends to enter into Paris with. Another rich suit is of purple satin, embroidered all over with rich orient pearls; the cloak made after the Spanish fashion, with all things suitable, the value whereof will be 20,000*l*. and this is thought shall be for the wedding-day in Paris. His other suits are all rich as invention can frame, or art fashion. His colours for the entrance are white pwatchett, and for the wedding crimson and gold.

Three rich suits a piece,

Twenty Privy Gentlemen; seven Grooms of his chamber; thirty Chief Yeomen; two Master Cooks

Of his own servants for the Household,

Twenty-five second Cooks; fourteen Yeomen of the second rank, seventeen Grooms to them; forty-five Labourers Selleters belonging to the kitchen.

Twelve Pages, three rich suits a-piece; twenty-four Footmen, three rich suits, and two rich coats a-piece; six Huntsmen, two rich suits a-piece; twelve Grooms, one suit a-piece; six Riders, one suit a-piece; besides eight others to attend the stable business.

Three rich velvet coaches inside; without with gold lace all over; eight horses in each coach, and six coachmen richly suited; eight-score musicians richly suited; twenty-two watermen, suited in sky-coloured taffety, all gilded with anchors, and my Lord's arms; all these to row in one barge of my Lord's. All these servants have every thing suitable, all being at his Grace's charge.

Lords already known to go.

Marquis Hamilton,
Earl Dorset,
Earl Denbigh,
Earl Montgomery,
Earl Warwick,
Earl Anglesea,
Earl Salisbury,
Lord Walden,
Mr. Villars,
Mr. Edward Howard,
Lord President's* two sons,
Mr. William Legar,
Mr. Francis Anslowe,
Mr. Edward Goring,
Mr. Walter Steward.

Besides twenty-four Knights of great worth, all which will carry six or seven Pages a-piece and as many Footmen. This whole train will be six or seven hundred persons at least. When this list is perfect, there will appear many more than I have named.

* Lord Manchester.

Francis Grose, *The Antiquarian Repertory*, 4 vols (London, 1807–9), vol. 2, pp. 13–4.

Notes

Notes to the Introduction

1 John Summerson, *Inigo Jones* (Harmondsworth, 1983), pp. 17–18.
2 H.M.C., Downshire Mss, vol. 4 (1940), p. 109.
3 Archivio di Stato, Florence, Mediceo 945, f. 102.
4 L. Pearsall-Smith, *The Life and Letters of Sir Henry Wotton*, 2 vols (Oxford, 1907), vol. 1, pp. 118–19*n*.
5 Roy Strong, *Art and Power* (Woodbridge, 1986), p. 15.
6 Ibid., p. 11.
7 For an account of how historians have differed as to the causes of the Civil War, see John Kenyon, *The History Men* (London, 1983), *passim*.
8 The sculptor who made English Renaissance tombs may not have carried them to their location, or even worked out the terms of the contract. Middle-men frequently played a role in what was often a major and expensive social statement.

Notes to Chapter 1: The Royal Palace

1 For Richmond Palace, see Simon Thurley, *The Royal Palaces of Tudor England* (New Haven and London, 1993), pp. 27–32.
2 Ibid., p. 54.
3 Ibid., p. 63.
4 Ibid., pp. 52–3.
5 George Parfitt (ed.), *Ben Jonson, The Complete Poems* (Harmondsworth, 1988), p. 97.
6 Royal Commission on Historical Monuments, England, *City of Cambridge*, 2 Parts (1959), Part II, p. 197.
7 A. W. Pugin, *An Apology for the Revival of Christian Architecture in England* (London, 1843), pp. 31–2. See also A. F. Kersting and David Watkin, *Peterhouse: An Architectural Record, 1284–1984* (Peterhouse College), plates 35–8.
8 E. S. De Beer (ed.), *The Diary of John Evelyn*, 6 vols (Oxford, 1955), vol. III, pp. 426–8.
9 Eileen Harris, *British Architectural Books and Writers* (Cambridge, 1990), p. 418.
10 Thurley, *The Royal Palaces*, p. 60.
11 Michael Kiernan (ed.), *Sir Francis Bacon, The Essayes or Counsels, Civill and Moral*, 2 vols (Oxford, 1985), 'Of Building XLV', vol. 1, pp. 135–8.
12 Ibid., p. 285.
13 Jules Lubbock, *The Tyranny of Taste: The Politics of Architecture and Design in Britain*,

1550–1960 (New Haven and Yale, 1995).

14 Ibid., pp. 164–5.

15 Oliver Hill and John Cornforth, *English Country Houses, Caroline 1625–1685* (London, 1966), p. 12.

16 Lubbock, *The Tyranny of Taste*, p. 164.

17 Mary F. S. Hervey, *The Life, Correspondence and Collections of Thomas Howard, Earl of Arundel* (Cambridge, 1921), p. 175.

18 For further reflections on the political uses to which Jones would put his practice see my essay 'The politics of Inigo Jones', in David Howarth (ed.), *Art and Patronage in the Caroline Courts* (Cambridge, 1993), pp. 68–89.

19 PRO, S. P., 124/131.

Loci genius
spectatori hospiti.
oculos maiestate ferientem Dominique
animam magnificentissime loquentem
hanc stratam
vix ante lateritiam marmoreis iam
per Europam quibusvis aequandam
JACOBUS
Magnae Britanniae monarcha primus
abusque solo extruxit, horis genialibus
spectaculis solennibus aulaeque Britannicae
pompis
destinatam, in aeternam nominis
eiusdem et pacatissimi imperii gloriam
posteris reliquit
Anno MDCXXI

20 F. H. Relf, 'Notes on the Debates of the House of Lords', *Royal Historical Society*, XLII (1929), pp. 48–50. I am grateful to Gregory Martin for drawing my attention to these documents.

21 Per Palme, *Triumph of Peace* (London, 1957), pp. 176–99.

22 Julius Held, *Rubens and his Circle* (Princeton, 1982), 'Rubens' Glynde Sketch and the Installation of the Whitehall Ceiling', pp. 126–37.

23 Kevin Sharpe, *The Personal Rule of Charles I* (New Haven and London, 1992), p. 666.

24 John Harris and Gordon Higgott, *Inigo Jones Complete Architectural Drawings* (London, 1989), cat. no. 29.

25 Mary F. S. Hervey, *The Life, Correspondence and Collections of Thomas Howard Earl of Arundel* (Cambridge, 1921), p. 390.

26 Linda Levy Peck and Jenny Wormald are the leading revisionists of the court of James I.

27 Thomas Locke to Dudley Carleton, 11 November 1620, C.S.P. (Dom.), CXVII, 71.

28 Arthur B. Chamberlain, *Hans Holbein the Younger*, 2 vols (New York, 1913), vol. 2, p. 293.

29 D. Harris Willson, *King James VI and I* (London, 1956), pp. 193–4.

30 R. Wittkower, 'Puritanissimo Fiero', *Burlington Magazine*, 9 February 1948, pp. 50–1.

31 *48th Annual Report of The Deputy Keeper of The Public Records* (London, 1887), Appendix 3, p. 474, no. 28. 'Jones, Inigo, Surveyor of H. M. Works. Privilege of exemption from juries, assizes, and inquests; subsidies, fifteenths, tenths, and other taxes, etc; and from serving as sheriff, constable, escheator, tithingman; with a pardon for not taking the order of knighthood. April 26/April 27 1633.'

32 PRO, S. P. 23/177, ff. 777–8.

33 For the Eltham Ordinances, G. R. Elton, *The Tudor Constitution* (Cambridge, 1960), pp. 93–4. For ceremonies and protocol at the court of Charles I, Albert J. Loomie, *Ceremonies of Charles I* (New York, 1987), *passim*.

34 M. Whinney, *John Webb's Drawings of Whitehall Palace* (Walpole Society, vol. XXXI, 1946).

35 Catherine Wilkinson Zerner, *Juan de Herrera Architect to Philip II of Spain* (New Haven and Yale, 1993), pp. 50–1.
36 I am grateful to Jeremy Wood for this revealing information on Charles I's accountancy methods.

Notes to Chapter 2: The God that Rules

1 J. S. Morrill, 'The religious context of the English Civil War', *Trans. Royal Hist. Soc.*, 5th series, 34 (1984), pp. 155–78, and *idem*, 'The attack on the Church of England in the Long Parliament, 1640–42', in D. Beales and G. Best (eds), *History, Society and the Churches* (Cambridge, 1985), pp. 105–24.
2 Maurice Howard, *The Early Tudor Country House* (London, 1987), p. 210.
3 D. H. Willson, *King James VI and I* (London, 1956), p. 207.
4 G. R. Elton, *The Tudor Constitution* (Cambridge, 1960), p. 344.
5 W. Scott and J. Bliss (eds), *The Works of the Most Reverend Father in God, William Laud*, 7 vols (Oxford, 1847–60), vol. 3, pp. 129–255.
6 Kenneth Clarke, *The Gothic Revival* (London, 1974), p. 170.
7 Kevin Sharpe, *The Personal Rule of Charles I* (New Haven and London, 1992), pp. 345–8, 'Henry Sherfield: a case study in complexities'.
8 J. Wickham Legg (ed.), 'English Orders for the Consecration of Churches', *Henry Bradshaw Society*, 41 (1911), pp. 101–12.
9 Per Palme, *Triumph of Peace* (London, 1957), pp. 23–4.
10 John Harris and Gordon Higgott, *Inigo Jones Complete Architectural Drawings* (London, 1989), cat. no 4.
11 John Summerson, *Inigo Jones* (Harmondsworth, 1983), p. 105.
12 William Kent's 1727 design of the elevation of the west front shows a balustrade with ten statues.
13 British Library, Harleian Ms, 5900, fol. 56 r.
14 J. Alfred Gotch, *Inigo Jones* (London, 1928), pp. 155–6.
15 Ibid., pp. 157–8.
16 Ibid., p. 159.
17 Ibid., p. 159.
18 Howard Colvin, 'Inigo Jones and the Church of St Michael Le Querne', *The London Journal*, 12, no. 1 (1986), pp. 36–40.
19 David Howarth (ed.), *Art and Patronage in the Caroline Courts* (Cambridge, 1993), the author's essay 'The politics of Inigo Jones', pp. 79–82.
20 Peter Heylyn, *Cyprianus Anglicus* (London, 1671), p. 209.
21 F. A. Patterson *et al.* (eds), *The Works of John Milton*, 18 vols (New York, 1931–8), vol. VII (1932), pp. 141–3, and vol. III, Part I (1931), pp. 54–5.
22 For the fullest account of Gage, Susan Barnes, 'Van Dyck and George Gage', pp. 1–12, in Howarth (ed.), *Art and Patronage*.
23 Tobie Matthew wrote to Sir Dudley Carleton, English ambassador to The Hague, on 25 February 1617, about a picture Rubens was painting for Carleton: 'If yr Lp be pleased to exchange your Chaine for the Picture I will take all the paines I can, and Mr Gage will gladlie use all the judgement he hath, to make the Maister doe it excellentlie.' W. Noël Sainsbury, *Original Unpublished Papers relating to Rubens* (London, 1859), p. 18.
24 British Library, Trumbull Ms. Alph. Correspondence vol. XLIV, item 52.
25 Joseph Jacobs (ed.), *Epistolae Hoelianae, The Familiar Letters of James Howell*, 2 vols (London, 1890), vol. 2, p. 45, Letter no. XXXVIII.
26 Joanna H. Harting, *Catholic London Missions* (London, 1903), p. 9.
27 Erica Veevers, *Images of Love and Religion: Queen Henrietta Maria and Court Entertainments* (Cambridge, 1989), pp. 165–71.

28 Ibid., p. 167.
29 Francis Haskell, 'Charles I's Collection of Pictures', p. 211, in Arthur MacGregor (ed.), *The Late King's Goods* (Oxford and London, 1989).
30 Ibid., p. 221.

Notes to Chapter 3: The Royal Portrait: The Tudors

1 David Starkey (ed.), *Henry VIII: A European Court in England* (London, 1991), p. 61.
2 Simon Thurley, *The Royal Palaces of Tudor England* (New Haven and London, 1993), p. 209.
3 Ibid., p. 39.
4 'Whether it was conceived as a design for a mural decoration, like those carried out by Holbein for The Steelyard, remains conjectural', K. T. Parker, *The Drawings of Hans Holbein in The Collection of His Majesty The King at Windsor Castle* (Oxford and London, 1945), p. 35.
5 In the revised catalogue raisonné of the paintings of Holbein, it is stated that the Solomon miniature is 'Another work in which Henry's new position of supremacy is shown'. John Rowlands, *Holbein* (Oxford, 1985), p. 91.
6 *Holbein and the Court of Henry VIII* (The Queen's Gallery, Buckingham Palace, 1978–9), no. 88.
7 There is a certain difficulty with the argument that the Holbein miniature is a record of a lost wall-painting. As Jeremy Wood has pointed out to me, if that had been the case, we might have expected a record in the inscription in Hollar's etching of 1642, where the miniature is recorded as 'ex Collectione Arundelia'.
8 Roy Strong, *The Cult of Elizabeth I* (London, 1977), p. 50.
9 Kevin Sharpe, *The Personal Rule of Charles I* (New Haven and London, 1992), pp. 52–62.
10 Margaret Aston, *The King's Bedpost* (Cambridge, 1993).
11 Roy Strong, *The English Icon* (London, 1969), p. 71.
12 For a refutation of this myth, see H. S. Ettlinger, 'The question of Sr George's garter', *Burlington Magazine*, 125 (1983), pp. 25–9.
13 Starkey (ed.), *Henry VIII*, pp. 140–45, Rory MacEntegart, 'Fatal Matrimony: Henry VIII and the Marriage to Anne of Cleves'.
14 Ronald Forsyth Millen and Robert Erich Wolf, *Heroic Deeds and Mystic Figures* (Princeton, 1989), p. 51.
15 M. Rooses and C. Ruelens, *Codex Diplomaticus Rubenianus: Correspondance de Rubens et Documents Epistolaires concernant sa vie et ses oeuvres*, 6 vols (Antwerp, 1887–1909), vol. 4, Doc. no. CCCCXLI.
16 Martin Warnke, *The court artist: On the ancestry of the modern artist* (Cambridge, 1993), p. 121.
17 Millen and Wolf, *Heroic Deeds*, p. 50.
18 Joanna Woodall, 'An Exemplary Consort: Antonis Mor's Portrait of Mary Tudor', *Art History*, vol. 14, no. 2 (1991), pp. 192–225.
19 Paul Johnson, *Elizabeth I: A Study in Power and Intellect* (London, 1974), p. 55.
20 Ibid., p. 12.
21 Warnke, *The court artist*, p. 195.
22 Janet Arnold, *Queen Elizabeth's Wardrobe Unlock'd* (Leeds, 1988), p. 122.
23 Gregorio Panzani to Cardinal Francesco Barberini, 26 September 1635, Vatican Library, Barberini Latina 8635, fol. 51.
24 Arnold, *Queen Elizabeth's Wardrobe Unlock'd*, *passim*, for the fullest account of the importance of dress and jewellery for the queen.
25 Arnold, *Queen Elizabeth's Wardrobe Unlock'd*, p. 122.
26 Strong, *The Cult of Elizabeth I*, pp. 50–52.

27 Roy Strong and Julia Trevelyan Oman, *Elizabeth R* (London, 1971), p. 44.
28 Jules Lubbock, *The Tyranny of Taste: The Politics of Architecture and Design in Britain, 1550–1960* (New Haven and Yale, 1995), p. 159.

Notes to Chapter 4: The Royal Portrait: The Stuarts

1 W. Noël Sainsbury, *Original Papers relating to Rubens* (London, 1859), p. 61.
2 This point was drawn to my attention by Anne Thackray.
3 Gregory Martin, 'The Banqueting House ceiling: Two newly-discovered projects', *Apollo*, February 1994, pp. 29–34.
4 Geoffrey Whitney, *A Choice of Emblemes* (Amsterdam and New York, 1969 reprint), p. 168.
5 I am grateful to Diana Scarisbrick for allowing me to make use of her researches on the symbolism of the jewellery in this portrait.
6 Rubens to Pierre Dupuy, London, 8 August 1629, in R. S. Magurn, *The Letters of Peter Paul Rubens* (Cambridge, Mass., 1955), p. 320.
7 See Graham Parry's essay 'Van Dyck and the Caroline Court poets', p. 250, in Susan Barnes and Arthur J. Wheelock (eds), *Van Dyck 350* (Washington, 1994).
8 Especially perhaps by Roy Strong, in *Henry, Prince of Wales* (London, 1986). Significantly, the book has as its sub-title *and England's Lost Renaissance.*
9 Peter Burke, *The Fabrication of Louis XIV* (New Haven and London, 1992), p. 9.
10 See David Howarth, 'Charles I: Sculpture and Sculptors', p. 74, in Arthur MacGregor, *The Late King's Goods* (Oxford and London, 1989). Whether this idea had any connection with the proposal of the House of Lords is not something which I have yet been able to unravel.
11 Martin Warnke, *The court artist: On the ancestry of the modern artist* (Cambridge, 1993), p. 196.
12 Oliver Millar, 'Abraham Van Der Doort's Catalogue of the Collections of Charles I', *Walpole Society*, 37 (1958–60), p. 62.
13 Oliver Millar, *The Tudor, Stuart and Early Georgian Pictures in the Collection of Her Majesty The Queen*, 2 vols (London, 1963), text vol., p. 94.
14 Ibid., text vol., p. 98.
15 Isaac D'Isreali, *Curiosities of Literature*, 3 vols (London, 1859), vol. 2, pp. 329–30.
16 John Evelyn, *Numismata* (London, 1698), p. 335.
17 Harold E. Wethey, *The Paintings of Titian*, 3 vols (London, 1969–1975), vol I, *The Religious Paintings*, Cat. no. 96: Lost Examples 2, London, Charles I 'A Saint kneeling before a Cross by Titian', Charles I Inventory of Sale, LR, 2/124, fol. 118v.

Notes to Chapter 5: The Tomb

1 John Weever, *Antient funerall Monuments* (London, 1631), p. 52, and Margaret Aston, *England's Iconoclasts* (Oxford, 1988), pp. 314–15.
2 Weever, *Antient funerall Monuments*, p. 5.
3 H. M. Colvin, D. R. Ransome, John Summerson, *The History of The King's Works*, vol. III, *1485–1660* (Part I) (HMSO, 1982), p. 187.
4 Thomas Astle, *The Will of King Henry VII* (London, 1775), pp. 5–6.
5 Colvin *et al.*, *History of The King's Works*, p. 220.
6 It is commonly assumed that Windsor Castle was the setting for this court ceremony but Per Palme, *Triumph of Peace* (London, 1957), p. 124, wrote that 'Whitehall was the favoured setting for the festival during the early part of the century.'
7 James Spedding *et al.* (eds), *The Works of Francis Bacon*, 14 vols (London, 1858), vol. vi, p. 245.

8 Colvin *et al.*, *History of The King's Works*, pp. 221–2.
9 John Speed, *The History of Great Britaine* (London, 1611), p. 784.
10 William Camden, *Britannia* (London, 1695), p. 435.
11 PRO, State Papers (Dom.), XXXVII, 41, 15 August 1565.
12 A. P. Stanley, *Historical Memorials of Westminster Abbey* (London, 1869), p. 177.
13 Cecil Papers (Marquess of Salisbury, Hatfield House), vol. 121, fol. 1.
14 Stanley, *Historical Memorials*, pp. 179–80.
15 Nikolaus Pevsner, *London 1: The Cities of London and Westminster*, The Buildings of England (Harmondsworth, 1957), p. 381.
16 William Camden, *Reges, Reginae, Nobiles, et alii in ecclesia collegiata B. Petri Westmonasterii sepulti.*
17 Roy Strong, *Henry, Prince of Wales*, p. 7.
18 J. S. A. Adamson, 'Chivalry and political culture in Caroline England', Kevin Sharpe and Peter Lake (eds), *Culture and Politics in Early Stuart England* (London, 1994), p. 191.
19 Ibid., pp. 191–3.
20 John Peacock, 'Inigo Jones's catafalque for James I', *Architectural History*, XXV (1982), pp. 1–5.
21 For the fullest account of royal funerary effigies, A. Harvey and R. Mortimer (eds), *The Funeral Effigies of Westminster Abbey* (Woodbridge, 1994).
22 John Harris and Gordon Higgott, *Inigo Jones Complete Architectural Drawings* (London, 1989), cat. no. 53.
23 PRO, L.C. 2/6.
24 Mary Edmond, 'Limners and Picturemakers – New light on the lives of miniaturists and large-scale portrait-painters working in London in the sixteenth and seventeenth centuries', *The Walpole Society*, 47 (1978–80), pp. 165–7.
25 N. E. McClure, *The Letters of John Chamberlain*, 2 vols (Philadelphia, 1939), vol. II, p. 564.
26 Weever, *Antient funerall Monuments*, p. xx.
27 Ronald Lightbown, 'The sculpture of Isaac Besnier', in David Howarth (ed.), *Art and Patronage in the Caroline Courts* (Cambridge, 1993), pp. 155–6.
28 David Howarth, 'Charles I: Sculpture and Sculptors', in Arthur MacGregor, *The Late King's Goods* (Oxford and London, 1989), p. 89.
29 Charles Avery, 'Hubert Le Sueur, "the unworthy Praxiteles of King Charles I" ', *The Walpole Society*, 48 (1980–2), p. 184.
30 Lightbown, 'Sculpture of Isaac Besnier', *passim*.
31 PRO, S.P., 105/8, fol. 28, Gerbier to the Duchess of Buckingham, Brussels, 16 October 1631: 'I will write to Mons[r] St Giles to have a care of the Epitafe . . .'.
32 Warwickshire County Record Office, Feilding Papers, C1. 9. Letter endorsed: 'Ans: 20 Sept. 1631 Geneva'. I am grateful to Philip McEvansoneya for pointing out that this reference must refer to the Portsmouth not the Westminster monument.
33 R. A. Beddard, 'Wren's Mausoleum for Charles I and the cult of the Royal Martyr', *Architectural History*, 27 (1984), pp. 36–47.
34 Tacitus, *Historiae*, IV. 15.
35 T. Dickinson and Heinrich Harke, 'Early Anglo-Saxon Shields', *Archaeologia*, 110 (1992), pp. 61–2.

Notes to Chapter 6: Patrons of Power

1 J. M. Fletcher, 'Isabella d'Este, Patron and Collector', in David Chambers and Jane Martineau (eds), *Splendours of the Gonzaga* (London, 1981), pp. 51–65
2 W. Knowler (ed.), *The Earl of Strafford's Letters and Dispatches*, 2 vols (London, 1739), vol. 1, p. 16.
3 Strafford to Conway, Fairwood Park, 13 August 1639, in ibid., vol. 2, p. 381.
4 Strafford to Carlisle, Westminster, 20 May 1633, in ibid., vol. 1, p. 85.

5 H. M. Colvin *et al.*, *History of The King's Works*, vol. IV (Part II) (HMSO, 1982), p. 362.
6 Philip A. Knachel (ed.), *Eikon Basilike: The Portraiture of His Sacred Majesty in His Solitudes and Sufferings*, Folger Documents of Tudor and Stuart Civilization (New York, 1966), p. 6.
7 Knowler, *Earl of Strafford's Letters*, vol. 1, p. 112.
8 10 March 1635, in ibid., vol. 1, p. 379.
9 12 August 1633, in ibid., vol. 1, p. 102.
10 16 December 1634, in ibid., vol. 1, p. 347.
11 Ibid., p. 348.
12 M. Craig, 'New Light on Jigginstown', *Ulster Journal of Archaeology*, col. 33 (1970), pp. 107–10.
13 20 November 1633, in Knowler, *Earl of Strafford's Letters*, vol. 1, p. 158.
14 24 December 1633, in ibid., vol. 1, p. 168.
15 31 January 1634, in ibid., vol. 1, pp. 200–1.
16 22 February 1633, Sheffield City Libraries, Wentworth Woodhouse Muniments, 13/201.
17 20 September 1634, in Knowler, *Earl of Strafford's Letters*, vol. 1, p. 301.
18 3 October 1634, in ibid., vol. 1, p. 303.
19 6 October 1634, in ibid., vol. 1, p. 306.
20 27 October 1634, Sheffield City Libraries, Wentworth Woodhouse Muniments, 14/197.
21 22 January 1635, ibid., 14/280.
22 16 March 1635, ibid., 8/205–7.
23 *46th Annual Report of The Deputy Keeper of The Public Records* (London, 1886), Appendix 11, p. 44.
24 For Christian IV's building works see 'Koldinghus', pp. 463–507, in *Christian IV and Europe: The 19th Art Exhibition of the Council of Europe* (Denmark, 1988).
25 14 September 1635, Sheffield City Libraries, Wentworth Woodhouse Muniments, 8/266.
26 R. Ollard and P. Tudor-Craig (eds), *For Veronica Wedgwood These* (London, 1986), Oliver Millar, 'Strafford and Van Dyck', pp. 109–23.
27 10 April 1638, in Knowler, *Earl of Strafford's Letters*, vol. 2, p. 158.
28 14 May 1638, in ibid., vol. 2, p. 170.
29 Charles Avery, 'Hubert Le Sueur, "the unworthy Praxiteles of King Charles I" ', *The Walpole Society*, 48 (1980–2), p. 184.
30 PRO, E 403/2751, fol. 60, consists of a payment of £411/11s/3d for providing three sets of tapestries 'for furnishing the presence drawing Chamber and Councell Chamber in the said Kingdom of Ireland'. I am grateful to Jeremy Wood for providing me with this reference.
31 Hugh Kearney, *Strafford in Ireland, 1633–41: A Study in Absolutism* (Cambridge, 1989), p. 173.
32 27 September 1637, in Knowler, *Earl of Strafford's Letters*, vol. 2, pp. 105–6.
33 ? December 1633, in ibid., vol. 1, p. 173.
34 For Shirley in Ireland, see John P. Turner Jr, *A Critical Edition of James Shirley's ST PATRICK FOR IRELAND* (New York and London, 1977).
35 PRO, State Papers, Ireland (Chas. 1), vol. CCLVI, 48, 21 August 1637.
36 6 January 1639, in Knowler, *Earl of Strafford's Letters*, vol. 2, p. 267.
37 David Howarth, 'William Trumbull and art collecting in Jacobean England', *British Library Journal*, vol. 20, no. 2 (Autumn 1994), pp. 152–4.
38 Brendan O'Hehir, *Harmony from Discords: A Life of Sir John Denham* (Berkeley and Los Angeles, 1968), p. 31.
39 Brendan O'Hehir, *Expans'd Hieroglyphicks: A Critical Edition of Sir John Denham's COOPERS HILL* (Berkeley and Los Angeles, 1969), pp. 130–1.
40 Martin Warnke, *The court artist: On the ancestry of the modern artist* (Cambridge, 1993), p. 184.
41 12 January 1640, in Knowler, *Earl of Strafford's Letters*, vol. 2, p. 390.
42 Kearney, *Strafford in Ireland*, p. xxxv.

Notes to Chapter 7: Collecting: Patronage and Display

1 E. F. Rogers (ed.), *St Thomas More: Selected Letters* (New Haven and London, 1961), p. 164.
2 John Rowlands, *Holbein* (Oxford, 1985), pp. 87–8.
3 Roy Strong, *Holbein and Henry VIII* (London, 1967), p. 67.
4 Arthur K. Wheelock and Susan Barnes, *Anthony Van Dyck* (Washington, 1990), cat. no. 17.
5 See David Howarth, 'Van Dyck Triumphant in Washington', *Apollo*, January 1991, p. 39,
6 Wheelock and Barnes, *Anthony Van Dyck*, cat. no. 17.
7 Freeman O'Donoghue, *Catalogue of Engraved British Portraits in The British Museum*, 6 vols (London, 1908–1925), vol. V (1922), p. 49, describes the print by Baron after Van Dyck as: 'Philip Herbert, 4th Earl of Pembroke and 1st Earl of Montgomery, W.L. seated with his first Countess Susan Vere'.
8 Malcolm Rogers, 'Van Dyck's Portrait of *Lord George Stuart, Seigneur d'Aubigny*, and some related works', pp. 263–81, in Susan J. Barnes and Arthur K. Wheelock (eds), *Van Dyck 350*, Studies in the History of Art, 46 (National Gallery of Art, Washington, Baltimore, 1994).
9 S. J. Gunn and P. G. Linley (eds), *Cardinal Wolsey, Church, state and art* (Cambridge, 1991), chapters 2–5 and 10, for his patronage of the arts.
10 David Howarth, *Lord Arundel and his Circle* (New Haven and London, 1985), p. 1.
11 John Wolley to Trumbull, 15 February 161[8]9, British Library, Trumbull Ms. Alph. vol. XLVIII, f. 8v.
12 Wotton to Isaac Bargrave, Venice, 5 July 1618. Logan Pearsall Smith, *The Life and Letters of Henry Wotton*, 2 vols (Oxford, 1907), vol 2, p. 151.
13 Ibid., vol. 1, no. 58.
14 W. Dunn Mackray (ed.), *The History of the Great Rebellion and Civil Wars in England*, 6 vols (Oxford, 1888), vol. 1, p. 82.
15 *46th Annual Report of The Deputy Keeper of The Public Records* (London, 1886), Appendix II, p. 48 '1623 21 March, N.S. Hague. Sir Dudley Carleton to Christian IV. Recommends Constantio Hugins for his service.'
16 Martin Warnke, *The court artist: On the ancestry of the modern artist* (Cambridge, 1993), p. 103.
17 Matthew de Quester wrote to Trumbull from London on 29 January 1607[8] about sending instruments to a musician in Brussels and mentioned 'Mr Bassano one of his Majesty's musicians who, maketh rare wind instruments'. H.M.C., *Downshire Manuscripts*, vol. 2 (London, 1936), p. 463.
18 W. Noël Sainsbury, *Original Unpublished Papers relating to Rubens* (London, 1859), p. 37.
19 H.M.C., *Downshire Manuscripts*, vol. 3 (London, 1938), p. 30.
20 W. Noël Sainsbury, *Original Papers relating to Rubens* (London, 1859), p. 49.
21 David Howarth, 'Rubens's"owne pourrtrait" ', *Apollo*, October 1990, pp. 238–41.
22 Ibid., p. 239.
23 J. B. Trapp, 'Quentin Matsys, Desiderius Erasmus, Pieter Gillis and Thomas More' (with Lorne Campbell, Margaret Mann Phillips and Hubertus Schutte Herbruggen), *Burlington Magazine*, 1978, 120, pp. 716–24.
24 Mary Webster, *Firenze e l'Inghilterra* (Florence, 1971), cat. no. 28.
25 House of Lords Record Office, 3 Car. 1, no. 10.
26 This was an argument I put forward in a paper on Lady Arundel at a conference entitled *New Perspectives on the Earl and Countess of Arundel: Collecting in the Stuart Court*, held at the Getty Museum in the autumn of 1995 in connection with the exhibition, *The Earl and Countess of Arundel Renaissance Collectors*.
27 Warwickshire County Record Office, Feilding Papers, C.1.16, n.d.
28 R. Malcolm Smuts, *Court Culture and the Origins of a Royalist Tradition in Early Stuart England* (Philadelphia, 1987), chapter 5 'The Discovery of European Art: Collecting and Patronage', pp. 117–138.

29 David Howarth (ed.), *Art and Patronage in the Caroline Courts* (Cambridge, 1993), the author's essay 'The politics of Inigo Jones', pp. 68–90.
30 British Library, Trumbull Ms. Misc. XVII.
31 Ronald Lightbown, *Mantegna* (Oxford, 1986), p. 442.
32 Per Palme, *Triumph of Peace* (London, 1957), pp. 255–66.
33 Howarth, *Apollo*, p. 238.
34 W. G. Thomson, *Tapestry Weaving in England* (London, 1914), p. 68.
35 Peter Heylyn, *Aulicus Coquinariae* (London, 1650), p. 66.
36 Mary F. S. Hervey, *The Life, Correspondence and Collections of Thomas Howard Earl of Arundel* (Cambridge, 1921), pp. 255–6.
37 By Giles Worsley at a conference on the theme of the London town house, held at the Institute of Historical Research, London University, in July 1993.
38 John Evelyn, *Numismata* (London, 1698), p. 50.
39 N. Pevsner *Cambridgeshire*, The Buildings of England (Harmondsworth, 1954), p. 110.
40 Paul Shakeshaft, 'To much bewiched with thoes intysing things', *Burlington Magazine*, 128, 1986, pp. 114–32; and Ellis Waterhouse, 'Paintings from Venice for 17th century England', *Italian Studies*, vii (1952), pp. 1–23.
41 Howarth, *Lord Arundel*, p. 142.

Notes to Chapter 8: Writers and Critics

1 Peter Gwyn, *The King's Cardinal* (London, 1990), p. 30.
2 Ibid., p. 29.
3 Ibid., pp. xxi–xxii.
4 Sir Thomas Elyot, *The Boke Named The Governour* (Everyman edn), p. 28.
5 Ibid., p. 30.
6 Lucy Gent, *Picture and Poetry, 1560–1620* (Leamington Spa, 1981).
7 Ibid., p. 35.
8 Ibid., p. 36.
9 William Shakespeare, Sonnet 55.
10 Gent, *Picture and Poetry*, p. 39.
11 PRO, S.P. 16/79/123. Note added by Filippo Burlamachi in the margins of a letter received from Nicholas Lanier datable after 17 October 1627.
12 Roger Lockyer, *Buckingham* (London and New York, 1981), p. 323.
13 William M. Lamont, *Marginal Prynne* (London, 1963), p. 6.
14 Martin Butler, *Theatre and Crisis, 1632–1642* (Cambridge, 1987), p. 314, n. 2.
15 S. R. Gardiner (ed.), 'Documents relating to the Proceedings against William Prynne in 1634 and 1637' (*Camden Society*, New Series xviii, 1877), *passim*.
16 William Prynne, *Histrio-mastix, The Player's Scourge; or, Actors Tragædie* (London, 1633), unpaginated preface.
17 Ibid., pp. 742–3.
18 Ibid., p. 901.
19 Ibid., p. 12.
20 W. Dunn Macray, *The History of the Great Rebellion and Civil Wars in England*, 6 vols (Oxford, 1888), vol. 1, pp. 62–3.
21 Kevin Sharpe, *The Personal Rule of Charles I* (New Haven and London, 1992), pp. 151–3.
22 Elizabeth DuGue Trapier, 'Sir Arthur Hopton and the Interchange of Paintings between England and Spain in the Seventeenth Century', *Connoisseur*, 164 (1967), pp. 239–43, and 165 (1967), pp. 60–3. Wethey, *The Paintings of Titian*, vol. II, *The Portraits*, cat. no. 115, under 'Lost Copies' of the Escorial version of the *The Martyrdom of St Lawrence*, notes: '2. London, Charles I Inventory of Sale, 1649 (Charles I: LR, 2/124, folio 117 v., no. 12)'.
23 5 February 1622, British Library, Trumbull Ms, Misc. vol. XIV, item 28.

24 British Library, Trumbull Ms, Misc. vol. XV (1623), Item 150 'Relation of Occurrences in England'. An unsigned newsletter in manuscript.
25 British Library, 30 May 1623, Trumbull Ms, Alph., vol. XLVIII, f. 97.
26 William Prynne, *Romes Master-Peece* (London, 1643), p. 24.
27 Ibid., p. 23.
28 Sir Kenelm Digby to Lord Conway, 27 July 1637, PRO, C.S.P. (Dom.), CCCLXIV, 68.
29 Virgil B. Heltzel (ed.), *The Complete Gentleman* (Ithaca, 1962), pp. 128–9.
30 Ibid., p. 128.
31 Allan Ellenius, *De Arte Pingendi* (Uppsala, 1960), p. 48.
32 Bodleian Library, Marshall Ms., 80 (Bod. Ms. 8661), f. 13 and ff. 18–19.
33 Michael Bryan's *Biographical and Critical Dictionary of Painters and Engravers* (London, 1813–1816).
34 Ellenius, *De Arte Pingendi*, p. 92.
35 Keith Aldrich, Philipp Fehl and Raina Fehl, *Franciscus Junius, The Literature of Classical Art*, 2 vols (Berkeley, 1991), vol. 1, *The Painting of the Ancients*, and vol. 2, *A Lexicon of Artists and Their Works*.
36 Ibid., vol. 1, p. xxvi.
37 Ibid., vol. 1, p. lxxxi.
38 Ibid., vol. 1, pp. xxvii–xviii.
39 Franciscus Junius, *The Painting of the Ancients* (Farnborough reprint, 1972), p. 13.
40 Ibid., p. 54.
41 Ibid., p. 81.
42 Ibid., p. 82.
43 David Howarth, 'Charles I: Sculpture and Sculptors', in Arthur MacGregor, *The Late King's Goods* (Oxford and London, 1989), pp. 92–3.
44 Avery, *Le Sueur*, op. cit., doc. 75.
45 Howarth, *The Late King's Goods*, pp. 89–90.
46 Junius, *Painting of the Ancients*, p. 140.
47 Ibid., p. 146.
48 Butler, *Theatre and Crisis*, pp. 130–2.
49 *The Dramatic Works of Richard Brome Containing Fifteen Comedies Now First Collected In Three Volumes* (London, 1873), vol. 2, *The Covent Garden Weeded*, pp. 1–2.
50 Ibid., p. 2.
51 Ibid., p. 2.
52 Malcolm Smuts, *Court Culture and the Origins of a Royalist Tradition in Early Stuart England* (Philadelphia, 1987), p. 128.
53 Brome, *The Covent Garden Weeded*, p. 1.
54 Ibid., p. 2.
55 Ibid., p. 8.
56 Ibid., p. 9.
57 British Library, Harleian Ms., 5900, fol. 57v.
58 The biography is Harleian Ms., 5900, ff. 57r–58v.
59 James F. Larkin and Paul L. Hughes, *Stuart Royal Proclamations*, 2 vols (Oxford, 1973), vol. 1, no. 152.
60 Richard Barber (ed.), *John Aubrey Brief Lives* (London, 1975), p. 259.
61 Richard Brathwaite, *The English Gentleman* (London, 1641), p. 37.
62 Richard Brathwaite, *The English Gentlewoman* (London, 1641), p. 380.
63 Graham Parry, 'The Great Picture of Lady Anne Clifford', pp. 202–19, in David Howarth (ed.), *Art and Patronage in the Caroline Courts* (Cambridge, 1993).
64 Martin Warnke, *The court artist: On the ancestry of the modern artist* (Cambridge, 1993), p. 227.

Index